# Everyday Life Skills

**AGS**®

American Guidance Service, Inc.
Circle Pines, Minnesota 55014-1796
800-328-2560

## Acknowledgments

The publisher gratefully acknowledges the students and staff of the Minnesota Life College, Minneapolis, Minnesota, for contributing to the writing of the self-assessment checklists in each chapter. In addition, the publisher gratefully acknowledges Chris Coffee Frazier, M. Ed., for her contributions to this book.

Page 383 was adapted from Elizabeth P. Aune and Jean E. Ness, *Tools for Transition Student Handbook*, AGS® American Guidance Service, Inc., 1991.

## Photos

Front cover: upper left—©Jose L. Pelaez/ Stock Market; lower left—Doug Fogg/ Workbook Co/Op Stock; right—©Michael Krasowitz/FPG International; background and back cover—Doug Wilson/Corbis; pp. i, 56, 87—©Doug Wilson/Corbis; pp. iii, 1, 6, 55—©F. Sieb/H. Armstrong Roberts; pp. x, 114, 143—©Larry Lefever/Grant Heilman Photography; pp. 1, 6, 75, 104, 131, 139, 185, 198, 226, 268, 303, 315, 346, 355—©Michael Newman/ PhotoEdit; pp. 4, 240, 273—©Walter Choroszewski/ Stock Connection; pp. 9, 414—©Myrleen Ferguson/PhotoEdit; p. 11—©Tony Freeman/PhotoEdit; p. 17a—©Lester V. Bergman/Corbis; p. 17b—©Dr. P. Marazzi/ Science Library/Photo Researchers, Inc.; p. 17c—©James Stevenson/Photo Researchers, Inc.; pp. 19, 22, 67, 81, 83, 116, 150, 170, 228, 261, 265, 389—©David Young-Wolff/PhotoEdit; p. 24—©James Darell/Stone; p. 30—©Robert Brenner/ PhotoEdit; p. 33—©Stephen Simpson/FPG International; p. 36—©A. Ramey/PhotoEdit; pp. 38, 243—©Bob Daemmrich/Stock Boston; pp. 41, 42, 47, 51—©Michael Crousek; p. 43—©Richard Lord/PhotoEdit; p. 56—©Ryan McVay/PhotoDisc; p. 59— ©Jim Whitmer Photography; p. 63— ©Patricia Barry Levy/Index Stock Imagery;

pp. 65, 98—©Rudi Von Briel/PhotoEdit; pp. 69, 349—©Bill Aron/PhotoEdit; pp. 76, 306—©Laura Dwight/PhotoEdit; pp. 76, 412, 416—©Chuck Savage/Stock Market; pp. 88, 113—©William Johnson/New England Photo; p. 88—©Camerique/ H. Armstrong Roberts; p. 101—©Frank Siteman/Stock Boston; p. 108—©Dave Martin/AP/Wide World Photos; p. 109— ©Jonathan Nourok/Stone; p. 114—©Dale Durfee/ Stone; pp. 121, 310—©Felicia Martinez/ PhotoEdit; p. 123—©Richard Hutchings/ PhotoEdit; pp. 127, 291—©Ron Chapple/ FPG International; p. 135— ©Cheyenne Rouse/Visuals Unlimited; pp. 137, 363—©Mary Kate Denny/ PhotoEdit; pp. 144, 169, 210, 239, 404, 421—©Westlight/ Corbis; pp. 144, 195, 300—©Don Mason/ Stock Market; p. 163—©Cameron Hervet/Stone; pp. 170, 209—©Michael Gadomski/ Animals Animals; pp. 172, 203, 342—©Spencer Grant/PhotoEdit; p. 175—©Norbert Schafer/Stock Market; pp. 179, 327— ©Dana White/PhotoEdit; p. 190—©David Young Wolff/Stone; p. 210—©Dave Krieger/Stone; p. 215—©Jon Feingersh/ Stock Market; pp. 240, 394—©Gary Conner/PhotoEdit; pp. 240, 273—©Walter Choroszewski/Stock Connection; p. 244—

©Rhoda Sidney/Stock Boston; p. 249— ©Myrleen Cate/Stone; p. 251—©Lori Adamski Peek/Stone; p. 253—©Index Stock Imagery; p. 255—©Lawrence Midgale/Stone; p. 266—©Bruce Ayres/ Stone; p. 274—©Brian Bailey/Stone; pp. 274, 299—©Adam Woolfitt/ Woodfin Camp & Associates; p. 276—©SW Produc- tion/Index Stock Imagery; p. 279—©James Martin/Stone; p. 284—©Bob Thomas/ Stone; p. 289—©Gabe Palmer/Mugshots/ Stock Market; pp. 292, 295—©Mugshots/ Stock Market; pp. 300, 339—©Chris Arend/ Alaska Stock; p. 331—©Don Smetzer/ Stone; pp. 334, 374—©David Hanover/ Stone; p. 340—©Tom McCarthy/ PhotoEdit; pp. 340, 379—©IFA Bilderteam/ Leo de Wys; p. 352—©David Roth/Stone; p. 357—©Mark Richards/PhotoEdit; pp. 359, 366, 370—©Walter Hodges/Stone; p. 362—©NJ/Hackensack/Visuals Unlimited; p. 380—©Bob Krist/Corbis; pp. 380, 403— ©Picture Finders Ltd./Leo de Wys; p. 382— ©Ulrike Welsch/PhotoEdit; p. 390— ©Michelle Bridwell/PhotoEdit; p. 392— ©William Taufic/Stock Market; p. 404— ©Ariel Skelley/Stock Market; p. 406—©Eric Larrayadieu/Stone; p. 410—©Barbara Filet/Stone; p. 418—©Brooke Slezak/Stone; p. 423—Custom Medical Stock Photo

## Publisher's Project Staff

Director, Product
   Development: Karen Dahlen
Editor: Julie Maas
Copy Editor: Maureen Meyer
Development Assistant: Bev Johnson

Designer: Virginia Sutton
Design Manager: Nancy Condon
Desktop Publishing
   Manager: Lisa Beller
Desktop Pub. Specialist: Linda Peterson

Purchasing Agent: Mary Kaye Kuzma
Executive Director
   of Marketing: Matt Keller
Marketing Manager: Brian Holl
Editorial services: Glen Phelan

Printed in the United States of America

ISBN 0-7854-2552-7

Product Number 91100

A 0 9 8 7 6 5 4

# Contents

# How to Use This Book: A Study Guide

Welcome to a study of transition skills. Everyone needs to develop skills that will help them make the transition from high school to the next step smoother. Whether you are going on to a job or a postsecondary school, transition skills will help you survive in the real world.

As you read the chapters and lessons in this book, you will learn skills that will help you live and function on your own. You will learn the importance of living independently and that you can take care of yourself and a home.

## How to Study

• Plan a regular time to study.

• Choose a quiet desk or table where you will not be distracted. Find a spot that has good lighting.

• Gather all the books, pencils, and paper you need to complete your assignments.

• Decide on a goal. For example, "I will finish reading and take notes on Chapter 1, Lesson 1, by 8:00."

• Take a five- to ten-minute break every hour to stay alert.

• If you start to feel sleepy, take a short break and get some fresh air.

## Before Beginning Each Chapter

• Read the chapter title and study the photograph. What does the photo say to you about the chapter title?

• Read the opening paragraphs and the self-assessment checklist.

• Study the goals for learning. The chapter review and tests will ask questions related to these goals.

• Read the chapter summaries to help you identify key issues.

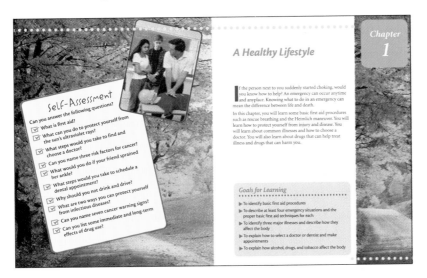

## Before Beginning Each Lesson

Read the lesson title and restate it in the form of a question. For example,

 **Lesson 1**   *Performing First Aid Procedures*  • • • • •

Write: *What are first aid procedures?*

Look over the entire lesson, noting . . .

• pictures        • bold words

• charts          • text organization

• tables          • questions in the margins

• figures         • lesson review

Also note the features . . .

- **Current Day**—Modern day information related to the chapter topic

- **Technology In Our Lives**—A technology advance related to the chapter topic

- **Online Resources**—Web sites related to the chapter topic

- **Everyday Tips**—
  Short, easy-to-use tips about making it on your own

## As You Read the Lesson

- Read the major headings. Each subhead is a question.

- Read the paragraphs that follow to answer the question.

- Before moving on to the next heading, see if you can answer the question. If you cannot, reread the section to look for the answer. If you are still unsure, ask for help.

- Answering the questions in the lesson will help you determine if you know the lesson's key ideas.

## Using the Bold Words

Knowing the meaning of all the boxed words in the narrow column will help you understand what you read.

These words appear in **bold type** the first time they appear in the text and are defined in the paragraph.

> **First aid,** the immediate emergency care given to a sick or injured person before professional medical care arrives

All the words in the narrow column are also defined in the **glossary.**

**First aid**—The immediate emergency care given to a sick or injured person before professional medical care arrives (p. 8)

---

**First aid**
*The immediate emergency care given to a sick or injured person before professional medical care arrives*

## Taking Notes in Class

As you read, you will be learning many new facts and ideas. Your notes will be useful and will help you remember when preparing for class discussions and studying for tests.

• Write the main ideas and supporting details.

• Use your own words.

• Keep your notes brief. You may want to set up some abbreviations to speed up your note-taking. For example: with = w/, and = +, United States = US, dollars = $

• Make notes on your self-assessment worksheets or in your Student Workbook. Use them to study.

• Use the same method all the time. Then when you study for a test, you will know where to find the information you need to review.

## Using the Summaries

• Read the summaries from your text to make sure you understand the chapter's main ideas.

• Make up a sample test of items you think may be on the test. You may want to do this with a classmate and share your questions.

• Review your notes and test yourself on vocabulary words and key ideas.

• Practice writing about some of the main ideas from the chapter.

## Using the Reviews

• Answer the questions under Identifying Facts.

• Answer the questions under Understanding Main Ideas.

• Write what you think about the questions under Write Your Opinion.

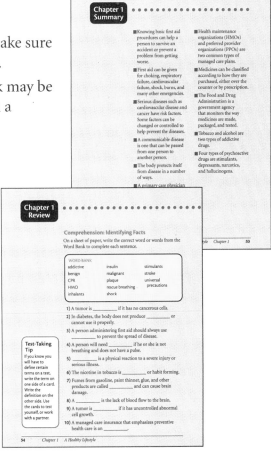

Some students prefer taking notes on index cards.

Others jot down key ideas in a spiral notebook.

# Introduction

Making the transition from high school graduate to living independently is a big step in life. Whether you choose to go on to a postsecondary school or to a job, this is an exciting time. You will face challenges. For example, you will need to find a place to live. Once you have done that, you will want to make it your home. You will need to manage a budget so you pay for food, clothes, and rent. You will want to start saving for your future so you have money when you retire.

You will need to choose a career and prepare for it. That process might include researching occupations and interviewing people in those occupations to learn more about them. You will need to find a position within the field that interests you. You will need to create job-search materials, and apply and interview for jobs. When you are offered a job that is right for you, you will want to consider the offer. Once you accept a position, you will need to apply your skills to make the most out of the job. This will involve learning how to communicate and work with your supervisor, coworkers, and other people in the company. Moving forward in your career may require more education and training.

You will also need to deal with day-to-day things such as transportation, doing laundry, eating well, and exercising.

This book can help you learn skills you will need to make the transition to being on your own. Good luck!

## Are You Ready to Live On Your Own?

Have you thought about what it means to go from high school to a job or on to a postsecondary school? Have you considered what it takes to have a successful marriage and raise children? Are you prepared to be out on your own, living independently?

**Directions:** Ask yourself the following questions. You do not need to share your answers with anyone. Can you answer *yes* to most of these questions? If you can, good for you! You are well on your way to making the transition from high school to the real world a successful one. If you answer *no* to most of these questions, do not worry. You can find the answers to these questions and many more in this book.

1) Do you know what steps to take to find a doctor?

2) Do you know how to choose an insurance company?

3) Can you explain why you should read and compare food labels?

4) Do you know how to set realistic goals?

5) Can you explain what it means to be a self-advocate?

6) Can you name five steps you could use to solve a problem?

7) Do you know what to do to vote in an election?

8) Can you name two responsibilities U.S. citizens have?

9) Do you know how to open a bank account?

10) Do you know what you need to connect to the Internet?

11) Do you know what information you need to complete a job application?

12) Do you know what a performance assessment is?

13) Do you know what to consider when selecting a postsecondary school?

14) Can you name the different learning styles?

15) Can you list two things that contribute to a successful marriage?

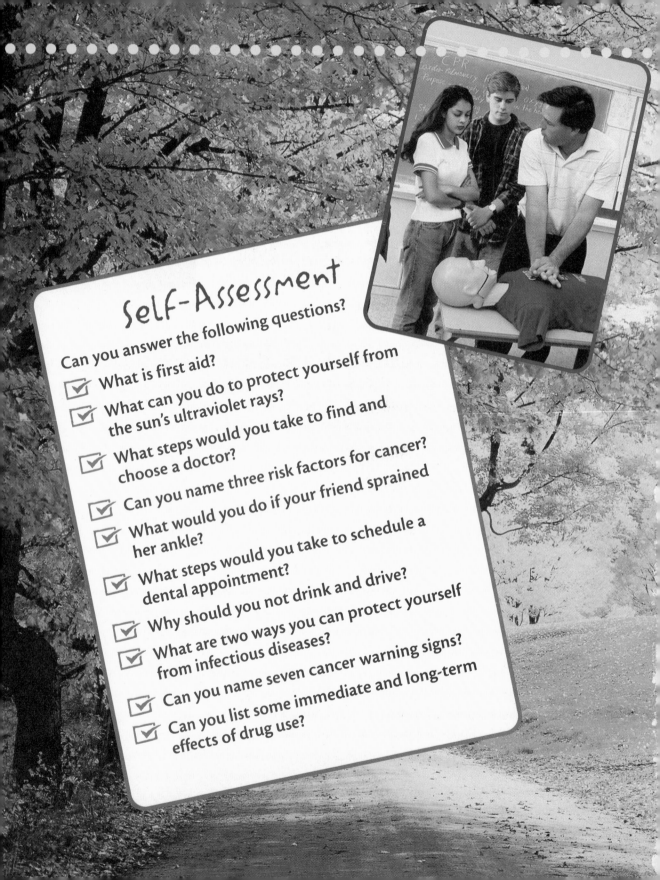

# Self-Assessment

Can you answer the following questions?

☑ What is first aid?

☑ What can you do to protect yourself from the sun's ultraviolet rays?

☑ What steps would you take to find and choose a doctor?

☑ Can you name three risk factors for cancer?

☑ What would you do if your friend sprained her ankle?

☑ What steps would you take to schedule a dental appointment?

☑ Why should you not drink and drive?

☑ What are two ways you can protect yourself from infectious diseases?

☑ Can you name seven cancer warning signs?

☑ Can you list some immediate and long-term effects of drug use?

# A Healthy Lifestyle

I f the person next to you suddenly started choking, would you know how to help? An emergency can occur anytime and anyplace. Knowing what to do in an emergency can mean the difference between life and death.

In this chapter, you will learn some basic first aid procedures such as rescue breathing and the Heimlich maneuver. You will learn how to protect yourself from injury and disease. You will learn about common illnesses and how to choose a doctor. You will also learn about drugs that can help treat illness and drugs that can harm you.

## Goals for Learning

▶ To identify basic first aid procedures

▶ To describe at least four emergency situations and the proper basic first aid techniques for each

▶ To identify three major illnesses and describe how they affect the body

▶ To explain how to select a doctor or dentist and make appointments

▶ To explain how alcohol, drugs, and tobacco affect the body

# Performing First Aid Procedures ● ● ● ● ●

**First aid**
*The immediate emergency care given to a sick or injured person before professional medical care arrives*

**A**ccidents happen without warning. Knowing basic first aid procedures and when to use them can mean the difference between life and death.

**First aid** is the immediate emergency care given to a sick or injured person before professional medical help arrives. Knowing how and when to use first aid techniques can help you relieve a person's pain and even save a life.

## What Are the Basic Guidelines for First Aid?

First aid is sometimes needed following a car accident or if someone has collapsed. One of the most important things you can do for a victim in an emergency is remain calm. By remaining calm, you can make clear, quick decisions and perform first aid correctly. Your calm will help the victim avoid panic. Follow these basic first aid guidelines:

Pre-program phone numbers for local police, fire department, poison control center, doctor's office, and vet (if you have a pet) into your phone. The numbers will be easily accessible in an emergency. Share this information with family members.

1. Grab your first aid kit if you have one with you. Look around the immediate surroundings to determine any dangers to the victim or yourself. You need to be safe in order to help others who are injured. Move the victim only if there is danger of an explosion, fire, or drowning.

2. Find out if the victim is conscious by tapping on the person's shoulder or loudly asking if he or she is all right. If the person is unconscious, ask someone to call for emergency medical help. Stay with the victim. If you are alone, call for emergency help and return to the victim.

3. Check to see if the victim is breathing and has a pulse and open airway. If not, clear the airway and perform rescue breathing. This procedure is discussed later in the chapter.

4. If the victim is conscious, ask permission to provide help. Check for other body injuries. Look for emergency medical bracelets or necklace nametags. They identify medical problems such as diabetes, epilepsy, or a heart condition.

5. Check for severe bleeding. If you have latex rubber gloves, put them on to protect yourself. Apply direct pressure to a wound to stop bleeding.

After you have done these things, stay with the victim until help arrives. Keep the victim comfortable and guard from getting too hot or too cold. Shade the person from the sun. Offer reassurance that help is on the way. Use common sense and only the skills you have been trained to use.

**Good Samaritan Laws**
*Laws that protect people who assist victims in an emergency*

## What Laws Protect You When Assisting Victims?

Many states have **Good Samaritan Laws** that protect people who assist victims in emergencies. The laws only require rescuers to use common sense and skills learned through training until help arrives. Rescuers are not expected to risk their own lives when providing emergency care. People can learn first aid skills through the American Red Cross, American Heart Association, and many other organizations.

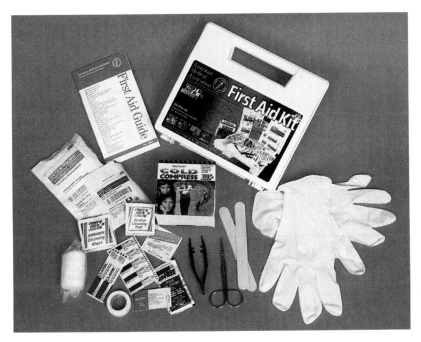

Keep a first aid kit stocked and ready for emergencies.

## What Are Universal Precautions?

To reduce the risk of infectious diseases such as AIDS or Hepatitis B, medical workers use **universal precautions**. These self-protection methods prevent contact with blood or other body fluids. For example, medical workers wear latex rubber gloves and other protective clothing such as masks. They carefully dispose of materials such as bandages that have come in contact with body fluids. They wash their hands after every procedure. First aid providers should use these methods to protect themselves and the victim.

**When you help a bleeding victim, what else could you use to protect your hands if you don't have latex gloves?**

### The American Red Cross

The Red Cross began in Switzerland in 1863. In 1881, Clara Barton helped start the American Red Cross. The organization helps people in wars, natural disasters, or other serious need. Each year, about 10 million Americans volunteer for educational programs, hospital duty, or disaster relief work. Red Cross Youth volunteer for hospital work and exchange gifts with needy young people. Volunteers donate much of the blood used by hospitals and during national emergencies. They contribute all of the money that supports Red Cross work. Volunteers are what truly make the Red Cross work.

## Lesson 1 Review

Write the answers to these questions on a sheet of paper, using complete sentences.

1) Why is it important to remain calm in an emergency?

2) When should you move a victim in an emergency?

3) What do the Good Samaritan Laws say?

4) What is the purpose of universal precautions?

5) Why would it be important to check a victim for emergency medical tags?

# *Reacting to Life-Threatening Emergencies* ● ●

Heimlich maneuver
*Firm upward thrusts below the rib cage to force an object out of the airway*

**S**ome conditions must be treated before others because they are life threatening. Choking, not breathing, cardiovascular failure, shock, and severe bleeding can all be life threatening. Minutes can mean the difference between life and death in these situations. Knowing what to do until help arrives can make that difference.

## What Is First Aid for Choking?

Thousands of people die from choking each year. Food or a foreign object can block a person's airway and prevent him or her from breathing.

Imagine your family is eating dinner in a restaurant. Suddenly your brother cannot speak and turns pale or blue. He clutches his throat between his thumb and index finger. He is using the universal distress signal for choking. Others signs of choking are gasping, a weak cough, inability to speak, and loss of consciousness.

Ask your brother if he can talk. If a choking victim can still speak or cough, some air is getting through. Allow him to try to cough up the object. Never pound on a person's back to try to force the object out. Pounding can cause the object to move further down the windpipe to completely block it.

If the victim cannot speak, cough, or breathe, perform the **Heimlich maneuver**. This emergency action calls for making firm upward thrusts just below the rib cage. The thrusts force air from the lungs through the windpipe to push the object out of the airway.

Follow the steps shown in Figure 1.1 to use the Heimlich maneuver:

1. Stand behind the choking victim and wrap your arms around the victim's waist.

2. Make a fist with one hand.

Universal distress signal for choking.

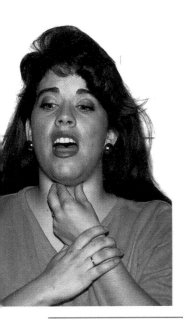

**Figure 1.1.** First aid for choking

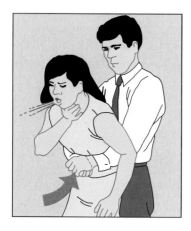

A. Heimlich maneuver

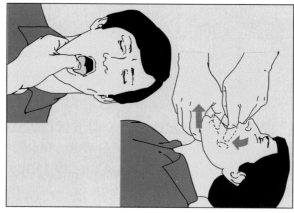

B. Finger sweep

3. Place the thumb side of the fist against the middle of the victim's abdomen or stomach, above the navel and below the ribs.

4. Use your other hand to grab your fist and give quick, upward thrusts into the victim's abdomen.

5. Repeat this procedure until the object is forced out.

If the person becomes unconscious, lower the person on his or her back to the floor. Have someone call 911 for emergency medical help. Open the victim's mouth and check the throat for the blockage using the finger sweep shown above.

To do the finger sweep, follow these steps:

1. Grasp the tongue and lower jaw between your thumb and fingers. Lift the jaw.

2. Use your other index finger in a hooking action at the back of the tongue to sweep the object out of the airway.

3. If this does not work, begin rescue breathing, which is described above.

● ● ● ● ● ● ● ● ● ●

**Why is it a good idea to chew your food well and not talk and chew at the same time?**

What if you are alone and choking? You can give yourself abdominal thrusts. Use your hands as you would to help a choking victim. You can also lean your abdomen over a sturdy chair or countertop. Press against the chair or countertop using quick thrusts.

## What Is First Aid for Respiratory Failure?

Choking is only one reason people stop breathing. Heart attack, drowning, electrical shock, or severe allergic reaction can also cause respiratory failure, or not breathing. People who are experiencing respiratory failure will have pale or blue skin, especially around their mouth and fingernails. If a person has a pulse but is not breathing, **rescue breathing** is required. Rescue breathing puts oxygen from the rescuer into an unconscious victim's lungs. Figure 1.2 shows the steps of rescue breathing, which is also known as mouth-to-mouth resuscitation. The best way to learn this technique is in a health class or through a first aid training class.

> **Rescue breathing**
> *Putting oxygen from the rescuer's lungs into an unconscious person's lungs to help the person breathe*

**Figure 1.2.** The steps in rescue breathing

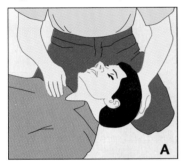
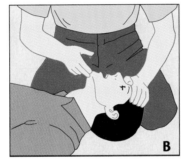
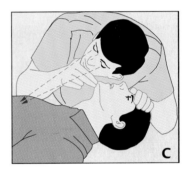
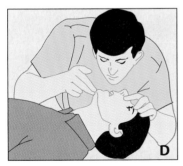
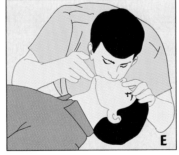
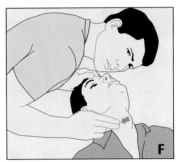

**A.** Tap on the person's shoulder or loudly ask, "Are you all right?" to find out if the victim is conscious. If the person is unconscious, send someone to call EMS for help.
**B.** Tilt the head back and lift the chin to open the airway.

**C.** Look, listen, and feel for breathing for 3 to 5 seconds.
**D.** Keep the head tilted back and pinch the nose shut.
**E.** Take a deep breath, seal your lips around the person's mouth, and give the victim two full breaths. For babies, seal your lips around both

the mouth and nose and give gentle breaths once every three seconds.
**F.** Check for a pulse on the side of the neck for 5 to 10 seconds. If you find a pulse, recheck breathing and continue rescue breathing as necessary.

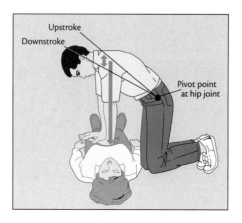

Figure 1.3. Cardiopulmonary resuscitation (CPR)

**Cardiac arrest**
*A condition in which the heart has stopped beating and there is no pulse*

**Cardiopulmonary resuscitation (CPR)**
*An emergency procedure for cardiovascular failure*

## What Is First Aid for Cardiovascular Failure?

The cardiovascular system may fail because of a drug overdose, a stroke, electrical shock, poisoning, or heart disease. Signs of failure include irregular pulse, moist face, difficulty breathing, and pale or blue skin. If the person's heart stops, the person is in **cardiac arrest** and has no pulse. Call emergency medical services (EMS) immediately when a person shows signs of cardiovascular failure or has a history of heart trouble. Until EMS arrives, perform **cardiopulmonary resuscitation (CPR)**. CPR combines rescue breathing with chest compressions, or presses. The goal is to open the person's airway and restore breathing and circulation. Follow these basic CPR steps which are shown in Figure 1.3.

1. Find the proper hand position.
   - Locate the notch at the lower end of the breastbone with your fingers.
   - Place the heel of your other hand on the breastbone next to your fingers.
   - Remove your fingers from the notch and put that hand on top of your other hand.
   - Use only the heels of your hands, keeping your fingers off the chest.

2. Give 15 compressions.
   - Position your shoulders over your hands.
   - Compress the breastbone 1½ to 2 inches.
   - Do 15 compressions in about ten seconds.
   - Compress down and up smoothly, keeping hand contact with the chest at all times.
   - After every 15 compressions, breathe two full breaths into the person's mouth.

The best way to learn CPR is in a health class or through a first aid training class.

## What Is First Aid for Shock?

**Shock** is a physical reaction to a severe injury or serious illness. The circulatory system fails to provide enough blood to the body. Even if the injury is not life-threatening, shock can lead to death. Take steps immediately to treat shock. Signs of shock include a rapid or weak pulse, fast or slow breathing, dilated pupils, and cold or moist skin. If a person appears to be in shock, call 911 immediately. Follow these steps until help arrives:

1. Keep the person lying down and raise the legs about 12 inches to help return blood flow to the heart. Do not elevate legs if you suspect injuries to the neck or spine.

2. Maintain normal body temperature by covering the person with a blanket.

3. Do not give the victim food or water.

## What Is First Aid for Severe Bleeding?

Severe bleeding can result in shock or death. Control the bleeding quickly. After taking self-protection measures, cover the wound with a sterile bandage or clean cloth. Press down on the wound using the palm of your hand. If the bandage becomes soaked with blood, leave it in place and add more layers. Continue to press until the bleeding stops. Elevate the wound above the level of the person's heart.

## Lesson 2 Review

Write the answers to these questions on a sheet of paper, using complete sentences.

1) What does the Heimlich maneuver do?

2) What is the difference between rescue breathing and CPR?

3) What is first aid for severe bleeding?

4) What happens when a person goes into shock?

5) What can you do if you are alone and choking?

> **Shock**
> *Failure of the circulatory system to provide enough blood to the body*

> **To help someone who is bleeding severely, follow these steps:**
> 1. Stop the bleeding.
> 2. Protect the wound from infection
> 3. Treat the person for shock.
> 4. Get EMS help immediately.

*First Aid for Other Injuries* • • • • • • • • •

**A** person trained in first aid can recognize the signs of poisoning, burns, and other problems and respond appropriately.

### What Is First Aid for Poisoning?

Poisons may be swallowed, breathed in, or absorbed through the skin. In any case, seek medical help quickly after giving first aid because some poisoning is life threatening.

Oral poisoning happens when a harmful substance such as a household cleaner is swallowed. Signs of oral poisoning are sudden severe abdominal pain, upset stomach, and vomiting. The person may become sleepy and lose consciousness. The person may also have chemical burns on the lips and a chemical odor on the breath. Call the local poison control center immediately. Follow the poison control expert's instructions.

• • • • • • • • •

**What would you do if your younger brother or sister ate leaves from a house plant?**

Inhalation poisoning happens when someone breathes in harmful fumes, or gases. Signs of inhalation poisoning are headache, dizziness, and unconsciousness. Move the victim out into fresh air at once. If the victim is unconscious, check for a pulse and breathing. Perform rescue breathing or CPR if the victim is not breathing. Take care not to breathe in any harmful fumes when helping the victim. Call for emergency help.

Contact poisoning happens when a harmful substance is absorbed through the skin. Poisons may be absorbed from plants such as poison ivy, household cleaners, and fertilizers. Signs include a severe rash, swelling, blisters, itching, and burning. Remove clothes that have touched the poison. Wash skin with soap and lots of water. Apply calamine lotion to relieve the itching.

## How Do You Treat Burns?

There are three kinds, or degrees, of burns. A first-degree burn injures only the outer layer of skin. This minor burn includes sunburn. A second-degree burn affects the top layers of skin. A third-degree burn extends through all skin layers to the tissues underneath.

First aid for first- and second-degree burns is the same. First, stop the burn by getting the person away from the burn source. Next, cool the burn with lots of cool water. Don't rub or clean the burn. Cover it with a dry, loose, sterile dressing to prevent infection. For a third-degree burn, call for emergency help immediately. Stay with the victim and watch for signs of shock.

**Heat exhaustion** *A condition resulting from physical activity in a very hot environment*

**Heatstroke** *A condition resulting from being in the heat too long*

 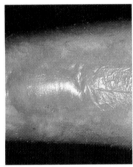 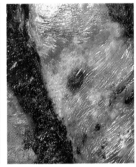

The three degrees of burns are treated differently.

## What Is First Aid for Exposure to Heat and Cold?

**Heat exhaustion** usually results from too much physical activity in a hot environment. Signs of heat exhaustion are heavy sweating, weakness, muscle cramps, headache, and dizziness. First get the person out of the heat. Loosen his or her clothing, cool with wet cloths, and offer cool water to sip. Call for emergency help if the person becomes unconscious.

**Heatstroke** can happen when a person has been in the heat for too long. Lack of sweating is the main sign of heatstroke.

Other signs are high body temperature, red skin, rapid pulse, confusion, vomiting, and sudden unconsciousness. Call 911 immediately and follow the steps for treating heat exhaustion.

**Hypothermia** is a serious loss of body heat from being cold too long. It happens mostly in moderately cold, damp weather when a person is tired and not dressed warmly. Signs are thick speech, shivering, and below-normal body temperature. Hypothermia can be deadly. If the person isn't breathing, perform rescue breathing and have someone call 911. Remove the person's wet clothing. Slowly warm the person with blankets. Give him or her warm liquids to drink.

**Frostbite** is a tissue injury caused by extreme cold. It usually affects hands, feet, nose, and ears. Frostbitten skin looks gray or yellow and feels numb, cold, and "spongy" or "doughy." To treat frostbite, slowly warm up the affected area by placing it in warm water. Don't rub the area. Cover it with clean, dry bandages and get medical help.

## What Is First Aid for Bone and Joint Injuries?

A **sprain** is the tearing or stretching of tendons or ligaments connecting joints. Usually sprains occur at wrists, ankles, or knees. To reduce pain and swelling, follow the RICE formula shown below.

### RICE Formula

R for rest. Rest the limb or affected part.

I is for ice. Cover the affected part with ice to reduce swelling.

C is for compression. Wrap the injured part with an elastic bandage to compress the part and reduce swelling.

E is for elevation. Elevate, or raise, the injured part above the heart level if possible to prevent swelling and bleeding.

If you suspect a **fracture** or broken bone, look for crookedness, bruising, severe pain, or inability to move. Keep the body part in the same position as you found it and apply a **splint**. A splint is a stiff object that prevents movement. If the bone has broken the skin, cover the wound with a sterile bandage without pressing on the bone. If you suspect a neck or back injury, do not move the person. Call for emergency help immediately.

> **Fracture**
> *A broken bone*
>
> **Splint**
> *A rigid object that keeps a broken bone in place*

## Lesson 3 Review

Write the answers to these questions on a sheet of paper, using complete sentences.

1) What are two signs of inhalation poisoning?

2) What do you do to treat first- and second-degree burns?

3) What could burns on a person's lips mean?

4) How do you treat a suspected sprain?

5) What do you do if your friend faints while at soccer practice on a hot day?

Wrap a sprain with an elastic bandage to reduce swelling.

## Lesson 4    *Recognizing Symptoms of Illness* • • • • • •

**Cardiovascular**
*Relating to the heart and blood vessels*

**Hypertension**
*High blood pressure*

Our bodies need food, plenty of fluids, exercise, and rest to stay healthy. However, there are times when the body does not work properly and an illness occurs. Being able to recognize the signs, or symptoms, of an illness will help you know when and how to get treatment.

### What Diseases Are Considered Common?

The most common disease in the United States is the cold. A cold usually lasts from several days to more than a week. Symptoms include sneezing, coughing, stuffy or runny nose, fever, headache, and sore throat. These symptoms differ throughout the time that you have the cold. They may also differ from person to person and from cold to cold.

The flu, or influenza, has some of the same symptoms as a cold. Flu symptoms are usually more severe. Symptoms include fever, headache, sore throat, and coughing. Aching muscles, chills, nausea, vomiting, and diarrhea are some other flu symptoms. These symptoms also differ throughout the illness and from person to person.

### What Are Some Cardiovascular Diseases?

**Cardiovascular** disease is a group of disorders that affects the heart and blood vessels. Cardiovascular disease is the leading cause of death in the United States. Some common cardiovascular diseases are high blood pressure and arterial diseases. Preventive measures such as not smoking, exercise, and low-fat, low-sodium diets have reduced diseases. In addition, advances in technology have improved cardiovascular disease treatment.

### *Hypertension*

One common cardiovascular disease is high blood pressure, or **hypertension**. Blood pressure is the force of blood against the walls of the arteries when the heart pumps. Blood pressure normally goes up during exercise and down during sleep or relaxation. When a person's blood pressure remains above 140/90, that person has high blood pressure or hypertension.

Hypertension symptoms are hard to spot. You need to have your blood pressure measured to find out if you have hypertension. High blood pressure cannot be cured. However, it usually can be controlled with diet and medicine. Regular exercise also helps lower blood pressure.

### Heart Attack and Stroke

A heart attack occurs when the supply of blood and nutrients to the heart is severely reduced. If the blood supply is cut off for a critical amount of time, the muscle tissues are injured and die. The seriousness of a heart attack depends on how much tissue dies.

Narrowed arteries can also lead to a **stroke**. A stroke occurs when the blood supply to the brain suddenly stops. When this happens, some brain cells cannot function and they die. A stroke affects the parts of the body that the damaged part of the brain controlled. For example, if the part of the brain that controls speech is affected, the stroke victim may not be able to speak. A stroke affects each individual differently.

## What Are Some Cardiovascular Risk Factors?

A **risk factor** is a habit or trait that is known to increase a person's risk of having a disease. Serious diseases, such as cardiovascular disease, have many risk factors. Some can be changed. Some cannot.

These risk factors for cardiovascular problems cannot be changed:

• **Heredity**—A person may inherit a tendency to develop cardiovascular disease. You cannot change your genetic makeup.

• **Gender**—Men have a greater risk of heart attack before middle age than women do. After middle age, women's risks increase.

**Risk factor**
*A habit or trait that is known to increase a person's chances of having a disease*

**Stroke**
*A cardiovascular disease that occurs when the blood supply to the brain is stopped*

- **Age**—The risk of heart attack increases with age. More than half of all heart attacks occur in people who are age 65 and older.

- **Race**—Some races have a higher risk of cardiovascular disease. For example, African Americans have an unusually high rate of hypertension.

You can change these risk factors to reduce your chances of having cardiovascular problems:

- **Smoking**—You can lower your risk by choosing not to smoke. Smoking can lead to hypertension and other cardiovascular diseases. A smoker is twice as likely as a nonsmoker to have a heart attack. When people quit smoking, their risk of cardiovascular disease decreases rapidly.

- **Cholesterol**—High blood cholesterol is another major risk factor of cardiovascular problems. You can lower the risk by limiting the amount of saturated fats you eat. Eat only small amounts of animal fat such as eggs, butter, and meat.

- **Being overweight**—Extra weight strains the heart and adds to cardiovascular problems. A well-balanced diet helps you maintain a safe body weight.

- **Physical inactivity**—Being inactive can limit your body's ability to withstand a sudden change in blood pressure. Physical activity helps increase blood flow to your heart and strengthen it. Walking, swimming, running, or biking for just 30 minutes a day can help.

## What Causes Cancer?

Cancer is the second leading cause of death in the United States. Quite a bit of progress has been made, however, in cancer prevention and treatment.

Eating healthy foods helps prevent cardiovascular problems.

An abnormal and harmful growth of cells in the body causes cancer. There are more than 100 types of cancer. When cancer invades normal tissue, those organs cannot function properly. Sometimes the abnormal growth of cells forms a mass of tissue called a **tumor**. If the cells' growth is uncontrolled, the tumor is called **malignant**. That means it is harmful. Some tumors do not spread and are not harmful. They are called **benign** tumors. More than 90 percent of tumors are benign. Appendix A includes information about the most common places for cancer in men and women.

Benign
*Not harmful to health*

Malignant
*Harmful to health*

Tumor
*A mass of tissue formed from the abnormal growth of cells*

## What Are the Symptoms of Cancer?

Cancer symptoms depend on the tumor's location. For example, someone with lung cancer may have a cough that does not improve with treatment. A woman with breast cancer may feel a lump in her breast. Some cancer symptoms are not specific. A person may not feel well but not have specific symptoms. Unusual weight loss and poor appetite may occur as a result of cancer.

Screening is the search for disease in people who do not have disease or who do not know they have disease. Early detection, though it does not prevent cancer, is the most important factor for cancer survival. Read the warning signs listed in the box below and see a doctor if you notice any of them.

### Seven Warning Signs of Cancer

C **hange in bowel or bladder habits**
A **sore that will not heal**
U **nusual bleeding or discharge**
T **hickening or lump in the breast or elsewhere**
I **ndigestion or difficulty in swallowing**
O **bvious change in a wart or mole**
N **agging cough or hoarseness**

## How Is Cancer Treated?

Three major treatments are used to fight cancer. They are surgery to remove tumors, drugs (chemotherapy) to kill cancer cells, or radiation to kill cancer cells. The kind of treatment depends on the kind of cancer. Often, a combination of treatments is used. Cancer treatments produce side effects that make people sick. For example, a person receiving chemotherapy may have an upset stomach or lose his or her appetite. However, these treatments allow people with cancer to live longer with the disease than they would without treatment. Many people survive cancer because of treatment.

## What Are the Risk Factors for Cancer?

Just as with cardiovascular disease, some major risk factors may cause cancer. If you understand the risk factors, you can avoid some of them.

• **Cigarette smoke**—Cigarette smoke contains 43 known chemicals that cause cancer. About 87 percent of lung cancer deaths and about 30 percent of all cancer deaths can be attributed to smoking. Avoid smoking and chewing tobacco. Second-hand smoke, or smoke breathed by a nonsmoker, is also a risk factor.

Smoking cigarettes is a cancer risk factor.

• **Toxic chemicals**—Toxic chemicals are substances that are harmful to human health or to the environment. Many chemicals used in industry, on farms, and in the home have been found to cause cancer.

• **Radiation**—Radiation is used to treat cancer, but too much of it can cause cancer. Have X rays only when you need them.

- **Sunlight**—Sunlight is a source of natural radiation that can cause skin cancer. People who sunbathe or use tanning booths expose themselves to harmful radiation. That puts them at risk for **malignant melanoma**, the most common form of skin cancer. See Appendix A. Wear sunblock lotion when you spend time outside on a sunny day. Sunblock will block more of the sun's rays than sunscreen. Clothing such as long-sleeved shirts, wide-brimmed hats, and sunglasses also protect you from the sun's rays.

- **Heredity**—A tendency to cancer may run in some families. If you have an inherited tendency to certain kinds of cancer, see your doctor regularly.

- **Viruses**—Viruses can cause cancer. A virus can insert its genes into human chromosomes. This causes a mutation, or change, that leads to cancer. Cancer caused by a virus cannot spread from person to person. Not everyone is vulnerable, or open, to cancers caused by viruses.

## What Is Diabetes?

Today, 15.7 million people in the United States have diabetes. **Diabetes** is a chronic disease in which the body does not produce or properly use insulin. Insulin, a hormone produced in the pancreas, converts sugar, starches, and other food into energy the body uses.

Type I and Type II are the two most common types of diabetes. Type I diabetes, or **insulin-dependent diabetes**, causes a person to depend on daily insulin injections for survival. Type I diabetes usually starts during childhood. Symptoms include frequent urination, extreme thirst and hunger, rapid weight loss, and fatigue. Type I diabetes accounts for 5 to10 percent of people with diabetes.

Type II diabetes, or **non-insulin–dependent diabetes**, usually occurs in adults over age 40. This is the most common form of diabetes. Type II diabetes is milder than Type I and has been linked to heredity, inactivity, and obesity. Type II diabetes can often be controlled through weight loss and exercise.

**Diabetes**
*A disease in which the body is not able to use glucose from food*

**Insulin-dependent diabetes**
*Diabetes that usually causes a person to depend on daily injections of insulin; type I diabetes*

**Malignant melanoma**
*A common form of skin cancer often caused by the sun*

**Non-insulin–dependent diabetes**
*Diabetes that usually does not cause a person to depend on insulin; type II diabetes*

When you are in the sun, use #15 or greater sunscreen or sunblock to protect your skin.

Symptoms include blurry vision, slow-healing sores, sleepiness, and tingling in hands or feet. Type II diabetes accounts for 90 to 95 percent of people with diabetes.

## What Is Arthritis and How Is It Treated?

**Arthritis**
*A group of diseases that result in swelling of the joints and rubbing on the bones*

**Cartilage**
*A cushion in the joints*

**Osteoarthritis**
*A condition in which the cartilage in joints wears away*

**Rheumatoid arthritis**
*A destructive inflammation of the joints*

**Arthritis** is a group of painful diseases that result in swelling of the joints and rubbing on the bones. Sometimes a person loses the function in the joints that are affected. The two main types of arthritis affect about 40 million people in the United States.

**Rheumatoid arthritis** is the most serious type of arthritis. It is destructive inflammation of the joints. The joints become stiff, swollen, and tender. A person with this disease may not be able to move the joints and may feel weak and tired. Rheumatoid arthritis may involve other tissues in the body and can result in deformity. Treatment usually includes medications to relieve the inflammation and pain.

The second most common type of arthritis is **osteoarthritis**. In this arthritis, the **cartilage,** a cushion in the joints, usually wears away. When this happens, the bones rub on one another. This wear and tear can change the structure and shape of a person's joints. It can also cause loss of movement. Treatment with rheumatoid arthritis medications has been tried. New studies, however, show that these drugs may hinder the body's natural process of fighting osteoarthritis.

· · · · · · · · · · ·

Why do you think a change in the weather affects people with arthritis?

## Lesson 4 Review

Write the answers to these questions on a sheet of paper, using complete sentences.

**1)** What is the difference between a heart attack and a stroke?

**2)** What are four risk factors for cardiovascular disease that you can control?

**3)** How does a benign tumor differ from a malignant tumor?

**4)** What is diabetes?

**5)** What are three warning signs of cancer?

## *Preventing the Spread of Illness* ● ● ● ● ● ● ●

> **Communicable disease**
> *A disease that can be passed from one person to another*

**H**ave you ever heard people say they "caught a cold"? How does a person catch a cold? How does the body get rid of it?

### How Are Diseases Acquired?

Many diseases are acquired. An acquired disease is caused by infection, human behavior, or environmental conditions that affect health. When infection causes an acquired disease, it is called a **communicable disease**. That means one person can pass the disease to another person. Another word for communicable is contagious. Germs that cause communicable diseases are passed from person to person. For example, you get a cold or the flu from another person's germs.

An acquired disease can also be caused by a person's behaviors. For example, consider a person who eats many fatty foods, avoids exercise, and smokes cigarettes. The person's continued behavior may cause high blood pressure or trigger a heart attack.

An acquired disease can also come from the environment. For example, small children who eat chips of lead-based paint can get lead poisoning. Nonsmokers who breathe other people's cigarette smoke may get lung diseases, including cancer.

**Wash your hands frequently with soap and water to prevent the spread of germs.**

## The Ways Germs Are Spread

- Through direct physical contact with an infected person
- By droplets that an infected person coughs into the air
- By contact with an object an infected person used
- By contact with food or water with a pathogen in it
- Through the bites of infected animals, including insects

## What Are the Stages of Infectious Disease?

Germs that cause communicable diseases are called **pathogens**. Bacteria, viruses, fungi, and one-celled organisms are some pathogens.

After a person is infected with a pathogen, the disease passes through several stages. Figure 1.4 shows the stages of infectious disease. The first stage is **incubation**. This is the time it takes after a person is infected for symptoms of the disease to appear. The incubation period can be days, weeks, months, or even years.

If the body's defenses are effective in fighting off the pathogen during incubation, the person may not get sick. The body's **immune** system fights the infection. If the immune system cannot fight off the pathogen, the person becomes ill. During an illness, the immune system continues to fight it. The person usually recovers in a few days.

Some illnesses, such as **acquired immunodeficiency syndrome (AIDS)** or cancer, lower the effectiveness of the immune system. When this happens, the body cannot protect itself from pathogens. A simple cold can be deadly. Fortunately, the immune system successfully fights most infectious diseases.

**Acquired immunodeficiency syndrome (AIDS)**
*A disorder of the immune system*

**Immune**
*Resistant to infection*

**Incubation**
*Time between the initial infection and the appearance of symptoms of a disease*

**Pathogen**
*An agent that causes disease*

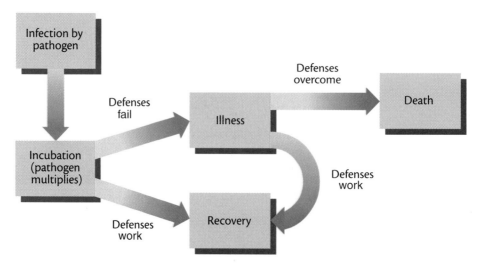

**Figure 1.4.** Stages of infectious disease

## How Does the Body Protect Itself from Disease?

The human body protects itself from infection and disease in many ways. Several physical and chemical barriers, or defenses, protect it. The skin forms the first line of defense. Regular washing with soap and water blocks germs from entering the body.

The skin and **mucous membranes** are physical barriers to infection. Mucous membranes are the moist linings of your mouth, nose, and other body passages. The body also has chemical barriers to infection. Saliva, tears, and sweat clear away pathogens. **Mucus**, the fluid the mucous membranes secrete, clears pathogens from the respiratory system. Urine carries pathogens out of the body. The stomach produces strong acids that kill pathogens when they enter the digestive system.

## How Does the Immune System Work?

In spite of your body's many barriers to infection, sometimes pathogens enter the bloodstream. This might happen because of a break in your skin such as a cut. Then your final line of defense—your immune system—goes to work.

**Mucous membrane**
*The moist lining of body passages*

**Mucus**
*Fluid the mucous membranes secrete*

• • • • • • • • • •

**What immunizations have you had?**

## Immunization Schedule

**Make a list of your vaccinations and the dates you had them. This chart lists some common vaccinations and the ages when they are recommended.**

| | |
|---|---|
| Haemophilus influenzae b (Hib) | 2, 4, and 6 months |
| Measles, Mumps, Rubella (MMR) | 2, 4, 6 and 15 months; booster after age 4 |
| Polio (IPV) | 2, 4, and 15 months; booster after age 4 |
| Diphtheria, Pertussis Tetanus (DTaP) | 2, 4, 6, and 15 months; booster after age 4 |
| Diphtheria-Tetanus (Td) | Age 11–12; booster every 10 years |
| Hepatitis B (Hep B) | Three-injection series for children older than age 2: more than one month between 1st and 2nd injection; more than four months between 2nd and 3rd injection. |
| Varicella (Chicken Pox) | After age 2 |

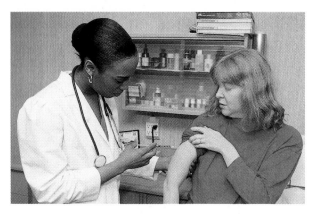

Vaccinations help the body build immunity to some diseases.

When a foreign substance enters the bloodstream, the blood makes **antibodies**. Antibodies are proteins that kill specific pathogens. If the correct antibodies are in the blood when an infection occurs, they can begin to fight it.

Antibodies form in the blood several ways. They develop during an illness. The antibodies help fight the illness and that speeds up recovery. Some antibodies remain in the body after you are over an illness. These antibodies give you **immunity** to the disease. Immunity is your body's ability to resist an infectious disease so you won't get it again. For example, once you have the mumps, you probably won't get the mumps again.

Another way to be immune to a disease is through a **vaccination**. A vaccination is an injection, or shot, of dead or weak viruses into your body. Enough virus is injected to make you immune to the disease. When you get a vaccination, your body makes antibodies against that disease.

Many states have developed immunization programs to make sure children are protected from certain diseases. An immunization schedule appears on page 29.

> **Antibody**
> *A protein that kills a specific kind of pathogen*
>
> **Immunity**
> *The body's ability to resist infectious diseases*
>
> **Vaccination**
> *An injection of dead or weakened virus to make the body immune to the virus*

## Lesson 5 Review

Write the answers to these questions on a sheet of paper, using complete sentences.

**1)** What is a communicable disease?

**2)** What are four ways germs can spread?

**3)** What is an incubation period?

**4)** How does a vaccination work?

**5)** Why might a country require a foreign visitor to have certain immunizations?

*Scheduling Medical Appointments* • • • •

**W**ise health consumers know when self-care is appropriate. They also know when it is a good idea to see a doctor.

### How Do You Practice Prevention?

Prevention is appropriate, ongoing self-care. Good nutrition, regular exercise, and safety practices help prevent illness or injuries. Not smoking and not breathing in second-hand smoke are also preventive measures. You practice prevention when you choose not to use tobacco, alcohol, or drugs other than those prescribed by a health professional. Eating right and maintaining a weight that is right for you help prevent heart and other problems.

When it comes to ordinary colds, the flu, and other minor illnesses, you can usually care for yourself. The key word is *ordinary*. Sound self-care for an ordinary cold or the flu includes drinking plenty of liquids and getting extra rest. But minor illnesses and injuries that do not show improvement within a few days require professional help.

### When Should You See a Doctor?

Sometimes it is best not to treat your own health problems. Knowing when to seek professional medical help is something you get better at over time. As a rule, you should consult a health professional whenever you notice something out of the ordinary about your body or how you feel. Here are some examples of situations where it is best to seek professional medical help:

• An injury to the head or face that is more than a scratch or bruise

• Blood in the urine or feces

• Any sharp abdominal or chest pain

• A mole that changes color or is an irregular shape

- A minor problem such as a cold, flu, sore throat, cough, fever, headache, vomiting, or body ache that lasts more than a week
- Numbness in any part of the body that doesn't go away
- A rash that doesn't clear up
- A cut or open sore that is not healing
- Depression that lasts more than a few days or recurrent thoughts of suicide or harming yourself

## Who Are Some Health Care Professionals?

Deciding who to see for health care involves many choices. Most people see a medical doctor called a **primary care physician (PCP)** for routine health care. A PCP gives annual physical exams, prescribes medications, and does routine tests or procedures. A **specialist** is a doctor who works only in a particular branch of medicine. The PCP will refer a patient to a specialist if regular treatment is not helping. A list of some medical specialists appears below.

### Some Medical Specialists

**Allergist**
Diagnoses and treats allergies such as hay fever and hives

**Cardiologist**
Diagnoses and treats heart diseases

**Gastroenterologist**
Diagnoses and treats stomach, intestinal, and liver disorders

**Neurologist**
Diagnoses and treats nervous system disorders

**Oncologist**
Treats cancers

**Orthopedic Surgeon**
Diagnoses and treats bone and joint problems

**Otorhinolaryngologist**
Diagnoses and treats ear, nose, and throat problems

**Pediatrician**
Provides primary care for babies, children, and adolescents

## How Can You Find a Health Care Professional?

Finding and choosing a doctor is part of caring for yourself. It helps to decide on a doctor before you actually need one. Your options for physicians may depend on certain factors—where you live and your insurance carrier. Another factor could be your eligibility for government-sponsored health programs. Word of mouth is a good first step in the process of selecting a physician. Ask a relative, friend, neighbor, or health care worker for a recommendation. Next, call your local hospital or physician referral center. Check your local library for a directory of physicians. It should list their names, their specialty, and their education. When you have a few names, consult your insurance provider to see if the doctors you selected are covered by your insurance. Many insurance providers have lists of health care professionals who accept their insurance.

Once you choose a physician, make an appointment to meet him or her. Call the office and ask the receptionist if you can make an interview appointment, or initial consultation with the doctor. Some physicians will make brief "get to know you" appointments with potential new patients.

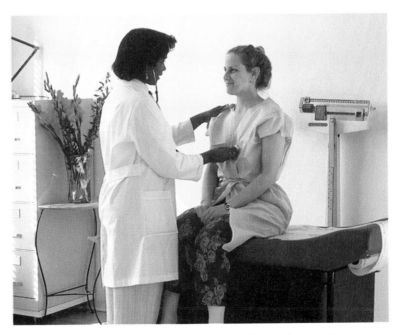

See a health professional when a minor illness doesn't improve.

This gives you a chance to meet and talk with the doctor. You can find out about the doctor's educational background and experience. Doctors are usually connected to specific hospitals. You can ask about this so you know in case you ever need hospital care.

Take time to ask at the reception desk about charges for phone calls or missed appointments. Some clinics charge you for missing an appointment and some have guidelines for canceling an appointment.

## Why Are Annual Checkups Important?

Most people go to a doctor only when they are sick. An annual physical exam or checkup can help keep you healthy. Through annual checkups, your doctor can detect illness and potential problems before they become an emergency. Write down any questions you have about your health. Bring the list and go through it with your doctor during your appointment.

If the doctor finds signs of illness during an exam, he or she may prescribe medicine to help your body heal. The doctor fills out a **prescription,** or a written order, for the medicine. Be sure to tell your doctor about any other medicines you are taking. Ask your doctor any questions you have about the medicine.

Take the prescription to a pharmacy to have it filled. Discuss the medicine with the pharmacist to make sure you understand exactly what it is for and how to take it. Ask about any side effects. Take the medicine as directed until it is gone, even if you feel better before then. If necessary, schedule a follow-up appointment with the doctor to make sure the illness is gone or to discuss further treatment.

● ● ● ● ● ● ● ● ● ● ●
**What would you do if you opened a refill of your prescription medicine and thought the pills looked odd or different?**

## What Are Some Health Care Facilities?

A **health care facility** is a place where people go for medical, dental, or other care. A dental or medical office is one kind of health care facility. Primary health care—routine exams and tests—is provided in these facilities.

**Outpatient clinics** offer same-day surgery health care for people who do not need to stay overnight. Other facilities provide **inpatient** care, meaning people receive care overnight or longer. Patients can receive nursing care and sometimes **rehabilitation**—therapy needed to recover from surgery or an illness or injury.

A **hospital** facility provides complete health care service. People can receive both outpatient and inpatient care at a hospital. Hospital emergency rooms and urgent care centers provide walk-in emergency care 24 hours a day.

Long-term care facilities such as nursing homes offer nursing care around the clock to elderly and young people. A **hospice** is another kind of long-term care facility for people who are dying from diseases such as AIDS or cancer.

## Who Pays for Health Care?

Most people cannot afford out-of-pocket medical expenses. **Health insurance** is a less expensive way to pay for health care. A health insurance plan, issued through a health insurance company, pays all or some medical costs. These costs may include medicines, surgery, tests, hospital stays, and doctor's visits. Health insurance covers major medical expenses that people cannot afford.

Three major kinds of health insurance are private, managed care, and government supported.

## What Is Private Health Insurance?

With an individual private health insurance plan, people pay for a policy themselves. Individuals regularly pay a premium, or fee, to an insurance company for a policy. In exchange, the insurance company agrees to pay part or all of their health care expenses.

Many employers offer a group plan as a job benefit to their employees. Premiums usually are lower in a group plan.

**Health insurance**
*A plan that pays all or part of a person's medical costs*

**Hospice**
*A long-term care facility for people who are dying*

**Hospital**
*A facility where sick and injured people receive medical care*

**Inpatient**
*Someone receiving health care who stays overnight or longer*

**Outpatient clinic**
*A place where people receive health care without staying overnight*

**Rehabilitation**
*Therapy needed for recovery from surgery or an illness or injury*

In both individual and group plans, each person usually pays a **deductible**. A deductible is a certain amount an individual pays each year for medical expenses before the insurance company pays anything. For example, if you have a $200 deductible, you must pay the first $200 on your medical expenses each year. After the deductible is paid, the insurance company usually pays a certain percentage and the individual pays the rest. An insurance plan specifies what is covered and what is not. The individual must pay for anything that is not covered.

## What Is Managed Care?

**Managed care** is one health care choice that private health insurance providers offer individuals. In this arrangement, an organization acts as a go-between for the patient and the physician. There are two common types of managed care plans: HMOs and PPOs.

**Health maintenance organizations (HMOs)** are corporations made up of member doctors and professional staff who provide complete medical care. Members pay a fixed amount each month for care for themselves and their families.

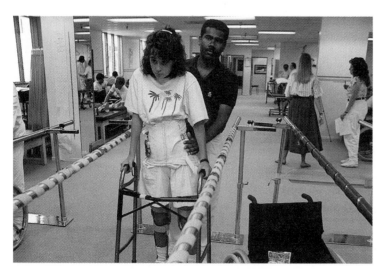

HMOs fall into two categories. Group HMOs require members to see specific doctors or go to specific medical clinics. Independent practice associations (IPAs) provide a list of participating doctors and hospitals from which to choose.

Many health insurance plans cover services such as physical therapy.

HMOs emphasize preventive health care such as regular physical exams, well-baby care, immunizations, and vision exams. Private insurance companies usually charge for preventive care.

**Preferred provider organizations** (**PPOs**) offer members more coverage if they choose health care providers in the plan, or PPO network. If a member sees a doctor or goes to a hospital outside the network, the member pays more.

## What Is Government Health Insurance?

The U.S. Department of Health and Human Services manages two types of government-sponsored medical insurance for special groups of people.

**Medicare** provides insurance for people age 65 and older. It also covers people who receive Social Security disability benefits. Medicare pays for hospital and nursing home care. People must buy additional insurance to cover physician and other medical expenses.

**Medicaid** provides medical aid for people whose incomes are below an established level. There is no age requirement for Medicaid. State and federal taxes pay for it. Individual states operate Medicaid and determine the benefits they will offer.

**Medicaid**
*State and federally funded health insurance for people with incomes below a certain level*

**Medicare**
*Health insurance for people age 65 and older and people with disabilities who receive Social Security benefits*

**Preferred provider organization (PPO)**
*A form of managed care*

## Lesson 6 Review

Write the answers to these questions on a sheet of paper, using complete sentences.

1) What is health insurance?

2) What is a primary care physician?

3) What is managed care?

4) What is the difference between an HMO and a private insurance company?

5) What steps would you take to find a doctor?

**Plaque**
*A sticky film of bacteria that grows on the teeth and gums*

**Tooth decay**
*The softening and wearing away of the hard part of the tooth*

**D**id you brush your teeth this morning? Did you floss? If you did, you helped keep yourself free of the world's most common disease—**tooth decay**. Tooth decay is the softening and wearing away of the hard part of the tooth. The good news is that tooth decay and most other dental problems can be prevented or cured. The bad news is that many people do not take the time to care for their teeth properly.

## What Is Good Oral Hygiene?

Good oral hygiene means keeping your teeth and gums clean and healthy. The goal is to remove food particles and bacteria. A sticky film of bacteria, called **plaque**, continually forms on your teeth and gums. Bacteria use the sugars in food to make acids. The acids change the hard white material of teeth into soft brown decay. Brushing well and flossing every day removes bacteria.

Here are some common questions about oral hygiene:

Regular brushing and flossing help keep teeth and gums healthy.

- **What is the best way to brush?** Angle the brush against the tooth where it meets the gum. Jiggle the brush gently, or move it in a circle. Repeat for each tooth. Do not scrub hard. You can hurt your gums when you brush too hard or overbrush.

- **What kind of toothbrush should you use?** Use a brush with soft bristles. You are removing only soft material—food and bacteria. Soft bristles will do the job. A brush with hard bristles can hurt your gums.

- **What kind of toothpaste should you use?** Most toothpastes that contain fluoride work well. Fluoride reduces tooth decay.

- **Is flossing really necessary?** Yes. Dental floss cleans the areas between the teeth, where a toothbrush cannot reach. Flossing is awkward at first, but gets easier with practice.

- **Why are candy and other sweets so bad for teeth?** Candy and other sweets contain a lot of sugar. Bacteria feed on the sugar and use it to make acids that decay teeth.

Six-month dental checkups are important to healthy oral hygiene. Regular checkups prevent minor dental problems from becoming major problems.

Brush your teeth three times a day and floss regularly to keep teeth and gums in good shape.

## Is Dental Insurance Available?

Many employers offer dental insurance as a company benefit. As with medical insurance, a deductible usually applies. It is typically less than a medical deductible because dental costs are often less than medical costs. Once the deductible is paid, the insurance pays a percentage of the dental costs up to a certain limit.

People used to consider professional dental care a luxury. Only within the last 100 years have people realized the positive effects of preventive dental care. Dental insurance has allowed people to have regular dental care they could not otherwise afford.

## How Do You Make a Dental Appointment?

As with a medical doctor, you will want to choose your dentist carefully. Ask relatives or friends to recommend dentists. Then check your dental insurance policy to see which dentists and services are covered. Call for appointments.

When you are at the dental office for your appointment, you will be asked to fill out a form. Be prepared to list any allergies you might have and to describe any dental problems.

Why do you think many people are nervous about going to the dentist?

Part of your appointment will probably be with the dentist and part will be with the **dental hygienist**. The hygienist may clean your teeth and do an initial check for tooth decay. If you ask, the hygienist will show you the proper way to brush and floss.

If the dentist finds a problem, he or she may suggest different ways to treat it. Listen carefully to the choices. Discuss the costs of each. The most involved and expensive treatment may not be necessary.

### Lesson 7 Review

Write the answers to these questions on a sheet of paper, using complete sentences.

**1)** What is tooth decay?

**2)** How does tooth decay happen?

**3)** What does good oral hygiene include?

**4)** How often should you have a dental checkup?

**5)** If toothpastes are so similar, why would you choose one over another?

## Current Day

### Fluoride Prevents Tooth Decay

Today's young people have far less tooth decay than any other generation in history. The main reason is not better dental care. It is not better toothbrushes. And it is not because people eat fewer sweets. The main reason for the decrease in tooth decay is the addition of fluoride to the drinking water supply. Beginning in the 1920s, studies were done in areas that had fluoride naturally in the drinking water. The studies showed that people who lived in those areas had very little tooth decay. In 1945, Grand Rapids, Michigan, became the first community to add fluoride to its water supply to control tooth decay. Since then, many communities have taken this action to improve dental health.

# Medicines ● ● ● ● ● ● ● ● ● ● ● ● ● ● ● ● ● ● ●

**Analgesic**
*A medicine that relieves pain*

**Drug**
*A chemical substance other than food that changes the way the mind and body work*

**Medicine**
*A drug that is used to relieve, treat, cure, prevent, or identify a disease or problem*

**Pharmacist**
*A druggist*

Everyone has problems that range from simple aches and pains to major illnesses. Sometimes a **drug** or **medicine** is necessary to relieve pain and restore health. A drug is a chemical substance other than food that changes the way the mind and body work. A medicine is a drug that is used to treat, prevent, or identify a disease or problem. All medicines are drugs, but not all drugs are medicines. The drugs described in this lesson are used for medical purposes.

## What Are the Two Types of Medicines?

The Food and Drug Administration (FDA) divides medicines into two types according to how they are bought. One type is available only with a prescription. The prescription must be taken to a pharmacy to be filled by a **pharmacist**, or druggist.

The second type is over-the-counter (OTC) medicine. Anyone can buy OTC medicines in stores without a prescription. Some OTC medicines are aspirin, cough drops, and antacid tablets.

Prescription medicines are generally stronger than OTC medicines. Because prescription medicines are strong, they can have some unwanted side effects. That is why only a doctor can prescribe them. OTC medicines can also have unwanted side effects. Read all medicine labels and follow the directions for safe use.

## What Purposes Do Some Medicines Serve?

Medicines are used for many purposes. Here are some major reasons to use medicines:

• **To relieve pain. Analgesics** are medicines that relieve pain. Some analgesics are mild. They work for headaches and minor pains. Most mild analgesics, such as aspirin or aspirin substitute, are OTC medicines.

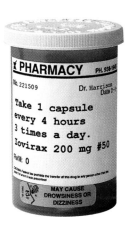

Labels on prescription medicines provide dosage directions.

- **To reduce or destroy pathogens. Antibiotics** are medicines that control infection by destroying bacteria and some other pathogens. Most antibiotics are prescription medicines. Some OTC medicines may contain a small amount of an antibiotic.

- **To restore normal organ function.** Some medicines are used to keep body organs working properly. For example, some medicines treat heart and blood vessel problems. These are prescription medicines. However, new studies show that aspirin, an OTC medicine, can help prevent heart attacks in some adults.

- **To replace body chemicals.** Some prescription medicines replace chemicals that the body cannot produce. Insulin, for example, is a prescription medicine. People with Type I diabetes take insulin because their bodies cannot produce it.

- **To relieve disease symptoms.** A drugstore may have an entire aisle of OTC cold medicines. These products can relieve uncomfortable cold symptoms.

- **To reduce anxiety.** Many medicines can reduce depression, nervousness, and other mental health problems. Most of these medicines are available only through prescription.

## How Are Medicines Taken?

It is important to know the purpose of a medicine and how you should take it. Usually a medicine is taken in the way that it will start working the fastest. For example, you may be instructed to swallow a medicine after a meal. That might be because the medicine can get into your system faster when your stomach is full. Or it may prevent an upset stomach to take it with food.

Read the packaging on OTC medicines carefully and follow label directions.

You may be instructed to take some medicines before meals. These medicines may work better when your stomach is empty.

Sometimes medicines are given as shots. The medicine goes directly into a vein or a muscle. Other medicines are breathed in and go through the lungs first. Some medicines such as creams, lotions, and medicated patches are absorbed through the skin.

## What Are Some Problems with Taking Medicines?

A person's size, weight, age, and body chemistry make a difference in how a medicine affects the body. For example, a short, thin teenager may experience unwanted side effects from a dose of medicine. A tall, heavy adult may experience no side effects from the same dose. Your doctor decides the amount of medicine that is right for you.

You and your doctor should also be aware of the medicines you cannot take in order to avoid problems. Four possible problems with taking medicines are unwanted side effects, dependence, mixing medicines, and misusing medicines.

Many medicines cause unwanted side effects. For example, you might get a rash or a headache from taking a certain medicine. Some other minor side effects include upset stomach or drowsiness. Some side effects such as hypertension or irregular heartbeat can be serious. It is important to understand even minor side effects before taking a medicine. For instance, you would not want to drive after taking a medicine that causes drowsiness. Prescription and OTC medicine labels list all known side effects of the medicine.

Contact your doctor if you experience any unexpected side effects from medicine.

Ask your doctor if you have questions about medication he or she prescribes for you. If you are still unsure, ask your pharmacist. Your pharmacist can answer your questions or give you printed information about the medication.

A person can become dependent on a medicine. For example, someone may take a medicine to sleep. In time, that person may not be able to sleep without taking the medicine.

Mixing one or more medicines can cause problems. Some medicines cancel out each other's effects if taken together. Other medicines can cause organ damage if mixed.

Misusing medicines is a serious problem. Here are some ways a person might misuse a medicine:

• Take more or less medicine than the recommended amount. Taking two pills instead of one for a cold could cause drowsiness while driving.

• Take a medicine for a longer or shorter time than recommended. If you stop taking an antibiotic too soon, the infection may flare up because it is not gone.

• Take a medicine for a purpose other than the intended one. Read the label or talk to a pharmacist to understand the medicine's purpose.

## How Does the Government Keep Medicines Safe?

The U.S. government has laws and agencies that control the safety of medicines. Before a company can sell any medicine, the FDA requires the medicine be tested carefully to prove its intended effect. The company must submit the test results to the FDA along with other information about the medicine. The FDA decides if the medicine can be sold. It also determines if the medicine must be sold with a doctor's prescription.

The FDA decides how medicines must be labeled. Labels must state the purpose of the medicine, the recommended amount, possible side effects, and safety cautions.

## What Are Some Cautions for Taking Medicines?

Medicines used appropriately can help a person stay healthy and improve life. Using medicines incorrectly can involve serious risks. To avoid any problems, you can follow these guidelines:

- Tell your doctor about any other medicines you are taking before you get a new prescription.

- Follow the directions for taking a medicine. Finish the prescription unless the doctor tells you otherwise.

- Call your doctor immediately if unwanted side effects occur.

- Take only medicines that are prescribed for you. Don't take anyone else's prescription medicine.

- Store medicines according to the instructions on the labels. Some medicines need refrigeration, while others need to be protected from light.

- Check the expiration dates. After these dates, the medicine may no longer work well and could even be dangerous. Throw away outdated medicines.

- To avoid dangerous results, never mix medicines, and never mix medicines and alcohol.

**Why do you think it is dangerous to take someone else's prescription medicine?**

## Lesson 8 Review

Write the answers to these questions on a sheet of paper, using complete sentences.

1) What should you do if you have questions about medicine you are supposed to take?

2) What is the difference between OTC medicines and prescription medicines?

3) List three purposes of medicines.

4) What are four possible problems with taking medicines?

5) Do you think taking medicine for every minor ache and pain is wise? Explain your answer.

## *Mood-Modifying Substances*

**Addictive**
*Habit forming*

**Emphysema**
*A serious respiratory disease that makes breathing difficult*

**Nicotine**
*A chemical in tobacco to which people become addicted*

**Stimulant**
*A drug that speeds up the central nervous system*

Some drugs harm the body. Tobacco and alcohol are drugs that have harmful physical and mental effects.

### How Does Tobacco Affect People?

Every time a person smokes, he or she breathes in about 2,000 harmful chemicals. One of the most damaging chemicals is **nicotine**. Nicotine is **addictive**, or habit forming. The nicotine in tobacco is a **stimulant**. It speeds up the central nervous system. Nicotine increases heart rate and blood pressure and narrows blood vessels. All forms of tobacco—cigarettes, cigars, pipe tobacco, and smokeless or chewing tobacco—contain nicotine.

Long-term tobacco use causes a buildup of materials in the blood vessels that can result in a heart attack, stroke, or cancer. In fact, smoking is responsible for 87 percent of lung cancer deaths. Smoking also causes chronic bronchitis and **emphysema**, a serious respiratory disease that makes breathing difficult.

Chewing tobacco can also lead to health problems. It can wear away tooth enamel, cause tooth decay, and cause gums to shrink so teeth become loose and fall out.

### How Does Cigarette Smoke Affect Nonsmokers?

Studies prove that healthy nonsmokers can get respiratory diseases and cancers  by inhaling smoke from burning cigarettes. Passive or second-hand smoke causes heart and lung diseases in nonsmokers. Second-hand smoke also irritates eyes and throats and causes asthma attacks and headaches. It makes existing illnesses worse.

Because of the harm second-hand smoke causes, laws forbid smoking in many public places and on public transportation. In addition, many workplaces are smoke free.

## How Can People Stop Smoking?

Many people who use tobacco realize the problems smoking causes and decide to quit. People who try to stop smoking will probably go through a period of **withdrawal** because of their addiction to nicotine. Withdrawal is a physical reaction to the absence of a drug in the body. During withdrawal from nicotine, people may have headaches, be unable to sleep, or have a hard time concentrating. They may be moody and anxious.

People who choose to quit smoking can find help. They can get prescriptions from their doctor for skin patches or special gum. These aids allow people to gradually decrease their need for nicotine. Classes, support groups, and health professionals are also available to help people stop smoking.

All forms of tobacco contain nicotine.

## How Does Alcohol Affect the Body?

People can become physically and psychologically addicted to ethyl alcohol. Ethyl alcohol is the kind of alcohol found in wine, beer, and hard liquor. People drink alcohol to feel more self-confident, to relax, or to escape uncomfortable emotions. In reality, alcohol doesn't help and instead often hinders people.

Alcohol is a **depressant** drug that slows down the central nervous system. It is also a **psychoactive drug**, which means it affects the mind. Twelve ounces of beer, 4 ounces of wine, or 1.5 ounces of hard liquor all have the same amount of pure alcohol. That means people can become just as addicted to beer as they can to whiskey.

**Depressant**
*A drug that slows down the central nervous system*

**Psychoactive drug**
*A drug that affects the mind and mental processes*

**Withdrawal**
*A physical reaction to the absence of a drug in the body*

Alcohol has a damaging effect on every major system in the body. Alcohol is not digested but absorbed directly from the stomach into the bloodstream and carried throughout the body. When people drink alcohol, their judgment, vision, reaction time, and muscle control are affected. Their blood-alcohol content (BAC) level begins to rise. Short-term effects of alcohol include slurred speech, reduced driving ability, dizziness, flushed skin, stumbling, and dulled senses and memory.

## What Is Alcoholism?

Physical and mental dependence on alcohol or lack of control over drinking is called **alcoholism**. Alcoholism is classified as a disease. Often medical and psychological help is needed to treat the disease. Organizations are available to help people who suffer from alcoholism.

**What is the BAC level limit in your state?**

## How Does Alcohol Affect Driving?

When a person has too much alcohol, the BAC level rises to the point of **intoxication**, or being drunk. Intoxication is excitement or stimulation caused by use of a chemical substance.

## Technology In Our Lives

### Software for Alcohol Testing

People who drink and drive are dangerous to themselves and others. Breath analyzers help police keep drunk drivers off the roads. These analyzers measure blood alcohol levels. One type of analyzer is called an "ignition interlock." It is put on the cars of people who have had problems with drinking and driving. The device is wired to the car's starter. Before starting the car, the driver blows into the device. Sensors check for alcohol in the breath. If they sense alcohol, the car will not start. The computer records the number of failed tests. Such technology keeps everyone safer.

In most states, a person over 21 with a BAC level of .08 or higher is legally intoxicated, or drunk. Driving at this level of intoxication is against the law.

Even if a person's BAC level is under .08, driving is still dangerous. Alcohol affects a person in the following ways:

- Vision and hearing are not as sharp
- Muscle coordination is impaired
- Reaction time is slower than normal
- Good judgment of actual speed and distance disappears
- Thought processes slow down; it causes drowsiness

## What Are Some Other Psychoactive Drugs?

Psychoactive drugs affect the mind and how a person acts. Some psychoactive drugs can be used as prescription medicines under a doctor's direction. Sometimes, however, these drugs are bought illegally. Other psychoactive drugs have no medical use and are made and bought illegally.

Stimulants are psychoactive drugs that speed up the central nervous system. They increase heart rate and cause high blood pressure. Stimulants cause dizziness, headaches, blurred vision, sweating, sleeplessness, and loss of appetite. In large amounts, stimulants cause irregular heartbeat, stroke, or heart failure. People can become physically dependent on stimulants. Strong stimulants include amphetamines, cocaine, and crack.

Depressants are psychoactive drugs that slow down the central nervous system. They produce a calming effect. Depressants lower blood pressure, heart rate, and metabolism rate. Large amounts of depressants can cause sleepiness, confusion, nausea, and loss of muscle control. An **overdose**, or too much of a drug, may cause heart, lung, and kidney failure, and sometimes even death. People can become physically and mentally dependent on depressants. Depressants include alcohol, **barbiturates**, and **tranquilizers**.

**Barbiturates**
*A category of sedative-hypnotic drugs*

**Overdose**
*An amount of a drug that is too large for the body to use*

**Tranquilizers**
*A category of sedative-hypnotic drugs*

**Hallucinogen**
*A drug that confuses the central nervous system*

**Heroin**
*An illegal narcotic made from the opium poppy*

**Narcotic**
*A psychoactive drug made from the opium poppy and used to relieve pain*

## The Sedative-Hypnotics

| Category | Prescribed for | Dangers |
|---|---|---|
| Barbiturates | Relaxation (rarely for sleep) | Produce negative side effects  Overdose can lead to death  Produce rapid dependence |
| Minor Tranquilizers | Anxiety, sleeplessness, muscle spasms | Produce dependence  Withdrawal causes severe shaking |
| Major Tranquilizers | Serious mental disorders | Strong, unpleasant side effects |

**How does the use of illegal drugs affect society?**

**Narcotics** are a third kind of psychoactive drug. Used to relieve pain, narcotics come from the opium poppy plant. Common medicines that are narcotics include morphine and codeine. Doctors give morphine and codeine to their patients to relieve severe pain after operations and during serious illness. However, doctors prescribe these drugs with great care because they can produce physical and mental dependence quickly. **Heroin**, another narcotic made from the opium poppy, is illegal in the United States. Heroin is addictive and deadly.

**Hallucinogens** are drugs that confuse the central nervous system. LSD and PCP, both illegal synthetic hallucinogens, fall into this category. Hallucinogens change the way the brain processes sight, sound, smell, and touch information. A person may feel, hear, or see things that are not there.

Hallucinogens increase the heart rate and blood pressure. The most dangerous effects, however, are mental. Users may become frightened and violent. Some injure or kill themselves because their thinking is distorted. Hallucinogens can cause permanent brain damage.

## What Are Some Other Dangerous Drugs?

Some drugs are dangerous because of the effect they have on a person's mind and body.

**Marijuana** is an illegal drug made from a hemp plant. Marijuana contains more than 400 chemicals. The main mind-altering chemical in marijuana is called THC. THC stays in the body for up to a month. Marijuana affects each person differently. It can cause memory, concentration, and judgment problems. Long-term use of marijuana damages the brain, kidneys, liver, lungs, and reproductive organs.

**Inhalants** are chemicals that people purposely breathe in. They include gasoline fumes, paint thinner, lighter fluid, glue, hair spray, and nail polish remover. Using these products as inhalants is considered illegal drug use. Inhalants can harm the mind and body by depressing the central nervous system.

A **designer drug** has a chemical makeup that is like the chemical makeup of a legal drug. Drug dealers, however, make designer drugs slightly different from the original drug and many times stronger. A person who takes a designer drug risks death because the drug's chemical makeup is unknown.

**Anabolic steroids** are synthetic drugs that resemble the male sex hormone testosterone. They are used legally to help people who do not produce enough testosterone naturally. Athletes sometimes use anabolic steroids illegally to boost muscle size and strength. These drugs can cause sterility in both men and women. Anabolic steroids produce both physical and mental effects. Physical effects include high blood pressure, heart and kidney disease, and liver cancer.

**Anabolic steroid**
*A synthetic drug that resembles the male sex hormone testosterone*

**Designer drug**
*An illegal drug with a slightly different chemical makeup than a similar legal drug*

**Inhalant**
*A chemical that is breathed in*

**Marijuana**
*An illegal drug made from a hemp plant*

Inhalants can cause brain damage and death.

Mental effects include anxiety, depression, hallucinations, and sudden mood swings.

## Lesson 9 Review

Write the answers to these questions on a sheet of paper, using complete sentences.

1) What substance in tobacco makes it addictive?

2) What are three ways alcohol affects a person's ability to drive?

3) What are some harmful effects of stimulants?

4) What are some products that give off harmful fumes?

5) What effects do hallucinogens have on a person's mind?

## Online Resources

**National Cancer Institute**

*cancernet.nci.nih.gov*

Current news on cancer treatments, suggestions on care, statistics, and more.

**U.S. Department of Health and Human Services**

*www.healthfinder.com*

Information about self-care and prevention, tobacco, food safety, cancer, diabetes, and more.

**U.S. Food and Drug Administration**

*www.fda.gov/*

Information about foods, cosmetics, human and animal drugs, tobacco, medical devices, and more.

**World Health Organization**

*www.who.int*

International focus on health concerns including disease, environment, family, policies, and technology.

■ Knowing basic first aid procedures can help a person to survive an accident or prevent a problem from getting worse.

■ First aid can be given for choking, respiratory failure, cardiovascular failure, shock, burns, and many other emergencies.

■ Serious diseases such as cardiovascular disease and cancer have risk factors. Some factors can be changed or controlled to help prevent the diseases.

■ A communicable disease is one that can be passed from one person to another person.

■ The body protects itself from disease in a number of ways.

■ A primary care physician is the main health care provider who does routine physicals, coordinates care with specialists, and provides prescriptions.

■ Health maintenance organizations (HMOs) and preferred provider organizations (PPOs) are two common types of managed care plans.

■ Medicines can be classified according to how they are purchased, either over the counter or by prescription.

■ The Food and Drug Administration is a government agency that monitors the way medicines are made, packaged, and tested.

■ Tobacco and alcohol are two types of addictive drugs.

■ Four types of psychoactive drugs are stimulants, depressants, narcotics, and hallucinogens.

## Comprehension: Identifying Facts

On a sheet of paper, write the correct word or words from the Word Bank to complete each sentence.

| WORD BANK | | |
| --- | --- | --- |
| addictive | insulin | stimulants |
| benign | malignant | stroke |
| CPR | plaque | universal precautions |
| HMO | rescue breathing | |
| inhalants | shock | |

**1)** A tumor is _____ if it has no cancerous cells.

**2)** In diabetes, the body does not produce _____ or cannot use it properly.

**3)** A person administering first aid should always use _____ to prevent the spread of disease.

**4)** A person will need _____ if he or she is not breathing and does not have a pulse.

**5)** _____ is a physical reaction to a severe injury or serious illness.

**6)** The nicotine in tobacco is _____ or habit forming.

**7)** Fumes from gasoline, paint thinner, glue, and other products are called _____ and can cause brain damage.

**8)** A _____ is the lack of blood flow to the brain.

**9)** A tumor is _____ if it has uncontrolled abnormal cell growth.

**10)** A managed care insurance that emphasizes preventive health care is an _____.

**Test-Taking Tip**

If you know you will have to define certain terms on a test, write the term on one side of a card. Write the definition on the other side. Use the cards to test yourself, or work with a partner.

11) The sticky film of bacteria that collects on teeth and gums is _____ .

12) Drugs called _____ speed up the central nervous system.

## Comprehension: Understanding Main Ideas

On a sheet of paper, write the answers to the following questions using complete sentences.

13) What is the best way to learn first aid?

14) Name one risk factor for cardiovascular disease that can be controlled and one that cannot be controlled.

15) Why is it important to finish all of a prescription?

16) What is the main purpose of the FDA?

17) How do stimulants, depressants, hallucinogens, and inhalants affect the central nervous system?

## Critical Thinking: Write Your Opinion

On a sheet of paper, write the answers to the following questions using complete sentences.

18) Why do you think it is important for rescuers to protect their own safety when trying to help someone in an emergency?

19) What do you think you could do to protect yourself from getting a cold or the flu from another person?

20) Why do you think some people use drugs illegally and some people never do?

## Self-Assessment

Can you answer the following questions?

☑ Where can you find information about apartments for rent?

☑ How would you choose an insurance company?

☑ How would you clean a wool garment?

☑ What are three reasons you would want to have renter's insurance?

☑ When should you change the batteries in your smoke detectors?

☑ Where can you find information about renter's insurance?

☑ Should you give your Social Security number to people over the phone?

☑ Do you know what could happen if you wash dark-colored clothes and light-colored clothes together?

☑ What does it mean to sign an apartment lease?

☑ How do you set up phone service in your apartment?

# Household Smarts

The idea of having your own place is exciting. It makes you feel like an adult. You feel independent. You can decide where to live and how to set up your home. You will be in charge.

Setting up a first apartment is an exciting time. It is also a time of many decisions. You want to make good choices, spend your money wisely, and feel secure in your new home.

In this chapter, you will learn about some of the decisions you need to make when setting up a household. You will discover some of the questions you will need to ask and answer.

## Goals for Learning

▶ To identify the steps involved in finding and renting an apartment

▶ To identify the types of household insurance and how to purchase it

▶ To know how to contact utility services

▶ To read and explain clothing care labels

▶ To know what information should not be given over the telephone

## *Finding an Apartment* • • • • • • • • • •

**Classified ad**
*Notice that describes property available for sale or rent*

**Lease**
*A written contract that describes a rental agreement*

**Rent**
*To pay a fee in order to use something*

• • • • • • • • • •

**Why should you not sign a lease you do not understand?**

For most people living on their own, an apartment is their first home. This lesson focuses on renting an apartment, but there are many other kinds of rental units. They include townhomes, mobile homes, duplexes, twin homes, and some single family homes.

When you **rent** something, you pay the owner a fee for using it. When you rent an apartment, you pay to use it each month. You make an agreement with the apartment owner. This agreement is a written contract called a **lease**. The lease states how much money you will pay the owner each month, and the date that payment is due. It describes what happens if your payment is late.

The lease describes what you are allowed—and not allowed—to do in the apartment. It outlines what the owner will do to keep the apartment in good condition. And it states how long the agreement will last. Most leases are for six months or one year. At the end of that time, you must sign a new lease or find a different apartment. If you do decide to leave when your lease is done, you must give notice. You must inform the building manager, in writing, that you are moving out when your lease is up. Most places require at least two months' notice. Ask your building manager about the requirements in your building.

A lease is an important legal contract. Read it carefully. It is a binding agreement that is difficult to break. If you do not understand it, ask someone else to read it with you. Be sure that you agree with all the conditions. Once you sign the lease, you have to keep your part of the agreement.

### How Can You Begin Your Apartment Search?

There are many ways to find an apartment that is right for you. One way to find an apartment is to read **classified ads** in your local newspaper. Classified ads are printed notices that describe properties available for sale or rent.

A classified ad gives important information about one property. Usually, words are shortened in the ad to save space. Some sample ads appear here.

**MAPLEWOOD**—Edgerton Estates 1 & 2 BR Apt. homes, Avail. June & July, Formal DR, CA, Indoor Pool, Party Room, Undgrnd Pkg, Elevator, Starting at $700/mo. Call 555-1234.

**MYRAN PARK**—248 Marsha Ave. Studio & 1 BR apts., AC, near busline, no pets, from $875. Call 555-1432.

**CROCUS LAKE**—Hudson Court, Lg. 1 BR in clean bldg., CA, refrig., near shops, no pets, nonsmoker. Garage avail. $755. Call 555-1324.

Another way to find a good apartment is by talking with family members and friends. Tell them you are looking for a place. Ask them if any apartments are available where they live. As you travel through your neighborhood, look for "apartment for rent" signs. Some owners simply put a sign in a building window rather than pay for a classified ad.

Many people find apartments through the Internet. Some commercial Web sites list hundreds of apartment listings. To use this source, you need a computer.

The classified ad section in the newspaper lists apartments for rent.

**Security**
*Safety system to keep people safe from harm*

If you do not have a computer, your local library may have one you can use. Using an Internet search engine, type the words *apartment rentals*. The names of different sites will appear. Scan the list for a site that covers your state, then select that site name. Follow the screen prompts for that site. You may need to enter more detailed information. You may need to type in the city and state where you want to live. Sometimes, you are asked to type in the rental amount you can pay. Answer all the questions as best you can. Your answers help the computer match an apartment to your needs.

## How Can You Get More Information?

Look through all the information you have gathered. Make a list of five apartments that seem to meet your requirements. Call each building manager and make an appointment to see each apartment. Arrive at your appointment armed with a list of questions and a notepad to take notes. Each appointment is your opportunity to learn as much as you can about each apartment. Here are some questions to ask:

• Is the apartment furnished?

• What is the rent? How much is the security/damage deposit?

• Does the building have laundry facilities?

• Is the building on a bus line or near the subway?

• How much parking space is available? Are individual garages available for rent?

• Are utility services included in the rent?

• What is the average age of the other tenants? How long have they lived there?

• Is there a **security** system in the building? Do you need a key, password, or card to enter?

• Do the apartment doors have deadbolt locks?

• Is the building in a low-crime area?

Knowing the answers to these questions will help you make a wise decision.

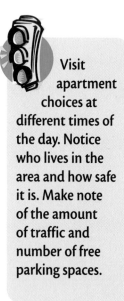

Visit apartment choices at different times of the day. Notice who lives in the area and how safe it is. Make note of the amount of traffic and number of free parking spaces.

## What Is the Next Step?

It is decision time! You visited a few apartments. You asked questions and reviewed the answers. You carefully considered the information you gathered and can now decide on one apartment.

Before you sign a lease, contact the local renter's association to ask if any complaints have been filed against the landlord or building owner.

### The Apartment Search

1. Find available apartments.
   - Look through classified ads.
   - Watch for "apartment for rent" signs.
   - Ask family and friends if they know of apartments for rent.
   - Check the Internet for listings.

2. Gather information about individual apartments.
   - Visit each apartment, walk inside, and look at each room.
   - Look at carpets, floors, walls, and appliances.
   - Meet the building manager.
   - Ask questions about the neighborhood, building owner, other renters, and building security.
   - Ask about costs: monthly rent and the deposit.
   - Ask about lease terms.

3. Compare the information you have gathered and make a decision.

4. Finalize the deal.
   - Read the lease carefully.
   - Sign the lease and pay the deposit.
   - Arrange a move-in date.
   - Give notice at your current residence that you are leaving.
   - Start packing.

You contact the building manager and set up a time to meet. At this meeting, you will read and sign the lease. You also will give the manager your **deposit**. A deposit is money the owner holds until you move out of the apartment. This money is put aside in case of damages. It is collected up front to cover any damages you or anyone else may do to your apartment during the time you lease it. If you move out of the apartment, you get the deposit back as long as you leave the apartment in good condition. Sometimes you have to pay first and last months' rent and a damage deposit. Be sure to ask about this when you visit your apartment choices. At the meeting, you will also set up a move-in date.

## Lesson 1 Review

On a sheet of paper, write the word or words in parentheses that correctly complete each sentence.

**1)** Renters sign a _____ when they choose an apartment. (will, deposit, lease)

**2)** When visiting apartment choices, you should ask questions about _____. (security, decorating, cooking)

**3)** You will probably enjoy living in an apartment building with other renters who are _____. (older than you, your old teachers, around your age)

**4)** If you leave your apartment in good condition when you move out, you will get _____. (an award, your deposit back, free rent)

**5)** An easy way to search for an apartment in another state is by _____. (using the Internet, traveling to that state, asking friends about the state)

Request a copy of Tenant's Rights from your state Attorney General's Office.

## *Organizing a Household* • • • • • • • • • • • •

You have just moved into your first apartment. Unpacked boxes are everywhere. Your furniture is in the correct rooms, but most of it needs to be assembled. As you look around, you realize that you have a lot of work to do.

### What Do You Do First?

The first thing you want to do is clean. The previous tenant may have cleaned before moving out. But you want to be sure the apartment is clean and it is easier to clean before you unpack. Cleaning is easy when you have the right tools. You will need sponges, a toilet brush, a broom and dustpan, a mop, and a bucket. And don't forget cleaning products for the bathroom, kitchen, and floors. If your apartment has rugs, you need a vacuum cleaner. Also, buy cleaning products such as soap for the dishes, detergent for clothes, and cleaners for the bathroom.

Once you have the necessary equipment, break the job into small pieces. Focus on one room at a time. In the bathroom, scrub the tub, sink, and toilet. Wipe down the counter, clean the mirror, and wash the floor. In the kitchen, wipe down the stove, oven, and countertops. Clean inside the refrigerator. Wash the floor. In the other rooms, vacuum the rugs and dust the lighting fixtures. This will take some time, but it is worth the effort. When you finish, your new home will sparkle.

Think about where to place items before unpacking.

• • • • • • • • • • •

**If you don't understand how to use the oven after reading the manual, what should you do?**

# How Do You Set Up the Rooms?

Now you are ready to unpack. The kitchen is a good place to start. Take a minute and think about how you want your kitchen set up. Store items in spots that make sense to you. Generally, you will want to store items near the place you will use them the most. Your pots and pans should be stored near the stove. Your plates and dishes can go near the sink. Arrange food items so that the things you use often are easiest to reach. Remember, you will be spending a lot of time in your kitchen. Take the time now to set it up right.

Put some thought into setting up your other rooms. How will you arrange them? In your bedroom, organize your clothing. Put the things you wear often in a spot that is easy to reach. The same goes for items in your bathroom.

After you finish unpacking, check out light switches. Note which light turns on when you flick a switch. Walk around and look for all the electrical outlets. Make sure you have placed your TV, radio, table lamp—anything that runs on electricity—near an outlet.

Make sure the door locks work properly. Insert your key in each lock to test it. Locate the smoke detectors and put new batteries in them. Make a note on your calendar to change the batteries twice a year—in the spring and in the fall. Test your smoke detectors once a month.

Study the stove, microwave, dishwasher, and any other appliances in your apartment. Learn how to use them. If you have user's manuals for the appliances, read them. A **manual** is a booklet that describes how to use and care for a piece of equipment. A sample user's manual appears here. Put the manuals in a safe, convenient place so you can find them when you need them. If you are not sure how to use the appliances, ask the building manager to show you.

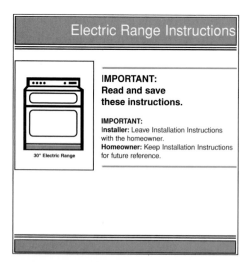

A user's manual

## Is Cleaning a One-Time Event?

You scrubbed your apartment from top to bottom and found the right spots for your things. Your apartment looks and feels like home.

Cleaning is not a one-time event, though top-to-bottom cleaning is not necessary every day. To keep your apartment in good shape, you will want to clean it regularly. You need to do some tasks every day. Daily tasks could include washing dirty dishes, wiping the kitchen table and counters, sweeping the floor, and making your bed. Other everyday tasks could include hanging up used towels, wiping down the bathroom counters, and putting away your clothes and shoes. When you keep up with simple daily tasks, your apartment is tidy all the time.

Some tasks don't need to be done every day. For example, you can change the bathroom towels and bed sheets once a week. Other once-a-week tasks include cleaning the bathroom fixtures and floor, dusting, and washing the kitchen floor.

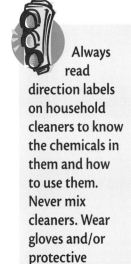

**Always read direction labels on household cleaners to know the chemicals in them and how to use them. Never mix cleaners. Wear gloves and/or protective clothing if the directions specify it.**

## What About Mail?

Find out where your mailbox is in your new apartment building. If the box has a lock, test the key so you know it works. Find out when the mail is picked up and delivered in your building. What happens to packages that come to you? Ask the building manager how packages are handled.

Make a trip to the local post office. Tell the clerk that you just moved into the area and want to set up mail delivery. The clerk will have you fill out a change of address form. The post office needs your name, new address, and former address to set up delivery.

Stop by the local post office to set up mail delivery.

## Who Else Needs to Know Your New Address?

Make a list of all the people and businesses that send you mail. Include in your list the place you work, your bank, and any credit card companies you use. Be sure to add any magazines or newspapers you receive by mail. Notify everyone on your list that your address has changed. In some cases, you might go to the business, such as your bank, to fill out a form. Sometimes you can make an address change over the telephone. To notify your credit card company, complete the change of address form. It is located on the back of most monthly credit card statements.

**Suppose someone asked you to name good shops in your neighborhood. How would you respond?**

## What Businesses Are Nearby?

You will want to explore the neighborhood once you are settled into your apartment. Take a drive or walk around the area. Notice the businesses near your home. Is there a grocery store within walking distance? How far is the bank? Where is the Laundromat? When you meet your neighbors, ask them where they shop or eat out. You also can ask the building manager for suggestions.

## Lesson 2 Review

Write the answers to these questions on a sheet of paper, using complete sentences.

1) What are some things to think about before you begin unpacking in your new kitchen?

2) Why is testing your smoke detectors important when you move into your apartment?

3) A user's manual for an appliance includes what kind of information?

4) Who needs to know your new address?

5) Why would you ask neighbors about the places they shop?

# *Managing Household Maintenance* ● ● ● ●

**Rate**
*A fee charged for a certain amount of a product*

**Utility company**
*A business that provides water, electricity, or gas to homes and businesses*

Have you ever gone camping? If you have, you know what it is like to spend a day without running water, electricity, or heat. You don't want your apartment to be like a campsite. You want to be able to switch on a TV and take a shower. You need to sign up for outside services.

## How Do You Sign Up for Service?

Determine if water, electricity, and heat are already covered in your rent. Ask the building manager if you need to pay for these services. If you do, you will need to establish service with local **utility companies.** Utility companies supply water, electricity, and gas to homes and businesses. In many areas of the country, one utility company supplies its product to a whole neighborhood. Ask the building manager for the names of the utility companies. You may need to contact more than one company. One may supply water while another supplies electricity and gas. Using the telephone book, call each company and ask to set up an account. Once that is done, you will receive bills for the products you use.

In some places, you can choose between two or more utility companies. Try to find the company that offers the best rate. A **rate** is the fee for a certain amount of a product. Different companies have different rates. Compare rates to find the one that will charge you the best rate for the product you use.

Call local utility companies to set up service to your home.

Often when you pay for something, you become aware of its cost. You can control your utility usage and sometimes lower your costs by conserving. Simple conservation methods include turning off lights and the TV when you are not using them. In addition to saving you money, your conservation actions can help the environment.

To arrange newspaper delivery, look up the newspaper's new subscription or general information numbers in the telephone book. Call and ask to start delivery. You will receive a bill for this service, too.

You also need to set up your telephone service. In some areas of the country, there is one local telephone company. Ask your building manager for the company's name. Call the company to set up an account. You will receive monthly bills for phone usage.

• • • • • • • • • •

**What are some other ways that you can reduce the amount of water or electricity you use?**

If you live in an area with more than one local phone company, you can contact each one to request rate and service information. Compare the information to get the best value for your money.

In some neighborhoods, people pay a trash removal company for weekly trash pickup. Ask your building manager. A portion of your rent may pay for this service. Also find out where trash is collected. Are there separate bins or dumpsters for **recycled** items, or items used over again? Sort recycled items as you use them to save time.

## What Does Household Equipment Do?

The **thermostat** controls the temperature in your apartment. Located in a central room, usually on a living room wall, it affects the temperature of every room. You can change the temperature in your apartment by moving the dial or button up or down. Moving the dial up increases the room temperature to make the apartment warmer. Moving it down turns off the heat to make the apartment cooler. On some newer thermostats, you have to enter a temperature number on a keypad.

Some thermostats also control air conditioners. The temperature can be set so that the air comes on when the room reaches that temperature. Many apartments have window or wall air conditioners, which are not controlled by thermostats.

Pilot light
*A small stream of burning gas that leads into a stove*

If you have a gas stove, find the **pilot light**. A pilot light is a small stream of gas that remains lit at all times. When you turn on the stove's burner, this flame ignites it. Sometimes the pilot light goes out. When the light is out, there is no flame under the burner when you turn it on. When this happens, turn off the burner and check the pilot light to confirm it is out. Then call the building manager and ask to have the pilot light lit.

Once in awhile, household appliances stop working. For example, your dishwasher is filled with dirty dishes. You put soap in the dispenser and close the door. You push the start button—and nothing happens. You can see the cord and know that it is still plugged into the wall. You open the dishwasher, close it, and push the start button again. Still nothing. What should you do? You call the building manager to report the problem. As a renter, you are not responsible for having apartment appliances repaired, unless that is part of your agreement. Let the building manager handle it. Ask to be kept informed of the process so you know when and how it will be fixed. A repair person will probably need to come into your apartment to fix the appliance.

Tell the building manager when an appliance doesn't work.

## What Is a Utility Bill?

Most utility companies send out monthly bills. The bill shows your name, address, account number, and how much of the product you used that month. It also shows the amount you owe for that usage and the date the payment is due.

The sample utility bill shows how much electricity a person used during a month. The bill also shows how much the user has to pay and when the payment is due.

**ZLX Power Company**

| Your Account Number 145-32-000 | Date Due 9/12/00 | Please Pay $164.46 | Amount Enclosed |
|---|---|---|---|

Please Return This Portion With Your Payment To:

P.O. BOX 1190
MPLS, MN 55768

SUSAN MANN
987045 ROLLING LANE
ROSEVILLE, MN 55113

X907890008799XXXXXXXXXYYYZZZZ0000000

Detach and Retain This Portion For Your Records

### Current Charges

**Electric Charges Usage Period: 7/15/00 to 8/16/00**
Residential - Underground        32 Days

| | |
|---|---|
| Basic Service Charge | $6.50 |
| Energy Charge - 1,610 kwh @ $.073500 | 118.34 |
| Subtotal | $124.84 |
| State Tax @ 6.50% | $8.11 |
| Total Amount | $132.95 |

**Meter Reading Information**
Meter xxx0009865433
Company Reading on 8/16........16466
Company Reading on 7/15........14856
Total    32 Days    kwh    1610

**Gas Charges Usage Period: 7/15/00 to 8/16/00**
Residential Service      32 Days

| | |
|---|---|
| Basic Service Charge | $6.50 |
| Distribution Charge | 5.74 |
| Cost of Gas | 17.35 |
| Subtotal | $29.59 |
| State Tax @ 6.50% | 1.92 |
| Total Amount | $31.51 |

**Meter Reading Information**
Meter #xxx9087788
Company Reading on 8/16........8586
Company Reading on 7/15........8556
Total    32 Days    ccf    30

A utility bill

You will receive a bill similar to this from your electric company and other similar bills from the telephone and water companies. Read your bills when you receive them. Mistakes can happen. If something on the bill looks unusual or you are not sure what it means, call the company to ask. Be sure to mail your payment a few days before the due date so it arrives on time. Some companies charge a late fee if payment is not received by the due date. That fee will be added to the next month's bill. Some companies will stop service if bills are not paid. Be sure to pay all your bills on time.

● ● ● ● ● ● ● ● ● ●
**What would be a comfortable room temperature?**

## How Do You Handle a Power Outage?

Problems with utility service sometimes occur. One morning you might turn on the faucet in the bathroom sink and nothing happens. Or one day your apartment suddenly seems cold. You turn up the temperature on the thermostat but the rooms remain cold. In both situations, you need to tell your building manager about the problem. You also need to call the utility company.

Find the customer service number on your monthly or quarterly bill, then call and explain the problem. Sometimes the problem can be fixed at the company's location. Other times, the company will need to send a repair person to your apartment to fix the problem. The person you speak with will tell you how the problem will be resolved. Be sure to ask the repair person to show you company ID before you let him or her into your apartment.

## Lesson 3 Review

Write the answers to these questions on a sheet of paper, using complete sentences.

1) How do you get water running into your apartment?

2) Why check the rates of different telephone companies before setting up an account with one?

3) Why do you need to set a thermostat?

4) What information appears on a utility bill?

5) How can you be sure that a stranger knocking at your apartment door is really a utility company worker?

## Lesson 4

# *Insurance* • • • • • • • • • • • • • • • • •

**Insurance policy**
*A written agreement between an insurance company and a buyer*

**Renter's insurance**
*A policy that protects the value of your property and your ability to replace it*

Think about all the things you own. Many are valuable to you. Some of the items, such as jewelry, clothing, furniture, and electronics, cost a lot of money. Could you afford to replace your belongings if they were stolen, damaged, or destroyed?

## What Is Renter's Insurance?

Many apartment renters have **renter's insurance**. Renter's insurance is a contract that protects the value of a renter's property. The contract or **insurance policy** is with an insurance company. An insurance policy is a written agreement between the company and a buyer. The renter pays the company a fee every month, every six months, or once a year for coverage. In return, the insurance company agrees to pay the renter a certain amount of money if the renter's apartment or belongings are damaged or stolen. The policy also protects the renter if someone is injured in the renter's apartment. The company pays expenses caused by the accident.

For example, a renter has personal property worth $20,000. In addition to this, he and his agent decide his liability coverage should be $500,000. This protects the renter if someone is hurt in his apartment. With a $250 deductible, the renter's annual premium would be around $150, depending on the building and its location. Insurance rates vary across the country, so check with a local agent to get rates where you live.

## Where Can You Buy Renter's Insurance?

Insurance agents sell many different kinds of insurance policies, including homeowner's insurance and auto insurance. Insurance coverage and costs vary depending on the policy. Coverage and costs also vary from one insurance company to another. When gathering information on renter's insurance policies, shop around. Meet with a few insurance agents from different companies. Take time to find the policy that meets your needs.

Begin your search for renter's insurance by contacting at least three agents with different insurance companies. The telephone book is one place to look for insurance agents. Agents are listed by company and, in some cases, grouped by location. Ask friends and family members for the names of their agents. You also can find insurance companies on the Internet.

Before calling the first agent on your list, think about the questions you want to ask. Write them down to keep yourself organized. Call each agent. Introduce yourself and tell the person you are interested in taking out renter's insurance. Explain that you want to learn about the agent's company, the kind of coverage offered, and rates. Some agents will share this information over the phone. Others will ask to meet with you. When you schedule an appointment, ask the agent what information you need to bring.

The agent will help you decide how much insurance you need. That amount of insurance determines the policy and what the policy will cost. Choose a policy that will cover the cost of replacing your belongings. The greater the policy's value, the more you pay for it. Be careful to choose a policy that covers your needs, not more or less.

Once the value of your policy is determined, the agent will tell you how much the policy will cost. Compare the cost and coverage of similar policies from three or more companies. Try to get the best rate you can. Decide on one company and call the agent again. The agent will draw up the policy and you will meet to review it. Make sure you understand how much the policy costs and when the payments are due. Always get a copy of the policy.

● ● ● ● ● ● ● ● ● ●

**How can you figure out how much insurance you need?**

## Checklist for Gathering Insurance Estimates

1. Make a list of your belongings; include everything of value to you.

2. Assign a dollar value to each item. If you have receipts for items on your list, use those figures. Use your best guess on other items.

3. If you have a video camera or can borrow one from a friend, use it. Walk around your apartment and videotape your belongings to provide a visual example of your valuables.

4. Make a list of at least three insurance agents to contact. Ask friends and family members about their agents. Look in the local telephone book or on the Internet for more names.

5. Write down the questions you want to ask before you contact agents. You want to compare policies and costs. Asking the same questions of all the agents you talk to will help you make a fair comparison.

6. Set up appointments. Ask a friend or family member to go with you.

7. At the meeting, ask questions if you don't understand something. Take notes. Make sure you understand what the policy covers and how much it costs.

8. Compare information. Review each policy and its cost. If you are having trouble deciding, discuss your choices with a family member to help you narrow the field.

9. Select an insurance policy. Contact the agent. Meet to review the policy and costs and to agree to the policy.

## What Are Some Other Kinds of Insurance?

Every person who has a driver's license needs auto insurance. Auto insurance protects drivers. When you are behind the wheel of a vehicle, you are responsible for anything that happens with that vehicle. If you cause an accident, you are responsible for damages to your vehicle. You are also responsible for damages to other vehicles involved in the accident. If anyone is hurt, you are responsible for that person's medical costs. Auto insurance will cover part or all of those costs.

Auto insurance also protects vehicle owners. If a vehicle is vandalized, the insurance company pays for repairs. If a vehicle is stolen, the insurance company gives the owner the amount of money the vehicle was worth.

Like renter's insurance, this coverage is available for a fee. The amount you pay depends on many things. Your age is a big factor. Younger drivers generally pay more for auto insurance than older drivers do.

People who have had accidents pay more than drivers who have not. Auto insurance rates vary. Check rates from different insurance companies before buying a policy.

If you have renter's insurance, contact the same agent. Tell the agent you want auto insurance and ask about discounted rates. You might be able to get one or both policies at a lower rate.

## Lesson 4 Review

On a sheet of paper, write the word or words in parentheses that correctly complete each sentence.

Compare policies and rates to get the most coverage at the lowest rate.

**1)** Renter's insurance protects you from losses due to _____. (family problems, fire, illness)

**2)** Before you take out renter's insurance, determine how _____. (much your belongings are worth, many people visit your apartment, long you expect to live in your apartment)

**3)** You can buy renter's insurance from _____. (the building manager, town hall, an agent)

**4)** Every person who has a driver's license needs _____. (renter's insurance, auto insurance, homeowner's insurance)

**5)** Comparing the insurance rates of different companies helps you to _____. (keep busy, meet new people, get the most for your money)

## *Communicating by Telephone* ● ● ● ● ● ● ●

How much time do you spend talking on the telephone each day? If you are like most people, you are on the phone a lot. People talk on phones at work, at home, and even in their cars. The telephone is an important part of modern life.

### How Can You Set Up Phone Service?

You know how to set up local telephone service. You may also choose to set up an account for long-distance phone service. Long-distance service allows you to make phone calls to people who live outside your area code. Depending on where you live, you may have several options for long-distance service carriers. You can set up an account with the same company that provides your local service or choose a different company.

People enjoy talking on the telephone.

Each long-distance carrier offers a variety of plans. To find the plan that's best for you, first think about your needs. How often do you make long-distance calls? Are the calls to the same area code? When do you make most of your calls—during the day, in the evening, or during the weekend? What is the average length of the calls? The answers to these questions will help you decide which calling plan to choose. Once you pick a plan, sign up for it and try it for awhile. If the plan is not right for you, you can change to a different plan.

## What About Cell Phones?

A cell phone is a portable telephone you can carry with you wherever you go. You can buy a cell phone in a department store, in an electronics store, or from your telephone service carrier. Cell phones come in a variety of models, sizes, and weights. Before you purchase one, you want to decide how often you will use it and where. Will you use it only in an emergency? Will you use it every day? Will you travel with it? Answering these questions will help you choose between analog, digital, and PCS phones.

The first cell phones were analog. This form of transmitting signals has the widest coverage area. An analog phone works in rural areas not yet serviced by digital providers. Analog phones use more power, so battery life is shorter. The phones need to be recharged more frequently, and calls can be intercepted.

Digital phones were introduced in the early 1990s. Digital phones offer better voice quality than analog and calls cannot be intercepted. Battery life for a digital phone is three to five times longer than for an analog phone. Airtime rates are usually lower, but the price of the phone may be higher. Voicemail, paging, caller ID, and other services are available with digital cell phones. Many new phones now have the ability to switch between analog and digital mode.

PCS is a new form of digital technology. It operates on a different frequency than digital. Internet data and streaming video can be transmitted on this frequency.

## Current Day

### Phone Service Choices

Not long ago, customers could not choose their long-distance carrier. Until recently, all long-distance calls made throughout the country were managed by one telephone company. The government decided that was not fair to consumers. It forced the company to break into smaller companies and new long-distance carriers were created. Now, people are free to choose their long-distance service carrier. People also can choose the features they want on their phone lines. Voicemail, call waiting, and caller ID are three well-known features. There are a few others.

New PCS phones also offer a Web browser option and the ability to send e-mail and faxes.

When you buy a cell phone, you need to arrange for service. Pick up any available service information wherever you buy the phone. You also can contact your local or long-distance phone carrier about cell phone service. Be sure to compare rates and service contracts before signing up for cell phone service.

## What Is Telephone Etiquette?

**Telephone etiquette** is the courteous behavior you use when talking on the telephone. Proper phone skills and courteous behavior help you deliver your message to your listener.

### Phone Tips

• Answer the phone with a friendly "hello."

• Use the proper tone of voice. For a business call, use a serious tone. For a personal call, a friendlier tone works well.

• Let the caller finish his or her statement before responding. Avoid interrupting.

- Do not eat while you are talking on the phone. If someone calls during a meal, explain that you are eating. Ask to call the person back when you are done.

- Always end a phone call with "good-bye," rather than just hanging up on the caller.

- Be kind to all callers, including those you do not know. The person on the other end of the line has feelings just like you.

- Telemarketers will call to sell you something or ask for a donation. If you are not interested, simply say "no thank you." If the caller persists, say again that you are not interested. Remain calm and pleasant, but firm.

## Technology In Our Lives

### Cell Phone Technology

Cell phones are a prime example of how technology changes our lives. The U.S. military was one of the first organizations to recognize the value of wireless technology. It used the technology for strategic purposes during World War II. Wireless technology allowed separate military units to communicate in real time without wires.

The first cellular tests were conducted in 1962. In 1981, the Federal Communications Center (FCC) established commercial regulation over the radio-telephone service. The first cellular technology used analog signals to send information.

Ten years ago, cell phones were almost as big as house phones. They had a limited calling area and calls were full of static. Today's cell phones are smaller and lighter. Advanced technology has minimized line static and increased range. Modern cell phones can now reach locations all over the world. Many provide features such as voicemail and caller ID. Before long, today's phones will be outdated as new cell phones with improved features are developed.

### Phone Security Tips

• Your Social Security number is the key that unlocks all your personal information. You must protect it. Do not give your Social Security number to anyone you don't know.

• Protect yourself by keeping your credit card number private. Do not give credit card numbers to anyone you don't know. Some people use others' credit card numbers to buy things. As the cardholder, you can be held responsible for paying all charges on your card.

### Answering Machines

You can set up an answering machine or arrange for voicemail service through your local phone carrier. Think about your message before you record it. Keep it short and pleasant. You can begin with a greeting and follow that with your phone number. Your phone number is enough to tell your callers that they have dialed correctly. You don't need to give your name. Ask your callers to leave a message and phone number so you can call them back.

● ● ● ● ● ● ● ● ● ●

**Why would you leave your name out of the message you put on your answering machine?**

### Lesson 5 Review

Write the answers to these questions on a sheet of paper, using complete sentences.

1) What are some things to think about before selecting a long-distance carrier?

2) What are two things you must do in order to have a working cell phone?

3) Why is it important to use courteous behavior when talking on the telephone?

4) Would a phone conversation with your boss sound the same as a phone conversation with your good friend? Explain your answer.

5) Why is it not ok to give out credit card numbers over the telephone?

## *Caring for Clothing* • • • • • • • • • • • • •

**B**uying new clothes can be fun, but it can also be expensive. Yet you have to wear clothes and you want them to look nice. One way to avoid the expense of buying new clothes is to take care of the clothes you have. If you take proper care of your clothes, they can last for years.

### What Statement Do Clothes Make?

Your clothes tell others about you. What you wear sends a message. Your clean, neat clothes tell people you care about yourself and take pride in how you look. Clean clothing shows that you are responsible because you care for your things. Dirty, torn, or wrinkled clothes send a different message. They say you don't value yourself, your appearance, or your possessions.

Caring for your clothing can lengthen its life span. Simple daily maintenance can keep your clothes in good condition. You may find you won't have to buy something new to replace something old as often. Cutting your clothing expense can make a difference when you live on your own. You can use the money you save on clothes for other things.

### How Can You Keep Clothing in Good Shape?

Clothes, or garments, are made of different fabrics. Each garment, because of its fabric content, requires specific care. How do you know how to care for a garment? Read the garment's label. Most clothing care labels are sewn into the collar, side seam, or waistband of the garment.

Clean, neat clothing tells others you care about yourself.

The front of the label usually states the size of the garment, where it was made, and the fabric content. On the back of most labels, you can find washing and drying instructions. Washing and drying instructions vary. Some labels list many details, including whether or not to use bleach when washing. Other labels have limited instructions and may simply state "machine wash cold, tumble dry low." Some clothing care labels appear below.

● ● ● ● ● ● ● ● ● ●

**Why must you show your receipt when picking up clothes at a dry cleaner?**

## Why Follow Care Instructions?

Ignoring clothing care instructions could result in damaged clothes. Wash your garments according to the instructions on their labels. Some fabrics shrink in hot water. Have you ever washed white socks that came out pink? That may have been the result of washing a red garment in hot water with white garments. Dark colors sometimes run when cloth is washed in hot water. Cold water usually prevents colors from running or shrinking. Follow instructions for drying garments, too. Some fabrics should not be put in the dryer. Some should be placed on a towel to dry flat so they keep their shape. Others should be hung on hangers to dry. Follow label instructions to prevent ruining your clothes.

## What About "Dry Clean Only" Labels?

Some garments require a special cleaning process. Clothing care labels that say "dry clean only" cannot be washed. Take them to a local dry cleaner. Dry cleaners clean wool and other garments using a special chemical process. Give the clerk your garments. The clerk fills out a form that includes the number and description of your garments. The clerk gives you a receipt and tells you when your garments will be ready. You need to show the receipt when you pick up your clothes. Also, if the dry cleaner loses your garments, the receipt is your claim to get them replaced.

Clothing care labels

# Where Can You Wash Your Clothes?

Most apartments do not have washers and dryers. But many apartment buildings have a laundry room with washing machines and dryers. Renters can pay to use these appliances to wash and dry their clothes. Most machines accept only quarters. One load of wash costs about one dollar. A dryer costs about 25 cents for 10 minutes.

Start the laundry process by sorting the clothes you plan to wash. Sort clothes by color. Make one pile of dark-colored items. Put white items in another pile. Put light-colored items in a third pile. You now have three loads of wash to do. Go through the clothes in each pile and read the care labels. Pull out clothes that are dry clean only to take to the dry cleaner later. When reading care labels, make a note of any items that should not go into the dryer.

Most washing machines are labeled with directions. Read and follow the directions to make your selections. Add laundry detergent by following the directions on the container. Some laundry rooms have vending machines with packets of detergent. You can purchase the packets but you may want to buy detergent at the grocery store. It will be cheaper.

While the washer is running, read the directions on the dryer. When the washer stops, move clothes to the dryer. Follow dryer directions to make your selections. When the dryer stops, pull out permanent-press garments and hang them up to minimize wrinkles. Then carefully fold your other garments.

Some garments wrinkle easily and require ironing. Check the garment's care label for ironing instructions. Some have no ironing information.

Many consumer washers and dryers are not large enough to handle large bedspreads or rugs. Take large bedspreads and rugs that are washable to a Laundromat, and use a large washer and dryer.

Follow the instructions on care labels when washing and drying clothes.

How would you care for a garment that does not have a care label?

For those that have no instructions, proceed with care. Using a barely warm iron, test the garment. Using an ironing board, iron a small hidden area of the garment to test iron temperature. If wrinkles persist, carefully turn up the heat a bit. Test the same area again. Continue this process until the iron is warm enough to remove the wrinkles without scalding the fabric. When you are finished, turn off the iron. Do not leave an unattended iron on. It can be a fire hazard.

## Lesson 6 Review

Write the answers to these questions on a sheet of paper, using complete sentences.

1) What message does wearing clean, neat clothing send to others?

2) Why would you hang some garments on hangers as soon as they finish drying?

3) What kind of information appears on a clothing label?

4) What effect does water temperature have on clothes?

5) Suppose your apartment building lacks clothes dryers. How could you dry your clothes?

### Online Resources

**U.S. General Services Administration, Federal Consumer Information Center**

*www.pueblo.gsa.gov/crh/toccah.htm*

The Consumer Action Handbook offers information and tips on home improvement, utilities, insurance, car repair, and more.

**U.S. Postal Service**

*www.usps.gov/moversnet*

Before and after moving tips, change of address form, forwarding mail, maps, and more.

# Chapter 2 Summary

● ● ● ● ● ● ● ● ● ● ● ● ● ● ● ● ● ● ● ●

■ You can find a good apartment by reading the classified ads, talking with friends and family, or searching the Internet.

■ When you rent an apartment, you pay to use it each month. You sign a written contract called a lease. The lease lists your responsibilities and those of the apartment's owner.

■ After you move into your new apartment, you must arrange for mail delivery and other services. You also need to let your bank and credit card companies know you have moved.

■ You need to contact phone companies to set up local and long-distance telephone service. Utility companies supply your apartment with important services such as water, electricity, and gas. You must contact these companies to set up new accounts.

■ Learn how to operate your appliances properly. Keep the owner's manuals in a safe place. You may need to refer to them.

■ Many apartment dwellers take out renter's insurance. Renter's insurance protects you in case your belongings are damaged or stolen.

■ You should not give out important information, such as your social security number or credit card numbers, over the telephone.

## Comprehension: Identifying Facts

On a sheet of paper, write the correct word or words from the Word Bank to complete each sentence.

> **WORD BANK**
>
> | | | |
> |---|---|---|
> | agent | electricity | rates |
> | classified ad | label | responsible |
> | clean | lease | thermostat |
> | credit card number | owner's manual | |
> | | post office | |

1) When you sign a _____, you agree to pay a fee to rent an apartment and to keep the apartment in good condition.

2) Available apartments are often listed in the _____ section of a newspaper.

3) You must fill out a form at the _____ to set up mail delivery to your new address.

4) Utility companies supply apartments with water, gas, and _____.

5) The air temperature of your apartment is controlled by a _____.

6) You can learn how to use an appliance by reading the _____.

7) You can obtain renter's insurance from an _____.

8) When setting up long-distance phone service, you want to compare different companies' _____.

9) Instructions for washing are listed on a garment's _____.

**Test-Taking Tip**

Sometimes it is easier to learn new vocabulary words if you make them part of your speaking and writing in other discussions and subject areas.

10) Clean, neat clothes tell others that you value yourself and are _____.

11) When you move into your new apartment, you want to _____ before you unpack.

12) Personal information such as Social Security number and _____ should not be given over the phone.

## Comprehension: Understanding Main Ideas

On a sheet of paper, write the answers to the following questions using complete sentences.

13) What are three ways to find an apartment?

14) What are some things to think about when setting up your kitchen?

15) Why do many apartment dwellers have renter's insurance?

16) What would you do to have running water in your apartment?

17) Why must you read clothing care labels before washing your garments?

## Critical Thinking: Write Your Opinion

On a sheet of paper, write the answers to the following questions using complete sentences.

18) Make your own list of five rules for telephone etiquette to hang near your telephone.

19) How would you end a telephone conversation with a persistent caller who did not want the call to end?

20) What would you do if the next door neighbor in your apartment building had his stereo blaring after 11 P.M.?

## Self-Assessment

Can you answer the following questions?

- ☑ How do you prepare for an earthquake?
- ☑ When buying a car, what safety features should you look for?
- ☑ How many fire extinguishers do you have in your home and where are they stored?
- ☑ When you will be away from home for a few days, what are three things you can do to make people think you are home?
- ☑ Do you know where to go if a tornado strikes?
- ☑ What supplies should you keep in your car during the winter months?
- ☑ What would you do if the power went out during a blizzard?
- ☑ How often should you change the batteries in smoke detectors?
- ☑ What steps can you take to plan for a fire?
- ☑ What should you do if a stranger knocks on your door?

# A Safe Lifestyle

**W**hen was the last time you rode a bicycle? Did you wear a helmet? In some places you can get a ticket for not wearing a helmet. Do you always wear a seat belt in the car? These are just two things you can do to lower your risk of injury.

Studies have shown that most Americans feel that life today is riskier than ever. Yet people continue to discover new ways to stay safe and healthy. Through laws, education, and technology, people are working to make their communities safe. In this chapter, you will learn how to reduce the risk of injuries at home and away.

## Goals for Learning

▶ To describe ways to reduce the risk of common accidents at home, work, and play

▶ To identify ways to avoid becoming a victim of a crime at home and away from home

▶ To explain how to increase vehicle safety on and off the road

▶ To describe ways to stay safe during natural disasters

# Safety at Home • • • • • • • • • • • • • •

**Nonskid**
*Rubber, plastic, or another sticky material that does not slip*

Most people would like to believe that their home is a safe place. However, accidents and crimes happen at home. Making your home safer is not difficult if you follow a few sensible safety practices.

## How Can You Reduce Accidents at Home?

More injuries happen at home than in any other place. In fact, every year people in the United States suffer almost 20 million injuries in their homes. Most injuries that happen in homes result from falls. Fires, poisoning, and electrical shock also cause home injuries. You can take steps to lower the risk of such accidents and injuries.

### Preventing Falls

Many falls happen on stairways. Safe stairways are well lit, in good repair, and free of litter. Handrails and carpeting help limit falls on stairs. Installing **nonskid** strips can also prevent falls on stairs. Nonskid strips or pads are made of rubber, plastic, or another sticky material.

People can slip or trip on spills or objects scattered on floors. Clean up spills when they happen. Keep toys and other objects off the floor. Throw rugs should have nonskid backing to keep them in place. If not, apply nonskid backing to them so they won't move. Many falls happen in the bathtub. To make tubs safe, you can install nonskid mats or stickers and grip bars.

People sometimes stand on wobbly chairs, boxes, or other items to reach high places. This is dangerous because a person can easily lose his or her balance and fall. To reach high places, use a sturdy stepladder or step stool.

### Preventing Fires

Smoking is dangerous to your health. It is also a big cause of fires. Careless smoking is one of the most common causes of death in home fires. An estimated 35 percent of all home fire deaths are caused by cigarette fires. Most cigarette fires are started when a lighted cigarette is dropped onto beds, upholstered furniture such as couches, or clothing. People who smoke need to make sure their cigarettes are out and ashtrays cool before they go to sleep.

**Electrical fires** are often caused by overheated wires and problems with electrical outlets. One way to prevent an electrical fire is to not overload electrical outlets. Overloading occurs when too many appliances are plugged into one outlet. Another way to prevent an electrical fire is to not use damaged electrical cords. A licensed electrician can repair damaged electrical cords and bad wiring.

Liquids that are **flammable** catch on fire easily. The word **inflammable** also means easy to light on fire. Flammable liquids include fuels such as gasoline or kerosene. Store flammable and inflammable liquids in tightly sealed containers. Keep them away from sources of heat and out of children's reach.

Use special care around burning candles, stoves, grills, and fireplaces. A burning candle can fall over and set fire to things around it. Cooking food left unattended on the stove for just a minute can cause a fire. Hot grease from a grill may catch fire during cooking. Children playing with matches start some house fires. Keep matches and lighters out of the reach of small children.

Some house fires start in fireplaces and chimneys. A fire in a fireplace should not be left unattended. Place a screen over the fireplace to contain sparks. Chimney fires can be prevented by having the chimney cleaned each year.

Space heaters and furnaces can also cause fires. All heating units should be cleaned regularly to make sure they are operating properly. Use only extension cords that match the requirements of a space heater. Keep space heaters away from drapes and other things made of cloth. Turn space heaters off when not in use or unattended.

**Electrical fire**
*A fire caused by a problem with the flow of electricity*

**Flammable** *or* **inflammable**
*Easily catches on fire*

Check the number and placement of smoke detectors in your home. Smoke detectors are most effective when placed on every level of a home, and near the kitchen and outside bedrooms.

Buy a shock-proof hairdryer. Look for a large, rectangular-shaped plug and a label saying that the dryer has been tested for safety.

## *Prevent Poisoning*

A poison causes injury, illness, or even death when it enters the body. Some household plants are poisonous if swallowed. Most household cleaning products such as laundry detergent, bathroom cleaner, and glass cleaner are poisonous if swallowed. Read labels carefully. Babies and young children especially are in danger of poisoning because they put things in their mouths. Medication not prescribed for you can be toxic. Store medicines, dangerous chemicals, and household products in their original containers out of children's reach or in locked places.

Some household products produce dangerous fumes or odors. Follow product label directions and allow plenty of fresh air into the room. Use the product outside when possible. One especially deadly fume is **carbon monoxide.** Carbon monoxide is a colorless, odorless gas that can cause death within minutes. Motor vehicles produce carbon monoxide fumes. Run a vehicle only in an open garage to avoid exhaust poisoning. Faulty furnaces and gas ovens can leak carbon monoxide. Install at least one carbon monoxide detector in your home. This device sounds an alarm if carbon monoxide is in the air. Place it near your bedroom so you can hear it if it goes off when you are sleeping.

## *Prevent Electrical Shock*

An **electrical shock** is a flow of electricity through the body. Electrical shock may cause serious burns, injuries to internal organs, and even death. Death by electrical shock is called **electrocution**. Shocks can happen when appliances are wet, do not work properly, or are used with too many other appliances. Here are some ways to prevent electrical shock or electrocution:

• Never use an electrical appliance if the floor, your body, or your clothes are wet. Hair dryers, radios, coffeemakers, and power tools are examples of electrical appliances.

• Pull on the plug, not the cord, when disconnecting lamps and appliances.

- Cover electrical outlets with safety plugs in homes with small children.

- Do not put anything other than a plug into an electrical outlet.

- Unplug electrical appliances that do not seem to be working right. Have them repaired or replace them.

- Stay away from aboveground and buried power lines.

## How Can You Protect Your Home from Crime?

Even though people would like to believe they are safe in their own home, sometimes crimes happen. However, taking security measures and being careful can prevent many crimes in the home.

To keep unwanted visitors out, check that all doors and windows have working locks. Keep your doors locked, even when you are home. If you are moving into a new apartment, change the locks. If you need to leave a key outside your home, hide it. Choose an unusual hiding place. Intruders know to look under the doormat, in the mailbox, or above the door.

Make sure you know who is at your door before you open it. Install a **peephole**. A peephole is a small hole in the door that allows you to see out. But the person outside cannot see in. Do not open the door to a stranger until he or she shows you proper identification. If a stranger at your door asks for help, do not let the stranger in. Offer to phone for help instead.

### *When You Are Away*

Here are some simple steps you can take to prevent crime while you are away.

1. Do not leave a note on the door or a message on the answering machine saying that you are away.

2. Cancel newspaper delivery.

3. Ask someone you trust to collect your mail.

4. Set timers on lamps to turn on and off at usual times, so people think you are home.

> **Peephole**
> *A small hole in a door that allows someone to see out but does not allow others to see in*

Change the batteries in your smoke detectors at least twice a year. Do it on the days daylight savings time switches—in late March and late October.

## What Steps Can You Take in an Emergency?

In an emergency, the most important thing to do is stay calm. When you are calm, you are more likely to make good decisions and take the right action.

### *Getting Help*

Often the first thing to do in an emergency is call for help. The 911 emergency telephone system is available in about half of the United States. If it is in use where you live, you can dial 911 to report crimes, accidents, medical emergencies, and fires. When you call, calmly provide information, answer questions, and follow directions until you are told to hang up. In areas where 911 is not available, call the local police or fire department. Keep emergency phone numbers near your phones.

## Current Day

### Internet Safety

The Internet has opened up new avenues of communication, learning, and ways of doing business with people throughout the world. However, the Internet can be a source of danger.

People who use the Internet to communicate with others need to be cautious. To protect yourself, follow a few commonsense rules:

- Choose a screen name that does not let people know whether you are male or female. Do not use your real name unless you know the person.

- Use special care when giving information about yourself online.

- Do not respond to rude, threatening, or angry messages.

- Save any threatening messages and report them to your Internet service provider.

## Taking Action

Many emergencies involve minor injuries and small fires. Minor injuries may be treated at home with first aid. Small fires can be put out with a **fire extinguisher** or other methods.

A fire extinguisher is a portable device that contains chemicals to put out small fires. A small fire is one that has not spread outside the area where it started. For example, an extinguisher can put out a fire on the stove, in a furniture cushion, or in a wastebasket. Read the labels on your fire extinguishers. Know how to use them before you need them. The parts of a fire extinguisher are shown here.

Some small fires can be extinguished other ways. Use baking soda to put out a small grease fire on a stove or in an oven. Turn off burners and the oven immediately. Put a tight lid on a pan that contains a grease fire . The lid cuts off oxygen to the fire. Do not put water on a grease fire. Water makes the fire spread.

## Escaping a Fire

When a fire has spread and cannot be extinguished, it is best to leave the home immediately. Do not stop for belongings. Drop to the floor and crawl to a door. Stay close to the floor where there is more oxygen and less smoke. Carefully touch the door and doorknob before leaving or entering a room. If the door or knob feels hot, take a different escape route, such as a window. Stop, drop, and roll on the ground if clothing catches fire. Go to a safe meeting place that you and your family have agreed on in advance. Call the fire department from there. The best way to successfully escape a fire is to be prepared.

> **Fire extinguisher**
> *A portable device containing chemicals that will put out a small fire*

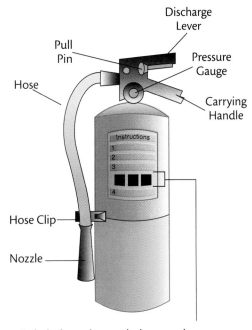

A slash through a symbol means do not use this extinguisher on that type of fire.

| Trash, Wood, Paper | Liquids, Grease | Electrical Equiment |

Use Symbols

The parts of a fire extinguisher

## Planning Escape Routes from Your Home

How would you get out of your home if there was a fire? Follow these guidelines to make a plan of escape from every room in your home.

1. Draw a floor plan of your home. Show two or more escape routes from each room to use in case of fire.

2. Choose an emergency meeting place for your family to gather once they're out of the home.

3. Post the floor plan where every family member can review it once in awhile.

4. Beneath the floor plan, write the names of two neighbors whose homes you can go to in case of emergency.

5. Have regular fire drills with all family members and communicate action plans.

• • • • • • • • • • •

**Why is it important to know how to use a fire extinguisher before you need it?**

## Lesson 1 Review

Write the answers to these questions on a sheet of paper, using complete sentences.

**1)** Where are two places that people commonly fall in the home?

**2)** What are two fire safety tools that can help if a fire starts in a home?

**3)** What are two actions that can prevent crime at home?

**4)** What are two actions that can prevent poisoning?

**5)** What would you do if a large fire started in your home?

# Safety at Work and Play ● ● ● ● ● ● ● ● ● ●

**Alert**
*Paying attention and being wide awake*

**Procedure**
*A way of doing something*

**Recreation**
*Activities people do for enjoyment*

Injuries also occur away from home. They happen in the workplace and during **recreational** activities—activities people do for enjoyment.

## How Can You Be Safe at Work?

If you have a job, you may already know about the importance of job safety. About 13.2 million work-related injuries occur every year. Nearly 6,500 people die each year from injuries while on the job.

Many work injuries and illnesses can be prevented. Employers are responsible for telling employees about possible dangers on the job. Employers must also remove dangers in the workplace, train workers well, and make them aware of safety rules. Employees are responsible for getting enough rest to be **alert**, or wide awake, at work to avoid injuries. Employees also need to follow all safety **procedures**, or ways of doing things. They need to use equipment properly and wear any required protective clothing or devices.

The Occupational Safety and Health Administration (OSHA) is a U.S. government agency that seeks to protect the safety and health of American workers. OSHA sets standards for industrial safety and provides education about safety procedures.

## How Can Recreational Injuries Be Reduced?

Everyone enjoys some kind of recreation. Every day, however, people are hurt or die during recreational activities. Water activities, sports, in-line skating, and bicycling are special concerns.

### Water Safety

Drowning usually results from swimming and boating accidents, often when people have been drinking alcohol. Knowing how to swim can decrease the chance of drowning.

Swimming classes are usually offered through schools or community recreation programs. Swim in places where a lifeguard is on duty and follow posted safety rules. Dive only where you know water is a safe depth. Stay clear of rocks, floating objects, or other swimmers.

Boating accidents can be reduced by practicing boating safety. Before going out in a boat, check weather conditions and make sure the boat is working properly. Everyone in a boat should wear an approved life jacket or life preserver at all times. If a boat overturns, stay with the boat until help arrives.

### Sports Safety

Sports injuries to people are common. Many sports accidents can be prevented by following a few simple guidelines. Know how to use recreational or sports equipment properly and safely. Make sure equipment is working correctly. Wear the protective gear that is required or recommended for a sport. Learn the skills needed to do the activity. Follow any recommended safety guidelines.

### Bicycle and In-line Skating Safety

Bicyclists are not protected as well as people riding inside vehicles. And drivers do not always see them. These facts increase bicyclists' risk for accidents. Bicyclists should wear helmets and make sure their bikes are in good repair. Here are some additional safety steps bicyclists should follow:

- Obey all traffic rules and signal all turns. Put the left arm straight out for a left turn and the forearm up for a right turn.

Wear a life jacket and use common sense while in a boat.

- Ride single file, keeping as far to the right as possible, and with the flow of traffic, not against it.

- Wear bright clothing to be seen in daylight and reflective clothing to be seen at night. Reflective clothing will shine in the dark.

- Keep a safe following distance from motor vehicles and other bicyclists.

In-line skating is growing in popularity every year. However, as popularity rises, so do accidents. An estimated 100,000 injuries resulted from in-line skating in 1997. Following a few safety tips can help prevent many of these accidents.

- If you have never skated before, take a lesson or watch an instructional video. Practice in a protected area before skating on the street.

- Avoid hills and skate only on smooth surfaces.

- Wear proper safety gear such as a helmet, knee and elbow pads, wrist guards, and light gloves.

- If you start to fall, curl up into a ball and roll to decrease your chance of injuries.

• • • • • • • • • •

**Do you think that people should be required by law to wear a helmet while bicycling or in-line skating? Explain your answer.**

## Lesson 2 Review

On a sheet of paper, write the word or words in parentheses that correctly complete each sentence.

**1)** One way to avoid injuries at work is to get enough rest so that you are always _____. (well trained, suspicious, alert)

**2)** While riding in a boat, a person should always wear a _____. (life preserver, helmet, mouth guard)

**3)** Bicyclists should ride _____ the flow of traffic. (with, against, across)

**4)** Sports players who do not have the correct _____ have a higher risk of injury. (teammates, equipment, win-loss record)

**5)** To signal a left turn, put your left arm _____. (up, straight out, down)

## *Vehicle Safety* ● ● ● ● ● ● ● ● ● ● ● ● ● ●

**Safety feature**
*Device on a vehicle that helps prevent accidents or protects the driver and passengers during accidents*

Staying safe in a vehicle means more than avoiding accidents. It also involves choosing the safest vehicle you can afford and maintaining that vehicle properly.

### How Can You Buy a Safe Vehicle?

Today's vehicles come with a number of **safety features**. Safety features help drivers avoid crashes or protect the driver and passengers during crashes. These features include antilock brake systems (ABS), air bags, seat belts, head injury protection, daytime running lights, and automatic-dimming rearview mirrors.

● ● ● ● ● ● ● ● ● ●
**Do you think it is worth paying extra money for optional safety features when buying a new vehicle? Explain your answer.**

### Technology In Our Lives

**Vehicle Safety Features**

Carmakers have designed new safety features and improved old ones. Here are some safety features created to protect drivers and passengers:

- Antilock brake system prevents a vehicle's wheels from locking when the driver brakes hard. This allows the driver to control the car when slowing down or turning.

- Air bags are large, balloonlike sacks stored inside the steering wheel and dashboard. The bag fills with air and bursts out during a crash. An air bag prevents the driver and front-seat passenger from hitting the steering wheel, dashboard, and windshield. Air bags for front-seat passengers are not standard in all vehicles. Some vehicles have side air bags.

- Seat belts have been improved. New features make them more comfortable to wear and increase the protection they provide. Seat belts tighten automatically during an accident to hold people in their seats.

- Automatic-dimming rearview mirrors adjust their brightness automatically. This reduces glare from the headlights of a following vehicle.

When shopping for a vehicle, ask the salesperson which safety features are **standard features**. Vehicles of a certain model come with the same standard features. **Optional features** can be added to a vehicle but the buyer pays extra for them.

Find out how the type of vehicle you are thinking about buying holds up in a crash. The National Highway Transportation Safety Administration (NHTSA) is a good place to get information. It performs crash tests on more than 200 makes and models of cars, trucks, vans, and sport utility vehicles. The NHTSA ranks each vehicle according to how likely it is that the driver and front-seat passenger will be injured in a head-on collision. The safest vehicles are awarded five stars, and the vehicles that offer people the least protection receive one star.

Before buying a vehicle, check out automobile insurance. Many factors, including the vehicle make, model, and year, affect insurance rates. Contact an insurance agent to get rate information on any vehicles you are considering.

> **Optional feature**
> *Device on a vehicle that a buyer pays extra to have*
>
> **Standard feature**
> *Device that comes in all vehicles of a certain model*

## How Can You Maintain a Safe Vehicle?

Maintaining your vehicle is one of the best ways to reduce the risk of accidents. Proper maintenance helps to avoid breakdowns, which are costly to repair and can be dangerous. For example, a tire blowout may cause you to lose control of your vehicle. A poorly maintained engine may catch fire.

Proper vehicle maintenance helps prevent costly repairs.

Carry emergency supplies such as a blanket, work gloves, jumper cables, a flashlight and batteries, flares, a few nutritional bars, water, and a cell phone in your vehicle.

You can take many actions to prevent accidents and breakdowns. Here are some things to do to prevent problems:

- Change the oil every 3,000 miles. Check the oil level every time you put gas in the vehicle.

- Check the coolant levels and the power steering and transmission fluids regularly.

- Check tires for cracks, punctures, wear, and incorrect air pressure.

- Check the vehicle's hoses for signs of weakness and replace them if necessary.

- Clear moisture and ice from windows so you can see clearly.

- Make sure windshield wipers and defrost fans work properly. Replace windshield wipers on a regular basis.

Another way to keep your vehicle safe is to get regular tune-ups. The vehicle manual will tell you how often your make and model of vehicle needs a tune-up. Pay attention to signs of trouble such as unusual noises and warning lights on the dashboard. Pulling to one side or wobbling and having to add oil frequently indicate problems. If any of these signs appear, have your vehicle checked at once.

## How Can You Avoid Vehicle Crashes?

In the United States, about 50,000 people die in vehicle crashes every year. Safe driving practices can prevent many of these crashes.

### Develop Safe Driving Habits

The best way to prevent accidents is to learn safe driving skills through a driver's training course. Students in these courses learn road rules and **defensive driving** skills. Defensive drivers watch out for other drivers and adjust to unsafe road conditions.

When road conditions are dangerous, traveling below the posted speed gives you better control of the vehicle. Reduce speed in fog, rain, snow, or ice.

To see and be seen, use headlights from dusk until just after sunrise. Use headlights in rain, snow, and fog. Leave enough distance between you and the vehicle in front of you to stop safely.

Wear a seat belt at all times to reduce injuries if an accident does occur. Buckle small children into car seats that meet state requirements.

Avoid using a cellular phone while driving. Pull off the road to a safe place before using the phone.

### Be Alert

A safe decision is never to use alcohol or other drugs and especially never to drive under their influence. Never ride with a driver who is under the influence of alcohol or drugs. About 40 percent of all traffic deaths involve drivers who are under the influence. Avoid driving when you are feeling angry, frustrated, stressed, or upset in any way. Strong emotions can cloud your judgment. If you become drowsy while driving, let someone else drive or pull over to a safe place and take a nap.

## Lesson 3 Review

On a sheet of paper, write the word or words in parentheses that correctly complete each sentence.

**1)** It is important to _____ speed when road conditions are dangerous. (increase, maintain, reduce)

**2)** If you become drowsy while driving, _____. (drive faster, pull over, call 911)

**3)** Drivers who adjust for unsafe road conditions practice _____ driving skills. (dangerous, defensive, optional)

**4)** The NHTSA finds out how safe new vehicles are by carrying out _____. (driving tests, maintenance checks, crash tests)

**5)** The driver and passengers should wear seat belts _____. (at all times, when driving over 55 miles per hour, only at night)

## *Pedestrian Safety* ● ● ● ● ● ● ● ● ● ● ● ●

**Jaywalking**
*Crossing a street at a place other than a corner or crosswalk*

**Pedestrian**
*A person who walks*

**W**henever you walk or run somewhere away from home, you are a **pedestrian**. Pedestrians need to protect themselves from accidents and crime.

### How Can Pedestrians Avoid Accidents?

When you are on foot, stay on the sidewalk whenever possible. If you must walk on the road, walk facing traffic. Avoid **jaywalking**. This is crossing a street at a place other than a corner or a crosswalk. Many communities have laws against jaywalking to protect pedestrians from accidents.

Some traffic lights have a button that pedestrians can push to signal traffic to stop. Some lights do not have buttons. The lights cycle automatically. Watch the traffic sign across the street. Wait until the "Walk" signal or a walking stick figure appears. This is your signal that traffic has a red light and should be stopping. Even when the signal appears, be sure you look both ways before crossing the street. Drivers do not always pay attention to traffic lights. You still have to watch out for your own safety.

According to the American Automobile Association (AAA), about 600 people are killed every year while walking on highways. Many accidents happen while people are crossing the highway, pushing or working on a vehicle, or standing on the shoulder.

Pedestrians need to pay attention to "Walk" and "Don't Walk" signals to avoid accidents.

To protect yourself, stay off busy highways when you are on foot. If your vehicle breaks down on a highway, pull over as far as possible on the right shoulder. Turn on your four-way flashers to signal you need help. Some states provide emergency call boxes and roadside assistance to help drivers with vehicle problems. In most cases, it is safest to wait inside your vehicle until help arrives.

## How Can Pedestrians Avoid Crime?

To protect yourself against crime, walk with confidence and act like you know where you are going. Stay alert and pay attention to what is happening around you. Do not daydream, wear headphones, or read while walking. If you carry a purse, hold it in front of your body. If you carry a wallet, put it in a front pocket. Try not to carry a large amount of money. Stay away from dark alleys and deserted parking lots.

Consider carrying a personal security device. Pepper spray and Mace both cause a painful burning when sprayed into an attacker's eyes. Before purchasing these devices, make sure they are legal where you live. Learn when and how to use them correctly. A handheld alarm is another option. It makes a loud noise when you turn it on. The noise may bring help or surprise an attacker so that you can escape.

Children are taught to look both ways before crossing the street. That is a good rule for people of all ages to follow.

● ● ● ● ● ● ● ● ● ●

Do you think jaywalking laws are fair? Explain your answer.

## Lesson 4 Review

Write the answers to these questions on a sheet of paper, using complete sentences.

**1)** Where should a pedestrian walk whenever possible?

**2)** Why should a pedestrian not wear headphones?

**3)** How do Mace and pepper spray help protect you?

**4)** What is one reason pedestrians are injured on the highway?

**5)** Which sign for not crossing a street do you think is best:
   • "Don't Walk" sign?
   • Stick walking figure in a circle with a line through it?

**Blizzard**
*A strong winter snowstorm*

**Evacuate**
*To leave home and go to a safe place*

**Hurricane**
*A strong tropical storm with heavy rains and winds above 75 miles per hour*

**Natural disaster**
*A sudden emergency that results from acts of nature*

**Tornado**
*A cone-shaped cloud with winds of up to 500 miles per hour*

**Warning**
*A dangerous storm is expected soon*

**Watch**
*A dangerous storm is possible*

Sudden emergencies that result from acts of nature are called **natural disasters**. Natural disasters include storms, floods, and earthquakes. People are injured or killed in natural disasters each year. With warning and preparation, however, people can lower the chance of injuries.

## How Can People Prepare for Storms?

Several types of storms happen in the United States. A storm can result in a natural disaster. Thunderstorms are common in much of the United States during the spring and summer months. A **hurricane** is a strong tropical storm with heavy rains and winds above 75 miles per hour. A **tornado** is a cone-shaped cloud with winds of up to 500 miles per hour. A strong winter snowstorm is called a **blizzard**. The National Weather Service (NWS) can predict all these types of storms, with different amounts of success.

### Safety in a Hurricane

The most important action to take if a hurricane is coming is to find shelter. People often have a few days to prepare for a hurricane. The southern and eastern coasts of the United States are prime hurricane targets. When a hurricane begins to develop, the NWS sends out a hurricane **watch** or **warning**. A watch means that a hurricane may hit. A warning means that a hurricane is expected to hit within the next 24 hours.

To protect a home from strong winds, put tape or boards over windows. Bring in items that can fly around in strong winds. Sometimes people are advised to **evacuate**. They are asked to leave their homes and go to a safe place away from the storm. Before they leave home, they need to shut off the gas and electric power.

## Safety in a Tornado

Tornadoes strike with less warning than hurricanes. The NWS issues a tornado watch when conditions in the air are right for a tornado to form. When a tornado watch is issued, store outdoor items that can blow around. This would include lawn chairs and tables. Check your battery-operated radio to be sure it is working. The NWS issues a tornado warning if a tornado is sighted in the area. If a warning has been issued, gather your family members and grab the battery-operated radio. Go to the basement and stay there. Keep away from windows. If you do not have a basement, go to the lowest floor of the building. Crouch or lie flat in a closet or bathtub and cover your head.

If you are outside, seek shelter indoors. Do not stay in a vehicle. A tornado can toss a vehicle around like a toy. If you cannot get indoors, lie down in a low spot such as a ditch. This will help shelter you from flying materials such as stones, tree branches, and pieces of metal.

Agree on a family emergency plan. Ask a relative or friend who lives out of state to be the "family contact." All family members should memorize the name, address, and phone number of the contact person. If family members are separated during a disaster, they can call the contact person, who will pass messages among them.

## Lightning Safety

Lightning is a huge electrical spark that occurs during thunderstorms. Here are some ways to avoid being electrocuted by lightning during a storm:

- Close doors and windows.
- Unplug electrical equipment and use the telephone only in an emergency.
- Avoid touching objects that are connected to metal pipes, such as bathtubs and sinks.
- If outdoors, find shelter in a closed vehicle or in a low area such as a ditch.
- Lightning often strikes water. If you are in water, get out at once.
- Do not seek shelter under a tree. Tall objects such as trees attract lightning.

**Flash flood**
*When a body of water quickly overflows without warning and covers dry land*

● ● ● ● ● ● ● ● ● ●

**Some communities have disaster relief plans. What kind of plan does your community have for dealing with a natural disaster?**

## Safety in a Blizzard

Local TV and radio weather people often alert people to possible blizzard or heavy snowstorm conditions. Pay attention to this information and stock up on food and supplies.

During a blizzard, stay in your home or a warm shelter. Avoid travel, even short distances. In a medical emergency, call local authorities for help. If the heat goes out in your home, call the local utility company. Dress in layers of warm clothing and sleep under several light blankets until heat is working again.

If you live in places where blizzards happen, carry emergency supplies in your vehicle during the winter. Include blankets, a flashlight and batteries, snacks, wool mittens and hat, extra socks, and warm boots. If your vehicle becomes stuck during a blizzard, stay in it. Run the vehicle only a few times each hour for heat. Clear snow away from the tailpipe to keep dangerous carbon monoxide exhaust out of the vehicle.

## How Can People Prepare for a Flood?

A flood is a natural disaster that occurs when a body of water overflows and covers dry land. Most floods can be predicted hours to days in advance. Sometimes very heavy rains cause dangerous **flash floods**, which happen suddenly and without warning.

If you live in a flood area, be prepared to evacuate. Know where to go if you are told to move to high ground. During a flood, do not try to cross a stream where water is at or above knee level. Do not drive over flooded roads or land. If your car stalls because of flood water, leave it and go to higher ground at once.

Flash floods happen suddenly and without warning.

After a flood, do not touch electrical equipment in wet areas. Throw away food and liquid the flood water touched. Drink only bottled or boiled water until you are told the water supply is safe again.

## How Can People Prepare for an Earthquake?

An **earthquake** happens when plates—major slabs of rock in the earth's crust—shift and move suddenly, causing the earth to shake. The shaking usually lasts less than a minute. Earthquakes may be followed by more shaking called **aftershocks**. Most earthquakes in the United States occur along the West Coast.

> **Aftershock**
> *A small earthquake that follows a larger earthquake*
>
> **Earthquake**
> *A shaking of the land that occurs when huge areas of rock move*

Scientists cannot tell when earthquakes will happen. Even so, people can store emergency supplies and prepare emergency plans. Earthquake emergency supplies include flashlights, a battery-operated radio, extra batteries, bottled water, canned food and can opener, and a first aid kit. If you are indoors when an earthquake strikes, duck under a strong table or desk and cover your head. Stay there until the shaking stops. If you are outside, stay in an open space away from buildings, walls, trees, and power lines. If you are driving, move to the shoulder of the road, stop, and stay in the car. Do not stop under bridges, overpasses, or power lines, all of which could fall.

Earthquakes cause tremendous damage.

## Lesson 5 Review

Write the answers to these questions on a sheet of paper, using complete sentences.

**1)** How are hurricanes and tornadoes different?

**2)** What should you do if you are caught outside in a tornado?

**3)** Why is a flash flood so dangerous?

**4)** Why should you stay away from trees, tall objects, and water during a lightning storm?

**5)** Why should you stay away from buildings, walls, bridges, overpasses, and power lines if you are outside during an earthquake?

### Online Resources

**Federal Emergency Management Agency**

*www.fema.gov/pte/prep.htm*

Information about preparing for and surviving natural disasters.

**National Highway Transportation Safety Administration**

*www.nhtsa.org/cars/testing/ncap*

Crash test results for more than 200 vehicles along with tips for how to choose a safe vehicle.

**U.S. Fire Administration's Fire Safety and Education**

*www.usfa.fema.gov/safety/safety.htm*

Information about preventing and surviving fires.

# Chapter 3 Summary

■ Installing simple equipment and taking some preventive actions can help people avoid falls.

■ Every home should have one or more smoke detectors, carbon monoxide detectors, and fire extinguishers.

■ Small fires in the home can be put out with fire extinguishers or in other ways. A family can prepare for a fire ahead of time holding fire drills.

■ A few simple precautions can prevent poisoning or electrical shock.

■ Keep doors and windows locked to protect your home. Ask strangers for proper ID.

■ The Occupational Safety and Health Administration (OSHA) sets standards for safety in the workplace.

■ Knowing how to swim and wearing a life preserver while boating can prevent drowning.

■ Sports and in-line skating injuries can be lowered by wearing protective gear and learning necessary skills.

■ Bicyclists can wear helmets, follow rules of the road, and take other preventive actions to lower accident risks.

■ Buy a vehicle with safety features and maintain it to help lower the risk of accidents. Practice safe driving skills.

■ People can prepare for hurricanes, tornadoes, blizzards, floods, and earthquakes.

## Comprehension: Identifying Facts

On a sheet of paper, write the correct word or words from the Word Bank to complete each sentence.

> **WORD BANK**
>
> | | | |
> |---|---|---|
> | defensive driving | gear | rest |
> | depth | heat | traffic rules |
> | earthquake | OSHA | safety helmet |
> | fire extinguisher | posted speed | seat belt |
> | falls | predicted | shock |

**1)** Stairs, tubs, showers, and wet or littered floors are places where _____ can happen.

**2)** Flammable liquids should be stored in tightly closed containers away from _____.

**3)** A _____ contains chemicals that put out small fires.

**4)** An electrical _____ is a flow of electricity through the body.

**5)** _____ sets standards for industrial safety.

**6)** Getting enough _____ can keep employees alert on the job.

**7)** Dive only in places where the water is a safe _____.

**8)** A person should wear the proper protective _____ when playing a sport.

**9)** Drivers should travel below the _____ when road conditions are dangerous.

**10)** Wearing a _____ can reduce injuries in a vehicle crash.

**Test-Taking Tip**

When studying for a test, use the titles and subtitles in the chapter to help you recall the information.

11) Bicyclists and in-line skaters should wear a _____.

12) Driver's training courses teach _____ skills.

13) Vehicle drivers and bicyclists should all obey _____.

14) Hurricanes, tornadoes, floods, and blizzards can all be _____.

15) During an _____, people indoors should duck under a strong table or desk.

## Comprehension: Understanding Main Ideas

On a sheet of paper, write the answers to the following questions using complete sentences.

16) Name one way to avoid crime against your home.

17) How should medicines and dangerous chemicals be stored to prevent small children from being poisoned?

18) Name one natural disaster and describe one way to stay safe during that kind of natural disaster.

## Critical Thinking: Write Your Opinion

On a sheet of paper, write the answers to the following questions using complete sentences.

19) What is one way you could make your own home safe?

20) How does the expression "an ounce of prevention is worth a pound of cure" apply to safety?

## Self-Assessment

Can you answer the following questions?

- ☑ Do you know how to make a balanced meal?
- ☑ How would you start a physical fitness program?
- ☑ What can you do to handle stress?
- ☑ What are the six essential nutrients?
- ☑ How do exercise and diet fit together?
- ☑ Is it ok to have a certain amount of stress?
- ☑ Why should you read and compare food labels?
- ☑ Why is your diet important to your health?
- ☑ How does having fiber in your diet help keep you healthy?
- ☑ What is your daily fat limit?

# Nutrition and Fitness

Y ou might say "Take care of yourself" to a friend you
may not see again for awhile. What does "taking care
of yourself" mean? Generally, it means making choices
that lead to a healthy, enjoyable life. For example, every day
you make choices about the food you eat. You also make
choices about the exercise you get. The choices you make
affect your health and the quality of your life.

In this chapter, you will learn about some ways to take care of
yourself and stay healthy. You will learn how to choose healthy
foods. You will also learn about the importance of fitness,
exercise, and rest to your health. Finally, you will learn how to
handle stress in healthy ways.

## Goals for Learning

▶ To use the Food Guide Pyramid to choose healthy foods

▶ To explain the importance of the six kinds of nutrients and
identify the foods that have them

▶ To use food labels to compare foods

▶ To identify the benefits of regular exercise and the parts of
an exercise program

▶ To identify healthy ways to cope with stress

## *Planning Nutritious Meals* • • • • • • • • •

**Calorie**
*A unit that measures the amount of energy in food*

**Diet**
*The food that you regularly eat and drink*

**Nutrient**
*A substance in food that your body needs to work properly*

Food is fuel for your body. Food provides the energy your body needs to work properly. Deciding what food to eat is important. Good food choices help you stay healthy. Poor food choices can lead to poor health. Eating too much or not enough food also can cause problems.

### Why Is Diet Important to a Person's Health?

Your **diet** is the food that you eat and drink. Your diet affects the way you look, feel, and perform. A healthy diet helps you look your best. It makes your hair shine and helps keep your skin clear. It gives you energy to do things you need or want to do. Eating healthy also contributes to your emotional health. It gives you energy to think clearly and to deal with stress.

Scientists have discovered that food contains about 50 substances that your body needs to work and grow properly. These substances are called **nutrients**. The nutrients are grouped into six classes. You will learn about these later in the chapter.

Active people and athletes need more calories for energy.

One thing you get from food is energy. Your body uses the energy in food for heat, movement, growth, and repair. A **calorie** is a unit that measures the amount of energy in food. Most people need between 2,200 and 2,800 calories a day. In general, males need more calories than females.

Foods vary in the nutrients and calories they provide. Some foods are high in calories but low in nutrients. For example, a teaspoon of sugar has 40 calories, while a teaspoon of green beans has 2 calories. Green beans have more nutrients and fewer calories than sugar. Foods that are good sources of nutrients but low in calories are called nutrient dense. A healthy diet includes nutrient-dense foods.

The number of calories you eat each day should just about match the number of calories your body needs. Too many calories can cause a person to become overweight. Too few calories can cause a person to become underweight.

If enough of the six essential nutrients are missing from the diet, a person may have **malnutrition**. A person might eat enough food but still not get enough nutrients because of poor food choices.

Some signs of malnutrition are frequent headaches, feeling tired, stomachaches, or depression. Malnutrition may lead to serious health problems.

Another problem that results from a poor diet is a **deficiency**, or lack of something. For example, a person who is not getting enough iron may have an iron deficiency. Deficiencies may lead to more serious health problems, such as damage to the nervous system or heart. Fortunately, there are some guidelines to help you plan healthy, nutritious meals.

Deficiency
*Lack of a certain nutrient in the diet*

Malnutrition
*A condition that results from a diet that lacks nutrients*

## Dietary Guidelines

The U.S. government has set guidelines to help people choose a healthy diet.

- Eat a variety of foods.
- Choose a diet with plenty of grain products, vegetables, and fruits.
- Choose a diet low in fat, saturated fat, and cholesterol.
- Choose a diet low in sugars.
- Choose a diet low in salt, or sodium.
- Balance the food you eat with physical activity.

### Food Guide Pyramid

The Food Guide Pyramid shown below can help you meet dietary guidelines. The pyramid groups food according to the number of servings a person should eat daily. Notice that the foods you should eat the most are in the bottom layer of the pyramid. These are breads, cereals, and other grains. Vegetables and fruits are in the next layer. Among the foods in the third layer are milk, yogurt, meat, and fish. Fats, oils, and sweets are in the small area at the top of the pyramid. Eat them sparingly.

The Food Guide Pyramid shows the number of servings of each kind of food you should eat every day. One serving is about the amount of a food you can hold in the palm of your hand.

● ● ● ● ● ● ● ● ● ●

**Think of everything you ate yesterday. How well did you meet the pyramid guidelines?**

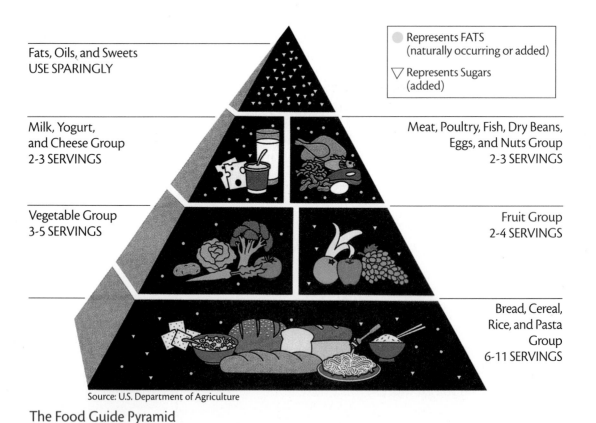

Fats, Oils, and Sweets
USE SPARINGLY

● Represents FATS
(naturally occurring or added)

▽ Represents Sugars
(added)

Milk, Yogurt,
and Cheese Group
2-3 SERVINGS

Meat, Poultry, Fish, Dry Beans,
Eggs, and Nuts Group
2-3 SERVINGS

Vegetable Group
3-5 SERVINGS

Fruit Group
2-4 SERVINGS

Bread, Cereal,
Rice, and Pasta
Group
6-11 SERVINGS

Source: U.S. Department of Agriculture

The Food Guide Pyramid

## Lesson 1 Review

Write the answers to these questions on a sheet of paper, using complete sentences.

1) Where in the Food Guide Pyramid will you find the foods that you should eat the most?

2) How does your diet affect your body?

3) What are nutrient-dense foods?

4) How many servings should you have from the fruit group?

5) What are three of the Dietary Guidelines?

## Current Day

**Can You Get a Healthy Meal at a Fast-Food Restaurant?**

Most fast-food restaurants provide nutritional information about their food. Pamphlets or flyers of nutrition facts are usually on display. They provide information about the calories, salt, and nutrients in each food on the menu. The next time you go to a fast-food restaurant, check out this information. Use it to order a meal low in fat and salt.

# *Identifying Essential Nutrients* • • • • • • •

**Carbohydrate**
*A nutrient that provides energy and includes sugar or starch*

**Digestion**
*To change food into a form the body can use*

**M**aking healthy food choices is easier when you understand the importance of the six essential nutrient groups. The six groups are carbohydrates, fats, proteins, vitamins, minerals, and water.

## What Are Carbohydrates?

**Carbohydrates** make up one nutrient group. Carbohydrates are sugars and starches that come mainly from plant food. They give your body much of the energy it needs each day. There are two kinds of carbohydrates—simple and complex.

### *Simple Carbohydrates*

Simple carbohydrates are sugars. Sugars have many different names. For example, sucrose is table sugar. Fructose is sugar in fruit. Lactose is sugar in milk. Sugar requires little **digestion** and enters the bloodstream quickly. Digestion changes food into a form the body can use. So sugar gives you quick energy. However, the energy boost you might receive from sugar wears off quickly. When it is gone, you feel tired and sleepy. This is because sugar has no other nutrients.

Avoid grocery shopping when you are hungry. You will be less likely to buy things you did not intend to buy.

Sugars in food are either natural sugar or refined sugar. Natural sugars are found in fruits, milk, honey, and syrup. Most of these foods contain other nutrients. Refined sugar, such as table sugar, has no other nutrients. Refined sugar is often added to cakes, candies, cookies, and soft drinks. Most foods with added sugar provide few nutrients and a lot of calories. Therefore, you might feel full without getting the nutrients you need for good health. Also, too much added sugar in your diet can cause tooth decay.

### *Complex Carbohydrates*

Complex carbohydrates are starches. Starches take longer to digest than sugars. They provide a longer-lasting source of energy than sugars. Complex carbohydrates are found in starchy vegetables such as potatoes, corn, beans, and peas.

They are also found in grain products such as pasta, rice, bread, and cereal. Most of these foods are nutrient dense because they provide many nutrients in a small amount of calories. The chart below lists some foods with a lot of complex carbohydrates.

The Dietary Guidelines recommend that most calories come from complex carbohydrates. Foods containing carbohydrates are found in the bottom two layers of the Food Guide Pyramid. Carbohydrates make up more than half of the pyramid.

Foods with complex carbohydrates are also good sources of **fiber**. Fiber is not a nutrient, but it helps you digest food. The fiber content of some foods is listed in Appendix B. Studies show that fiber in the diet helps protect the body from some forms of cancer.

Dietary Guidelines recommend that most calories come from complex carbohydrates.

Foods high in complex carbohydrates

| Single Serving | Total Carbohydrates (grams) | Simple Carbohydrates (grams) | Complex Carbohydrates (grams) |
|---|---|---|---|
| Corn flakes, 1 oz (low sugar) | 24 | 2 | 22 |
| Pasta or rice, 1/2 cup, cooked | 20 | 0 | 20 |
| Beans, 1 cup cooked | 40 | 0 | 40 |
| Potatoes, corn, or peas, 1 cup | 30 | 6 | 24 |

Fiber
*A substance that helps you digest food; it is found in foods that contain carbohydrates*

• • • • • • • • • • •

**How many foods with complex carbohydrates have you eaten today?**

## What Are Fats?

Like carbohydrates, fats are a group of nutrients that supply the body with energy. Fats are stored energy. They are part of all body cells and are needed for the growth and repair of cells. Fats help protect your internal organs, such as your heart and liver, from temperature changes. They protect the body from outside blows and are part of the protective covering of nerves. Fats also add flavor to foods.

There are two kinds of fats—saturated and unsaturated. **Saturated fats** come mostly from animal products. These fats are usually solids at room temperature. Foods high in saturated fat include fatty meat, whole milk, butter, and ice cream. **Unsaturated fats** come mostly from plants. These fats are usually liquids at room temperature. Foods with unsaturated fat include vegetable oils, nuts, and fish.

A diet high in saturated fats can be unhealthy. Too many saturated fats can raise **cholesterol** levels. Cholesterol is a waxy, fatlike substance found in the body cells that aids in making hormones. It also helps digestion. This cholesterol, called blood cholesterol, is carried in the bloodstream. Eating too many foods high in saturated fats can cause a buildup of cholesterol in blood vessels. Too much cholesterol in the blood can cause strokes and heart attacks.

One way to reduce the risk of high cholesterol levels is to avoid foods high in saturated fats. You can replace saturated fats with foods containing unsaturated fats. For example, you can eat more fish and cut back on red meat. You can also use olive, canola, or vegetable oil for cooking instead of lard or butter. You can drink reduced fat milk instead of whole milk.

Health experts recommend limiting fat to no more than 30 percent of total calories. For most people, a range of 20 to 30 percent fat is a realistic target that delivers significant health benefits.

## What Are Proteins?

Proteins are nutrients that help build muscle and repair body tissue. Protein is part of every cell in your body. Muscles, bones, blood, and skin all contain protein. Since cells are always being repaired or replaced, you need protein in your diet. Protein also provides energy, but not as much as carbohydrates and fats do.

Proteins are made up of chains of building blocks called **amino acids**. There are many kinds of amino acids. Your body is able to make all but nine of them. These nine are called essential amino acids. You must get these essential amino acids from your diet. Your body can make new proteins from these nine.

Animal products such as fish, meat, eggs, milk, and poultry usually contain all nine essential amino acids. Some foods provide only a few of the essential amino acids. These are plant foods such as grains, nuts, peas, and beans. People who do not eat animal products need to eat a variety of plant products. They need to do this to get all nine essential amino acids.

**Amino acid**
*A small chemical unit that makes up protein*

**Mineral**
*A substance formed in the earth, needed for fluid balance, digestion, and other body functions*

**Vitamin**
*A substance needed in small amounts for growth and activity*

## Why Are Vitamins, Minerals, and Water Important?

You have learned about three groups of nutrients: carbohydrates, fats, and proteins. The other three kinds of nutrients are **vitamins, minerals,** and water. While these nutrients do not provide energy, they help the body change food into energy.

Proteins help build muscle and repair body tissue.

Your body needs small amounts of vitamins and minerals. You need enough water to replace the amount you lose every day.

## Vitamins

Vitamins are substances the body needs for normal growth and to maintain life. The chart on the next page lists some vitamins, their purposes, and sources.

Some vitamins can be lost during food preparation. For example, the B vitamins and vitamin C dissolve in water. When you cook vegetables that contain these vitamins, many of the vitamins are released into the water. When you pour off the water, you lose the vitamins. To prevent this, use a small amount of water to cook vegetables, and avoid cooking them too long. Raw vegetables contain more vitamins than cooked vegetables.

## Minerals

Minerals are substances formed in the earth. You need small amounts of minerals every day. Like vitamins, minerals perform many important jobs. For example, the minerals **calcium** and **phosphorus** help build strong bones and teeth. Calcium is found in dairy products, such as milk and cheese, and green leafy vegetables. Calcium helps control certain body functions and maintains strong bones and teeth. Phosphorus is found in peas, beans, milk, meat, and other foods. Phosphorus combines with calcium to keep bones firm. The body needs larger amounts of calcium and phosphorus than other minerals.

The best way to get sugar in your diet is to eat naturally sweet foods such as fruit and juices.

Sodium, or salt, is another mineral that helps control the amount of fluids in your body. You need only a small amount of sodium in your diet. Too much may cause high blood pressure. Sodium is found in many foods. The sources and purposes of minerals are listed in Appendix B.

Many good sources of vitamins are also good sources of minerals. You can get the vitamins and minerals you need by eating a variety of foods every day.

Essential vitamins

| Vitamin | Purpose | Sources |
|---|---|---|
| **Vitamin A** | Helps skin, hair, eyes, lining of nose and throat | Milk, egg yolk, beef liver, carrots, sweet potatoes, yellow squash, spinach, other greens |
| **B Vitamins**<br>Niacin | Protects skin and nerves, aids digestion | Beef, chicken, turkey, liver, whole wheat, milk, cereals, mushrooms |
| Thiamin | Protects nervous system, aids appetite and digestion | Pork, sunflower seeds, whole grains, cereal, green beans, peanuts, organ meats |
| Riboflavin | Increases resistance to infection, prevents eye problems | Milk, milk products, pork, liver, eggs, bread, rolls, crackers, green leafy vegetables |
| **Vitamin C** | Helps to form bones and teeth, increase iron absorption, resist infection and stress | Tomatoes, most citrus fruits, kiwi, potatoes, fruit juices, green pepper |
| **Vitamin D** | Needed for strong bones and teeth | Fish oils, milk, sunlight |
| **Vitamin E** | Helps maintain cell health, has possible role in reproduction | Vegetable oils, margarine, peaches |
| **Vitamin K** | Aids in blood clotting | Green leafy vegetables, soybeans, bran, peas, green beans, liver |

## *Water*

Water does not contain calories, but it is important to your body. Water makes up about two-thirds of your body's weight. The water in your blood carries nutrients to your body cells. It carries waste out of your body. Water also helps control your body temperature.

Each day, your body loses about eight glasses of water. You lose water when you sweat, when you release waste, and when you breathe out. You need to drink about eight glasses of water every day to replace what you lose. You can drink plain water or get water from juices, soups, and other drinks.

## Do People Have Different Dietary Needs?

The Dietary Guidelines and the Food Guide Pyramid provide general guidelines for people to follow. People must adjust their diet to their own specific needs.

Teenagers have special dietary needs that other people may not have. Because teens are growing and changing, they need more calories, calcium, and iron.

Calcium is an important mineral necessary for bone growth. Some of the best sources of calcium are milk, yogurt, and cheese (see Appendix B).

Iron is important for getting oxygen into the blood and cells. Iron is found in meat, dried fruits, whole grain foods, and leafy green vegetables.

Very active people and athletes require more calories for energy. It is safest for athletes to eat a healthy, balanced diet with enough calories to match their increased activity level.

## Lesson 2 Review

Write the answers to these questions on a sheet of paper, using complete sentences.

**1)** How are carbohydrates, fats, and proteins alike?

**2)** Why are the minerals calcium and phosphorus important?

**3)** Why is it important to eat a variety of foods?

**4)** How many glasses of water does a person need each day?

**5)** Fruits and vegetables are healthy for you. Is it healthy to have only fruits and vegetables in your diet? Explain your answer.

## *Comparison Shopping* • • • • • • • • • • •

Understanding good nutrition and caring about being healthy can make you a better food shopper. In fact, food shopping is often where good nutrition begins. Yet how can you choose wisely among the thousands of food items in the store?

### What Does a Food Label Tell You?

Most foods in a grocery store come in a labeled package. By reading food labels, you can identify foods that are the most nutritious at the best price.

The government has set guidelines for the information that must appear on a food label. The information includes what is in the package and how to store the food. The label also gives the weight and lot number of the product. Some labels have freshness dates. The product should be used by this date to ensure freshness.

Food labels also provide information about the nutrients and ingredients in the food product. This information appears under the heading **nutrition facts**. Nutrition facts tell the size of one serving and how many servings are in the package. They also list the number of calories per serving as well as the number of calories from fat.

Within the nutrition facts is the percent of the **Daily Value (DV)** for each nutrient in the product. This percent tells how much of a nutrient is in the food compared with the total amount needed each day. The DV is based on a diet of 2,000 calories per day. For example, the DV for sodium is 2,400 milligrams (mg).

Good nutrition often begins with careful food shopping.

**Nutrition Facts**

Serving Size 2 bars (42g)
Servings Per Container 6

| Amount Per Serving | 2 bars | | 1 bar | |
|---|---|---|---|---|
| **Calories** | 180 | | 90 | |
| Calories from Fat | 50 | | 25 | |
| | **% DV\*** | | **% DV\*** | |
| **Total Fat** | 6g | **9%** | 3g | **5%** |
| Saturated Fat | 0.5g | **3%** | 0g | **0%** |
| **Cholesterol** | 0mg | **0%** | 0mg | **0%** |
| **Sodium** | 160mg | **7%** | 80mg | **3%** |
| **Total Carbohydrate** | 29g | **10%** | 15g | **5%** |
| Dietary Fiber | 2g | **8%** | 1g | **4%** |
| Sugars | 11g | | 6g | |
| **Protein** | 4g | | 2g | |
| | | | | |
| Iron | | 6% | | 2% |

Not a significant source of vitamin A, vitamin C and calcium.

\*Percent Daily Values are based on a 2,000 calorie diet. Your daily values may be higher or lower depending on your calorie needs:

| | Calories: | 2,000 | 2,500 |
|---|---|---|---|
| Total Fat | Less than | 65g | 80g |
| Sat Fat | Less than | 20g | 25g |
| Cholesterol | Less than | 300mg | 300mg |
| Sodium | Less than | 2,400mg | 2,400mg |
| Total Carbohydrate | | 300g | 375g |
| Dietary Fiber | | 25g | 30g |

**INGREDIENTS:** WHOLE GRAIN ROLLED OATS, SUGAR, CANOLA OIL, CRISP RICE (RICE FLOUR, SUGAR, MALT, SALT), HONEY, SOY PROTEIN, BROWN SUGAR SYRUP, SALT, CINNAMON, SOY LECITHIN, BAKING SODA, ALMOND FLOUR, PEANUT FLOUR. **CONTAINS SOY, ALMOND AND PEANUT INGREDIENTS.**

A food label

The label shown here is for a product that has 160 mg of sodium per serving. That amount is about 7 percent of the sodium you should have for the day. In other words, one serving is 7 percent of the Daily Value for sodium. The Daily Value information helps you tell how many nutrients you are getting in one serving of that food.

The amounts of total fat, cholesterol, sodium, total carbohydrates, and protein also are provided under nutrition facts. Amounts appear in grams or milligrams. Next to the amounts are the DV percentages. The label may also include the amount of vitamins A and C, calcium, iron, and other vitamins and minerals.

The food label also lists all the ingredients in the product. The ingredients are listed in order by weight, from the most to the least. For example, whole grain rolled oats is the first ingredient listed on the granola bar label.

The information on a food label can help you choose foods wisely. For example, you may have an allergy to a food. Check the list of ingredients to see if a product contains that food. If you are trying to limit salt in your diet, the label tells you what percent of sodium, or salt, is in one serving.

• • • • • • • • • • •

**Look at the food label. What percent is the percent Daily Value of protein for two servings of this food?**

## Food Shopping Tips

• Make a list of the foods you need before you shop. Stick to the list as you shop.

• Look for sales. Use coupons from newspapers and magazines.

• Do not buy foods in damaged packages or foods with broken seals.

• Check expiration or freshness dates on foods such as meats and dairy products.

**Additive**
*A substance added to food in small amounts*

You can also use the label to compare prices. Divide the price by the number of servings to know how much each serving costs. Then compare that amount with other brands of the same food to see which one is the best value.

## What Are Food Additives?

When you read a list of ingredients, you may notice some uncommon words. Many are the names of food **additives**. An additive is a substance added to food to change it in some way. Some additives are used to change the color, flavor, or texture of food. Additives such as sugar or salt are sometimes added to help prevent food from spoiling. Sometimes nutrients are added to foods. For example, vitamin C is added to some fruit drinks.

**Learn where** things are located in your grocery store. Memorize the layout of the store and make your grocery list accordingly. This will make shopping easier and faster.

Some people question whether additives are safe. The U.S. government has passed laws about food additives. Additives must be tested and must not be found to cause cancer in animals or humans. Food producers must test the additives and give their results to the Food and Drug Administration (FDA). The FDA decides whether the additive is safe.

Choose a variety of foods—packaged, natural, and fresh—to give you the nutrients you need. With all the foods available and a little planning, a healthy diet is within your reach.

## Lesson 3 Review

Write the answers to these questions on a sheet of paper, using complete sentences.

**1)** What are two kinds of information found in the nutrition facts of a food label?

**2)** What does the order of ingredients on a food label tell you?

**3)** How can you use a food label to compare prices?

**4)** What are three reasons that food additives are used?

**5)** Suppose a food has 60 percent of the Daily Value for sodium. Do you think this is a healthy food? Explain your answer.

## Technology In Our Lives

### Using Electron Beams Instead of Additives

Some additives are added to food to keep bacteria from growing and spoiling the food. Still, millions of people in the United States become sick each year from eating foods that have harmful bacteria.

Now, a new process kills almost 100 percent of the bacteria in food without using additives. The process uses an electronic beam to kill bacteria in meats, fruits, vegetables, and grains. The FDA has already approved the process, called electronic pasteurization. It may be used most widely on ground beef.

## *Personalizing a Fitness Program* ● ● ● ● ●

**P**hysical fitness is your body's ability to meet the demands of daily living. That means having enough energy to do all the things you want to do. Physical fitness is a key part of your overall good health. It affects your emotional, social, and physical well-being. Exercising regularly to be physically fit is another way you can take care of yourself.

### Why Is Physical Fitness Important?

You can improve your physical fitness with regular exercise, good nutrition, and enough rest. To exercise means to move the larger muscles of your body, such as those in your arms and legs.

Regular exercise can improve your health. It helps build a strong heart and lungs. It helps build strong, firm muscles. It improves your body's ability to move in ways you want it to move, such as by twisting and turning. Exercise gives you more energy so you can do more without becoming tired. Active people sleep better, feel better, and are less depressed than people who are not active.

Exercise can reduce the chance for illness. For example, regular exercise reduces the risk of heart disease. Regular exercise can also shorten the time it takes to get well if you become sick.

Regular exercise can improve a person's health.

Another benefit of exercise is weight control. Exercise burns up extra calories so that your body does not build up too much fat. Exercise can be fun and is a great way to make friends.

## What Are the Parts of Health-Related Fitness?

Physical fitness is made up of different parts. Some of these parts are skills such as speed, reaction time, and coordination. Most sports and other activities require certain combinations of skills.

Other parts of physical fitness are related to health instead of skills. **Health-related fitness** helps you stay healthy. There are five parts of health-related fitness.

1. *Cardiovascular fitness* is the ability to exercise your entire body for a long time. Your heart and blood vessels move oxygen efficiently through your blood to your lungs. A person with good cardiovascular fitness has a strong heart and healthy lungs.

2. *Strength* is the amount of force your muscles can make. A person who is strong can do everyday tasks more easily.

3. *Muscular endurance* is the ability to use your muscles for a long time. A person with good muscular endurance can lift, push, and pull objects without unusual muscle fatigue.

4. *Flexibility* is the ability to twist, turn, bend, and stretch your body easily. Flexibility helps prevent muscle pulls and strains and increases range of motion in body joints. A person with good flexibility has fewer muscle injuries and often has improved posture.

5. *Body fat* is the percent of your body weight that is fat. Teenage girls should have 11 to 25 percent body fat. Teenage boys should have 6 to 20 percent body fat. Having a healthy amount of body fat can help prevent illness and give you enough energy for activities.

**Do not overdo exercise, especially if you have not exercised regularly for a long time. Start out slowly, and gradually increase the amount of time spent exercising.**

Types of exercise

| Type of Exercise | Purpose | Examples |
|---|---|---|
| **Aerobic exercise** (steady, continuous activity) | Helps heart and lungs work more efficiently | Walking, running, bicycling, swimming, cross-country skiing |
| **Anaerobic exercise** (short spurts of activity) | Improves body's ability to operate at peak performance | Sprinting, tennis |
| **Isokinetic exercise** | Builds muscle strength with tension resistance through slow motions | Workout with machines that control force of pushing and pulling |
| **Isometric exercise** | Builds muscle strength through muscle tension | Pushing against a wall |
| **Isotonic exercise** | Builds muscle strength with weights | Any body movement, push-ups, pull-ups |

## What Are Some Kinds of Exercises?

Exercises have different purposes. The chart that appears here lists some types of exercise and their purpose. Exercise is one of the best ways to keep your mind and body healthy. Some fat-blasting exercises are listed in Appendix C.

## What Is a Good Fitness Program?

A good fitness program includes three main parts: a warm-up, a workout, and a cool-down.

### Warm-Up

Warm-up exercises stretch your muscles and improve your flexibility. Warming up reduces the risk of injury and soreness. It allows your heart rate to increase gradually rather than suddenly. It gets your heart ready to handle more brisk exercise. A warm-up should take about five minutes. You can warm up by walking and doing stretching exercises.

**Aerobic exercise**
*Activity that increases a person's heart rate*

**Anaerobic exercise**
*Activity that quickly uses up oxygen in the body*

**Isokinetic exercise**
*Activity that builds muscle strength when muscles resist tension through a full range of slow motions*

**Isometric exercise**
*Activity that uses muscle tension to build strength*

**Isotonic exercise**
*Activity that builds muscle strength with weights*

Maximum heart rate
*Heartbeats per minute during hard, fast, and long exercise*

. . . . . . . . . . .

**What are some chores you can do every day that can be part of your fitness program?**

## Workout

After the warm-up comes the workout, which is the main period of activity. The workout should include activities that improve heart and lung endurance, muscle fitness, and flexibility. Often, a variety of activities works best. For example, you might enjoy sports such as basketball and softball. Other activities such as hiking, dancing, swimming, and bicycling can also be included in workouts.

In order for exercise to improve your fitness, you need to exercise three to six days a week. You also need to exercise for 30 to 60 minutes at a time. Exercising only a couple of days a week or for only a few minutes at a time is not enough. You might enjoy the activity, but it will not improve your fitness.

## Improve Heart and Lung Endurance

Your **maximum heart rate** is heartbeats per minute when you exercise as hard, fast, and long as you can. Although maximum heart rate differs among people, it is about 220 minus your age. For example, if you are 17, your maximum heart rate is 203 beats per minute.

If you want to decrease your exercising heart rate, slow down. To increase it, pick up your pace. Be careful to not push yourself too hard. You should be able to carry on a conversation with someone next to you.

Aerobic exercise is especially important in a workout because it improves your heart and lung endurance or cardiovascular fitness. An aerobic exercise is an activity that is steady and continuous. Aerobic exercise increases the heart rate and allows the heart to supply all the oxygen the muscles need.

Running, swimming, bicycling, walking, or any other exercise you do at a steady, continuous pace without stopping is aerobic. Sports such as baseball or softball are not aerobic because the activity is not steady and continuous.

### Improve Muscle Fitness

Improving muscular fitness involves resistance. Your muscles need to overcome some sort of resistance to become stronger. Push-ups, sit-ups, and pull-ups improve muscle strength and endurance. Weight lifting and isometric exercises also improve muscle strength and endurance.

### Improve Flexibility

Slow stretching exercises can improve body flexibility. Stretching causes muscles to relax and lengthen. Slow, gradual movements are best for building flexibility. Avoid fast, bouncy movements, which cause muscles to contract instead of lengthen.

### Cool-Down

End your workout with a cool-down. Your body needs a chance to slow down gradually. Your blood needs time to flow back toward the heart from the muscles. If you stop suddenly, you could become light-headed or you could even faint. To cool down, continue to exercise, but at a slower pace. You might also do stretching exercises you did in the warm-up to improve flexibility. A cool-down should take about five minutes.

Stretching exercises relax muscles and improve body flexibility.

## Why Is Rest Important to Fitness?

Rest is a necessary part of a person's well-being. When you are tired, your body is not able to function properly. You have a harder time paying attention and often feel more stressed. Your body also is at greater risk for illness and injury when you are tired. Sleep and rest are necessary to feel better and to stay healthy.

Most young people need between eight and nine hours of sleep each night. Depending on your level of activity, you might need more rest. Rest does not always have to involve sleep. Reducing your level of activity or relaxing is a good way to rest during the day.

## Lesson 4 Review

Write the answers to these questions on a sheet of paper, using complete sentences.

**1)** What are four benefits of exercise?

**2)** What are three main parts of a fitness program?

**3)** Why is warm-up an important part of a fitness program?

**4)** How often should a person exercise to improve fitness?

**5)** Is it possible that a body builder might not be physically fit? Explain your answer.

## *Living with Stress* ● ● ● ● ● ● ● ● ● ● ● ● ●

> **Stress**
> *A state of physical or emotional pressure*

You probably face some amount of **stress** every day. Stress is the body's reaction to a demanding situation. It is a state of physical or emotional pressure. Stress is a reaction to anything that places demands on the body or mind to which people must adapt. Stress is normal, and it can be either good or bad. Happy events such as graduations, dates, and weddings can all be sources of good stress. Good stress helps people reach goals and make positive changes. Bad stress has harmful effects. The death of a loved one can cause bad stress. Too much stress can cause problems and interfere with healthy living. When people talk about stress, they are usually referring to bad stress.

### How Do People React to Stress?

Different people react to stress in different ways. For example, some people eat when they are stressed. Others lose their appetite. Some people become nervous, talkative, and active. Others become quiet.

When people face stress, they try to identify what is wrong and whether it is dangerous. A person's response to stress often takes the form of fight or flight. The fight-or-flight impulse is natural and often happens automatically. When something threatens or angers you, you may feel an impulse to fight it. When you fight, you attack what threatens you. Fighting may simply be using words to stand up for what you believe. The other response is to flee. When you flee, you leave the situation but nothing changes.

In a stressful situation, chemical changes happen in your body to prepare you to either fight or flee.

Sometimes it helps to talk with others about a stressful situation.

## Common Stressful Events for Teens

- Death of a parent
- Beginning a date
- A visible deformity
- Death of a brother or sister
- Parents' divorce or separation
- An outstanding personal achievement
- Being involved with alcohol or other drugs
- A change in parents' financial status
- Being a senior in high school
- A change in acceptance by peers
- Being accepted to college

For example, your eyes take in more light, your heart rate increases, and your muscles tense. Usually, physical reactions to stress help people resist stress. They help people react quickly and remain alert while choosing the best way to respond.

### What Are Some Ways to Manage Stress?

One of the best ways to relieve stress is to focus on the things you enjoy in your life. Take time to laugh and have fun.

Because stress is a common part of our lives, it is important to learn to manage it in healthy ways. You can learn to **cope**, or find a way to deal with stress or other problems. Coping with a situation relieves the stress. When you cope with a problem, you can do four things:

1. Identify the cause of the problem.
2. Decide on a way to solve the problem.
3. Carry out your plan.
4. Evaluate your plan to see if it solved the problem and relieved your stress.

For example, you might feel stress about getting a job. To cope with this problem, plan ways to get help. Check the newspaper and ask adult family members or friends for suggestions. Find and read a library book about how to apply for a job. Set a plan and act on it. Your chance for success in finding a job is better because you are actively doing something about it. You are coping with the problem.

When you succeed in solving a problem, you relieve stress. Learning to cope with one problem may help you deal with other problems. You can learn from your successes as well as your mistakes.

Experience and time also help relieve stress. When people try something new, they often feel stress. The more you do something and gain experience, the less stress you will feel. For example, giving a speech in class can be stressful. The more you practice talking in front of people, the less stressful it will be to give speeches.

Studying is one way to relieve school-related stress.

Here are some other ways you can cope with problems in your life and relieve stress:

- Sit or lie down in a quiet place. Take several deep breaths. Breathe in through your nose and out through your mouth.

- Stretch your muscles to relieve tension.

- Do exercises or other physical activity.

- Identify the cause of the stress. For example, if you are angry, figure out what is making you angry.

- Take one thing at a time. You may have several problems piling up. Decide which ones to handle now and which ones to handle later.

- List several ways to solve your problems. Consider the results of each way, then choose the best.

- Accept what you cannot change. For example, if you did something in the past that causes you stress, accept that you cannot change the past. However, you can learn from mistakes and change your behavior.

- Think positively. Keep an "I can" attitude. Instead of viewing a situation as a problem, look at it as a challenge.

**What is something positive you have learned from a success? What is something positive you have learned from a failure?**

- Avoid situations that you know are going to cause stress. For example, if you know that illegal drugs will be at a party, you can choose not to go to the party.

- Take responsibility. Do not count on wishful thinking or wait for others to solve your problems.

## Lesson 5 Review

Write the answers to these questions on a sheet of paper, using complete sentences.

**1)** What is stress?

**2)** How can stress be helpful?

**3)** What are four things you can do to cope with a problem?

**4)** What are three other ways to deal with stress?

**5)** Think of a problem that is causing you stress. How would you cope with the problem and relieve the stress?

## Online Resources

**American Dietetic Association**

*www.eatright.org*

Information about nutrition, health, food safety, finding a dietitian, and more.

**U. S. Department of Agriculture**
**Center for Nutrition Policy and Promotion**

*www.usda.gov/cnpp*

Information about dietary guidelines for Americans, the Food Guide Pyramid, healthy eating, and recipes.

**U.S. Food and Drug Administration**
**Center for Food Safety and Applied Nutrition**

*vm.cfsan.fda.gov/*

Information on dietary supplements, food additives, and food labels and nutrition.

# Chapter 4 Summary

- The Dietary Guidelines and the Food Guide Pyramid help you choose foods for a healthy diet.

- The body needs six kinds of nutrients: carbohydrates, fats, proteins, vitamins, minerals, and water.

- Teenagers have special dietary needs including more calcium and iron.

- Food labels provide information about the product. Labels include nutrition facts, Daily Value information, and a list of ingredients.

- Additives are substances added to foods to change them in some way. Some additives help prevent food from spoiling.

- Physical fitness is your body's ability to meet the demands of everyday life.

- You can improve your physical fitness with exercise, good nutrition, and rest.

- Regular exercise improves all parts of your health, including increasing energy, reducing the chances of illness, and managing stress.

- Five parts of health-related fitness are cardiovascular fitness, strength, muscular endurance, flexibility, and body fat.

- A good fitness program includes a warm-up, a workout, and a cool-down.

- Stress is the body's reaction to a demanding situation. Stress is a normal part of life.

- Coping with stress involves identifying the cause of the problem, deciding how to solve it, carrying out your decision, and evaluating it.

- You can do many things to cope with and manage stress.

## Comprehension: Identifying Facts

On a sheet of paper, write the correct word or words from the Word Bank to complete each sentence.

> **WORD BANK**
>
> additives
> amino acids
> balanced
> carbohydrates
>
> cardiovascular
>   fitness
> cool-down
> cope
> Daily Value
>
> Food Guide
>   Pyramid
> physical fitness
> stress
> weight

1) You can use the _____ to choose foods that meet the Dietary Guidelines.

2) Potatoes, pasta, and bread are good sources of _____.

3) The body needs nine _____ that are the building blocks of protein.

4) A _____ diet includes a variety of foods that give you all the nutrients you need.

5) The _____ of a food is based on a diet of 2,000 calories per day.

6) On a food label, the ingredients are listed in order by _____.

7) Sometimes _____ are put in foods to keep them from spoiling.

8) The body's ability to meet the demands of everyday living is called _____.

9) A person with good _____ has a strong heart and healthy lungs.

**Test-Taking Tip**

Always read directions more than once. Underline words that tell how many examples or items you must provide.

10) You should always end a workout with a _____.

11) The body's reaction to a demanding situation is called _____.

12) To handle stress, it is important to find ways to _____.

## Comprehension: Understanding Main Ideas

On a sheet of paper, write the answers to the following questions using complete sentences.

13) What are the six groups of nutrients?

14) What are three of the Dietary Guidelines?

15) What foods form the smallest part of the Food Guide Pyramid and should be eaten the least?

16) What information is on a food label to help you choose healthy foods?

17) What are three ways exercise improves your health?

18) What are four ways to cope with stress?

## Critical Thinking: Write Your Opinion

On a sheet of paper, write the answers to the following questions using complete sentences.

19) In what ways could you change your diet to make it healthier?

20) What is an exercise plan you could try for a week?

# Self-Assessment

Can you answer the following questions?

☑ What are three common eating disorders?

☑ What are some of your personal values or beliefs?

☑ What is self-esteem and why is it important to your well-being?

☑ What are the four forms of well-being?

☑ How do the forms of well-being work together?

☑ What three social skills should you have to strengthen your social well-being?

☑ Do you know how to set realistic goals?

☑ What are two self-defeating behaviors?

☑ What is clinical depression?

☑ What does it mean to be a self-advocate?

# Emotional Health and Self-Advocacy

Getting to know yourself and becoming aware of your values and beliefs can make a difference in your emotional well-being. That can make a difference in your outlook on life and the quality of your relationships, too. You can do many things to improve and maintain good mental and emotional health.

In this chapter, you will learn about influences on mental health and the characteristics of mentally healthy people. You will also learn about self-advocacy and how that ties into your well-being.

## Goals for Learning

▶ To describe actions that promote mental well-being

▶ To explain the effect of positive self-esteem

▶ To identify signs of poor mental health

▶ To apply self-advocacy skills

## *Assessing Individual Well-Being* ● ● ● ● ●

**E**very day you see ads urging you to buy something. These ads often claim that the item will make your life better in some way. Product advertising is designed to make you feel that you will be happy if you buy the product. But happiness is not something that comes from things. Happiness is a feeling that comes from within you, from your thoughts and feelings about yourself.

### What Is Well-Being?

Well-being is feeling healthy, happy, and content. Well-being involves balancing many different behaviors and needs. If a person feels healthy and content, all four forms of well-being are working together successfully. The four forms are emotional, social, physical, and personal well-being.

• Physical well-being is your body's ability to meet the demands of daily life. You are physically healthy and free from pain and illness.

• Emotional well-being is the ability to handle problems and stress in daily life. You have a positive outlook and are in control of your emotions.

• Social well-being is the ability to get along with others. Social well-being is important because you interact with other people many times every day.

• Your satisfaction with your own beliefs and values contributes to your sense of personal well-being. Values and personal beliefs develop and change over time. As long as your beliefs and values are right for you and respectful of others, they increase your well-being. Your belief system can guide you and help you make decisions.

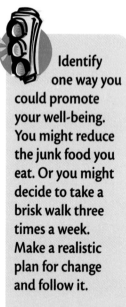

**Identify one way you could promote your well-being. You might reduce the junk food you eat. Or you might decide to take a brisk walk three times a week. Make a realistic plan for change and follow it.**

## How Are the Forms of Well-Being Related?

Your overall well-being depends on how all the forms of well-being work together. They all are equally important and support each other. For example, when you are physically healthy, you are better able to handle stress. Likewise, a good mental attitude promotes physical health.

Problems in one area of well-being can affect another area. If you don't feel well physically, you may also feel sad or depressed. If you are worried about something, you may withdraw from those around you. This lack of emotional well-being may hurt your relationships with others for awhile. Establishing support for all four forms of your well-being is the key to good mental health.

**How did you feel when you woke up this morning? Why do you think you felt this way?**

## Create Your Own Support System

One important piece of good mental health is having your own support system. You can assemble some resources for times when you feel down.

- Make a list of things you can do to solve problems such as talk it over, get another opinion, or ask for help.
- Add the names of your closest friends and their phone numbers.
- Review your list whenever you are hurting or feel down.
- Call one of your friends on the list if you need to talk about it.

## What Actions Promote Well-Being?

You can do many things to promote your well-being. Physical well-being requires being healthy. This includes eating right, getting enough sleep, and exercising regularly. People are also more likely to stay healthy if they understand illnesses and know how to prevent them.

One piece of emotional well-being is knowing how to cope with stress. Physical activity helps relieve stress. Understanding and dealing with your emotions also helps relieve stress.

**Have your values and beliefs ever changed? If so, why?**

Developing your social skills will strengthen your social well-being. Here are some social skills you can develop:

- Communication skills—listen, pay attention when others speak, ask questions, be honest in what you say

- Friendship skills—be a good friend, ask others' advice, show respect and loyalty, keep promises and confidences

- Citizenship skills—follow the rules of society, respect others, do your part, volunteer to help

Promoting personal well-being involves forming beliefs about what is important to you and what you believe is right. Is it right to help a friend? Is it right to steal? Is it right to stay out past curfew? You face many choices every day. Your sense of personal well-being can help you make the right choices. Working on all four forms of well-being helps to promote your positive mental health.

## Lesson 1 Review

Write the answers to these questions on a sheet of paper, using complete sentences.

**1)** What are the four forms of well-being?

**2)** How can physical well-being affect emotional well-being?

**3)** What are some things you can do to promote your physical well-being?

**4)** What are some things you can do to promote your social well-being?

**5)** Why is it important to know what you value?

## Lesson 2  *Handling Social-Emotional Health*  ● ● ● ●

**Self-esteem**
*How one feels about oneself; self-respect*

**N**o one lives a trouble-free life. Things happen. Problems crop up. Emotionally healthy people learn to solve problems and adjust to occasional setbacks. People can learn the skills and behaviors needed to be emotionally healthy.

### What Are Some Indicators of Emotionally Healthy People?

Emotionally healthy people have high **self-esteem**. Self-esteem is how you feel about yourself. High self-esteem is feeling good about yourself, but not thinking you are perfect. It is knowing that you are good at some things and not so good at other things. Feeling happy and content is usually an indicator of high self-esteem.

Low self-esteem is just the opposite. People with low self-esteem feel unimportant and unsatisfied. They believe that many things they do are wrong. They usually are not eager to try new things because they think they will fail.

You can do things to develop high self-esteem. Accept the fact that everyone makes mistakes—even you. Try not to let your mistakes upset or embarrass you. Instead, try to learn from them. Learning from each mistake helps you avoid repeating it.

Many people find it hard to change their ways. Breaking old habits is hard. But a person grows through change. Through change, you can grow into the kind of person you want to become. Emotionally healthy people are constantly learning, changing, and growing. They try their best at everything they do.

● ● ● ● ● ● ● ● ● ●
**Think of a person you know who has high self-esteem. What is this person like? How do you feel when you are with this person?**

## How Can People Reach Their Goals?

**Compromise**
*Both sides give in a little to reach an agreement*

**Optimism**
*Tending to expect the best possible outcome*

**Pessimism**
*Tending to expect the worst possible outcome*

Emotionally healthy people set realistic, or reasonable, goals. Realistic goals are balanced between **pessimism** and **optimism**. Pessimism means tending to expect the worst possible outcome. Optimism means tending to expect the best possible outcome. If a goal is too high, or too optimistic, you may spend too much time and effort trying to reach it. You may overlook other things that are important to you and still not reach your goal. If you feel pessimistic about a goal, you may give up without trying. Setting reasonable goals can be difficult. A goal is reasonable if you can reach it with some effort. Setting reachable goals leads to high self-esteem. You feel good when you reach your goal because you know you have accomplished something.

## How Can People Solve Problems?

Sometimes people compromise to solve a problem.

Frustration is a common feeling when people cannot reach their goals. If another person seems to cause the frustration, two people may experience conflict. Rather than dwell on these conflicts, it is important to find solutions to them. Emotionally healthy people know how to look at problems and solve them. They look at a problem from different sides. They try to work out a solution that suits everyone involved.

Sometimes people **compromise** to solve a problem. To compromise means that both people or parties involved in the problem agree to give in a little to solve it. When the problem is resolved, both sides get something out of the solution. For example, you want to buy a new stereo system. Your parents think it is too expensive.

Rather than argue, you ask your parents to work with you to find a solution. You explain to them why you want the system. Your parents explain why they want you to save your money. Your parents bring up good points. You stop and consider your resources rationally. Together, you and your parents work out a **rational** compromise. Rational means being reasonable. You might agree to buy a less expensive system. Or you might buy only part of a system. Or you might agree to wait until you have more money saved before you buy the system. By compromising, you and your parents know each other's views were heard and respected. And the solution is acceptable to everyone involved.

> Rational
> *Reasonable*

## How Can People Manage Their Emotions?

Emotions signal needs. These signals are not always adjusted to the correct "volume." For example, when you are tired, you may react too strongly, or overreact, to a situation. If you were rested, you might react with more control.

Everyone has certain impulses. When someone bumps into you, your impulse might be to strike back. Your impulse might even cause you to overreact. But you don't have to give in to that impulse. Emotional health depends on learning to control impulses and express feelings appropriately.

**What are some things you do to control your emotions?**

People often are able to predict the consequences, or results, of their actions ahead of time. To do this, they consider what might happen if they react a certain way. They can change their actions to avoid a negative consequence. For example, you notice that your friend has a new haircut. You think it is too short. Your impulse is to say, "I think your hair is too short." Before you say it, you realize that comment might hurt your friend's feelings. Instead you say, "I see you have a new hair style." By thinking about the results of your comment ahead of time, you did not hurt your friend's feelings.

## What Are Some Healthy Ways of Thinking?

Emotionally healthy people think in ways that help them reach their goals. They set and work toward goals that are challenging but reachable. They recognize what can and cannot be controlled in their lives. They also have faith in themselves and hope that events will work out for the best.

Emotionally healthy people also know how to cope with stress. They know that things don't always go as planned. They think about how their actions are causing the stress. They change behaviors that are not working.

Keeping a journal can help you identify and cope with your emotions. Write about the events in your life and how you feel about them. Read your entries occasionally and reflect on them.

## School Violence Warning Signs

You may notice some of these warning signs of violence in a friend or classmate. Be alert if someone

• plans violent acts.

• carries a weapon.

• has a violent temper or frequently gets into fights.

• uses threats and abusive language.

• prefers violent entertainment and Web sites.

• produces violent writing or art.

• uses drugs or alcohol.

• exhibits cruelty to animals.

• vandalizes things.

• takes extreme risks.

• has few or no friends.

• feels disrespected or bullied.

Follow your instincts. If you feel uncomfortable about someone's behavior, share how you feel and why with a trusted teacher, counselor, or parent.

## Tolerance: A Tool for Keeping the Peace

Sometimes people are violent toward others because they have been treated badly themselves, just because they are "different." Accepting everyone's right to be different is called *tolerance*. Here are some examples of *intolerance*:

- Calling people names that disrespect their race, sex, accent, religion, intelligence, sexual orientation, or looks.

- Mistreating people who don't fit your idea of what a "man," a "woman," or an "American" should be.

- Making hurtful remarks or asking rude questions about someone's differences.

- Not allowing people to join in activities or "belong" because they are different.

- Picking on people just because they are easy to pick on.

## Positive Thinking

Emotionally healthy people use positive thinking to explain events. People can learn to replace negative, or pessimistic, thinking with realistic, positive thinking. When surprising or unpleasant events occur, you may automatically wonder why they happened. Your reaction to unexpected events can influence the quality of your life. For example, a student receives a poor grade on a test. She reacts by thinking, "This isn't fair! Why is it happening to me?" A more positive reaction would be "That test was hard. I can do better next time."

Emotionally healthy people make sure their actions blend with their ideas and values. Their values become part of them and guide their thinking and behavior. Emotionally healthy people reflect on their feelings and thoughts instead of worrying about what others think. They face and overcome disadvantages and find meaning in their work and play.

## Lesson 2 Review

On a sheet of paper, write the word or words in parentheses that correctly complete each sentence.

**1)** A person with high self-esteem feels that everything he or she does is _____. (perfect, unworthy, valuable)

**2)** One way to develop high self-esteem is to _____. (learn from your mistakes, set high goals, refuse to try new things)

**3)** A healthy way to solve a problem is to _____. (fight, reach a compromise, avoid the situation)

**4)** A healthy way to deal with stress is to _____. (blame others for the stress, work harder, note how your actions add to the stress)

**5)** When telling a friend that his tardiness is annoying, you should _____. (laugh as you send your message, consider what you will say before you say it, yell at the person)

## Technology In Our Lives

### Online Resources for People with Disabilities

The Internet has opened up new avenues for people with disabilities. Here are some things available online:

• **Information.** The Internet lists many sites for people with special needs. Some sites offer information about disabilities. Others describe support groups, their work, and how to get in touch with them.

• **Communication.** Online magazines and newsletters are written by, for, and about people with disabilities. These publications carry related news and discuss health, advocacy, and lifestyle issues.

• **Community.** Using online chat rooms and bulletin boards, people with disabilities can share experiences and concerns. During online forums, experts speak on disability topics and answer questions from online audiences.

# *Handling Mental Health Issues* ● ● ● ● ● ●

**Abnormal**
*Unusual; different from normal*

**Psychologist**
*A person who studies people's mental and behavioral characteristics*

**H**ave you ever wondered about the difference between mentally healthy and unhealthy behavior? Mental health covers a wide range of behavior. Most mental health problems and disorders can be treated successfully.

A person is usually neither completely healthy nor completely mentally ill. The most helpful indicator of mental health is how well a person gets along in his or her world. Healthy people have problems, make mistakes, and behave in self-defeating ways. It is the same for people with mental health problems. The difference between mentally healthy and unhealthy people has to do with behavior patterns. Behavior patterns are either normal or not normal.

## What Does Behavior Indicate About Mental Health?

A **psychologist** studies the mental and behavioral characteristics of people. Most psychologists evaluate mental health by determining the level of normal (usual) behavior. If a person has many **abnormal** behaviors, that person may not be mentally healthy. Abnormal means unusual or not normal. The more abnormal a person's behavior or thinking pattern is, the greater the *possible* risk of mental illness.

Psychologists define normal and abnormal behavior in many ways. One way is to see how well a person adjusts to different situations. People who care for themselves and set and meet personal goals show a normal pattern of behavior. They function independently and get along with others. Mentally healthy people are usually willing to try new things.

People who have trouble getting along with others show behavior usually considered abnormal. People who depend on others too much or who are defeated repeatedly by failure also exhibit abnormal behavior.

## What Are Self-Defeating Behaviors?

**Defense mechanism**
*A mental device one uses to protect oneself*

**Phobia**
*An irrational or unreasonable fear of something*

**Self-defeating behavior**
*An action that blocks a person from reaching a goal*

**Self-defeating behaviors** are actions that block a person from reaching his or her own goals. For example, you want to try out for the track team. You know you must practice and increase your speed. The day before the tryouts, you work out twice the normal time. You are so exhausted the next day that you do not perform well at tryouts. The decision to practice too much was self-defeating. Your actions blocked you from reaching your goal.

Sometimes self-defeating behavior is a sign of poor mental health. Self-defeating behavior can take many different forms. Two common forms are anxiety and **defense mechanisms.**

### Anxiety

Anxiety is a feeling of uneasiness or fearful concern. You feel anxious when you sense that something bad will happen or when you try something new. You might even feel anxious when you are around a certain person. For example, suppose you are attracted to a classmate. You really want to get to know him or her better. But you are worried you might do something foolish and the person won't like you. So you avoid him or her. Instead of dealing with your anxiety, you avoid someone you really want to know better. Your behavior is self-defeating.

Sometimes people use drugs or alcohol to reduce anxiety, but the effects are only short-lived. Drugs and alcohol do not get rid of the source of the anxiety. In fact, when the effects of a substance wear off, the anxiety may be worse.

A **phobia** is one form of anxiety. It is an irrational fear of something. Claustrophobia, a fear of being in enclosed spaces, is a phobia you hear about a lot. This fear is irrational, or unreasonable, because enclosed spaces cannot really hurt a person. A person with a phobia creates a problem for himself or herself. For example, a man won't use elevators because of his claustrophobia. He avoids them and has to find stairs, escalators, or some other way to get around. This disrupts his normal behavior.

Make a list of five things you do well. Post it someplace you will see it daily to remind you that you are special.

## Defense Mechanisms

People use various defense mechanisms to hide anxiety instead of dealing with their problems. A defense mechanism is a mental device people use to protect themselves. Escaping or avoiding the source of anxiety is an example of a defense mechanism. The most common defense mechanisms are **repression, denial, projection,** and **displacement**.

- Repression is refusing to think about something that upsets you. For example, you may "forget" about a doctor appointment you don't want to go to.

- Denial is a conscious refusal to take something seriously. For example, you are having a difficult time in class and are worried about your grade. You have a big test soon but you do not study or ask for help. You tell yourself that reviewing your notes just before the test will be enough to get a good grade. You take the test and fail.

- Projection is accusing someone of your attitudes, feelings, or purposes. For example, if you are angry with your sister, you might project your anger on her. You might say to her, "What are you so angry about?"

- Displacement is shifting an emotion from its real object to a safer one. For example, you are angry with your teacher for making you stay late to make up work. When you get home, your mother asks why you are late. You yell back that you are sick of being treated like a baby. You shift your anger from its real object to someone with whom you feel safe.

Defense mechanisms are normal when used occasionally. Using them too much leads to self-defeating behavior.

## How Are Disorders Treated?

Mental health problems can interfere with a person's ability to lead a healthy life. Fortunately, trained mental health professionals can treat most of these problems. Many disorders can be cured or people can learn to cope with them.

**Denial**
*A conscious refusal to take something seriously*

**Displacement**
*Shifting an emotion from its real object to a safer or more immediate one*

**Projection**
*Accusing someone of having your attitudes, feelings, or purposes*

**Repression**
*The unconscious dismissal of painful impulses, desires, or fears from the conscious mind*

• • • • • • • • •

**Have you ever received someone's displaced emotions? How did it make you feel?**

Anxiety disorder
*A mental problem that makes normal life difficult because of intense anxiety*

Behavior modification
*A form of psychotherapy that teaches a person to replace an unhealthy behavior pattern with a healthy one*

Panic attack
*A feeling of terror that comes without warning and includes chest pains, rapid heartbeat, shaking, sweating, or shortness of breath*

Psychotherapy
*Psychological treatment for mental or emotional disorders*

Substance abuse disorder
*An unhealthy dependence on alcohol or other drugs*

## How Are Substance Abuse Disorders Treated?

A **substance abuse disorder** is an unhealthy dependence on drugs or alcohol. Most substance abuse begins as a defensive behavior pattern. For example, a person may drink because he thinks he will feel less shy or self-conscious. Someone else may use a drug because it makes her feel confident and happy. But alcohol and drugs do not solve problems. They wear off and the problems remain. The person must rely on the drug more and more. Many substances are habit-forming. Before long, the person may become hooked on the substance.

People who abuse substances can get help. How well they respond to treatment depends on their desire to get well. The most important step is admitting a problem exists. For this reason, most treatment programs begin with developing self-awareness and admitting the need for help. Treatment may involve individual counseling, behavioral change programs, or support groups.

## How Are Anxiety Disorders Treated?

An **anxiety disorder** is a mental problem that makes normal life difficult because of anxiety. A phobia is one type of anxiety disorder. A **panic attack** is another type. A panic attack is a feeling of terror that comes without warning. Its symptoms include chest pain, rapid heartbeat, shaking, sweating, or shortness of breath. It can be triggered by a stressful situation.

Some anxiety disorders are physical and some are psychological. Physical problems can be treated with prescription medicine. Medicine can reduce the symptoms long enough for a person to learn how to prevent more problems. Psychological problems can be treated with **psychotherapy**, including **behavior modification**. Psychotherapy is psychological treatment for mental or emotional disorders.

Behavior modification is a form of psychotherapy. It teaches a person how to replace unhealthy behavior patterns with healthy ones. For example, through behavior modification, a person can learn to use deep breathing to relax and avoid panic.

## How Are Affective Disorders Treated?

An **affective disorder** is a mental disorder marked by disturbed or uncontrolled emotions. **Clinical depression** is the most common affective disorder. Clinical depression is a long-lasting, intense sadness. Experiencing mild depression once in awhile is normal. For example, you may feel depressed when you break up with someone. You may feel sad, angry, and tired, and your eating or sleeping habits may change. For most people, the level of depression is related to the loss. If it is not a serious loss, you will feel better in a few days.

People who have clinical depression stay sad for a long time. They cannot handle normal situations easily. Clinically depressed people may experience new symptoms because of the depression. They may not eat and begin to lose weight. This makes them even more tired and depressed. The problems compound and the situation gets worse. They tend to have negative thoughts and often withdraw from social contact. Clinically depressed people need both social contact and energy to recover.

In its most dangerous extreme, depression may lead an individual to attempt **suicide**, or killing oneself. Depression and suicide affect many teens. Suicide is the third leading cause of death among young people, ages 15 to 24. More teenagers and young adults die from suicide than from cancer, heart disease, AIDS, birth defects, stroke, pneumonia and influenza, and chronic lung disease combined. A suicidal person needs immediate mental health treatment. Mental health professionals can treat clinical depression. Through psychotherapy, professionals help people change their behavior patterns. Some treatment plans include antidepressant medicines.

**Affective disorder**
*A mental problem characterized by disturbed or uncontrolled emotions*

**Clinical depression**
*An affective disorder involving long-lasting, intense sadness*

**Suicide**
*Killing oneself*

**Suicide Warning Signs**
- Depression, lack of energy
- Change in sleeping patterns
- Change in appetite
- Withdrawal from social activities
- Drop in grades
- Personality changes—moody, withdrawn, doesn't care
- Increased risk taking
- Earlier suicide attempt

**Bipolar disorder**
*A mental problem involving wide uncontrollable shifts in a person's feelings*

**Delusion**
*A false belief*

**Hallucination**
*A distorted idea about a person or event that is not real*

**Thought disorder**
*A mental problem characterized by distorted or false ideas and beliefs*

One way to deal with depression is to become involved in an activity. Working toward a reasonable goal gives the depressed person a new direction. He or she becomes active and involved in life again. Some examples are taking up a hobby such as painting, photography, or gardening, or caring for a pet. Physical activity is also a positive way to relieve depression.

**Bipolar disorder** is another example of an affective disorder. Bipolar disorder causes people to experience wide shifts in their feelings. Their behavior changes from one extreme to another. They are extremely happy and full of energy one minute, then sluggish and depressed the next. A person who has bipolar disorder needs professional help.

## How Are Thought Disorders Treated?

A **thought disorder** is the most serious kind of mental disorder. Thought disorder symptoms are distorted or false ideas and beliefs. An example of a distorted idea is a **hallucination**—an idea about a person or an event that is not real. A person who hallucinates may see things that do not exist. An example of a distorted or false belief is a **delusion**. A person who has delusions might falsely believe that he or she is an entirely different person.

A person with thought disorders is out of touch with what is real. This loss of touch with reality may range from mild to severe. He or she may say and do strange things. His or her behavior can be frightening, even dangerous. Only mental health professionals can treat thought disorders. Some medicines can reduce the symptoms. However, no cure has been found.

## How Are Eating Disorders Treated?

**Eating disorders** are attempts to deal with psychological problems through eating habits. People falsely believe they do not look good and have to change their appearance. They make harmful changes in their eating habits. An eating disorder can be a way to avoid the pain of real life. Every feeling and problem becomes a war between the individual and food. The person may believe she is in control but she is not. The disorder controls her. Eating disorders most often affect females. Anorexia, bulimia, and compulsive eating are three common eating disorders. An eating disorders chart appears in Appendix B.

If you know someone with an eating disorder, urge him or her to seek professional help. Encourage the person to talk about his or her feelings.

Help is available for people with mental health problems. Many can live normal lives with treatment.

> **Eating disorder**
> *An attempt to deal with psychological problems through eating habits*

## Lesson 3 Review

On a sheet of paper, write the word or words in parentheses that correctly complete each sentence.

1) Someone who _____ may be exhibiting an abnormal behavior pattern. (gets along with others, depends too much on others, is late)

2) Self-defeating behaviors stop you from _____ . (learning, reaching your goals, losing weight)

3) Phobias and panic attacks are types of _____ . (anxiety disorders, affective disorders, eating disorders)

4) Mild depression can be reduced through _____ . (time alone, physical activity, extra rest)

5) Hallucination and _____ are examples of thought disorder symptoms. (depression, panic attack, delusion)

# Advocating Personal Needs ● ● ● ● ● ● ●

**Accommodation**
*An adjustment that helps a person successfully complete a task*

**Disability**
*A condition that causes a person to be unable to do a task in the usual way*

**Self-advocacy**
*The ability to identify and meet needs connected to one's disability without loss of dignity to oneself or others*

People who have **disabilities** do many things well. A disability hinders a person from doing a task the same way most people do it. Some disabilities are physical. Other disabilities affect how a person learns. In many cases, a person with disabilities needs **accommodations** in order to complete a task. An accommodation is an adjustment that allows a person to successfully accomplish a task. **Self-advocacy** is the ability to identify and meet needs specific to one's disability without loss of dignity to oneself or others. Self-advocacy involves facing a problem and using a possible strategy to overcome it. Being an effective self-advocate requires a high level of knowledge about oneself in any situation. Success comes from knowing oneself so well that there is no doubt regarding likes, dislikes, strengths, and weaknesses.

## What Are Some Ways to Have Needs Met?

Each person is unique. Each person has his or her own strengths and weaknesses. People with high self-esteem and self-confidence accept their weaknesses. They focus on their strengths and take actions to deal with their difficulties. For a person with physical disabilities, this may mean seeking specific accommodations.

Suppose you move from place to place in a wheelchair. You are starting a new job. In order to reach your job, you must cross a busy street. As you reach the curb, you look for a ramp, but you do not see one. Getting your wheelchair over a steep curb is very difficult. You need an accommodation. Your safety depends on it. What can you do to solve this problem? You can contact a local government organization such as the Public Works department. Find the phone number for the Public Works department in your local phone book. Call the organization and explain the situation.

Advocating personal needs also applies to people with nonphysical disabilities. People with learning disabilities need to seek accommodations, too. People with learning disabilities need to practice their self-advocacy skills so they are comfortable talking about their needs. Practice involves describing the person's learning disability as well as the person's specific strengths and weaknesses. Learning to speak up for yourself and knowing what to ask for are vital to living and functioning independently. Knowing when and whom to ask for help, and asking for help are also critical skills to learn.

Arrange in advance for any assistance you may need, so that the support is available immediately.

For example, a young woman with an auditory disability may need to remind her supervisor that she misses some of his verbal instructions when he gives them. Though she told him about her disability before she was hired, she needs to remind him again. Because she knows her strengths, she can also offer a solution to the problem. She tells her supervisor that she has noticed that she misses some of his instructions. She says she wants to be sure this does not to happen again because she wants to do a good job. Then she suggests that perhaps she can write down his instructions as he gives them. She asks him to review her notes to be sure she hasn't missed anything.

Disadvantages can be overcome.

He agrees. By her actions, the young woman proves that she is a self-advocate who is in touch with her own needs. She also shows her supervisor that she is a problem-solver and a dedicated employee.

**What accommodations do you need in the workplace, at home, or at school?**

Various organizations provide post-high school services to people who have learning disabilities. These organizations include vocational rehabilitation agencies, mental health agencies, independent living centers, postsecondary services, employment services, and the Social Security Administration.

Students who choose a postsecondary education path after high school need to decide whether or not to self-disclose. Self-disclosure to your postsecondary school can help you succeed by giving you access to disability services. Seeking accommodations through the school's disabilities service office from the beginning sets you up for a positive postsecondary experience.

## Current Day

### Mental Illness

In the past, people with mental illness were thought to be possessed, criminals, or weak-minded. They were locked in asylums, hidden by their families, or mistreated.

Now mental illness is recognized as often having biological causes as well as emotional causes. It is like being born with a physical problem that a person must learn to live with. Some mental illness has emotional causes. Again, it is something a person can live with. Today, many people with mental illness are treated with therapy, medication, and sometimes hospitalization. They frequently live in mainstream society and are productive citizens. Mental disorders are estimated to affect about 20 percent of the U.S. population during a given year.

## How Does ADA Meet the Needs of People with Disabilities?

The Americans with Disabilities Act, or ADA, is a civil rights law that protects the rights of people with disabilities. The law has two goals.

1. The ADA seeks to make American society more accessible to people with disabilities.

2. The ADA prohibits discrimination, or unfair treatment, of people with disabilities.

The ADA protects any individual with a disability who

1. has a physical or mental impairment that substantially limits one or more life activities, or

2. has a record of such an impairment, or

3. is regarded as having such an impairment.

In an employment situation, a qualified individual with a disability must be able to perform the essential functions of the position he or she has or desires, with or without a reasonable accommodation.

The ADA protects more than 40 million people with disabilities. You can get information about the ADA by calling (800) 514-0301, or by visiting its Web site at www.usdoj.gov/crt/ada/adahom1.htm. Information about how to obtain an accommodation and how to report a violation of the law is offered.

 Use the career resource information available in your school or local library to research careers you are interested in pursuing. Identify academic skills and training requirements that are important to reach your goal.

## Lesson 4 Review

On a sheet of paper, write the word or words in parentheses that correctly complete each sentence.

**1)** People with mental health problems _____ . (cannot work, do many things well, are always sick)

**2)** Some accommodations help keep a person with disabilities _____ . (busy, learning, safe)

**3)** The ADA is a law that protects the rights of _____ . (people with disabilities, families, drivers)

**4)** You can get information about groups that help people with special needs by _____ . (talking with friends, calling the operator, searching the Internet)

**5)** When you report an ADA violation, you may _____ . (cause trouble, help others with disabilities, waste your time)

## Online Resources

**Americans with Disabilities Act**

*www.usdoj.gov/crt/ada/adahom1.htm*

Information about the ADA, the people it protects, rights of the disabled, and how to report a violation.

**National Institute of Mental Health**

*www.nimh.nih.gov*

Information about mental health disorders, depression in children and adolescents, suicide, and more.

**U.S. Department of Health and Human Services**

*www.healthfinder.gov*

Under "Just for you," click on "teens" for information about eating disorders, substance abuse, suicide, and more.

# Chapter 5 Summary

- Well-being involves a balance of physical, social, emotional, and personal well-being. Some ways to promote well-being are staying healthy, learning how to handle stress, working to understand others, and forming beliefs and values.

- Some characteristics of emotional health are learning from experience, changing to improve oneself, and setting realistic goals.

- Self-esteem is how you feel about yourself. High self-esteem means being happy and content with yourself. Low self-esteem means feeling unimportant and unsatisfied.

- People with severe emotional problems may need professional help.

- Self-defeating behaviors block a person from reaching goals. Self-defeating behavior patterns can be a sign of poor mental health.

- Defense mechanisms are mental devices people use to protect themselves. Some common defense mechanisms are repression, denial, projection, and displacement.

- Substance abuse disorders involve a dependence on alcohol and other drugs.

- Eating disorders are attempts to cope with problems through harmful eating habits. Three common eating disorders are anorexia, bulimia, and compulsive overeating.

- Individuals with special needs have the right to ask for accommodations to help them carry out their life activities.

## Comprehension: Identifying Facts

On a sheet of paper, write the correct word or words from the Word Bank to complete each sentence.

> **WORD BANK**
>
> | | | |
> |---|---|---|
> | abnormal | compromise | respect |
> | anxiety | decisions | social |
> | appearance | goals | stress |
> | comfortable | psychologist | unfair |

1) Self-defeating behaviors can stop you from reaching your _____.

2) A person who never seems to get along with others shows _____ behavior.

3) A _____ is someone who studies mental and behavioral characteristics.

4) Eating disorders involve unrealistic emphasis on _____.

5) Emotional well-being is the ability to handle problems and _____ in daily life.

6) People with high self-esteem are _____ with themselves.

7) Defense mechanisms and _____ are two common forms of self-defeating behavior.

8) Sometimes you need to _____ in order to solve a problem.

9) Communication, friendship, and citizenship skills are all social skills needed to strengthen _____ well-being.

**Test-Taking Tip**

When you have vocabulary to learn, make flash cards. Write a word on the front of each card. Write the definition on the back. Use the flash cards in a game to test your vocabulary skills.

**10)** One way to keep a relationship healthy is to show that you _____ the other person.

**11)** You use your system of values and beliefs to make _____ that are right for you.

**12)** The Americans with Disabilities Act prohibits the _____ treatment of people with disabilities.

## Comprehension: Understanding Main Ideas

On a sheet of paper, write the answers to the following questions using complete sentences.

**13)** How do most psychologists evaluate mental health?

**14)** What are the four forms of well-being?

**15)** Give an example of a link between two forms of well-being.

**16)** How can you promote personal well-being?

**17)** What does it mean to be a self-advocate?

**18)** What are some ways to solve a conflict between two people?

## Critical Thinking: Write Your Opinion

On a sheet of paper, write the answers to the following questions using complete sentences.

**19)** You are applying for a job and require an accommodation. What do you do?

**20)** Suppose you believe that a good friend has an eating disorder. What could you do to help your friend?

# Self-Assessment

**Can you answer the following questions?**

- ☑ What can you do to save for retirement?
- ☑ What is a budget?
- ☑ Do you have to have a bank account to use an ATM?
- ☑ Do you know how to open a bank account?
- ☑ Why should you apply for a credit card?
- ☑ What is direct deposit?
- ☑ Do you know how to use a check register?
- ☑ Why should you limit the number of credit cards you have?
- ☑ What is a PIN and why would you need one?
- ☑ What is sales tax?

# Financial Responsibilities

**W**hat would you do if someone gave you $1,000? Would you spend it on something you have wanted for awhile? Put it all in a bank? Leave it in a drawer until you needed it? Spend part of it and save the rest? The way you handle your money is important. Making wise decisions about money helps you make sure that you have enough when you need it.

In this chapter, you will learn how to manage your money. You will learn how to save money in a bank or credit union. You will also learn how to use a checking account. You will discover some good and bad things about credit. You will learn some tips about buying wisely. You will find out about taxes. Finally, you will learn why it is never too early to save money for retirement.

## Goals for Learning

▶ To set up and use a budget

▶ To explain how to open and use a savings account and a checking account

▶ To describe when credit is helpful and when it is harmful

▶ To judge products and services in order to get the most for your money

▶ To list ways to save money

*Paying with Cash* • • • • • • • • • • • • • •

**Credit card**
*A card that allows a person to buy something now and pay for it later*

Think of the last time you bought something. It might have been food, clothing, or a CD. Perhaps you paid cash for it. Cash is paper money and coins. Bills and coins are what most people think of when they think of money.

## What Are Some Kinds of Money?

Money is anything that people accept in exchange for goods and services. Throughout history, all sorts of things have been used as money. For example, peppercorns, the seeds of the pepper plant, were used as money 200 years ago. Pepper was used to cover up the taste of spoiling meat, so peppercorns were valuable.

Today, cash is just one of several kinds of money. Another kind of money is a check. A check is a written order to a bank to pay an amount of money to a person or company. People also use **credit cards** as money. A credit card is a card that allows a person to buy something now and pay for it later. You will learn more about checks and credit cards later in this chapter.

Always carry a small amount of cash.

## When Should You Use Cash?

Having some cash on hand when you go out is always a smart practice. This is true even if you do not plan on using it. For example, if your car breaks down, you may need cash to pay for a taxi. You might need some coins to make a phone call.

Some other things you might want to have cash for—both bills and coins—include

- food.
- beverages.
- toll booths or parking fees.
- tips.
- vending machines.

## When Should You Not Use Cash?

Carrying some cash is a good idea, but carrying too much is not. If your wallet or purse gets stolen or lost, your money is gone. Keeping too much cash at home is also not wise. It can be stolen. A bank is a much safer place for large amounts of money.

Cash should never be sent through the mail. Mail could be lost or stolen. Use checks to pay bills through the mail. What if the company that you are paying does not receive the check? You can call your bank to stop payment on the check.

## How Do You Make Change?

When you buy something with cash, do you always know that you are getting the right amount of change back? How can you tell? Consider this example. A bottle of water costs $1.50. You give the cashier, or the person at the checkout counter, a $5 bill. You should receive $3.50 in change. The amount of money you give minus the cost of the item equals your change.

$$\begin{array}{r} \$5.00 \\ -\$1.50 \\ \hline \$3.50 \end{array}$$

Sometimes with odd amounts, making change is easier if you pay a little more. For example, suppose the bottle of water cost $1.51. If you pay with a $5 bill, your correct change would be $3.49. The 49 cents might be one quarter, two dimes, and four pennies. However, if you pay $5.01 (one penny more), it would be the same as if the water cost $1.50 (one penny less). Then your change would be $3.50. The 50 cents would probably be two quarters, which gives you fewer coins to carry around.

$$\begin{array}{r} \$5.01 \\ -\$1.51 \\ \hline \$3.50 \end{array}$$

## Current Day

### The Golden Dollar

In 1979, the U.S. Mint created a new silver dollar with a portrait of Susan B. Anthony. She was a leader of women's rights in the 1800s. The coin was not used much because it looked too much like a quarter. So in the year 2000, the mint created the Golden Dollar. Its gold color makes it look very different from any other coin.

The front of the Golden Dollar has a portrait of Sacagawea. She was the Shoshone Indian who guided Lewis and Clark on their famous expedition. From 1804 to 1806, they explored the Northern Great Plains and Pacific Northwest. Without Sacagawea's help, the expedition would likely have failed.

Describe a situation in which you would want to have cash instead of other kinds of money.

Many stores have containers of pennies beside the cash register. Cashiers use the pennies to make it easier to make change.

### Lesson 1 Review

Write the answers to these questions on a sheet of paper, using complete sentences.

1) What are three kinds of money?

2) What are three things for which it is good to have cash on hand?

3) Why is it not a good idea to carry a lot of cash?

4) If you are sending money through the mail, what kind of money should you use?

5) You buy a CD that costs $12.25. You give the cashier a $20 bill. How much change should you receive?

# Managing a Budget

I t's payday! You receive a paycheck for $174.45 for your part-time job. You cash your check and head to the store. You buy a pair of jeans and a shirt that cost almost $80. There is plenty of money left over, so you decide to buy concert tickets for yourself and a friend. They cost $90. You have $4.45 left. The next payday is two weeks away, and $4.45 won't even buy snacks at school for one week. Besides, you have a car payment of $75 due this month. Where did all your money go? How could you have avoided this situation?

## How Can a Budget Help You?

A **budget** is a plan for spending money. It helps you manage your money so that you spend it wisely. With a budget, you keep a record of your income, or money that you get. You also keep a record of your expenses, or ways that you use money. This includes money that you save.

A budget can show you where your money goes. Keeping track of your money makes you think about how you spend it. If you set up a budget and follow it, you will know what you can afford to buy. You might even spot places where you can cut spending. Then you will have more money for other things.

## What Are the Parts of a Budget?

Every budget has two parts: income and expenses. Income is all money coming in to you. Income includes money you earn from a job. It also includes money you might get from an allowance and from gifts. Your income might change from week to week or month to month.

Budgeting involves making choices.

Expenses are all the ways you use your money. Expenses include bills such as rent, car payments, insurance payments, electricity and water bills, and credit card payments. Expenses include other things that you spend money on such as food, clothing, and recreation.

Expenses also include money that you put away to use later on. This is savings. You might save money to buy a car or for college. You might also save just so that you have money in the future, in case you need it.

## How Do You Set Up a Budget?

Setting up a budget is easy when you follow some simple steps. Notice how the following information is included in the sample budget.

### Monthly Budget

| Income | |
|---|---|
| Job | $1,812.00 |
| **Expenses** | |
| Rent | $600.00 |
| Car payment | 115.00 |
| Car insurance | 85.00 |
| Health insurance | 77.00 |
| Credit card payment | 100.00 |
| Electric | 50.00 |
| Phone | 48.00 |
| Water | 30.00 |
| Food | 400.00 |
| Gas | 42.00 |
| Clothing | 40.00 |
| Recreation | 75.00 |
| Vacation | 50.00 |
| Savings | 100.00 |
| TOTAL Expenses | $1,812.00 |
| GRAND TOTAL | $0.00 |

1. List all your income.

2. List your regular expenses. Begin with bills such as rent and phone. Then list other things that you usually spend money on such as food, gas, bus fare, and recreation.

3. List any new expenses that you expect such as a birthday present or a vacation. You might have to estimate, or guess, the amount.

4. List savings. You might be saving for something special or saving for the future.

5. Check to see that your total income matches or is greater than your total expenses.

This budget is for one month. However, you can set up a budget for a week, for two weeks, or for any amount of time.

## How Can You Stay on a Budget?

Setting up a budget is easy. Staying on a budget is often hard. It is tempting to spend money, but that will throw off your budget. For example, you might see a pair of shoes you would really like to have. But buying them would put you $45 over your clothing budget. What should you do?

You have several choices if you want to stay on budget. The easiest choice might be to wait until the following month to buy the shoes. If you decide not to wait, you might try increasing your income. Perhaps you can work more hours at your job to earn extra pay. You could try lowering some of your other expenses. For instance, you could try using less gas in your car and walking more. Maybe you could lower your recreation budget by skipping a movie. You might decide to put less money toward your vacation fund this month.

By taking money from other parts of your budget, you could probably afford the shoes this month. Remember, though, that some parts of a budget cannot be changed. You cannot change the amount of rent or your car payment, for example.

As you can tell, budgeting involves making choices. You cannot spend your money on everything you want. Spend it wisely and keep track of where it is going.

**How much money do you spend in an average week? What do you spend it on? How could you spend less and save more?**

## Lesson 2 Review

Write the answers to these questions on a sheet of paper, using complete sentences.

1) How does a budget help you manage your money?

2) What are the two parts of a budget?

3) What are five steps to setting up a budget?

4) What is one way to stay on budget even if you spend more money from another part of the budget?

5) The example in the beginning of the lesson refers to a high school student with a part-time job. Set up a two-week budget for that person.

# *Opening Bank Accounts* • • • • • • • • • •

**P**utting your money in a bank or credit union is much smarter than keeping it all at home. Your money is safe in a bank. Also, you can earn money just by having your money in the bank. That is because a bank pays **interest** on certain accounts. Interest is money that a bank pays you for keeping your money in the bank. (For simplicity in this chapter, the term *bank* is used. However, credit unions offer many, if not all, of the same services.)

## How Can You Choose a Bank?

Most communities have several banks. They are not all the same. You must choose a bank that is best for you. There are a number of things to consider when choosing a bank.

### *Convenience*

• • • • • • • • • •

**What would you keep in a safe-deposit box?**

A bank should be convenient for you to visit. First, look for banks that are near where you live or work. Then find out how long they are open each day. Some banks are open in the evening. Some are open on Saturday, too. If a bank has a drive-through window, the window may be open longer than the main part of the bank. The longer the bank is open, the more convenient it is for you to use.

### *Services*

Learn about the services the bank offers. Make sure that it offers savings accounts and checking accounts. Banks that serve mostly businesses are called commercial banks. You may not be able to open a personal account at a commercial bank.

Ask questions to find out what services the bank offers. For example, some banks offer the use of a **safe-deposit box.** This is a secure fireproof box that is shoebox size. People use safe-deposit boxes to hold jewelry, important papers, and other items that they do not want stolen or damaged.

## Fees

Banks often charge their customers money, or **fees,** for different banking services. For example, some banks charge a monthly fee for having a checking account. They might charge another fee if you do not keep a **minimum balance,** or a specific amount of money, in the account.

Banks might also charge a fee for printing the checks you use. That is because the checks must be printed specially for you, with your name, address, phone number, and driver's license number on them. Some banks charge you for every check you write. Banks also charge a yearly fee of around $30 for a safe-deposit box. And some banks charge you for closing an account.

Ask about the bank's other charges and fees. Add up the fees for the services you think you will use. Having this information will help you choose a bank that meets your needs and budget.

### Interest Rates

Most banks pay you interest on your accounts. The interest rate varies but it may be 2 to 3 percent per year. How does interest work? Suppose you put $100 in the bank. The interest rate is 2 percent. After a year, the bank pays you 2 percent of $100, or $2. The higher the interest rate the bank pays, the better for you.

## What Is a Savings Account?

To save money in a bank, you can open a **savings account.** Money in a savings account is not only safe but earns interest too. The more money you put in and the longer you leave it there, the more interest you earn. It is good to have a savings account so that you always have some money if you need it.

> **Fee**
> *Money charged for a service*
>
> **Minimum balance**
> *The smallest amount of money a person can keep in a bank account without having to pay a fee*
>
> **Savings account**
> *Money that earns interest in a bank*

A safe-deposit box is a secure place to store important papers, jewelry, rare coins, and other items.

**Deposit**
*Money put into a bank account*

**Deposit slip**
*A slip of paper you fill out to show how much money you are putting into a bank account*

**Withdrawal**
*Money taken out of a bank account*

**Withdrawal slip**
*A slip of paper you fill out to show how much money you are taking out of a bank account*

## Opening a Savings Account

When you go to the bank to open a savings account, take identification with you. You will also need your Social Security number. Call the bank ahead of time to find out which forms of identification you need to bring. Also, find out the minimum amount of money you need to open the account. It might be as little as $10 or as much as $100.

At the bank, you will sign a signature card so the bank has a sample of the way you sign your name. The bank uses this card as a security measure. It is a way to protect you from other people accessing your account.

## Using a Savings Account

When you put money into your savings account, you make a **deposit.** When you take money out of your savings account, you make a **withdrawal.** Each time you make a deposit, you fill out a **deposit slip.** Each time you make a withdrawal, you fill out a **withdrawal slip.** Samples appear here.

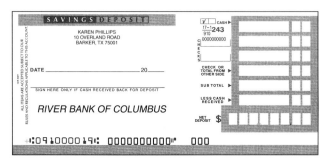

A deposit slip

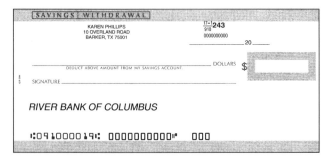

A withdrawal slip

• • • • • • • • • •

**You might use money in your savings account for what kind of an emergency?**

When you open your savings account, the bank usually gives you a **savings book register.** This is a book you use to record each deposit and withdrawal. Recording deposits and withdrawals helps you keep track of how much money is in your account. At the end of each month or every three months, the bank sends you a statement. The statement shows each deposit and withdrawal, how much interest you earned, and the **balance,** or amount of money in the account.

At some banks, you may be given a passbook instead of a register. The bank records each deposit and withdrawal in the passbook.

## What Is a Checking Account?

A checking account is money in a bank that can be taken out by writing a check. Some banks pay interest on checking accounts. However, banks also usually charge a fee for having the checking account.

Checking accounts are convenient because you can pay for things by writing checks. Then you do not have to carry a lot of cash. You can also safely send checks through the mail.

### *Opening a Checking Account*

Opening a checking account is like opening a savings account. You will have to show ID, sign a signature card, and fill out a couple of forms.

When you open the checking account, you will fill out a deposit slip. You fill out a deposit slip every time you put money into the account. When you deposit money, the bank will give you a receipt. Before you leave the bank, make sure the amount on the receipt is correct. Save the receipts at home in a safe place. You can keep them in a file folder, a shoebox, or a large envelope. Use the receipts to check against your monthly bank statement.

**Balance**
*The amount of money left in an account after the withdrawals are subtracted from the deposits*

**Savings book register**
*A small book you use to record each deposit and withdrawal*

• • • • • • • • • •
**Why is it important to sign your name the same way each time?**

## Using a Checking Account

You withdraw money from a checking account by writing a check. A check tells the bank how much money to take from your account to pay to someone else. You can get checks from the bank that have your name, address, phone number, driver's license number, and account number printed on them. This may take a few days. When you open your account, the bank will probably give you special checks to use in the meantime. As you use your checking account you will eventually run low on checks. When this happens, you can order more checks using the reorder form that comes with your checks.

Look at the sample personal check below. Notice the parts that are printed and the parts you have to fill out. Always use a pen to write a check . If you write in pencil, someone could erase it and write in different information. Be neat and clear when you write a check. If you make a mistake, tear up the check and write a new one. The bank may not accept a check with crossed-out mistakes.

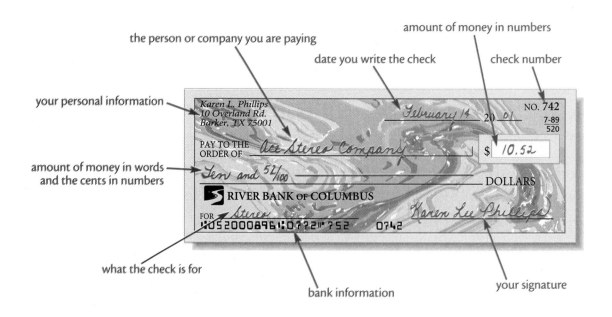

A personal check

## Balancing a Checkbook

When you write a check, be sure you have enough money in your account to cover it. Use your **check register.** This is a booklet in your checkbook. Record every deposit you make and every check you write in the register.

A sample page from a check register is shown below. Notice how the balance changes with each deposit or check that is written. You add your deposits and subtract your withdrawals to keep your balance up to date.

Keeping correct records of the checks you write is important. To make sure your records are correct, you will want to balance your checkbook every month. This means comparing your register to each bank statement you receive. Some of the checks you have written may not reach your bank in time to make it onto the current bank statement. If the check register does not match the bank statement, check the register again. Make sure you have not forgotten to record a check you wrote. If you think the statement might be wrong, call the bank and ask.

> **Check register**
> *A booklet in a checkbook to keep track of checks and deposits*

| NUMBER | DATE | DESCRIPTION OF TRANSACTION | PAYMENT/DEBIT (-) | CODE | FEE (-) | DEPOSIT/CREDIT (+) | $100 | 52 |
|---|---|---|---|---|---|---|---|---|
| | 11/1/00 | Deposit ABC check paycheck | $ | | $ | $ 906 00 | 1006 | 52 |
| 822 | 11/1/00 | Myran Park Apartments November rent | 600 00 | | | | 406 | 52 |
| 823 | 11/6/00 | Cards Are Us credit card payment | 100 00 | | | | 306 | 52 |
| 824 | 11/7/00 | Bob's Fuel gas | 42 00 | | | | 264 | 52 |
| | 11/15/00 | Deposit ABC check paycheck | | | | 906 00 | 1170 | 52 |

A check register

## Lesson 3 Review

Write the answers to these questions on a sheet of paper, using complete sentences.

1) Is it better to have a savings account that pays 3 percent interest or 2 percent interest? Explain your answer.

2) What are three services for which a bank might charge a fee?

3) How are a savings account and a checking account similar? How are they different?

4) Why should you not use a pencil to write a check?

5) How can you use a check register to keep track of the bills you pay?

# Using ATMs

**W**hat acts like a bank teller but works 24 hours a day, 7 days a week, without a break? An **automated teller machine (ATM)**.

## How Can You Use an ATM?

An ATM is a machine that lets you put money into your bank account or take money out. You can also use an ATM to transfer money between accounts. If you just want to check your account balance, you can do that too.

ATMs are convenient. You can find them at banks and other places around town such as shopping malls, grocery stores, and train stations. You can even find them in other cities, states, and countries.

## How Does an ATM Work?

An **ATM card** allows you to use an ATM. You get an ATM card at the bank. You also need a **personal identification number (PIN).** This is a code that lets your ATM card work. If the ATM does not recognize your PIN, you cannot use the ATM.

**Describe a time when you might want to use an ATM.**

---

## Keep Your PIN to Yourself

Do not tell anyone your PIN, not even your best friend. A dishonest person might get hold of it and try to use the number to withdraw money from your account. When you are using an ATM, make sure no one can see you input your PIN. If you lose your ATM card, tell the bank right away.

---

Using an ATM is easy when you follow the instructions that appear on the ATM's screen. When you put your ATM card into the machine, questions will appear on the screen. When you answer one question, the next question appears. The ATM first asks for your PIN. Then it asks what you want to do, such as withdraw or deposit money.

Suppose you want to withdraw money. The ATM asks if you want to withdraw from your savings account or checking account. Then it asks how much you want to withdraw and if you want a receipt. The money comes out of one slot and the receipt comes out of another.

Remember that an ATM is not a "magic money machine." The money you get from an ATM is yours to begin with. Keep the receipt you get from the ATM and record the withdrawal or deposit in your account register.

An ATM accepts deposits and withdrawals, and can give you the balance on your account.

An ATM is a service a bank offers, but the service is not always free. Most banks charge $1 to $2 every time you use an ATM. This fee is automatically taken from your account and should show up on your bank statement.

## Lesson 4 Review

Write the answers to these questions on a sheet of paper, using complete sentences.

**1)** What does an ATM let you do?

**2)** Where can you find ATMs?

**3)** What two things do you need in order to use an ATM?

**4)** Why should you not tell anyone your PIN?

**5)** If you are at the bank, why is it probably better to go inside to a teller than to an ATM?

# Lesson 5 Handling a Paycheck

**Paycheck**
*A check from an employer to an employee*

Have you ever earned money from babysitting or cutting lawns? You were probably paid in cash. When you work for a business, however, you receive a **paycheck.** Your paycheck shows how much money your employer is paying you for your work.

Most people get a paycheck either every two weeks or twice a month. However, some people get a paycheck every week or only once a month. Before accepting a job, you will want to ask how often you will receive a paycheck.

Some jobs pay by the hour. For example, a person might earn $6 per hour working in a clothing store. The amount of money on the person's paycheck would depend on how many hours he or she worked. Some jobs pay a salary, which is a fixed amount of money. The person's paycheck is always the same no matter how many hours he or she works.

## What Are the Parts of a Paycheck?

The sample paycheck shown here is similar to a personal check you would write. For example, the name of the person receiving the money is on the paycheck. The amount is written in words and in numbers. The paycheck has the date it was written.

SUNSHINE REAL ESTATE
555 NORTH SUNSHINE DRIVE
RAINBOW, IL 60608

CHECK NO: 010238

DATE: 11/24/00

PAY TO JENNIFER PEREZ $183.10

ONE HUNDRED EIGHTY-THREE AND 10/100 ---------------------------------------- DOLLARS

BIG BANK CORPORATION

A paycheck

# What Are the Parts of a Paycheck Stub?

A **paycheck stub** is a piece of paper attached to the paycheck. The paycheck stub has a lot of information about the money earned.

For example, look at the Current Hours section on the sample stub shown below. It shows that Jennifer worked 32 hours during the last pay period. She earns $7 per hour. She can check the amount by multiplying this rate by the number of hours worked. So $7 per hour times 32 hours equals $224. The amount in the Current Earnings section is $224.

The Year to Date (YTD) section shows how many hours Jennifer has worked since the beginning of the year. It also shows how much she has earned this year.

**SUNSHINE REAL ESTATE**

CHECK NO: 010238
CHECK DATE: 11/24/00
PERIOD ENDING: 11/24/00
PAY FREQUENCY: SEMIMONTHLY

JENNIFER PEREZ

ID NUMBER: 01234
BASE RATE: 7.00/HOUR

**IMPORTANT MESSAGE**

**HOURS AND EARNINGS**

| DESCRIPTION | CURRENT HOURS/EARNINGS | | Y-T-D HOURS/EARNINGS | |
|---|---|---|---|---|
| HOURLY | 32.00 | 224.00 | 147.25 | 1030.75 |
| | | | | |
| TOTAL HOURS/EARNINGS | 32.00 | 224.00 | 147.25 | 1030.75 |

**TAXES AND DEDUCTIONS**

| DESCRIPTION | CURRENT AMOUNT | Y-T-D AMOUNT |
|---|---|---|
| SO SEC TAX (FICA) | 13.89 | 63.91 |
| CITY TAX | 3.25 | 14.95 |
| FED INC TAX | 17.04 | 74.98 |
| STATE TAX | 6.72 | 30.93 |
| | | |
| TOTAL TAXES | 40.90 | 184.77 |

| | GROSS | PRE-TAX | TAXABLE WAGES | LESS TAXES | LESS DED | NET PAY |
|---|---|---|---|---|---|---|
| CURRENT | 224.00 | .00 | 224.00 | 40.90 | .00 | 183.10 |
| Y-T-D | 1030.75 | .00 | 1030.75 | 184.77 | .00 | 845.98 |

A paycheck stub

If you are paid every two weeks, how many paychecks will you get in a year? How many checks will you get in a year if you are paid twice a month?

The total amount of money earned is called **gross pay.** Jennifer's gross pay for this pay period is $224. But the amount of her check is only $183.10. This is because the paycheck has some **deductions.** A deduction is money taken out of a paycheck. Most deductions are taxes.

See if you can find these deductions on Jennifer's check stub:

• Federal income tax

• Social Security tax (FICA)

• State tax

• City tax

Notice that the amounts for these deductions are given for the current paycheck and for the year to date. The total amount of deductions for this paycheck is $40.90. The gross pay minus the total deductions equals the **net pay.** So $224 minus $40.90 equals $183.10. That is Jennifer's net pay. That is the amount of her paycheck.

When you receive a paycheck, look over the information on the stub to make sure it is correct. For example, make sure the number of hours you worked is correct.

## How Do You Deposit or Cash Your Paycheck?

Your paycheck is just a piece of paper until you deposit it or cash it. If you have a savings account or a checking account, you can deposit the check into those accounts. You must fill out a deposit slip and sign, or endorse, the back of your paycheck. The backs of most paychecks have a line near the top showing you where to sign.

Suppose Jennifer wants to deposit $100 of her paycheck in a savings account and receive the rest as cash. On the deposit slip, she would write the total amount of $183.10. Then, next to Less Cash Received, she would write $83.10. Finally, next to Net Deposit she would write $100.00. Most banks require a picture ID from someone who is cashing a check or part of a check.

# What Is Direct Deposit?

Many companies offer **direct deposit** to their employees. This means the paycheck is automatically deposited in the employee's bank account. The employee receives the check stub but not the check. Direct deposit is convenient for a person who deposits the check in the bank anyway.

Direct deposit can help you save money. If the money is put directly into the bank, you may be less likely to spend it all at once. Try to build up three to six months' worth of earnings in a savings account. This money will be useful in case of an emergency or if you lose your job.

Direct deposit
*Having a paycheck deposited directly into a bank instead of receiving the check*

## Lesson 5 Review

Write the answers to these questions on a sheet of paper, using complete sentences.

1) What are five parts of a paycheck?

2) What do Current and YTD mean on a paycheck stub?

3) How does gross pay differ from net pay?

4) What must you do on the back of a paycheck when you deposit it or cash it?

5) If you make $7 per hour and work 20 hours per week, how much will your gross pay be after two weeks?

**Credit**
*Money that is borrowed with the promise to pay it back*

**Loan**
*Money borrowed for a certain amount of time*

Suppose you buy lunch for a friend, and your friend promises to pay you back. You just gave your friend **credit.** Credit is money that is borrowed with the promise to pay it back.

## How Can You Use Credit?

Buying on credit means borrowing money from a bank, a store, or a credit card company to pay for something. But buying on credit is not exactly like borrowing money from a friend. You usually have to pay the money back with interest or a fee. Therefore, the item you buy ends up costing more than its original price.

One kind of credit is a **loan.** A loan is money borrowed for a certain amount of time. Usually the money is borrowed from a bank or a loan company. People typically get loans for expensive items, such as a car or a house. They pay the loan back by making monthly payments. Each payment includes part of the original price plus interest.

Another common way to use credit is with a credit card. Every time you use a credit card, you are borrowing money from the credit card company. You are using that money to buy something. The credit card company pays the store for your purchase. Then you pay the credit card company.

A credit card can be a useful way to make some purchases as long as the card is used wisely.

## How Do People Establish Credit?

It is dangerous to depend on credit too much. However, establishing some credit is good. Why? Most people need to take out loans at some time in their lives. It may be to buy a house or a car or to help pay for college. Getting a loan is much easier if you have a history of paying credit card bills on time.

The best way to get a credit card for the first time is to be responsible. You must show the credit card company that you are able to handle money. One way to do this is to have a job. This shows that you have an income and will have money to pay your credit card bills. You can also show you are responsible with money by depositing money regularly in a savings account.

A department store credit card is usually the easiest kind of credit to get for the first time. You have to fill out an application. You need to provide information about where you work, how long you have worked there, and how much you earn. The application may ask for bank account numbers. The store will check the information you put on the application. For example, the store might call your employer to confirm you work there.

If you are getting your first credit card, you may need a **cosigner.** This is a parent or other adult who has a good credit history. You both sign the application. If you cannot pay a credit card bill, your cosigner will have to pay it for you.

If you get the credit card, you will probably have a limit on how much you can charge. You might have a limit of $500, for example. The more money you earn, the higher your limit will be.

## Why Not Use Credit for Everything?

Credit cards make buying easy. Sometimes, it is too easy. People often use credit cards too much. They end up owing so much money that they spend years trying to pay it back. How does this happen? Part of the answer has to do with how credit card companies make their money.

**Cosigner**
*A person with a good credit history who will pay a credit card bill if the cardholder cannot pay it*

Credit card companies make their money in these three main ways:

• annual fees

• finance charges

• late fees

Some credit card companies charge their customers a yearly fee for using the card. The fee might be $30 or more. Not all companies charge an annual fee. For example, stores and gasoline companies usually do not charge annual fees.

Credit card companies make most of their money through **finance charges.** A finance charge is a fee you pay based on the amount of money you have borrowed from the company. Finance charges are added to an outstanding balance on a credit card.

Some companies allow you to pay just part of the credit card bill each month. This is called a **minimum payment,** or the least amount of money you must pay. If you pay only part of the bill, you must pay a finance charge on the rest. You also must pay a finance charge on any new purchases. Finance charge rates are often between 13 percent and 21 percent. How can minimum payments and finance charges get you into trouble? Suppose you use a credit card to make these purchases:

| | |
|---|---|
| Bike | $230.00 |
| Dinner | 38.00 |
| Earphones | 32.00 |
| CD | 17.00 |
| TOTAL | $317.00 |

The total bill is $317. But the minimum payment is only $42. You need money for other expenses this month, so you decide to make only the minimum payment. You might expect next month's bill to be $275 ($317 minus $42). Instead, it is $278.43. The extra $3.43 is the finance charge on the unpaid part of the first bill. If you still do not pay the entire bill, more finance charges will be added to the balance.

A finance charge will also be added to any new purchases you made in the month. If you pay only part of a credit card bill, it can take you a long time to pay it off.

A third way that credit card companies make money is by charging late fees. Notice the Payment Due date on the sample bill shown below. What happens if you do not make the payment by that date? The bill next month will have a late fee added to it. The late fee may be more than the minimum payment.

**What is one reason a teenager should have a credit card?**

**What is one reason a teenager should not have a credit card?**

## How Can You Use Credit Cards Wisely?

If you are responsible with your credit, credit cards can be a useful way to make some purchases. Here are some ways to use credit cards wisely.

1. Pay the entire amount of a credit card bill if you can. Then you will not have to pay a finance charge.

2. Do not use a credit card if you know you cannot pay the entire amount when the bill comes.

3. Do not use your credit card for every purchase. Pay with cash or a check when you can.

4. Save all the receipts from purchases you make on credit. Then you will have a record of your purchases in case a mistake shows up on your credit card bill. If a mistake does appear on your bill, call the credit card company.

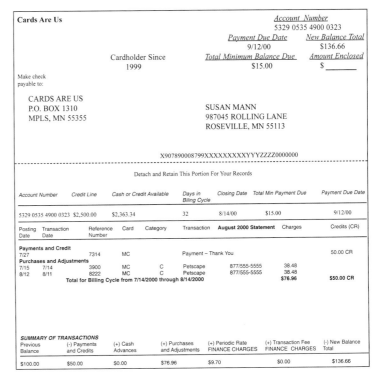

A credit card bill

Credit report
*A summary of a
person's credit
history*

5. Do not apply for too many credit cards. It will be easier to keep track of your credit card bills if you limit yourself to one or two and you won't have as many annual fees.

6. Write down the card number and the name of the credit card company for each card. Keep this information in a safe place.

7. If your credit card is lost or stolen, call the company. It will cancel the account so that someone else cannot charge things on your card.

8. Never give your credit card number to anyone who calls on the phone. The caller may be dishonest.

9. If you get a new credit card, cut up your old one into several pieces and throw it away. Do not leave it whole, otherwise someone might find it and use it.

## What is a Credit Report?

Before you can get a credit card or a loan, the company will pull a **credit report.** A credit report is a summary of your credit history. It shows whether or not your made payments on time. The report gives you a credit risk score. If you have made many late payments, it will be more difficult to get credit or a loan.

## Lesson 6 Review

Write the answers to these questions on a sheet of paper, using complete sentences.

**1)** When you buy something with a credit card, who pays the store for the purchase?

**2)** Why is it a good idea to establish credit?

**3)** What are three ways that credit card companies make money?

**4)** What should you do if your credit card is lost or stolen?

**5)** Why is it dangerous to have high credit limits?

## Be a Wise Consumer ● ● ● ● ● ● ● ● ● ● ● ●

> **Consumer**
> *A person who buys goods and services*

**Y**ou have learned a lot about managing your money. You will be able to manage your money better if you are a wise **consumer.** A consumer is someone who buys goods or services. You already know how to be a consumer. But do you know how to be a wise consumer?

### What Is a Wise Consumer?

● ● ● ● ● ● ● ● ● ●

**How have you been a wise consumer during the past month? How have you not been a wise consumer?**

A wise consumer is someone who does not waste money. A wise consumer is not someone who is "cheap." Wise consumers buy the best products and services they can afford.

A wise consumer understands the difference between wanting something and needing something. A need is something you must have. A want is something you would like to have but can do without.

For example, you may *need* to buy a new pair of jeans. You may *want* a certain brand of jeans. The pair of jeans you want is almost twice as expensive as other jeans. You have budgeted only a certain amount of money this month for clothes. If you buy the designer jeans, you will not have enough money for gas, recreation, and other things. You choose the less expensive jeans. You are a wise consumer.

Wise consumers buy quality products at prices they can afford.

## What Advantages Does a Wise Consumer Have?

One advantage to being a wise consumer is saving money. Here are some ways to do that:

• Find out as much as you can about what you are shopping for. Consumer magazines, such as *Consumer Reports*, compare different brands of products. They can help you choose a product that will last longer and save you money.

• Read ads in newspapers. Find out if the item you want is on sale.

• Shop at several stores to compare prices.

• When shopping, ask yourself these questions: Do I need this item? How much will I use it? Can I afford it? Should I use the money for something else?

Another advantage to being a wise consumer is getting the best products possible. Suppose you are looking for a CD player. You read about many different brands. The CD player you were going to buy is given a poor rating. You decide to buy one that is higher quality for just about the same price. Because you took time to research the product, you bought a quality CD player that you could afford.

Another advantage to being a wise consumer is having a good self-image. If you know you spent your money wisely, you will probably feel good about it. You will feel proud of yourself for taking the time to get the most for your money.

## What Influences Consumers' Choices?

Many factors influence the choices consumers make. One factor is advertisements. Ads can influence people without their realizing it. For example, you keep singing a catchy tune that you have heard advertising a product. Without thinking about the reason, you buy that product.

Ads use many different kinds of messages to convince you to buy the product or service. How many of these messages have you seen or heard?

- **Join the crowd:** These ads tell you that everyone is using the product and that you do not want to be left out.

- **You deserve the best:** These ads try to flatter you or compliment you. They say that you should use the product because you deserve the best.

- **Famous people:** These ads use famous people to sell products. They want you to believe that if you use the product, you will be like the famous person.

- **Enjoy life**: These ads show people having fun and enjoying life. The product may have little to do with what the people are doing. The ad wants you to think they are enjoying life because of the product.

Just because an ad uses one of these or other messages does not mean the product or service is not good. When you hear or see an ad, separate the selling message from the useful information. Then use that information to help you make a choice.

Another influence on consumers is advice from family and friends. For example, if your friend says a shampoo works wonders on his dandruff, you might try it. You also might buy a product because your family has always used it. Word-of-mouth recommendations can be helpful when you consider a purchase. Keep in mind, however, that what is right for another person may not work for you.

Price also influences choices. Well-advertised brand-name products are familiar but usually cost more than lesser-known brands. The place you buy a product also affects price. Stores that are more elegant often have more expensive products. Sometimes the same brand-name product is cheaper at a different store. Check out factory outlet stores and discount stores for some good buys.

## How Do You Return a Product?

Did you ever buy something and wish you had not? Maybe it was the wrong color. Maybe it did not fit right or work right? Or maybe you just decided that you really did not want it.

Usually, you can return an item to the store for a **refund.** A refund is a return of money. Instead of a refund, you might ask for an **exchange.** That means you trade the item you are returning for another item.

Make sure you understand a store's return policy before you buy an item. Some stores will give exchanges but not refunds. When you return an item, you might have to go to the store's customer service department. Be polite. Explain why you want to return the item. Then ask for a refund or an exchange. If the store accepts refunds, you will probably need your sales receipt. The receipt proves that you bought the item at that store and how much it cost. Some stores will allow refunds only for a certain amount of time after the purchase, for instance, three months.

Ask about a store's return policy in case you need to return or exchange an item.

## Why Is a Warranty Important?

Some products have **warranties.** A warranty is a written statement that promises the product will work for a certain amount of time. Most products that have motors come with a warranty. For example, an electric razor probably has a warranty card inside the package. You might have to fill out the card and mail it to the manufacturer for the warranty to take effect. Spending a few minutes to fill out a warranty card is part of being a wise consumer.

> **Warranty**
> *A written statement that promises the product will work for a certain amount of time*

## Lesson 7 Review

Write the answers to these questions on a sheet of paper, using complete sentences.

1) How would you describe a wise consumer?

2) What are three ways to save money when shopping?

3) What are two ways that ads try to sell products?

4) What should you keep in case you need to return a product?

5) What do you think of a product whose ads do not give any useful information?

## *Paying Taxes* ● ● ● ● ● ● ● ● ● ● ● ● ● ● ●

**Income tax**
*A tax paid on the money that people earn*

**Tax**
*Money that people pay to the government*

I f you take a short walk near your home, you probably will see streets, sidewalks, parks, schools, and libraries. Everyone uses or benefits from these things. Therefore, everyone pays for them. We pay for them with taxes. A **tax** is money that people pay to the government. The government uses the taxes to pay for the services it provides. Some of these services include schools, libraries, roads and bridges, police and fire protection, and the armed forces.

### What Are Some Different Kinds of Taxes?

There are many kinds of taxes. People who work pay an **income tax.** Income tax is the amount of money a person pays on what he or she earns. The amount of income tax people pay depends on how much income they earn. The chart below shows the amount of income tax the federal government collects from people who earn different incomes. As you can see, the more you earn, the more taxes you pay.

Income taxes are taken out of your paycheck and recorded on your paycheck stub. You pay income taxes to the federal, state, and local governments.

### Federal Income Tax for a Single Person

| Income per Year | Percent Taken Out |
|---|---|
| $0 to $25,750 | 15% |
| $25,750 to $62,450 | 28% |
| $62,450 to $130,250 | 31% |
| $130,250 to $283,150 | 36% |
| More than $283,150 | 39.6% |

People pay other taxes besides income tax. For example, you pay tax on the interest earned from a savings account. People who own property pay a property tax. If you inherit money or win a lottery, you pay taxes on that money. Companies pay taxes on the profits they make.

Think about the last time you bought something. Did you pay the price marked on the item? You probably did not. You also had to pay **sales tax.** This is an amount of money added to the price of goods and some services. It is a percent of the cost of the item. If the sales tax is 6 percent, a gallon of milk that sells for $2.69 would cost $2.85. Sales tax amounts vary from state to state.

Another tax you pay is Social Security tax. Social Security is a government program that provides money for people who are retired. This money comes from the Social Security tax that is taken out of each employee's paycheck. Employers also pay taxes to Social Security for each employee.

## What Is a Tax Deduction?

You do not have to pay income tax on all the money you earn. You can use tax deductions. A **tax deduction** is a cost that you can subtract from your income when figuring out your income taxes. Then you owe taxes on the amount that is left instead of on your entire income.

Some tax deductions include property taxes, interest on a home mortgage, and money gifts to religious groups and charities. You can list each deduction when you fill out your tax form for the year. However, many people use a **standard deduction** instead. This is an amount of money set by the government. A standard deduction takes the place of all your separate deductions.

Standard deductions may change each year. It might be $4,300 for a single person and $7,200 for a married couple. This means a single person could subtract $4,300 from his or her taxable income. In this example, a single person does not have to pay taxes on $4,300 of his or her income.

**Sales tax**
*An amount of money added to the price of goods and some services*

**Standard deduction**
*An amount of money set by the government that takes the place of separate tax deductions*

**Tax deduction**
*A cost that you can subtract from your income when figuring out your income taxes*

● ● ● ● ● ● ● ● ● ●
**How might your life be affected if all taxes were cut in half?**

An **exemption** is a tax deduction for each family member. The more people you have to support, the more exemptions you get. For example, you get one exemption for yourself. A married couple gets two exemptions. A single parent or married couple gets another exemption for each child. That exemption might be as much as $2,800 per child. Exemptions are set by the government and can change each year.

So what do these deductions mean for you when paying your taxes? Suppose you are a single person earning $23,000 per year:

| | |
|---|---|
| Income | $23,000 |
| Standard deduction | − 4,300 |
| One exemption | − 2,800 |
| | $15,900 |

This means you would owe taxes on only $15,900 even though you earned $23,000. The amount of taxes would be 15 percent of $15,900. That equals $2,385. Most or all of this tax is taken out of your paycheck in small amounts throughout the year. So when you fill out your tax forms for the year, you may not owe any more taxes. In fact, because of tax deductions, too much money might have been taken out for taxes. Then, the government would refund, or return, this money to you.

## Lesson 8 Review

Write the answers to these questions on a sheet of paper, using complete sentences.

**1)** What are taxes used for?

**2)** What are two kinds of taxes taken out of a paycheck?

**3)** What kind of tax do you pay when you buy most things?

**4)** How does an exemption help you?

**5)** Using the example on this page, how much income would you owe taxes on if you had two exemptions?

> **Exemption**
> *A tax deduction for each member of a family*

# *Planning for Retirement* ● ● ● ● ● ● ● ● ●

Y ou have already learned that Social Security is a program that provides money for people when they retire. It is like having a bank account with the government. Each month, the U.S. government sends a check to every retired person who paid Social Security taxes. However, a Social Security check may provide only a few hundred dollars. That helps, but it is not enough to pay all the bills.

## How Can You Save for Your Retirement?

In order to enjoy your retirement years, you must plan for them. It may sound silly to plan for your retirement when you are still a teen or young adult. But the money you set aside for the next 40 years will earn you more money. Then when you retire, you will have enough money to do the things you would like to do. You can make your money work hard for your retirement in several ways.

Certificates of deposit, savings bonds, and IRAs are some retirement investment options.

### CDs

A savings account called a **certificate of deposit (CD)** is one good way to save money for a long time. CDs earn higher interest than a regular savings account. But you have to leave your money in the account for a certain amount of time. The time varies. Some CDs are for six months or a year. Others are for five or ten years. When the time is up, you can renew the CD. CDs may pay 6 percent interest or more, instead of about 2 percent for a regular savings account.

### Savings Bonds

How would you like to loan money to the government and have the government pay you interest? That's what happens when you buy a **savings bond.** A savings bond is a certificate of a loan to the government.

You can buy savings bonds at most banks. Bonds come in several amounts, such as $25, $50, $100, and $500, but you do not pay that much. You buy a bond for half of its face value. That means a $50 bond costs you only $25. The bond will be worth its face value of $50 when it **matures,** which could be in ten years. At that time you can cash it in and get $50. However, if you leave it alone, the bond continues to earn interest. After 30 or 40 years, a bond can be worth many times its face value.

### IRAs

• • • • • • • • • •

**Why do savings bonds make good gifts for infants and children?**

An **individual retirement account (IRA)** is a savings account that is set up to encourage people to save for their retirement. You can put up to $2,000 into an IRA each year. But you cannot take any money out until you are at least 55½ years old. The benefit of an IRA is that you do not pay taxes on the money that you put into the account. You pay taxes on the money only when you take it out.

## Tax-Deferred Savings Plans

Many companies offer their employees savings plans to save for their retirement. These plans, such as the 401k plan, allow you to set aside part of your salary in a **tax-deferred** account. That means you put off paying taxes on that money until you withdraw it.

A tax-deferred account works like this. The government might allow you to put from 1 to 15 percent of your income into the tax-deferred account. Suppose you earn $25,000 a year. You decide to put 5 percent of your income into the account. That is $1,250. A portion of that money is taken out of each paycheck before you pay income taxes on it. At the end of the year, $1,250 has gone into the account. You pay taxes on $23,750 instead of on $25,000. You pay less in taxes and you save money for your retirement. And the money you put in the account earns more money.

At age 59½, you can start withdrawing money from the account without paying a **penalty.** A penalty is a sum of money you forfeit, or lose, because you withdraw money early. You have to pay taxes on the money at that time. However, you probably will pay a smaller amount of tax because you will not be earning as much after you retire.

**Penalty**
*A sum of money you forfeit for not meeting all the requirements of an agreement*

**Tax-deferred**
*Not taxed until withdrawn*

## Technology In Our Lives

### Online Banking

If you have a computer, you may be able to do most of your banking from home. More and more banks are offering the service of online banking. Online banking lets you link your personal computer directly to your bank's computer. You can check your account balances, transfer money from one account to another, and open new accounts. You can even pay bills online. With online banking, there are fewer paper records to keep.

## Lesson 9 Review

Write the answers to these questions on a sheet of paper, using complete sentences.

**1)** Which pays higher interest: a CD or a regular savings account?

**2)** How much does buying a savings bond cost?

**3)** What happens when a savings bond matures?

**4)** What is a tax-deferred account?

**5)** Is an IRA a tax-deferred account? Explain your answer.

### Online Resources

**Better Business Bureau**

*www.bbb.org*

Connect with the Better Business Bureau in your state, check on a company or a charity, or get consumer tips.

**Department of the Treasury Internal Revenue Service**

*www.irs.gov*

Tax information for consumers and business owners, electronic tax services, taxpayer help, and tax forms and publications.

**FDIC Learning Bank**

*www.fdic.gov/about/learn/learning/index.html*

Information about how banks work.

# Chapter 6 Summary

● ● ● ● ● ● ● ● ● ● ● ● ● ● ● ● ● ● ● ●

■ Taking some cash with you when you go out is a good idea. But you should not carry too much in case it gets lost or stolen.

■ Never send cash through the mail.

■ When you budget your money, you keep track of income and expenses and plan how you will spend your money.

■ Budgeting involves making choices so that you spend your money wisely.

■ When choosing a bank, consider convenience, services, fees, and interest rates.

■ You can open a savings account and a checking account at a bank. Then you can deposit and withdraw money.

■ Using an ATM is a convenient way to do some of your banking.

■ A paycheck stub includes important information about the money that you earn.

■ Establishing credit is good. But you must be careful about how you use credit cards. Do not charge more than you can easily pay off when the bill comes.

■ Wise consumers do not waste money. They get the best goods and services they can afford.

■ Ads, friends, family, and price affect consumers' choices.

■ A tax is money that people pay to the government for services the government provides.

■ People pay several kinds of taxes including income tax, sales tax, and Social Security tax.

## Comprehension: Identifying Facts

On a separate sheet of paper, write the correct word or words from the Word Bank to complete each sentence.

> **WORD BANK**
>
> | | | |
> |---|---|---|
> | ATM | consumer | interest |
> | budget | deposit | minimum balance |
> | cash | expenses | PIN |
> | check register | income | withdrawal |

**1)** A _____ is a plan for spending money.

**2)** The longer you keep money in a savings account, the more _____ that money will earn.

**3)** When you take money out of a bank account, you make a _____.

**4)** You should never send _____ through the mail.

**5)** The ways you spend or use money are called _____.

**6)** The money that you get from a job is called _____.

**7)** In order for an ATM to work, you need to input your code, or _____.

**8)** When you put money into a bank account, you make a _____.

**9)** When you write a check, you record it in your _____.

**10)** A person who buys goods or services is a _____.

**Test-Taking Tip**

If you do not know the meaning of a word in a question, read the question to yourself, leaving out the word. Then see if you can figure out the meaning of the word from its use in the sentence.

11) You can do some of your banking at a machine called an
_____.

12) A bank might charge a fee if you do not keep a
_____ in your checking account.

## Comprehension: Understanding Main Ideas

On a sheet of paper, write the answers to the following
questions using complete sentences.

13) What is the difference between gross pay and net pay?

14) You want to stay on budget but still buy something that
you cannot afford. What are some choices you can make
in order to do both?

15) Why are checking accounts useful?

16) What is direct deposit and why is it helpful?

17) Why is it good to establish credit?

18) Why is it dangerous to use credit cards to pay for most
things you buy?

## Critical Thinking: Write Your Opinion

On a sheet of paper, write the answers to the following
questions using complete sentences.

19) If a friend says that taxes are unfair, how would you
respond?

20) What are the three most important things you have
learned in this chapter? Why is each important to you?

## Self-Assessment

Can you answer the following questions?

- ☑ How can you protect a personal computer from computer viruses?
- ☑ What are some examples of online etiquette?
- ☑ Can you download anything you want from the Internet?
- ☑ What do you need to connect to the Internet?
- ☑ What is a search engine?
- ☑ What are the steps involved in doing a search online?
- ☑ How does e-mail work?
- ☑ How do you create a new document?
- ☑ What is an Internet service provider and why do you need one?
- ☑ How do you create a folder?

# Accessing Computer Technology

**Y**ou can find a computer in just about any place you go these days. Sales clerks use computers to record sales. Bank tellers use them to check accounts. Students use them to find information. People who wait tables in restaurants even use them to place food orders.

Computers have become so popular because they are powerful tools. They can help you do simple tasks such as write a letter. They can help you complete harder tasks such as finding information in a library far away.

In this chapter, you will learn how to operate a computer. You will discover how to create documents and folders. You will find out about the Internet and learn how to communicate with friends by e-mail.

## Goals for Learning

▶ To identify the parts of a computer

▶ To create, save, and print a document

▶ To understand the need for file management

▶ To access and search the Internet

▶ To use e-mail

## Lesson 1 — Performing Basic Computer Operations

**Hardware**
*The equipment that makes up a computer—the base unit, monitor, mouse, keyboard, and printer*

**Personal computer**
*A small computer used by one person at a time*

**Select**
*To click on a character, word, or words using a mouse, which highlights that item so you can change it*

A **personal computer,** or PC, is a small computer used by one person. Personal computers are made by a variety of manufacturers and come in different shapes, sizes, and colors. Both Windows-based and Macintosh computer basics are discussed. As is often the case, there is more than one way to perform most of the functions described here.

Five different pieces, or **hardware,** are common to most PCs. The main, essential piece of hardware is the computer base unit. It houses everything that runs the computer, including the electronics, hard and floppy drives, and the power supply. Another piece of hardware is the monitor, a screen that displays information. You use the keyboard to type or input information into the computer. The mouse lets you **select,** or highlight, information displayed on the monitor. The last piece of hardware is the printer, which prints hard copies of your work.

Common pieces of computer hardware

# How Do You Start the Computer?

To start up a computer, turn on the control switch. The switch is usually on the side or back of the base unit. The monitor and printer each have their own control switches. On some computers, the control switch is a button on the keyboard. The instructions that come with the computer will tell you exactly how to get started. Generally, you turn on the base unit, then the monitor, followed by the printer. Turn them off in the same order.

# What Is a Document?

Information that you put into the computer is called a **document**. A document is a page or pages of text in a word processor file. A letter, report, recipe, or list—all are examples of documents. The computer uses **software** to create a document. Software is the program that tells the computer how to take in and process, or use, information.

After you turn on the computer, the **operating system software** takes over. The operating system software runs the computer. On many computers, a *Start* button appears on the screen. Click on it and a **menu,** or list of operations, appears. On other computers, there is no button; the menu just appears on the screen. **Icons,** or small images, also appear on the screen. You might see icons of the **hard drive,** folders, and *Recycle* bin or *Trash* bin. The hard drive is a data storage device installed in the computer base unit. Other icons may appear on the screen as well, depending on how the computer is set up.

# How Do You Create a Document?

There are a couple of ways to create a new document. One of the easiest ways is to select the Programs icon under *Start.* When the menu appears, find the word processing program and click on it. A blank page or document pops up. A **cursor,** or blinking line, appears on the blank page. When you start typing, the characters appear under the cursor.

---

**Cursor**
*A blinking line that indicates where you are working within a document*

**Document**
*A page of text in a word processor file or a spreadsheet*

**Hard drive** *or* **hard disk**
*A data storage device that is usually installed in the computer base unit*

**Icon**
*A small image on a computer screen that represents something stored on the computer*

**Menu**
*List of operations or directions*

**Operating system software**
*Software that runs the computer*

**Software**
*Program that tells the computer how to take in and process information*

---

## How Do You Correct a Document?

After inputting information, check it for errors and clarity. Carefully read each line on the screen. You might want to use the spelling feature built into the word processing software to check for errors. If you find a mistake, you can fix it easily. Using the mouse, place the cursor over the error. Click and **drag** the cursor to select the character, word, or words you want to change. To drag, you first point on an item. Then you press and hold the mouse button as you move the mouse to a new location. The items you selected should now be highlighted. Press the *Backspace* or *Delete* key to erase the error. Now type the correction. You can follow the same steps to correct a document on a Macintosh computer.

## How Do You Save a Document?

After checking your document, you will want to save it. When you save a document, you store a copy of it on the computer's hard drive. Using your mouse, select *File* from the menu bar and a menu appears. **Scroll,** or move the mouse, down the menu to *Save* and click on it. A *Save As* window pops up. You may notice a box in the window that tells you which folder your document will be saved in. You can select a different folder by clicking on the box. You will also see a box that is highlighted. Type the name of your document in the box and click the *Save* button.

**Complete and return registration cards that come with computer hardware and software you purchase. Record identification or registration numbers in the manuals.**

### Creating a Document on a Macintosh Computer

To create a new document, use the mouse to select the hard drive icon that appears on the screen. You need to open a software program or an existing document to create a new document. Find the word processing program icon and click on it. A blank page or document pops up and a blinking cursor appears. When you start typing, the characters appear under the cursor.

Choose a name that is short and easy to remember. What is your document about? Consider using that information in its name. For example, a name for a report about trees might be *TreeReport.* Get into the habit of saving your document while you are working on it. Saving on a regular basis—every few minutes—can protect your work from disappearing.

To close the document, select *File* and click on *Close.* To get out of the word processing program, select *File* and click on *Exit.*

Computers are powerful tools that help us do simple and complex tasks.

## Saving a Document on a Macintosh Computer

Use your mouse to select *File* in the menu bar and a menu appears. Click, hold, and scroll down the menu to *Save.* Click on *Save* and a window pops up. In that window a horizontal box with the heading *Save Current Document As* appears. Type the name of your document in that highlighted box. Choose a name that is short and easy to remember. Click on the *Save* button. Save your document often while you are working on it.

To close the document, select *File* and click on *Close.* To get out of the word processing program, select *File* and click on *Quit.*

## How Do You Delete a Document?

To delete a document from your hard drive, first find the document you want to delete. It might be stored in a folder. Do not open the document when you find it. Instead, click on the icon, hold, and drag it to the *Recycle* bin. Position the icon over the bin and let go. The document icon disappears into the bin. On most computers, a message appears asking if you are sure you want to delete the document. Select *Yes* to delete the document from your folder. Now double-click on the *Recycle* bin and you will see the document icon inside. A right mouse click on the *Recycle* bin deletes the item. When you delete a document, you remove it from the computer's hard drive. Deleting documents you do not need anymore frees up space on your hard drive.

● ● ● ● ● ● ● ● ● ●

**What should you check if your computer does not go on after you turn on the control switches?**

### Deleting a Document on a Macintosh Computer

Find the document, but don't open it. Click on the icon, hold, and drag it to the *Trash* bin. Position the icon over the bin and let go. The document disappears into the bin. Open the *Trash* bin to confirm it's there, then close it. Find *Special*, which is on the same menu bar as *File*. Click on *Special* and a menu appears. Select *Empty Trash* from the menu and the document is deleted.

## How Do You Print a Document?

After saving your document, you might want to make a hard copy of it. Using your mouse, select *File*. Scroll down to *Print* and click on it. The print window appears. Many programs let you type in the number of copies you want to print. The "number of copies" box may already display the number 1. This is the **default,** or preprogrammed information, supplied by the software that operates the printer.

If you want to print more than one copy of your document, type that number in the "number of copies" box.

Otherwise, go ahead and click on the *OK* or *Print* button. The computer sends a message to the printer to print your document. You can follow the same steps to print a document on a Macintosh computer.

## How Do You Open an Existing Document?

Sometimes you will want to open a document that already exists on the computer or on a **diskette.** A diskette is a small square made of plastic and metal, used to store information. Find the document you want to open on your computer. Double-click on the document icon and the first page of the document appears on the screen. Use the same steps to open a document on a diskette and to open a document on a Macintosh computer.

Keep all your computer manuals in a safe place. If a piece of hardware stops working, you can read its manual to find out how to fix the problem.

## Lesson 1 Review

Write the answers to these questions on a sheet of paper, using complete sentences.

**1)** What are the names of five pieces of computer hardware?

**2)** What is computer software?

**3)** How do you create a document?

**4)** What should you consider when naming a document?

**5)** Why would you delete a document?

**File**
*A text document, spreadsheet, database, or program that is identified by a unique name*

**Folder**
*A section in a computer's hard drive where documents are stored*

You can save hundreds of documents on most computers. Each one is stored on the computer's hard drive under its own **file,** or document, name. A file is a text document, spreadsheet, database, or program that is identified by a unique name and stored as a unit. Often, you hear people refer to a graphics document as a graphics file. The word *file* is sometimes used in place of *document.*

You probably will not be able to remember the name of each of your files, but don't worry. The computer remembers your files' names. You can view them in alphabetical order, which may be the fastest way to find the one you need. Select *View,* which is on the same menu bar as *File.* Then click on *List* or *as List.* The files appear in an alphabetical list.

### How Do You Organize Files?

When you organize items, you arrange them a certain way. You have probably organized your clothes. You put socks in one drawer and shirts in another drawer. This arrangement makes it easy for you to find the clothes you need.

**Folders** help you organize the documents on your computer's hard drive. A folder represents a section of the computer's hard drive. One folder might hold all your letters. Another folder might hold a report. A third folder might hold work or school documents.

### How Do You Create a Folder?

To create a folder for your letters, open an existing folder. Click on *File,* scroll down to *New,* then scroll over to *Folder.* Click on *Folder.* A *New Folder* icon appears on your screen within the existing folder. Notice that the name *New Folder* is highlighted. Type the name of the folder in the highlighted space. Click away from the *New Folder* icon.

Now click back on the *New Folder* icon. Hold and drag the icon outside the existing folder area and let go. Close the existing folder. You should see the icon for the new folder you created.

> ## Creating a folder on a Macintosh Computer
>
> To create a folder for your letters, open the hard drive icon. Select *File*, scroll down to *New Folder*, and click on it. An *untitled folder* icon appears within the list of documents on the hard drive. Notice that the name *untitled folder* is highlighted. Type the name of the folder in the highlighted space. Click away from the folder when you finish.

## How Do You Move a File into a Folder?

To move a document or file into a folder on the hard drive, first close both the document and the folder. Now you see the icons. Using the mouse, click on the document icon, hold, and drag it to the folder icon. Position the document icon over the folder and let go. The document disappears. Now open the folder and you will see the document. You can follow the same steps to move a document into a folder on a Macintosh computer.

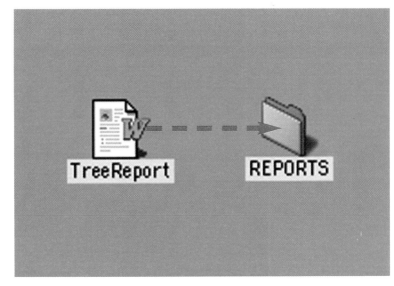

Moving a file into a folder

## How Do You Move Files Between Folders?

• • • • • • • • • • •

**Why would you want to put all your letter files in one folder?**

To move a document or file from one folder to another, first open the folder that holds the document. Click on the document icon, hold, and drag it over to another folder. Position it over the other folder, let go, and the document disappears into that folder. Open the folder to see it. Open the first folder and you will see it is gone. You have moved the document from one folder to another. A copy does not remain in the original folder. You can follow the same process to move documents between folders on a Macintosh computer.

## Lesson 2 Review

Write the answers to these questions on a sheet of paper, using complete sentences.

1) What is the difference between a document or file and a folder?

2) What are the steps for moving a file from one folder to another folder?

3) What should you consider when naming a folder?

4) How long does a file remain stored in a folder?

5) What are some folders you could create to organize your files?

*Using a Browser* ● ● ● ● ● ● ● ● ● ● ● ● ● ● ●

> **Web site**
> *A file server (hard drive) on a remote computer network*

A computer is a powerful tool. It can process information quickly and organize it in a form that is easy to understand. A computer can also connect you with the Internet.

## What is the Internet?

The U.S. government designed what we now call the Internet back in the 1960s. It was set up to be a communications web with alternate message routes that would survive a nuclear attack. In the 1990s, the Internet was opened to commercial access. Once companies could use the Internet, they started selling access to individuals. The Internet is a worldwide network of computers that connect to each other through telephone and cable lines. The computers on the network use a common language to communicate.

Some popular features you can find on the Internet:

• Electronic mail, or e-mail, allows you to send and receive messages almost instantly anywhere in the world.

• Newsgroups or public bulletin boards offer information on specific topics.

• Listservs or mailing lists offer information on specific topics. You subscribe to a mailing list on a specific topic for free. You automatically receive e-mail about that topic.

• World Wide Web is the most popular part of the Internet. Information on the World Wide Web appears as point-and-click pages or screens. **Web sites** use pictures, text, video, and sound. When you connect to a Web site, you log into a file server (hard drive) on a remote computer network.

Some nicknames for the Internet are the Net, the Information Superhighway, and I-Net. Whatever you call it, the Internet gives you access to information from all over the world.

● ● ● ● ● ● ● ● ● ●

**What should you consider when selecting an Internet service provider?**

## What Is a Web Browser?

A **Web browser** is a special software program that allows a personal computer to communicate with other computers on the Internet. A browser interprets information transmitted over the Internet and changes it into a readable form. The actual information your computer gets is coded text—a computer language called **HyperText Transfer Protocol (http).** The browser translates this coded text. Every Web address starts with *http.* Many different Web browsers are available.

## What Is a Modem?

Suppose you have your own computer. You also have a browser program on your computer. Can you connect to the Internet? Not yet. You need two more things before you can explore the Net.

You need a **modem.** A modem is a piece of hardware that connects your computer to a telephone line. The telephone line then connects your computer to the Internet. Information travels to and from the Internet and your computer through this line.

## What Is an Internet Service Provider?

You also need to subscribe to an **Internet service provider (ISP)** to connect to the Internet. An Internet service provider is a company that connects your telephone line to the Internet. The company charges a fee for this service. Fees are based on how much time you spend on the Internet. For example, some ISPs offer five hours of access per month for a set fee. If you go over the five-hour limit, you may pay an hourly fee. Some charge one set monthly fee for unlimited use. That means you pay a certain amount each month no matter how much time you spend on the Internet. The ISP will bill this service to your credit card account. Hundreds of Internet service providers exist. Some telephone and cable companies also offer Internet service.

Shop around when you look for an ISP. Ask your friends for recommendations, read the newspaper business section, or consult computer magazines. Make a list of four or five companies. Compare their fees for monthly service and installation. Compare the features they offer. Find out if they provide software or if you need to provide your own software. Ask about the computer requirements needed to run the software. Some ISPs offer free Internet access for a short period of time. You can try the service before you commit. When you decide, set up an account.

> **Bookmark**
> *A shortcut to an Internet site*
>
> **Online**
> *Connected to the Internet*

## How Do You Get Online?

Once you have set up an account with an ISP, you can go **online.** When you are online, you are connected to the Internet. Each Internet service provider has its own set of instructions for going online.

When you are online, you can visit any of the computers on the Internet. Each computer, or Internet site, has its own address. You type the address into the *Address* box and press the *Enter* or *Return* key. The site—usually its front or main page—appears on your screen. If you don't know a site's address, you can do a search for it. You will learn more about performing a search later in the chapter.

If you find a site you really like, you might want to **bookmark** the location. When you bookmark a site, you create a shortcut to it. Each Internet service provider's software has its own way of making and deleting a bookmark. Bookmarks may have different names, depending on the software you use. Common names include *Favorites* and *Bookmarks.*

**Add a page to favorites**

---

**Apartments online** ☺
**Feel–good diets** ☺
**Fun–filled things to do** ☺
**Healthy food to go** ☺
**Healthy you** ☺
**Job finder** ☺
**Rock music rocks** ☺
**Social butterfly club** ☺
**Tasty snacks** ☺
**Travel bug** ☺
**Volunteers unite** ☺

Bookmarked sites

Most often, you go to a Web site and then click on the *Favorites* button on your menu bar. A screen pops up with a message asking if you want to bookmark the site. You select *Yes* and the site address is stored in that box, or bookmarked. The next time you want to go to that site, you can select the bookmark. Instead of typing in the site's address, select the *Favorites* button. Click on the site's name in the bookmarked list and the site appears on your screen.

## How Can You Get Help?

All Internet service provider programs have a *Help* command. Whenever you have a question about using the computer or the Internet, click on *Help*. Type in the topic you want to know more about, such as bookmarks. Information about the topic will appear on your screen.

## Lesson 3 Review

On a sheet of paper, write the word or words in parentheses that correctly complete each sentence.

1) A software program that allows a PC to communicate with other computers on the Internet is a _____. (address, browser, Internet service provider)

2) A modem connects a computer to a _____. (printer, screen, telephone line)

3) An Internet service provider connects a telephone line to the Internet for _____. (free, all of its workers, a fee)

4) A shortcut to a favorite site on the Internet is called a _____. (diskette, address, bookmark)

5) When choosing an Internet service provider, you should look at _____. (the calendar, the monthly fee, your schedule)

# Downloading Files from the Internet ● ● ●

**Download**
*To move a copy of a file from one computer to another*

**W**hat are your interests? Sports? Music? Cooking? Whatever your interests, you can learn new things by visiting the Internet. You can find out the latest scores of your favorite teams, the lyrics to a song, or a new recipe. Sometimes, you may want to have a copy of something you find on the Internet. To do this, you can **download** the file.

## How Do You Download a File?

When you download a file, you move a copy of it from one computer to another. You can download documents, images, sounds, or even videos from the Internet. But not everything on the Internet can be downloaded.

The downloading process is not the same on all computers. Following are some common things you may see when you try to download files.

● ● ● ● ● ● ● ● ● ●
**Can you download a file to a diskette? Why might the hard drive be a better location for storing downloaded files?**

Click on the image you want to download. On some computers, when you click and hold on an image, a menu box appears. You may be able to select *Download Image to Disk* or *Save Picture As.* The computer may let you choose a folder for storing the downloaded file. Sometimes  a message appears to tell you when the file is downloading.

Many computers perform the download function automatically when you click on the file icon or file name. Watch for the file icon to appear on your screen. Then move it to your hard drive or a diskette to store it. If a file can't be downloaded, its icon won't appear on your screen.

## How Do You Open a Downloaded File?

You have downloaded a file and now you want to open it. First select the folder it is stored in. Double-click on it and look at the files inside. Double-click on the downloaded document to open it.

## What Is a Computer Virus?

If you have ever caught a flu virus, you know that a virus causes your body to not work properly. Computers can catch viruses, too. A computer virus is a program that makes many copies of itself. Some viruses fill up all the empty space in the computer's hard drive. Other viruses destroy all the information stored in the computer.

You can do two things to protect your computer from catching viruses. First, never download a file from a stranger. Second, load an **antivirus program,** or virus protection program, on your computer and activate it. The program will scan all files, including any you download, and tell you if a file has a virus.

## How Can You Get an Antivirus Program?

Many Internet service providers offer free software to their customers. You can download these programs to your computer. To find out which programs are available, go to the main screen of your ISP software. Click on the *Search* command on the main screen. Type in the word *downloads*, and a list will appear on your screen. Look for an antivirus program. You may have to use *Help* to find it. Then follow the directions for storing the program on your computer. You can also purchase antivirus software and install it on your computer.

> **Antivirus program**
> *A program that protects a computer from viruses*

New computer viruses can hit at any time. Update your virus protection software as new versions become available.

Make sure your computer has a current antivirus program.

## Lesson 4 Review

Write the answers to these questions on a sheet of paper, using complete sentences.

**1)** What kinds of files can you download?

**2)** What is a computer virus?

**3)** What are two things you can do to keep your computer safe from viruses?

**4)** How could you find out if your ISP offers free software?

**5)** Suppose you want to store an antivirus program on your computer. You search for antivirus programs you can download but don't find any. What could you do?

## Current Day

### Permission to Download

Every document found on the Internet has an author. The author owns the document. He or she decides whether others can copy the work. Most documents state whether or not their authors allow them to be copied. When you want to copy a document, look for this statement: Not to be copied. If the document says that, don't copy it. If you do, you are breaking the law. If the document says that it can be copied, you are free to download it. However, you are not allowed to pass off the document as your own words and ideas. If you use information from the document in a report, note the file on the reference page of the report. That means listing the name of the file, its author, and the Internet address where it is located.

**E-mail**
*Electronic mail; messages that are written and/or read on-screen and sent through a modem*

**M**ost Internet service providers offer their customers an **e-mail** address. E-mail stands for electronic mail. It works much like mail delivered by the post office, except e-mail is much faster. If you have an e-mail address, you can receive messages on your computer. You can also send messages to other people's e-mail addresses. When you choose an address, consider how you will be using e-mail. Will you use it to communicate with friends, or to contact businesspeople?

People communicate quickly and easily through e-mail.

## How Do You Write E-mail?

The first step in sending e-mail is to open the e-mail program. Often, e-mail is part of the Internet service provider software. Now select the *Write* command on your screen. Some programs use the command *Compose.* Wording depends on the software. A form pops up. At the top of the form is a line marked *Send To* or *To.* Type in the e-mail address of the person you want to send a message to. Be careful to type the address correctly. A small mistake, such as forgetting a period, can stop delivery of your message. If you send an e-mail message with an error in the address, it will probably be returned to you. Most e-mail programs automatically put your e-mail address in the *From* line. You can type the subject of your e-mail message in the *Subject* line.

In the middle of the form is a large blank space. This is where you type your message. Use the same format you would use to write a letter. Begin with a greeting, such as *Dear*, and the person's name. Press the *Enter* key. Then type the body of the message, using complete sentences and correct punctuation. End the message with a closing, such as *Best regards*, and your name.

## How Do You Send E-mail?

Read your message and correct any errors. When you are sure it is in good form, you can send it. Click on the button marked *Send* that appears on the top or right side of the screen. With a simple click of the mouse, your message is sent.

Most programs store e-mail messages that have been sent. To review the list, click on *Sent Mail*. A new screen pops up with a list of e-mail messages you have sent. The program stores e-mail messages you have received unless you delete them. Click on *Old Mail* or *In Box* and a list of e-mail messages you have read appears.

**What would you do if you received e-mail with a return address you didn't recognize?**

## How Can You Read E-mail?

How do you know you have received e-mail? The computer tells you. When you sign on to the Internet, a picture appears at the top of the screen. This indicates that a new message is waiting for you. Some programs have a voice alert so you hear, "You've got mail."

To read the message, click on *New Mail*. The message pops up on your screen. To respond to the message, click on the *Reply* button on the screen. The same form you use to write new mail pops up. Type your response and click on *Send*.

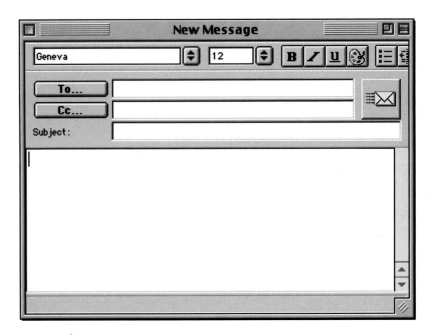

An e-mail form

To forward a message you received to someone else, open the message. Click on the *Forward* button at the top or side of the screen. The same form you use to write new mail pops up. In the *Send To* or *To* spot, type in the address of the person you want to forward the message to. Type a message in the large message space below that. Click on *Send*. The message you have just written and the original message are forwarded to that person.

### *Be Cautious*

Computer viruses can travel through e-mail. They are often sent as attachments, but sometimes are in the body of the message. To avoid computer viruses, read the return address and subject line of all new e-mail you receive before opening it. Be wary of return addresses you do not recognize.

# Online Etiquette

When you are online, you are in a public place with thousands of other people from all over the world. These simple tips will help you communicate effectively.

- **Do not type in all capital letters.** Online, words in all caps mean you are shouting. This is a turnoff for other readers, who will think you are angry about something. Avoid typing in all caps unless you really *are* shouting.

- **Avoid flaming.** Flaming is uncontrolled complaining about someone or something. Keep in mind that once you send your e-mail, you cannot get it back. It is out there for everyone to read, so avoid saying anything you might regret later.

- **No one can see you smile.** Online, there is no body language, no laughter, no frowns or smiles, only your words. Pay attention to your tone when you write, and consider how someone else might incorrectly interpret your words. One simple way to put some emotion into your messages is to use a smiley face or other similar faces. You can make them using keys on your keyboard. A few examples follow. But keep in mind that some people dislike them.

| | |
|---|---|
| :) | Happy |
| :-) | Happy, with a nose |
| :( | Unhappy |
| ;-) | Wink, with a nose |
| :0 | Surprise or shock |
| 8-) | Wearing shades |

- **Learn the meanings of shortened words or expressions used online.** Because people are typing and not talking, they have found ways to speed up their typing. Here are a few examples:

| | |
|---|---|
| BAK | Back at the keyboard |
| BRB | Be right back |
| IMHO | In my humble opinion |
| IMNSHO | In my not-so-humble opinion |
| LOL | Laughing out loud |
| OIC | Oh, I see |
| ROTFLOL | Rolling on the floor laughing out loud |
| TTYL | Talk to you later |

## Lesson 5 Review

On a sheet of paper, write the word or words in parentheses that correctly complete each sentence.

**1)** E-mail is electronic mail sent to and from your _____. (home, school, computer)

**2)** You set up an e-mail message the same way you write a _____. (letter, list, report)

**3)** Clicking on _____ brings up a list of all the e-mail messages you have sent. (New Mail, Sent Mail, Old Mail)

**4)** You can respond to an e-mail message by clicking on the _____ button. (New Mail, Send, Reply)

**5)** Typing an extra letter in an e-mail address will cause your message to _____. (go to the wrong person, not be delivered, be sent many times)

## Technology In Our Lives

### Shopping Online

A growing number of people are shopping on the Internet. Thousands of companies sell items at their sites. Clothing, household products, books, and sporting goods are just some of the products available for sale online. Sometimes the price of an item sold through the Internet is lower than its price in a local store. Online shopping has some other advantages, too. You do not have to deal with a busy shopping center or crowded parking lot. You can shop any time of the day or night because the Internet never closes. You don't have to carry your purchases home. They are delivered right to your doorstep. In addition, you can buy items from companies all over the world. You just might find the perfect gift in a shop thousands of miles away.

# Accessing Online Resources ● ● ● ● ● ● ● ●

> **Search engine**
> *A site that offers an index of other sites*

**Y**ou are planning a surprise party for a close friend. Your friend loves Mexican food, so you decide to serve your guests a traditional Mexican meal. The only problem, is you don't know how to cook traditional Mexican food. You need recipes—and fast. Where can you find them? On the Internet.

## What Is a Search Engine?

Suppose you wanted to find a book of Mexican recipes in a local library. You would probably look up the word *cookbooks* in the card catalog. There you would find a list of all the cookbooks available in the library.

The Internet is like a library. Both contain a vast amount of information. However, the Internet does not have a card catalog. To find the information you need on the Internet, you use a **search engine.**

A search engine is a Web site that offers an index of other Web sites. The main screen of an Internet service provider's program usually has a *Search* box. When you click on this box, a screen pops up. Type in the name of the topic you want information on. With another click of the mouse, the search engine starts looking for sites containing the word or words you input.

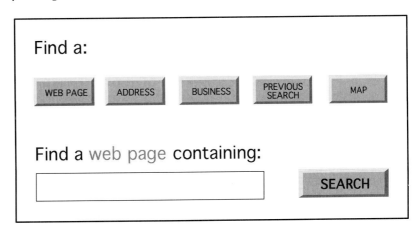

Find a:

| WEB PAGE | ADDRESS | BUSINESS | PREVIOUS SEARCH | MAP |

Find a web page containing:

[                    ]  SEARCH

A search box

## How Do You Choose Search Words?

The computer searches for the word or words you type into the *Search* box. You need to put some thought into the words you choose. Avoid choosing a word that is too broad. Performing a search on a word that is too broad will turn up hundreds of sites, too many to investigate.

For example, if you input the word *cooking*, your search will find every site that contains the word *cooking*. Your cooking search will turn up cooking recipes, cooking tools, and other cooking-related items.

• • • • • • • • • • •

**What search word or words would you use to find information on each of these topics?**

• Treatment for dogs with arthritis

• Mountain climbing in Colorado

• Apartments for rent in your city

## Different Kinds of Sites

The ending of a Web site address gives you a clue about the kind of site it is. Here are some address endings and their meanings.

• Sites ending in *.com* are companies.

• Sites ending in *.org* are organizations such as Girl Scouts of America or the Red Cross.

• Sites ending in *.edu* are educational institutions such as high schools and universities.

• Sites ending in *.gov* are government agencies such as the Internal Revenue Service and the U.S. Department of Labor.

• Sites ending in *.net* are Internet administrative sites.

## How Can You Narrow the Search?

The purpose of a search is to find a list of sites that contain specific information. You don't want the search engine to find hundreds of related sites. You want it to find a small number of specific sites, so your search words must be specific.

For example, inputting the words *Mexican* and *cooking* would narrow the search. The search engine looks for sites that contain both words (see Figure 7.1). Enter a type of Mexican food such as *Mexican beef burritos*, and the search becomes even narrower (see Figure 7.2).

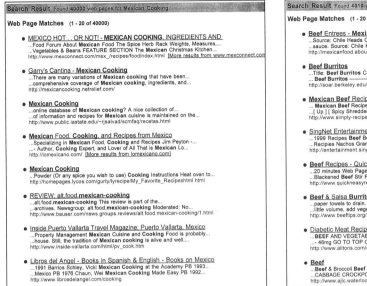

**Figure 7.1.** *Mexican cooking* search results

**Figure 7.2.** *Mexican beef burritos* search results

Generally, the more words you input, the narrower your search. The result should be a list of Web sites or Web pages that are likely to contain the information you need.

## How Do You Read Search Results?

When a search engine has finished looking for the words you used, a search results list appears on your screen. Some search engines rate search results. Others do not. For those that do, a number precedes each item in the list. The number tells you how well that site matches your search words. A site marked 100 percent is a strong match. A site marked 30 percent is a weak match. Often, the list includes each site's Internet address, and some provide a short description of each site. Click on the sites you think are the best matches. Use the *Back* button to return to the page with your search results.

What other words besides *Mexican cooking* might you choose to narrow the search even more?

## What Are Some Other Ways to Get Information?

Sometimes you can get the information you need without using a search engine. Many companies put their Web site addresses on packaging for their products.

Organizations often include their Web sites on posters and handouts. You can call a company or organization and ask for its Web site address.

## Lesson 6 Review

Write the answers to these questions on a sheet of paper, using complete sentences.

1) What is a search engine?

2) What should you consider when choosing a search word or words?

3) Is it better to input a single word or many words when beginning a search?

4) What do numbers on search results show?

5) Suppose you want to learn more about a company that made an item you just bought. Where would you look for the company's Internet address?

Online Resources

**Better Business Bureau Online**

*www.bbbonline.org*

Consumer tips as well as information about shopping online, identifying reliable Web sites, and privacy issues.

**Federal Consumer Information Center
U.S. General Services Administration**

*www.pueblo.gsa.gov/*

Consumer tips and information.

**Federal Trade Commission
Bureau of Consumer Protection**

*www.ftc.gov/bcp/menu-internet.htm*

Information about e-commerce and the Internet.

# Chapter 7 Summary

■ A personal computer is made up of five main pieces of hardware. They are the computer base unit, monitor, keyboard, mouse, and printer.

■ Any information that you put into a computer is called a document. When you save a document, you store a copy of it on the computer's hard drive.

■ A folder is a section in a computer's hard drive where files are stored. Organizing files into folders helps you find your documents more easily.

■ The Internet is a worldwide system of computers that are joined by telephone wires and cables. To access the Internet, you need a computer, a modem, a browser, and an account with an Internet service provider.

■ Most Internet service providers offer their customers e-mail addresses. If you have an e-mail address, you can send and receive mail electronically.

■ The Internet contains information about thousands of subjects. A search engine can help you find information you need on the Internet.

## Comprehension: Identifying Facts

On a sheet of paper, write the correct word or words from the Word Bank to complete each sentence.

> **WORD BANK**
>
> | | | |
> |---|---|---|
> | communicate | electronic | modem |
> | computers | fee | save |
> | delete | folder | short |
> | document | hardware | software |

1) When you _____ a document, you remove it from the computer's hard drive.

2) All the equipment that makes up a computer is called _____.

3) A _____ is any information that you put into a computer.

4) The Internet is a worldwide network of _____.

5) Keep the name of a document _____ to make it easier to find later.

6) A program that tells a computer how to take in and process information is called _____.

7) A _____ connects a computer to a telephone line.

8) A _____ is a section in a computer's hard drive where documents are stored.

9) E-mail is _____ mail sent from one computer to another.

10) An Internet service provider is a company that connects a telephone line to the Internet for a _____.

11) When you _____ a document, you store a copy of it on the computer's hard drive.

12) A Web browser is a computer program that allows a computer to _____ with other computers on the Internet.

## Comprehension: Understanding Main Ideas

On a sheet of paper, write the answers to the following questions using complete sentences.

13) What is the difference between hardware and software?

14) What are some ways to find the Internet address of a company?

15) What is the difference between a document and a folder?

16) What kinds of things can you download?

17) What are two things you can do to protect your computer from a virus?

18) How can you find useful information on the Internet?

## Critical Thinking: Write Your Opinion

On a sheet of paper, write the answers to the following questions using complete sentences.

19) You have just received e-mail from a friend. He wants to know if you would like to go to a concert with him next Saturday. Write an e-mail response to your friend.

20) If you type the same words into two different search engines, will the results be exactly the same? Explain your answer.

# Self-Assessment

Can you answer the following questions?

☑ What can you learn from socializing with a variety of people?

☑ What are five steps you could use to solve a problem?

☑ Can you describe a healthy relationship?

☑ What are three examples of discourteous behavior?

☑ Why would you want to use time-management techniques every day?

☑ Why is honesty so important in a relationship?

☑ What is the best way to avoid sexually transmitted diseases?

☑ Does dating always lead to a serious relationship?

☑ Where can you meet people who are different from you?

☑ Do you know how to resolve a conflict?

# Social Awareness

**H**ave you ever watched a young bird learning to fly? At first it flaps its wings, but it doesn't go anywhere. A few days later, it may flutter to a nearby branch. Its takeoffs and landings are clumsy. Day by day it gets stronger and can make longer flights. Before long, the bird is soaring above the treetops.

Birds are natural-born flyers, but they still have to learn the skills necessary to fly well. In the same way, people are naturally social. This means that relationships with other people are important. But people are not born knowing how to be social. Just as birds need to learn flying skills, people need to learn social skills. This chapter will describe some of the skills you need to have healthy and successful social relationships.

## Goals for Learning

▶ To identify the characteristics of healthy relationships

▶ To explain the importance of valuing others

▶ To describe common sexually transmitted diseases and explain how to avoid them

▶ To identify time management skills

▶ To describe the steps involved in successful problem solving and decision making

# Having Healthy Relationships

**Intimate**
*Very personal or private*

**Nurture**
*Helping someone or something grow or develop*

Everyone has the need to belong and be loved by others. The most common way people meet this need is to form and maintain close relationships. Some close relationships, such as connections with family members, are chosen for you. You choose other close relationships such as friendships. Friendships are based on something people have in common. Friends share interests and activities or have similar backgrounds. Healthy close relationships can make your life happier and more fulfilling.

## What Makes a Relationship Healthy?

A healthy close relationship has these important characteristics:

• Emotional attachment

• Mutual, or common, dependence between partners

• Satisfaction of both partners' needs

Make time for yourself.

A close relationship can satisfy the need for **intimate** communication and the need to **nurture.** Intimate means something very personal or private. Intimate communication means confiding in someone you trust. To nurture means to help someone or something grow or develop.

### Relationships That Work

There are things you can do to maintain healthy relationships. Self-acceptance is one of the most important ingredients of a healthy relationship. When you accept yourself, it is easier to accept and not feel threatened by others' differences. In healthy relationships, people are allowed to be themselves.

Good self-esteem is another key ingredient of a healthy relationship. When people value themselves and their own goals, they feel good about who they are. Continue to develop your interests and improve your skills. Feel good about yourself.

The more you like yourself, the healthier your relationships will be. And favorite subjects or hobbies can satisfy you even when you are alone. People who are not anxious for a relationship are less likely to become involved in unhealthy relationships.

Friends share interests or have similar backgrounds.

Showing respect for each other also contributes to a relationship's success. Showing respect and courtesy includes being kind and realizing that what another person says and feels is important, even if you do not agree with it.

**Dysfunctional**
*Not working properly*

### Unsatisfying Relationships

Relationships that are full of conflict or are not satisfying are **dysfunctional**. Dysfunctional means something that does not work properly. Relationships that restrict people from being themselves or that involve fear of being pushed away are unhealthy. Poor communication is the most common form of dysfunction in a relationship. For example, you are worried about something but refuse to confide in a trusted person about it. Therefore, that person cannot offer help or understand what is wrong. When you avoid sharing information or only share partial information with someone you trust, you hurt the relationship. Your actions tell the other person you do not want to be close to him or her. That person feels shut out and may withdraw from you. Unfortunately, you may be cutting yourself off from other people's support when you need it most.

Use "I" statements kindly and respectfully when communicating with others.

You can avoid this pattern of shutting others out by identifying the people you trust. When you are troubled, you can talk with them about your feelings. In addition, you need to let them know you are there for them.

Low self-esteem and lack of confidence are other common problems in dysfunctional relationships. A person with low self-esteem lacks confidence and feels unworthy. When you feel unworthy, you may have conflicting emotions. You may want someone to help you feel better. But your low self-esteem makes you believe that no one wants to be close to you. Your own conflicting feelings make it difficult to have a healthy relationship with others.

On the other hand, when you share your problems continually, you put demands on trusted friends or family members. If you need constant reassurance, people must spend a lot of time and energy reassuring you. They get tired of this. Expecting other people to make you happy is unreasonable and unhealthy. People who love you will help you, but they are not responsible for your happiness. Fortunately, if you think you demand too much of your friends and family, you can change your behavior. Learn to help yourself. Taking care of yourself will lead to improved self-esteem, independence, and healthier relationships.

Good self-esteem is a key ingredient of a healthy relationship.

## Why Is Communication So Important?

Communication is a basic element in a relationship. It can mean talking, writing, touching, listening, smiling, and even knowing when to be silent. Open and honest discussion helps people understand each other.

It prevents misunderstandings. While expressing your feelings or thoughts can be difficult, it is an essential element in a healthy relationship.

Every communication has a sender and a receiver. The sender wants to send a message to the receiver. The message the receiver gets affects him or her. Communication is effective, or successful, when the sender's intended message matches the effect on the receiver. For example, you (the sender) want to compliment your friend (the receiver) on her new dress. If your words make her feel good, your communication is successful. Communication is unsuccessful when the sender's intended message doesn't match the effect on the receiver. For instance, if you sound insincere or smirk when you compliment your friend on her new dress, she would be insulted. Your tone of voice and **body language** make the message sound insincere. Body language is facial expressions, hand gestures, and other forms of communication that do not use words.

Another tip for communicating successfully is to use "I" statements. Starting a statement with "I" helps others understand and respond to you. Follow the "I" statement with an explanation of why or when you feel the way you do. Here are examples: "I feel hurt when you tease me about my hair." "I like the notes that you leave for me because they let me know you're thinking about me." "I" statements also show that you are taking responsibility for your feelings.

Careful listening is another important piece of successful communication. Good listening skills include actively listening and using body language to show you are listening. Look directly at the person who is talking to you. You can also show interest by leaning toward him or her with your arms comfortably relaxed at your sides. Tune out your own thoughts and any quick responses and really listen. Listening includes commenting at times on what you are hearing. For example, a friend might say, "I can't seem to do anything right." You could respond, "It sounds like you are disappointed in yourself."

> **Body language**
> *Facial expressions, hand gestures, and other forms of communication that do not use words*

• • • • • • • • • •

**What body language might you use when you tell someone that you are sorry for missing an appointment?**

Your response shows your interest, and can confirm that you understand what your friend is expressing.

Keep in mind that some people are not good communicators. The messages they send may be mixed or unclear. When you receive unclear messages, avoid reacting until you have asked questions to clarify them.

### Honesty

Good communication depends on people being honest with each other. Honesty helps build trust in a relationship. Trust comes with time. It does not happen right away. Be honest about what you want to get out of the relationship. Tell the truth about what you like and don't like. Share how you feel when you are with the other person. Being truthful with each other builds mutual trust and a caring, stable foundation in your relationship. Be prepared to receive the same kind of information from the other person.

Sometimes it may seem easier to be dishonest in a relationship. You want to avoid hurting someone's feelings or avoid conflict. For example, your roommate always eats the food you buy and never replaces it. You are angry about this, but you do not say anything because you do not want to argue. If you bottle up your feelings, you may become even angrier. Your anger may come out at some other time and in a way that causes hurt feelings. In other words, it is almost always best to deal with feelings honestly as they happen. You can even express angry feelings without anger if you haven't bottled them up and allowed them to control you. Choose a time to talk when you are calm and use "I" statements to express your feelings.

## How Do You Handle Conflict?

**Conflict** is a disagreement between two or more people who have different ideas. Conflicts can be minor or serious. A minor conflict with a family member could be about chores at home. You may have a minor conflict with a friend because you hurt his or her feelings.

**Some Ways to Manage Anger**

When you get angry, give yourself time out to avoid saying or doing something you may regret later. During a time-out, you can

- take a deep breath.
- wait and count to ten.
- exercise, if possible, to reduce your energy level.
- identify your own part in the problem.
- think of nonviolent solutions.
- be prepared to apologize if necessary.
- avoid name-calling.
- ask a respected adult for advice.

A major conflict may be with a friend who wants you to do something you think is wrong or dangerous. For example, your friend may want you to lie to another friend. Conflict can cause an argument or it may be an ongoing issue about which two people strongly disagree.

You may think that you can simply avoid conflict, but it is not that easy. Conflict is all around us. Sometimes the best way to deal with conflict is to walk away. When conflict arises, ask yourself: Is this issue really such a big deal? Is the conflict based on a rumor that may not be true? How will I feel if I just forget about it? Think about what is happening. Maybe the other person is having some serious problems at home or at school. Perhaps the person never intended to cause a conflict. The best idea may be to let it go, and accept that the other person may just be having a bad day.

Some conflicts cannot be ignored. When you must resolve a conflict, talking with the person alone is the best action to take. Having other people around only increases the chance that the situation will get out of control. Don't talk with someone who is under the influence of alcohol or other drugs.

As you explain your feelings, try to remain calm and keep your emotions under control. Insults will not help you end the conflict peacefully. Use "I" statements and focus on your feelings rather than on the other person's actions. Give the other person a chance to do the same thing. If you have hurt the other person, don't be afraid to say, "I'm sorry."

When you are faced with a serious conflict, you may need to get help to deal with it. Talk with a trusted teacher, counselor, or parent. Everyone has conflicts. Asking for help does not mean you are weak. It means you care enough about yourself and other people to take control of your life.

Everyone, at one time or another, gets into conflicts that cannot be resolved in a way that is acceptable to those involved. For example, this kind of conflict often arises over political discussions. People often have strong political views and arguing about them usually does not resolve anything.

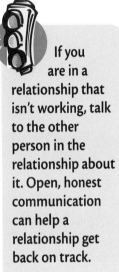

**If you are in a relationship that isn't working, talk to the other person in the relationship about it. Open, honest communication can help a relationship get back on track.**

● ● ● ● ● ● ● ● ● ● ●

**Why is it impossible to avoid some conflicts?**

## Warning Signs of Conflict

- Shouting
- Name-calling
- Spreading rumors
- The silent treatment
- Insults
- Mean looks

- Making fun of someone
- Getting others to take sides
- Threats or threatening gestures
- Pushing or hitting

In these situations, it is ok to agree to disagree and let the subject drop. We all face situations that involve conflict. Remember not to let conflict make you so angry that you act unwisely.

## Lesson 1 Review

Write the answers to these questions on a sheet of paper, using complete sentences.

**1)** Name two characteristics of a healthy close relationship.

**2)** How does low self-esteem lead to dysfunctional relationships?

**3)** What are two things you can do to maintain a close relationship?

**4)** What is an "I" message?

**5)** How would you answer an overweight friend who asks you, "Do you think I need to lose weight?"

*Practicing Group Relationships* ● ● ● ● ● ● ●

Learning to form and maintain group relationships is an essential part of growing up. During adolescence, teens are ready for new experiences. It is a good time to meet and get to know a variety of people. Teens are forming ideas about themselves and are ready to form ideas about others. Socializing in groups and dating are two of the ways teens learn to function successfully in social situations.

## What Is Socializing?

Socializing is getting together with others to enjoy leisure-time activities. It includes spending time with many male and female friends. Through socializing, people decide which traits or qualities they like and dislike in others. They discover more about themselves and the kind of future they hope to have. They recognize interests they have in common with others. For example, they may discover they enjoy in-line skating because they try it with others in the group. They also find out about interests they do not share. Some people may enjoy seeing movies while others would rather go to dances.

There are many ways to meet new people. Friendships begin at school, at work, and through religious activities. Recreational activities such as hobby clubs and sports leagues offer another healthy way to meet and spend time with people.

Through socializing, people get to know others who have similar interests.

Volunteering can also introduce you to a variety of people. All these activities give you opportunities to meet people who share your interests and values.

## What Is Dating?

● ● ● ● ● ● ● ● ● ●

**How does being independent strengthen a relationship?**

As a young person gets to know others through group activities, he or she may meet someone special. One way to get to know another person better is through dating. Dating is socializing with another person as a couple. Dating as a single couple or in a group with other couples can be a good experience.

A young person usually dates a variety of people. He might enjoy spending time with some of them more than with others. He may go on one date with one person and decide he doesn't want to go out with that person again. He might make this same decision after he has dated someone several times. Or he might decide to continue to date one or more people without getting serious about any one person.

Two people may find that they enjoy being with each other more than with anyone else. They may decide to date only each other exclusively. Being exclusive, or going steady, can help two people become closer and learn more about each other. However, when they make a commitment to see only each other, they give up the chance to date other people.

## What Are Some Dating Challenges?

Communication is one of the most important challenges in all relationships. Open, honest discussion and careful listening help you understand each other. Expressing your thoughts and feelings is hard, but critical to creating and maintaining a lasting relationship.

Avoiding sexual contact is the best way to prevent a sexually transmitted disease.

As a couple grows closer, they face another challenge—the decision about their physical relationship. A healthy romantic relationship is based on many elements. These elements include shared values, interests, and goals; the ability to communicate; and physical attraction.

Sometimes a relationship is based mainly on physical attraction. This attraction may lead two people into a sexual relationship. If this happens too early in a relationship, the couple may experience problems. For example, the sexual relationship may result in an unwanted pregnancy. Or it could result in spreading an infection that is transmitted sexually.

Many couples who are dating or going steady practice **abstinence**. Abstinence is choosing to avoid a sexual relationship. It allows a couple to get to know each other in many ways before beginning a sexual relationship. It gives them more time to mature, to make better decisions, and to avoid unwanted problems. It allows them time to find other meaningful ways of being close, such as sharing deep personal thoughts. Abstinence is the best way to avoid an unwanted pregnancy or a sexually transmitted disease.

Another challenge is breaking up. Not all relationships last forever. In fact, almost everyone experiences the end of a romantic relationship. You may decide the person you are dating is not right for you. Or, the person you are dating may decide you are not right for him or her. Breaking up can be difficult because it is a loss and may involve grief. A person may feel unhappy, depressed, lonely, or insecure. These feelings are normal. Finding ways to raise your self-esteem and seeking support from others are healthy ways to deal with your grief. However, if these bad feelings become too strong and interfere with a person's life, the person should seek professional help.

Two people can get to know each other better through dating.

## Lesson 2 Review

Write the answers to these questions on a sheet of paper, using complete sentences.

**1)** Is going steady always a good decision? Explain your answer.

**2)** What is the best way to avoid pregnancy?

**3)** What are two things that healthy romantic relationships are based on?

**4)** What are two normal feelings that people experience after a breakup?

**5)** Why are socializing and dating important parts of growing up?

## Technology In Our Lives

### HIV Home Test Kit

In 1985, the FDA licensed the first test to detect HIV antibodies. Through this testing, people who are HIV-positive receive counseling on how to prevent spreading the virus. They are also told how to get early treatment. Until 1996, only health professionals could do the testing.

In May 1996, the FDA approved the first HIV home test system. A person can now test for HIV at home. The system includes materials for blood sample collection and analysis. Pretest and posttest counseling are also part of the system.

A person who uses the home test system is assigned a confidential and anonymous PIN. She collects her own blood sample on special paper and mails it to the lab. It is analyzed by trained medical personnel.

To get her results, she calls a toll-free number and uses the PIN. Only one FDA-approved system is currently available. For more information, visit the FDA site: www.fda.gov U.S. Food and Drug Administration, Office of Special Health Issues (select *AIDS* in the index)

# *Valuing Others*

**D**o you know your neighbors? Do you know other people in your comunity? Are any of these people visibly different from you? Do you treat everyone you know with courtesy and respect?

The ability to value other people is critical to individual health and healthy relationships. Valuing others creates strong communities. When people value one another, they care about each other's successes and failures. They help and support each other. Two ways people show they value one another are by treating each other with courtesy and accepting each other's differences.

## What Is Courteous Behavior?

Courtesy is behaving in a way that makes people feel comfortable and good. It means avoiding behavior that makes life unpleasant for others. It means being polite. No laws force people to behave courteously, but people usually disapprove of discourteous behavior. For example, you cannot be arrested for talking in a theater during a movie. But it is discourteous because it is distracting and it prevents other people from enjoying the show. Everyone deserves to be treated with courtesy—family and friends, acquaintances, and strangers.

Almost everyone knows some basic rules of courtesy such as saying "please," "thank you," "excuse me," and "no thank you." Why are these rules so important? Because they show you care about the people around you. They tell others that you value and respect them. Being courteous to others shows them you want to be treated courteously too. Basic courtesy rules help people get along by providing guidelines for expected behavior.

Being courteous to others shows you respect and value them.

Here are some common courtesy do's and don'ts:

## Do

• respond (RSVP) to invitations promptly.

• show up on time.

• pay your fair share of the bill at a restaurant.

• return borrowed objects or money promptly.

• write a thank-you note when you have been given a gift or have been a guest in someone's home.

• dress correctly for the occasion.

• say "excuse me" or "pardon me" when you bump into someone.

## Don't

• burp, spit, or do other rude things in public.

• talk loudly in movies or other places where people are trying to hear what's going on.

• overstay your welcome in someone's home.

• throw trash on the ground.

• be late.

• ignore people when you bump into them.

• litter.

• • • • • • • • • • •

**How do the rules of courtesy help people get along better?**

## How Can You Accept Differences Between People?

No two people are exactly alike. Even identical twins think differently. Some differences between people can be seen. Other differences are not visible. Some visible differences are age, race, sex, height, and eye color. Some differences that are not visible are thoughts, feelings, and behaviors. You can learn to value differences by truly getting to know the people who are different from you.

Unfortunately, a person may form negative, or unfavorable, opinions about another person who is different.

He or she may have little knowledge about this person who is different, but still dislikes him or her. This is called **prejudice**. Prejudiced people tend to **discriminate** against others who are different from themselves. To discriminate means to treat differently on the basis of something other than individual worth. Prejudice creates an unhealthy situation. For example, imagine learning that people you have never met dislike you. You are different from them in some way. You, in turn, may find it hard to like these people. You believe they are being unfair. This cycle is difficult to break. Prejudice is unfair. It can destroy a community's goodwill.

People can overcome prejudices by getting to know members of different groups. One way to learn cooperation and discover similarities is to work together toward a common goal. Through this process, people begin to have **empathy** for each other. Empathy is identifying with and trying to understand someone else's feelings. You put yourself in that person's shoes and imagine how he or she feels. Empathy is part of healthy close relationships.

Here are some ways you can get to know a variety of people:

- Meet people from different ethnic backgrounds through a common interest such as sports, music, or art.

- Get to know a person of the opposite sex as a friend rather than a possible date.

- Spend time with older adults—grandparents, aunts and uncles, or family friends. They can offer different outlooks on life based on their own experiences.

**Discriminate**
*To treat differently on the basis of something other than individual worth*

**Empathy**
*Identifying with and trying to understand someone else's feelings*

**Prejudice**
*Negative, or unfavorable, opinions formed without grounds or sufficient knowledge*

Learn from older adults, who can offer different outlooks on life.

## Lesson 3 Review

On a sheet of paper, write the word or words in parentheses that correctly complete each sentence.

**1)** Behaving courteously and accepting other people's differences are ways people show that they _____ one another. (dislike, value, understand)

**2)** An example of courteous behavior is _____. (spitting, discriminating, returning borrowed things promptly)

**3)** Visible differences between people include _____. (hair and eye color, beliefs, feelings)

**4)** _____ is forming negative opinions about a person based on something other than personal worth. (Discrimination, Prejudice, Courtesy)

**5)** Prejudiced people tend to _____. (act discourteously, discriminate, throw trash on the ground)

## Current Day

### A Safe Blood Supply

At the beginning of the AIDS epidemic, some people were infected with HIV through blood transfusions. A transfusion is the transfer of blood that was donated by one individual to another. Since 1985, blood donated for transfusions is tested for HIV. Blood is released for transfusions only when the test for HIV is negative. Any infected blood and blood products are safely thrown away. In addition, testing procedures have improved so that early signs of infection can be detected. Because of this improved testing, the blood supply in the United States is among the safest in the world. The risk of infection with HIV through a blood transfusion or blood products is extremely low.

# Preventing AIDS and Sexually Transmitted Diseases ● ● ● ● ● ● ●

**Human immunodeficiency virus (HIV)**
*The pathogen that causes AIDS*

**Sexually transmitted disease (STD)**
*Any disease that is spread through sexual activity*

In the United States, one in four people under age 21 has a **sexually transmitted disease (STD)**. Any disease that is transmitted, or spread, through sexual activity is a sexually transmitted disease. For example, acquired immunodeficiency syndrome (AIDS) is an STD because it can be spread through sexual activity. More than 20 diseases are transmitted sexually. Some of the most common and serious STDs are gonorrhea, chlamydia, syphilis, and genital herpes.

## What Is AIDS?

AIDS is a disorder of the immune system. The first AIDS cases in the United States were identified in 1981. Since then, AIDS has spread at an alarming rate not only in the United States but throughout the world. Many people have died from AIDS. Figure 8.1 on the next page shows the number of reported AIDS cases in the United States.

Between 650,000 and 900,000 people in the United States are infected with **human immunodeficiency virus (HIV)**. HIV is the virus that causes AIDS. By the end of 1999, 733,374 cases of AIDS had been reported in the United States. More than 420,000 people in the United States have died of the disease. The United Nations estimates that about 14 million people worldwide have died of AIDS.

## Causes of AIDS

HIV infects body cells and cripples the human immune system. As a result, the body cannot fight off opportunistic pathogens. Opportunistic pathogens—normally harmless germs—cause infection when a person's immune system is greatly weakened.

Like all illnesses caused by a virus, AIDS is contagious, or can be passed from one person to another. Therefore, knowing how AIDS is acquired is important. HIV is spread in these ways:

• • • • • • • • • •

**What would you say to a friend who is concerned about catching HIV from an infected coworker?**

1. **Body fluids**—HIV is transmitted through blood, semen, vaginal fluids, and the breast milk of infected women. It is spread through exchange of these fluids from one person to another. It is not transmitted through other body fluids such as tears, saliva, sweat, and urine.

2. **Sexual activity**—It can be spread through sexual activity with an infected partner. Each new partner in turn can infect others.

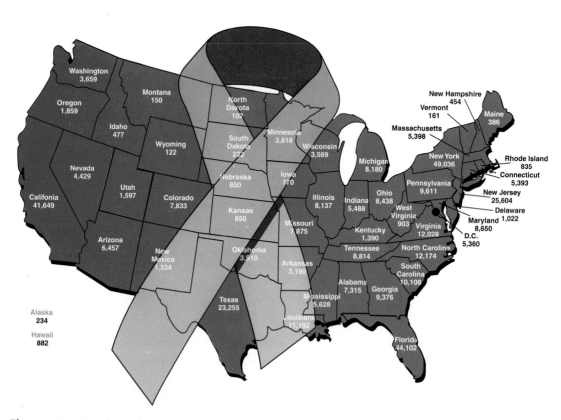

**Figure 8.1.** Number of adults, adolescents, and children living with HIV infection and with AIDS reported through June 1999.

3. **Sharing needles among drug users**—Any needle that has been used to inject a drug or medicine into the body has blood on it. Drug users who share needles risk getting HIV.

4. **Mother to child**—HIV can be passed from a mother to a baby before, during, or after birth. It can also be passed to a baby when the baby drinks its mother's breast milk.

A blood test can show whether a person is infected with HIV or has AIDS. People who have HIV but don't know it do not realize that they may already have AIDS. They also do not realize that they may be passing it on to others.

## *How AIDS Is Not Acquired*

Some people have incorrect ideas about how AIDS is acquired. They believe they can get AIDS through casual social contact with an infected person. They are afraid to be around people with AIDS.

AIDS is not acquired by casual social contact because HIV cannot survive outside the body. For that reason, neither HIV nor AIDS is spread through

• touching, hugging, or kissing a person with HIV or AIDS.

• sharing cups, dishes, and other eating utensils with an infected person.

• bathing in the same pool or hot tub as an infected person.

• crying, coughing, and sneezing.

• bites from sucking insects such as mosquitoes.

## *AIDS Symptoms*

AIDS is an illness that can have a long incubation period. A person infected with HIV may not show outward signs of AIDS for six to ten years or longer. During that time, however, HIV is weakening the person's immune system. Some HIV treatments available now may help slow the virus's progress.

When AIDS symptoms appear, they are similar to HIV infection symptoms. Some of these symptoms are a dry cough, chills and fever, night sweats, and shortness of breath.

Other symptoms are fatigue, stiff neck, headache, weight loss, skin rashes, diarrhea, and swollen **lymph nodes**. Lymph nodes are knotlike lumps in the body that contain disease-fighting cells. Lymph nodes in the neck and armpits and above the groin are near the skin's surface. Another symptom is mouth sores.

Because HIV weakens the immune system, people who are infected with it can also catch other serious diseases. The other diseases are caused by opportunistic pathogens that the body cannot fight. For example, a person might have a certain kind of **pneumonia**. Pneumonia is a lung infection. **Kaposi's sarcoma**, a rare type of cancer, is another serious illness a person can have. **Cytomegalovirus retinitis**, a potentially severe AIDS-related eye infection, can lead to blindness. Other serious problems can result from AIDS attacking the nervous system. The disease can also cause brain damage.

### What Is Gonorrhea?

**Gonorrhea** is an STD. One-quarter of the people who have gonorrhea are between 10 and 19 years of age. An infected woman can transmit the disease to her baby during delivery. Gonorrhea can cause an eye infection in babies that can lead to blindness.

People can have gonorrhea and not even know it. In males, symptoms are a white discharge from the urethra and a burning feeling while urinating. Between 20 percent and 40 percent of infected males have no symptoms and do not know they have gonorrhea. Females may have a vaginal discharge and some swelling and redness in the genital area. However, most females have no symptoms and do not know they are infected. The bacteria that cause gonorrhea can also infect the throat and the **rectum**, which is the lower part of the large intestine.

Fortunately, gonorrhea can be treated successfully with a shot or pill of the antibiotic penicillin. All newborns are treated with eye medicine immediately after birth to prevent the eye infection.

Untreated gonorrhea can lead to **sterility** in males, or the inability to produce a child. Untreated gonorrhea in females can spread throughout the reproductive system and cause sterility. Gonorrhea can also spread to the bloodstream. Once it is in a person's bloodstream, the bacteria can infect other body parts. This can lead to heart valve problems and other diseases. Gonorrhea in the joints can cause arthritis. Gonorrhea is an important health concern because people who do not have symptoms can spread the disease unknowingly.

## What Is Chlamydia?

An estimated 3 million cases of **chlamydia** occur each year. Chlamydia symptoms are similar to gonorrhea symptoms. For some females, symptoms may be a vaginal discharge and pelvic pain. Usually, however, females have no symptoms. Males may have a discharge from the urethra and pain when they urinate. It may also cause complications such as swollen and tender testicles. Like gonorrhea, chlamydia can infect a baby during delivery. It can also cause an eye infection that causes blindness. Left untreated, chlamydia in females can cause infertility, serious pregnancy problems, and chronic pelvic pain. Chlamydia can be treated with an antibiotic.

## What Is Syphilis?

**Syphilis** progresses in three stages if left untreated. The first stage of syphilis is marked by the appearance of a **chancre.**

**Chancre**
*A painless, hard sore with a small amount of yellow discharge*

**Chlamydia**
*A sexually transmitted disease with symptoms similar to gonorrhea*

**Sterility**
*The inability to produce a child*

**Syphilis**
*A sexually transmitted disease*

Part of staying healthy is avoiding contact with pathogens that cause diseases, including sexually transmitted diseases.

A chancre is a painless, hard sore. The chancre usually appears on the penis, anus, or rectum in men. It appears on the **cervix** and genital area in women. The chancre can also appear on the lips and in the mouth. If a person does not get adequate treatment, the infection progresses to the second stage.

The second stage starts with a rash that usually does not itch. The rash often appears on the palms of hands or bottoms of feet as rough, "copper penny" spots. Other symptoms include headaches, muscle aches, fever, sore throat, and weight loss.

After second stage symptoms disappear, syphilis begins to damage internal organs. In about one-third of untreated people, the internal damage shows up many years later in the third stage of syphilis. Third stage signs include paralysis, gradual blindness, and tumors. The damage can cause death. Penicillin can cure a person in the early stages of syphilis.

## What Is Genital Herpes?

**Genital herpes** is a chronic infection. The main symptom of genital herpes is clusters of painful small blisters in the genital area. The blisters break, heal, and come back. Herpes is spread by contact with the broken blisters. Avoiding contact with the pathogen that causes herpes can prevent this disease.

Genital herpes can cause other problems. Repeated infections in females sometimes lead to cancer of the cervix. Genital herpes can infect a baby during delivery and can cause brain damage in the baby. The disease has no cure. A pill controls the symptoms. It speeds up healing but doesn't get rid of the infection. Over time, the infections tend to be less severe, but the disease never goes away.

## Is Help Available for Sexually Transmitted Diseases?

Except for genital herpes and AIDS, most sexually transmitted diseases can be cured when they are treated early. For diseases without cures, medical treatment can make people more comfortable.

Many clinics concentrate on diagnosing and treating individuals and their partners who think they might have a sexually transmitted disease. Clinic staff members appreciate a person's strength and good judgment in seeking medical attention. They protect the identity of their patients.

There are no vaccines for sexually transmitted diseases, and the body is not immune to them. Treatment with medicine is effective for some STDs that are caught early. For others, like AIDS, there is no known cure. Some treatments increase the quality and length of life for people with AIDS. Eventually, however, AIDS is fatal. Scientists are actively searching for a cure, but it could be years before they find one. For now, the only way to protect yourself from AIDS is to avoid contact with HIV-infected blood or other body fluids. Abstinence from sexual activity is the best way to protect yourself from a sexually transmitted disease.

## Lesson 4 Review

On a sheet of paper, write the word or words in parentheses that correctly complete each sentence.

**1)** HIV cripples the body's _____ so that it cannot fight disease. (pathogens, immune system, power source)

**2)** Neither HIV nor AIDS is spread through _____. (casual social contact, sharing needles, sexual activity)

**3)** Chlamydia, gonorrhea, and syphilis can be treated with _____. (an antibiotic, a vaccine, abstinence)

**4)** The main symptom of _____ is clusters of small, painful blisters on the genital area. (AIDS, chlamydia, genital herpes)

**5)** Right now, AIDS cannot be _____. (prevented, cured, explained)

### Hospices

A hospice is a place where people who are dying can receive the long-term health care they need. Hospice patients are so seriously ill that they can no longer be helped in a hospital.

A hospice has a homelike atmosphere to make patients comfortable. Support services for patients and families are usually offered.

A hospice volunteer may feed, dress, talk, or read to patients. Family, friends, and volunteers who have no formal medical training are often the people who provide hospice care.

# Solving Problems and Making Decisions ● ●

**Obstacle**
*Something that interferes with achieving a goal*

For most people, problems are part of life. You can find problems everywhere you look—at school, at work, at home, and in the community. It seems you cannot do anything without running into a few problems. That is why knowing how to solve problems when they arise is an important survival skill to have. Fortunately, there are some problem-solving steps you can learn and follow.

You also need to know how to make decisions. Some decisions seem easy, like what to eat for breakfast. Other decisions are so hard that you may not want to make them. Making decisions is a skill you must learn to survive on your own. What you decide affects your life. For example, your decision to go to school will benefit you for years to come.

## How Can You Solve Problems Successfully?

You have a problem if you want something and **obstacles** block you from getting it. An obstacle is anything that interferes with achieving a goal. For example, not knowing how to get what you want is one kind of obstacle. Not having enough or the right kind of experience when applying for a job is another. You can even have internal obstacles. For instance, you may need help at work. You don't ask people to help you because you want to do it yourself. You are the obstacle to people helping you.

You can respond to a problem in a number of ways. Sometimes your response is successful, and sometimes it is not. You might not always get the outcome you want or expect for a variety of reasons. In some situations, your approach might not be right. In others, you might choose to ignore the problem. Or you might act tough and demand that the problem be solved your way. There are times when you choose to give in and go with someone else's solution. Sometimes meeting someone halfway, or compromising, is the best solution.

You need to develop your own problem-solving and decision-making skills. It is part of growing up and becoming responsible for yourself. Using the following five-step approach can help.

1. **Define the problem.** Collect as much information as you can about the problem. Ask and answer these questions: "Why is this a problem?" "How did the problem start?" "Where did the problem occur?" "How long has this been a problem?" "Who is involved in the problem?" Avoid placing blame for the problem on another person or yourself. Part of this step is to uncover the main cause of the problem. When you identify that, you have a better chance of solving the problem successfully.

2. **Come up with possible solutions.** Make a list of solutions to your problem. Add suggestions from other people.

3. **Consider the consequences of each solution.** For each solution, ask yourself, "What might happen next?" Based on how you answer that question, select the solution that can best solve your problem.

● ● ● ● ● ● ● ● ● ●
**What would you do if you missed your ride to school?**

Problems are part of life. Following some simple steps can lead to solutions.

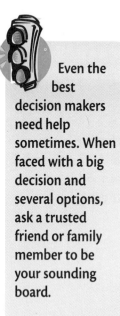

Even the best decision makers need help sometimes. When faced with a big decision and several options, ask a trusted friend or family member to be your sounding board.

4. **Put your plan into action.** Once you identify the best solution, you are ready for the next step: Do it. As part of this step, consider what is required to make the solution work.

5. **Evaluate the outcome.** After you have used your solution, decide how well it worked. Learn from your decision and use that information for future problem solving. If there are new or remaining problems, consider another solution. You may also choose to ask others for help.

## How Can You Make Good Decisions?

Decisions give you power and control over your life. But making decisions is not always easy. Sometimes people are afraid they won't make the right decisions. Some people spend too much time thinking about making a decision and fail to act. Others act before they think and then regret their actions later.

Discussing a problem with someone else can help uncover a solution.

One way to avoid falling into these traps is to follow decision-making guidelines. You can use several different techniques to help you decide something. You can ask others what they would do. You can make a list of **options**, or choices. You can rank your options from best to worst. Then narrow the list by crossing off options you do not like or that you do not think will work. You can consider the consequences of each option and weigh the pluses and minuses. Finally, you may want to combine options to reach a better decision than if you chose only one. Following these guidelines can help you make informed decisions.

> **Option**
> *A choice*

## Lesson 5 Review

Write the answers to these questions on a sheet of paper, using complete sentences.

**1)** What is an obstacle?

**2)** Name the five problem-solving steps.

**3)** What is one reason that decision making can be difficult?

**4)** How can making a list of options help you make a decision?

**5)** Describe a problem that may be solved by compromising.

# *Managing Time* • • • • • • • • • • • • •

**H**ave you ever heard people say, "I don't have time"? You have probably said it yourself. Controlling how you spend your time will help you accomplish more. As your control over your own time grows, your feelings of success and self-esteem will grow too.

## What Are Some Time-Management Techniques?

Time-management techniques include creating schedules and lists and ranking list items in order of importance. Using these techniques help people spend their time wisely.

You can create a weekly schedule beginning with Sunday and ending with Saturday. Break each day into hour increments, or blocks. Write the activities you must do every day on your schedule and the amount of time it takes to do them. Look at the amount of time that is left. This is time you have for leisure and other activities. You can use this schedule to manage your time each day and accomplish things you want and need to do. For example, you have a test on Tuesday and a softball game on Monday night. You need to figure out when to study for the test. According to your schedule, you could study for several hours during a free period and right before your softball game. A schedule can also help you plan ahead and get things done.

Scheduling activities can help you make the most of your time.

One way to plan your day effectively is to spend a little time each morning creating a list. Put on your list the things you have to accomplish that day. When you have made your to-do list, decide which activities are the most important. Write the letter *A* next to these activities. Write the letter *B* next to those tasks that are important but do not have to be done immediately.

Write the letter *C* next to tasks that are least important. You have just prioritized, or ranked, your list. Beginning with letter *A* items, follow your list and check off activities as you complete them. If you cannot finish everything on your list today, put the uncompleted tasks at the top of tomorrow's list.

For longer tasks or projects, you can create a schedule to accomplish a small part each day. Use a list similar to your daily list, but do not plan to complete the tasks in one day. For example, you are planning to move across town in three months. Your list may include tasks such as finding an apartment, packing, renting a truck, cleaning, and filling out change-of-address forms. Each of these tasks needs to be broken down into smaller tasks in order to get them done. All need to be done within the three-month period, before you move.

## What Are Some Time-Management Obstacles?

When we have many things to do, time often seems to get away from us. When this happens, it is hard to get everything done. People make several common mistakes that prevent them from using their time wisely. Perhaps the most common obstacle is **procrastination**. Procrastination means putting off things you need to do. When we procrastinate, we may feel rushed and overwhelmed. We may end up not doing a good job, forgetting things, or making needless mistakes.

Another obstacle people face is interruptions that knock them off course. Some interruptions cannot be avoided. For example, an illness may interrupt your time-management plans. You find you have to change your plan to make up for the interruption. However, some interruptions can be avoided. For instance, when you are working you can let your answering machine pick up calls to avoid phone interruptions.

One more obstacle to time-management is not knowing which of your activities is most important. Sometimes you must decide whether spending time with your family or doing some extra studying is more important.

**Procrastination**
*Putting off things you need to do until the last minute*

• • • • • • • • • •
**What would you do if you had two important tasks that had the same deadline?**

Making your list and ranking the activities on your list in order of their importance are useful steps. They can help you decide which tasks you need to finish first and keep you on track.

### Lesson 6 Review

On a sheet of paper, write the word or words in parentheses that correctly complete each sentence.

1) _____ makes completing tasks easier. (Procrastination, An obstacle, Time management)

2) Making _____ in the morning helps you plan your day. (a to-do list, three phone calls, an appointment)

3) Interruptions can _____ be avoided. (never, sometimes, always)

4) As your control over your own time grows, your feelings of success and _____ will also grow. (wealth, self-esteem, speediness)

5) When planning your day, it is useful to rank your activities in order of their _____. (difficulty, lateness, importance)

## Online Resources

**Centers for Disease Control and Prevention, National Center for HIV, STD, and TB Prevention**

*www.cdc.gov/hiv/pubs/faqs.htm*

Includes frequently asked questions about AIDS and HIV.

**Centers for Disease Control and Prevention, Division of Sexually Transmitted Diseases**

*www.cdc.gov/nchstp/dstd/dstdp.html*

Information about sexually transmitted diseases.

# Chapter 8 Summary

- Healthy relationships involve emotional attachment, mutual dependence, and satisfaction for both partners.

- Maintaining healthy relationships involves open communication, good self-esteem, self-acceptance, and honesty.

- The best way to resolve conflict is to talk openly and honestly with the other person or parties involved. People need to remain calm, control their emotions, and avoid insults. Using "I" statements can help.

- Getting to know other people through dating is part of learning how to have adult relationships.

- Entering into a sexual relationship is a big decision. Abstinence can help avoid problems such as unwanted pregnancy and sexually transmitted diseases.

- People show they value others who are different by treating them with courtesy and respect. Courteous people expect to be treated with courtesy too.

- AIDS is a disorder of the immune system with no cure. It is caused by HIV which weakens the immune system, leaving it open to other infections.

- Following simple guidelines can help a person learn effective problem-solving and decision-making skills.

- People can accomplish their goals by using daily time-management techniques.

## Comprehension: Identifying Facts

On a sheet of paper, write the correct word or words from the Word Bank to complete each sentence.

> **WORD BANK**
>
> abstinence       discriminate       self-esteem
>
> body language    dysfunctional      social contact
>
> chronic          intimate           socializing
>
> courtesy         procrastination    time
>
> cure             prejudice          management

1) One need a close relationship can satisfy is the need for _____ communication.

2) Relationships are healthy when people have good _____.

3) A _____ relationship is one that does not work well.

4) If your words do not match your _____, your message might be misunderstood.

5) Getting together with others to enjoy leisure-time activities is known as _____.

6) The best way to avoid an unwanted pregnancy or a sexually transmitted disease is to practice _____.

7) Saying "please" and "thank you" are basic rules of _____.

8) _____ is a negative opinion formed without enough experience or knowledge.

### Test-Taking Tip

Studying together in small groups and asking questions of one another is one way to review material for tests.

9) Prejudiced people tend to _____ against people who are different from themselves.

10) AIDS is not acquired through casual _____.

11) There is no _____ for AIDS at this time.

12) Genital herpes is a _____ disease with no cure.

13) Using _____ techniques can help people use their time wisely.

14) _____ is an obstacle to using time wisely because it forces a person to do things at the last minute.

## Comprehension: Understanding Main Ideas

On a sheet of paper, write the answers to the following questions using complete sentences.

15) What are five steps you could take to solve a problem?

16) What could you do to resolve a conflict?

17) What are the four main ways that HIV is spread?

18) How does lack of honesty harm relationships?

## Critical Thinking: Write Your Opinion

On a sheet of paper, write the answers to the following questions using complete sentences.

19) What are two questions you would ask yourself before starting a new relationship? Why do you think these questions are important?

20) What is one way that discrimination harms communities? Give an example.

# Self-Assessment

Can you answer the following questions?

☑ Where can you find out about volunteer opportunities?

☑ Why is it better to use traveler's checks instead of cash or personal checks when you travel?

☑ Do you know what to do to vote in an election?

☑ What are four things you could volunteer to do?

☑ What are some ways people can express themselves?

☑ Can recreational activities be nonphysical?

☑ Where can you find out more about candidates running for office?

☑ What are five things to consider when planning recreational activities?

☑ What are two responsibilities U.S. citizens have?

☑ What is community awareness?

# Express Yourself

**W**hat are some ways you can show who you are—your thoughts, abilities, opinions, and feelings? You might create a painting or compose a song. You might give your opinion about something. You might plant a garden, plan a trip, or volunteer for a community project. These actions are just a few examples of things you can do to express yourself.

In this chapter, you will learn more about activities you can do in your free time. You will learn how to match your values with fun and meaningful activities. And, you will learn how to get involved with your community and improve life for yourself and others.

## Goals for Learning

- ▶ To state reasons why it is important to include recreation in your life
- ▶ To create and carry out a recreational activity plan
- ▶ To explain why it is important to vote
- ▶ To list ways you can get involved in your community
- ▶ To describe how certain laws in your community affect you

## *Participating In Physical Activities* • • • •

What do you do during your free time? Do you spend time watching TV, riding a bike, or playing a sport? Maybe you like to surf the Internet, read, paint, or go for walks. All these activities are kinds of recreation. Recreation is any activity that you do for enjoyment. Some forms of recreation involve very little physical activity, such as reading or listening to music. Other forms of recreation, such as swimming or doing aerobic exercise, are very active.

### Why Is Recreation Important?

Recreation is an important part of your physical, mental, and social health. Recreational activities that involve exercise improve your physical health. Regular exercise helps build a strong heart and lungs. It gives you more energy and can reduce your chances of getting sick. Recreation also gives you a chance to rest your body and let it repair itself.

Recreation improves your mental health by helping you cope with stress. Recreational activities help take your mind off your job, school, or a problem you may have. You get a break from stress and can then deal with these things when your mind is clear. Recreation also can build your self-esteem and pride, and provide a sense of accomplishment. For example, suppose you play a musical instrument as a hobby. You learn to play a certain song all the way through without mistakes. You can take pride in accomplishing that goal.

Recreational activities can build self-esteem and provide a sense of accomplishment.

Some physical recreational activities

| | | |
|---|---|---|
| Aerobics | Field hockey | Roller skating |
| Archery | Football | Rowing |
| Backpacking | Golf | Skiing |
| Badminton | Gymnastics | Soccer |
| Baseball | Handball | Softball |
| Basketball | Hiking | Swimming |
| Bicycling | Horseback riding | Surfing |
| Bowling | | Table tennis |
| Canoeing | Ice hockey | Tennis |
| Chores such as yard work | Ice skating | Volleyball |
| | Jogging | Walking |
| Climbing | Jumping rope | Weight training |
| Dancing | Martial arts | Wrestling |
| Fencing | Racquetball | |

Recreation improves your social health by providing opportunities to meet people and share interests. Many people make friends through recreational activities.

## What Are Some Physical Activities?

"What do you want to do?" "I don't know. What do *you* want to do?"

You and your friends have probably had this conversation many times. Often people do not think about the variety of physical activities they can do in their free time. Or they get into a rut and do the same activities over and over. However, many physical activities, such as those shown above, are good for recreation.

● ● ● ● ● ● ● ● ● ●

**What recreational activities might be especially good for making friends?**

Some types of museums

| Museum | What You Will Find There |
| --- | --- |
| Air and Space | Aircraft and spacecraft |
| Military | Usually military aircraft and other vehicles |
| Science and Industry | Displays of scientific discoveries and how they affect people |
| Natural History | Displays on ancient civilizations; dinosaur skeletons |
| Art | Works of local artists or world-famous masters |
| Hall of Fame | Items connected to sports heroes |
| Historical | Information about a community's past |
| Aquarium | Live displays of fish and other marine life |
| Planetarium | Information about stars, planets, and outer space |
| Arboretum | Trees and shrubs from different regions in an outdoor setting |

## What Are Some Other Recreational Activities?

How could a visit to a local historical museum lead you to care more about your community?

Not every form of recreation is a sport or an intense exercise. Many recreational activities involve little activity other than walking. In a city park, you may see people playing baseball and jogging. You may also see people reading, talking, listening to music, picnicking, walking, or just relaxing on a park bench.

Your community probably provides dozens of recreational opportunities. Museums are a good example. Museums are places where people can learn about the world around them. Name any item from buttons to boats and chances are good that you could find a museum for it. Some types of museums are listed here. You might find some of them in your city.

Many museums today have interactive exhibits. That means you can touch and work with the exhibits. For example, some art museums have large computer images of famous paintings. With the touch of your finger, you can change a painting to see how it would look with different colors.

Many other places offer recreational activities. These include playgrounds, gymnasiums, swimming pools, beaches, parks, forest preserves, and nature centers.

## What Should You Consider When Planning Activities?

You may want to consider several things before choosing recreational activities. Ask yourself the following questions to help you decide.

1. What do I enjoy doing? What interests me?

2. What goals do I have?

3. Where can I do the activities?

4. Are there costs?

5. What equipment is needed?

6. How can I find time for the activities?

7. Can I do any of these activities with a friend?

### Interests

To get the most out of your recreation, choose activities that you enjoy and that match your interests. For example, look back at the list of activities mentioned earlier in this lesson. Which of them do you enjoy? Perhaps some are activities you have always wanted to try but never have. You might also be interested in hobbies such as gardening, taking photographs, or sewing. What other hobbies can you think of?

Choose activities you enjoy.

### Goals

One way to choose activities is to think of goals you have. You can choose activities that help meet those goals. For example, if you want to be more physically fit, you could choose physical activities. You might have a goal to meet new people. Then you might choose activities that involve other people such as taking a cooking class or joining a bicycling club.

When you plan a recreational activity, invite a friend along.

### Location

The location of an activity might affect your recreational choices. Some activities can be done only in certain places. Racquetball, for example, can be played only on a racquetball court. On the other hand, activities such as reading and photography can be done just about anywhere.

### Costs

Many activities involve some costs. Examples include concert tickets, museum entrance fees, sports equipment expenses, bowling lane fees, and book fees for a class. You also need to consider the cost and availability of transportation to and from the activity.

---

## Exercise Attire

- Wear loose-fitting clothing, so you can move freely. It also helps your body cool down faster.
- Dress in layers when you are outdoors in cool weather. You can remove layers as you warm up and put them on as you cool down.
- Wear thick sport socks. They provide a cushion, absorb sweat, and help prevent blisters.
- A good pair of multipurpose gym shoes is fine for most exercise. Leather or cloth shoes are best because they let air pass through to cool your feet.

---

## Equipment

You need equipment to participate in most sports activities. For organized sports, one fee usually covers the cost of uniforms, gym time, or other team expenses. Many hobbies require special equipment or materials. The amount of equipment you use, however, may be up to you. Camping is one example. You can buy a lot of equipment designed especially for campers. However, you may need to buy only a few basic items such as a tent, sleeping bag, camp stove, and lantern.

## How Can You Fit Activities into Your Schedule?

A common reason people give for not doing activities is that they do not have time. Here are ways you can manage your time better to include recreational activities in your life.

1. Begin to manage your time by keeping track of how you spend it. Keep a written record of what you do throughout the day. Record the time you spend sleeping, eating, at school, at work, studying, and doing other activities.

2. After a week, review your records to see how you spend your time. Are you spending it the way you want to? You may find that you spend a lot of time watching TV or doing nothing at all.

3. Now you can start managing time better so that you can do more of the things you want to do. Ask yourself these questions:

   • What activities did I spend more time on than I wanted to?

   • What is the most time I want to spend on each activity?

   • What activities do I want to spend more time doing?

   • How much more time do I want to spend on each activity?

4. Make a schedule and note how you will spend your time in the coming week. A written schedule will help you assign enough time to the things you need to do and want to do.

• • • • • • • • • •

**Why might it be a good idea to let friends know when you plan on doing recreational activities?**

## How Can You Develop an Activity Plan?

You have learned some things to consider when planning activities. Now you can use that knowledge to create an activity plan.

First, review how you spend your time so that you can see how much time is available for recreation. Then, decide which activities you would like to do during your free time. Find out where and when you can do the activities. Find out about the equipment or materials you need and the costs involved. You might invite a friend to join you for certain activities. Write your activities on a calendar. This will remind you that you have scheduled specific times for specific activities that are important to you. Finally, follow through and enjoy the recreational activities you have planned.

## Lesson 1 Review

Write the answers to these questions on a sheet of paper, using complete sentences.

1) How does recreation improve your physical health? Your mental health? Your social health?

2) What are three physical activities and three nonphysical activities that you have never tried before?

3) What are seven things to consider when planning activities?

4) Why is it important to keep track of how you spend your time?

5) What are two recreational activities you would like to make time for? How do you think these activities would improve your health?

# Making Travel Arrangements  ● ● ● ● ● ●

If you could take a trip anywhere in the world, where would it be? Some people might choose a tour of Europe. Others might want to explore the cultures of China. Still others would prefer a rugged camping trip in a national park.

Many people enjoy traveling as a form of recreation. While you may not be able to take your "dream trip" right now, you still have many travel choices. A trip does not have to be expensive or long to be enjoyable. Wherever you go, you can take certain steps to make sure your trip is fun, relaxing, and enjoyable.

## Where Can You Get Travel Information?

When taking a trip, some people like to just jump in the car and go. This may seem like an exciting and carefree way to travel. To get the most out of your traveling, however, be sure to do some planning.

Your planning might start with finding out about your **destination**, or the place you want to go. It might be a city, a national park, a part of a state, or an entire country.

Many places offer information about your destination. You can start with travel guidebooks in the library's travel section. Travel books are designed to help people plan trips. They provide information on where to stay, where to eat, what to do and see, and how to get there. They include easy-to-read maps. Guidebooks also give information such as hotel rates and phone numbers, restaurant meal prices, and the best time of year to visit.

Guidebooks are helpful, but they are only current up to the year they were printed. For up-to-date information, check out other sources. For example, the Sunday editions of many newspapers have a travel section. You can read articles on selected destinations. Some travel sections list the lowest air fares to certain cities.

**Reservation**
*An arrangement made to keep something available for your use*

Another travel information source is a city's or state's department of tourism. The Web sites for these tourism departments have road construction updates and seven-day weather forecasts. The sites also include maps, a calendar of events, things to do and see, and information on lodging. You can even print out a map for your trip.

## How Do You Make Reservations?

You would like to stay at a certain hotel when you reach your destination. You could take the chance that a room will be available when you arrive. But to avoid disappointment, you should make a **reservation**. A reservation is an arrangement to keep something available for your use. Call the hotel to make a reservation. You probably will need to give your credit card number to reserve a room. When traveling, you might also need to make reservations to ride in an airplane or rent a car. You might need reservations to eat in a restaurant or attend special events.

**How would knowing the weather forecast help you plan a trip?**

Many people travel for fun and relaxation.

Consider using a travel agency to make reservations. Travel agencies are listed in the phone book. A travel agent can find the lowest airfares and make hotel reservations for you. The travel agency's fee is paid by the airline and hotel. You can also make airline reservations yourself. Most airlines have a toll-free 800 number to call. Remember to ask for any special rates or offers.

**Traveler's check**
*A check that is bought from a bank and can be replaced if lost or stolen*

When making reservations, be sure you understand the conditions. For example, find out if you have to pay extra to change the arrival or departure date on an airline ticket. When renting a car, find out if you have to pay by the mile as well as a flat daily fee.

## Should You Use Traveler's Checks?

You are going on vacation and plan to spend a few hundred dollars on your trip. It would be wise to purchase and use **traveler's checks** instead of carrying a few hundred dollars in cash. A traveler's check is a check bought from a bank. It is used like cash, but can be replaced if it is lost or stolen. Traveler's checks usually cost $5 for every $100 worth of checks you buy. You sign each check when you buy it and then sign it again when you cash it.

You might choose to use personal checks rather than cash or traveler's checks. However, some places do not accept personal checks, especially out-of-state checks. A credit card is a good way to pay for large expenses, such as lodging and food, when you travel. You can use your traveler's checks or your bank debit card to pay for expenses under $100. Smart travelers estimate trip expenses ahead of time, so they have an idea of how much they can spend. They also keep track of their daily expenses by writing them down in a notebook.

When going on a trip, have a friend pick up your newspapers, or stop delivery while you are gone. A collection of newspapers on the doorstep is a sign to burglars that no one is home.

# Traveler's Checklist

Some things to consider when you plan your next trip:

- Collect information about your destination.
- Decide on travel dates. Find out the best time of year to go. Sometimes airline and hotel rates are lower if you stay past Saturday.
- Decide on transportation to your destination: car, bus, train, boat, or plane.
- If you are not traveling by car, decide whether to rent one at your destination.
- Let family members and close friends know about your trip.
- Arrange to have mail picked up or stopped while you are gone.
- Find out what the weather will be like and pack suitable clothes.
- Choose a route and alternate routes.
- If you are traveling in a group with more than one vehicle, decide when and where to meet others.
- If you are flying, find out if your hotel offers a free ride from the airport.
- Budget your money for the trip, both before and during the trip. Consider costs of transportation, food, lodging, sightseeing, and other entertainment. Keep track of expenses in a small notebook.
- Buy traveler's checks at the bank.
- Find out about exchange rates on money if you are traveling out of the country.
- Get a passport for traveling out of the country.

## Lesson 2 Review

Write the answers to these questions on a sheet of paper, using complete sentences.

**1)** What are four kinds of information you would find in a travel guidebook?

**2)** What are two other travel information sources besides guidebooks?

**3)** Why is making reservations for such things as hotel rooms and restaurant meals a good idea?

**4)** What is one advantage of using traveler's checks instead of cash on a trip?

**5)** What item or items would you add to the Traveler's Checklist?

---

### Tips on Tipping

Here are some suggested standard amounts to tip various people for the services they provide when you are traveling. A tip is a way to express satisfaction. Larger tips can be given for extraordinary service; smaller tips or no tip when service is poor.

| | |
|---|---|
| Airport skycap | $1 or more per bag |
| Taxi driver | 15% of fare |
| Hotel bellhop | $5 for bringing you and your luggage to your room |
| Room service waiter | 15% of the bill |
| Chambermaid | $5 a night; more if your stay is longer than a week |
| Restaurant waiter or waitress | 15% of the total bill |
| Coat check attendant | $1 for one or two coats |
| Restroom attendant | 50 cents |

**Candidate**
*A person running for government office such as for mayor or president*

**Citizen**
*A member of a country*

**Issue**
*A question or problem that people discuss and make a decision about*

**Responsibility**
*A duty*

One of the most important ways you can express yourself is to vote. When you vote, you express your opinion about **candidates**, or people running for a government office. You show how you feel about **issues**, or questions that people must make a decision about. When you vote, you take part in shaping the kind of future you want.

## What Are Some Rights and Responsibilities of U.S. Citizens?

Voting is one of the responsibilities of being a **citizen**, or member, of the United States. A citizen has certain rights. For example, you have the right to practice any religion, or no religion at all. You have the right to express your feelings about anything, as long as you do not harm others. You have the right to a trial if you are charged with a crime. These are just a few of the many rights that U.S. citizens enjoy.

Along with rights come certain **responsibilities**, or duties. U.S. citizens have these responsibilities:

- To support the government by paying taxes.
- To learn about laws and obey them.
- To express their opinions about laws they think should be changed.
- To stay informed about government.
- To vote in elections.
- To defend the country in times of war.

## Why Should You Vote?

Voting is an important part of being a citizen. When you vote, you help choose your leaders. You vote for people you want to represent you. You vote for national leaders such as president and senator. You vote for state and local leaders such as governor, county commissioner, and mayor.

These leaders make decisions that affect your life. You need to know who the candidates are and what kinds of decisions they are likely to make.

Besides voting for leaders, you also vote on issues. Sometimes issues are placed on the **ballot**. A ballot is a card or paper on which a voter marks his or her vote. This

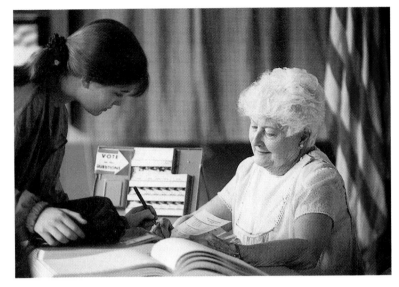

Voting allows citizens to express their opinions about candidates and issues.

gives you a chance to vote directly on an issue instead of leaving it up to government leaders to decide. For example, you might be asked to vote on raising taxes to build a new library.

## How Can You Vote?

In most states, you must **register**, or sign up, before you can vote. You must be a U.S. citizen and at least 18 years old to register. When you register, you fill out a voter registration form. This form is available at the post office, at the library, or from the board of elections. Fill out the form and mail it as directed. You will receive a voter registration card in the mail. You will be assigned a place to vote near your home, such as a school or library. On election day, you go to that place to vote.

Learn as much as you can about the candidates and the issues before you vote. Read newspaper articles. Listen to the candidates' speeches. Discuss issues with family and friends. Contact voting organizations such as the League of Women Voters to get information on the candidates and the issues. Consider all the choices and make your own decisions.

> **Ballot**
> *A card or paper on which a person marks his or her vote*
>
> **Register**
> *To sign up to vote*

• • • • • • • • • •

**In many elections, less than half of the adult citizens vote. Does this surprise you? Explain your answer.**

## Lesson 3 Review

Write the answers to these questions on a sheet of paper, using complete sentences.

**1)** What are two rights of U.S. citizens?

**2)** What are two responsibilities of U.S. citizens?

**3)** How old must you be to register to vote?

**4)** What are three ways to find out about the candidates and issues in an election?

**5)** How would life in the United States be different if people were not allowed to vote?

### Technology In Our Lives

### Voting Over the Internet: A Good or Bad Idea?

Many people use computers to do shopping and banking from home over the Internet. Some people think citizens should be able to cast their votes over the Internet too. People who favor Internet voting say that it will make voting easier, so more people will vote. According to one survey, 78 percent of computer users said they would like to vote this way.

People who are against Internet voting say that it will invite unfair election practices. For example, campaign posters and signs, or people trying to influence how others vote are illegal at a voting place. But these laws cannot be enforced in homes. Also, computer hackers might be able to break into the computer election system and change the election results. Computer viruses could affect results. Experts are looking into these and other problems with Internet voting. What do you think?

## *Community Awareness and Involvement* ● ●

You already know that a good citizen votes and performs other duties. A good citizen also is involved in the community. A community in which people are involved is a healthier, happier place to live.

### What Is Community Involvement?

Community involvement means taking part in things that affect the people where you live. Citizens can become involved in their community in many ways. One way is by serving on a **jury**. A jury is a group of people chosen to listen to both sides of a case in a trial. Then the jury decides if the person on trial is innocent or guilty. Most people are called for jury duty at least once in their lives. Serving on a jury is a duty of every U.S. citizen.

Another way to become involved in the community is by **volunteering**. This means giving your time to help others without getting paid.

Perhaps you would like to volunteer but do not know how to go about it. There are many places you can call to find out who needs help. Some towns have volunteer centers. You can also contact community centers, schools, religious groups, senior centers, the YMCA or YWCA, and the United Way. The local chamber of commerce and community service groups, such as the Salvation Army, offer volunteer opportunities as well. And check for a "Volunteers Wanted" section in your local newspaper.

Serving on a jury is a citizen's duty.

Volunteering gets people involved in their communities.

Visit your neighborhood library to see what it has to offer. In addition to books, libraries lend CDs and videotapes. Many libraries offer programs and speakers. Ask for a list of events at your library.

You can become involved in your community simply by staying informed. Make a habit of reading the local newspaper and community newspaper. Find out what issues are affecting your community. You can voice your opinion by writing letters to the newspaper editor. Such opinions appear in the newspaper's editorial section.

The newspaper will also print notices of public meetings. These notices give a time and place to meet to discuss community issues. The issues might involve new building or road projects, taxes, crime problems, and more. Local government bodies, such as city councils, planning commissions, and zoning boards, often have public meetings. By attending these meetings, you can stay informed.

The more you know about your community, the more you are likely to care about it. And when people care, life is better for everyone.

## How Does the Government Help Communities?

People in communities depend on one another. They help one another. But sometimes people need more or different help than individuals or organizations can provide. In these cases, the government usually offers help.

Different levels of government provide different services. For example, your local government provides police and fire protection. The city or county has a health department. The health department protects community health by

- providing vaccines against certain diseases.

- operating free clinics to treat medical problems.

- providing information about health.

- offering classes about parenthood for new mothers and fathers.

- testing school children for certain medical problems such as vision, hearing, and emotional problems.

Volunteer in your community. You'll help others and feel good about yourself.

What are some issues up for discussion in your community?

## Some Volunteer Opportunities

- Visit patients in a hospital or nursing home.
- Visit senior citizens who seldom leave their homes.
- Help people at home who are ill or confined to a wheelchair by doing errands and cleaning house for them.
- Organize a community cleanup to pick up litter.
- Become a "big brother" or "big sister" to a lonely child.
- Help out in summer day camps.
- Offer to work in a library or museum.
- Serve meals to homeless people in shelters.
- Teach someone to read.
- Help organizations such as Meals on Wheels deliver hot food to people who cannot leave their homes.
- Help out at a food shelf.

- checking the safety of the water supply.
- checking the safety of food in restaurants, stores, and food manufacturing facilities.

Governments have many different **agencies**, or departments, that provide help. You can usually find these agencies in the white pages or blue pages of a phone book. Look under Government Offices.

## What Laws Do Communities Have?

"Ignorance is no excuse." You might hear this if you accidentally break a law and tell the police officer that you did not know about the law. Knowing the law is your responsibility.

Some laws are the same throughout the United States. For example, stealing is against the law no matter where you are in the country. Some laws vary from state to state. For instance, in some states the speed limit on most highways is 55 miles per hour. In other states, the limit may be 65 miles per hour.

## Current Day

### Good Samaritan Laws

All states have Good Samaritan laws. Under these laws, people who assist emergency victims are protected from being sued. For example, suppose you see someone fall and break an arm. You try to help the victim by putting the arm in a sling. In doing so, you make the break worse. The victim cannot sue you.

Some states also have Good Samaritan laws that say a person *must* help a victim. The person who is helping, however, is not required to put himself or herself in danger. For example, if you see a person being robbed, the law might say you have to call the police. However, you would not be expected to physically stop the robber because that would put you in danger.

Some laws vary from town to town. For example, some towns have **curfew** laws. A curfew is the time by which people must be at home or off the streets and other public property. For instance, people under the age of 18 might have an 11:30 P.M. curfew. Curfews usually do not apply to young people who are with adults.

Most towns have laws against **littering,** or leaving trash on property that is not your own. Examples of littering include spitting gum on the ground, tossing a can out a car window, and leaving food wrappers on a park bench. Most streets, parks, and public buildings have plenty of trash cans. Hold on to trash until you can throw it away properly.

Some communities have laws against these actions:

• Making too much noise.

• Walking dogs in parks.

• Spitting on public property.

• Jaywalking, or crossing a street other than at a corner.

• Parking your car on the street overnight.

**Curfew**
*A time by which people must be off the streets*

**Littering**
*Leaving trash on property that is not your own*

• • • • • • • • • • •

**What would you do if you lost track of time and discovered you were out past curfew?**

Learn and follow community laws.

Some laws may sound unreasonable, but laws help keep people safe. They help us get along with each other. Whether you live in a community or are just visiting, you are responsible for knowing and obeying the laws.

## Lesson 4 Review

Write the answers to these questions on a sheet of paper, using complete sentences.

1) What are four ways to volunteer in the community?

2) What are four places to call to ask about volunteering?

3) What government agency checks the safety of food in restaurants?

4) What are curfew laws?

5) What are five things the city or county health department does to protect a community's health?

## Online Resources

**Federal Election Commission**

*www.fec.gov*

Information about national candidates' campaign financing, voting, and voter registration.

**State Home Page**

*www.state.[insert state's two-letter abbreviation].us/*

When planning a trip, find information about a state by contacting the state's home page. (Example: www.state.mn.us/)

# Chapter 9 Summary

- Recreation is important to your physical, mental, and social health.

- There are a variety of activities you can do for recreation. Some are physical, such as a sport. Others, such as reading, involve little physical activity.

- Before choosing recreational activities, consider these things: what you enjoy, your goals, location, costs, equipment, and time.

- You can make an activity plan to help you include recreational activities in your life.

- Some planning helps make sure that a trip is enjoyable.

- Guidebooks, newspapers, and tourism departments provide helpful information for planning a trip.

- Voting is a responsibility of every U.S. citizen.

- When you vote, you choose your leaders in government and decide on issues.

- You must be a U.S. citizen and at least 18 years old to register to vote.

- A community is a better place to live when people are involved.

- You can get involved in your community by volunteering, staying informed, and attending public meetings.

- Local, state, and federal governments have different agencies that help communities.

- You are responsible for knowing and obeying your community's laws.

• • • • • • • • • • • • • • • • • • • • • • • •

## Comprehension: Identifying Facts

On a sheet of paper, write the correct word or words from the Word Bank to complete each sentence.

> **WORD BANK**
>
> | | | |
> |---|---|---|
> | ballot | jury | responsibility |
> | candidates | littering | traveler's check |
> | citizen | recreational | volunteering |
> | destination | register | |
> | issue | reservation | |

1) If a _____ is lost or stolen, it can be replaced.

2) When you take a trip, the place you are going to is your _____.

3) You vote for _____ who are running for government office such as mayor or president.

4) _____ activities can be physical or nonphysical.

5) Voting is one of the duties of being a _____ of the United States.

6) You must be at least 18 years old and a U.S. citizen in order to _____ to vote.

7) Before taking a trip to a hotel, it is a good idea to make a _____ at the hotel.

8) The card or paper on which you vote is called a _____.

9) Paying taxes is a citizen's _____.

10) Giving your time to help others is called _____.

**Test-Taking Tip**

To prepare for a test, study in short sessions rather than one long session. In the week before the test, spend time each evening reviewing your notes.

11) When you vote, you might make a decision about a certain _____ or problem in the community.

12) As a citizen, you might be chosen to be on a _____ and help decide if a person on trial is innocent or guilty.

13) Throwing a can out of a car window is an example of _____.

## Comprehension: Understanding Main Ideas

On a sheet of paper, write the answers to the following questions using complete sentences.

14) What are three ways you can express yourself?

15) What steps can you take to manage your recreational time?

16) Where can you find information about candidates running for office?

17) What are some ways that you can get involved in your community?

## Critical Thinking: Write Your Opinion

On a sheet of paper, write the answers to the following questions using complete sentences.

18) Describe something you have done recently that shows you are a good citizen.

19) Why do you think it is important to vote?

20) Look at the laws listed in Lesson 4. Choose three and explain why each one is a good law.

# Self-Assessment

Can you answer the following questions?

- ☑ What information do you need to complete a job application?
- ☑ What is the purpose of a resume?
- ☑ How would you follow up after a job interview?
- ☑ Where can you find information about job openings?
- ☑ What is networking?
- ☑ What is the purpose of an informational interview?
- ☑ How do you get to and from work?
- ☑ Can you describe your ideal job?
- ☑ What are some typical items in a benefits package?
- ☑ What is a pocket resume?

# Career Planning

**P**lanning your career is a little like getting ready to climb a mountain. Before you start, you would ask yourself, "What supplies will I need?" "Who can help me?" "What skills have I mastered that can help me reach the top?" Career planning takes the same kind of preparation.

The words *career, occupation,* and *job* are used in this chapter. A career is a profession for which a person prepares. It generally involves upward movement from one job to another as a person gains more experience. An occupation is the type of work in which a person is regularly employed. Job refers to a specific employment position in a specific company. In this chapter, you will learn how to choose an occupation that fits your abilities and interests. You will also find out how to go about getting a job.

## Goals for Learning

▶ To discover your career-related abilities, interests, and values

▶ To identify appropriate occupations based on your abilities, interests, and values

▶ To prepare job-search materials

▶ To learn to be an effective interviewer and interviewee

▶ To identify ways to negotiate employment needs

## Lesson 1 — *Discover Your Abilities and Interests* • • •

**Self-assessment**
*The process of studying your own interests, needs, abilities, and values*

If you are like most people, you will spend half your life—or more—working. So choosing a career that will satisfy you makes good sense. Start by figuring out what you like to do. What do you do well? What rewards do you want to get out of working? This process is called **self-assessment.** Taking a career interest inventory, can help you determine your career interests and possible occupations.

### What Are Qualities and Skills?

A skill is something you do well. You may be skilled at writing, telling jokes, fixing machines, growing plants, cooking, or using a computer. Some of your skills will help you find a job and do it well.

Qualities are traits, or characteristics, that you have. Qualities are part of your personality. To explore your qualities, ask yourself the following questions: Am I outgoing or private? Do I like to take risks and have adventures, or am I more cautious? Am I optimistic? Or do I believe that life is full of problems?

People value qualities differently. Qualities that people value in themselves and others are thought of as strengths. Some qualities that are considered strengths include kindness, humor, patience, dependability, trustworthiness, honesty, and cheerfulness. Some qualities that are generally thought of as weaknesses include laziness, grumpiness, dishonesty, rudeness, and selfishness. Everyone has both strong and weak qualities. Some situations bring out people's strengths, while other situations bring out their weaknesses.

In choosing the best occupation for you, look at which situations bring out your strengths and your weaknesses. You may not like to sit at a desk for hours. Doing so may make you grumpy. You may need to get up often and walk around.

If this sounds like you, you may not want to seek a job in an office environment. You might feel more comfortable doing other activities. For example, you might enjoy building things. Carpentry might be an occupation you would enjoy. We spend a lot of time and energy on the job. For that reason, we should choose occupations that are right for us.

## How Do You Discover Your Abilities?

Sometimes people have trouble identifying their abilities. Recognizing other people's abilities is often easier than seeing your own. One way to begin to identify your abilities is to look at your interests. Interests are subjects or activities that attract your attention and excite you. Many people are interested in sports, music, movies, and TV. Unfortunately, not many jobs are available in these areas. You may have to look deeper to find interests that you can relate to job skills.

Which class subjects do you enjoy? Are they the ones you get the best grades in? Think about the skills you use in your favorite classes. In math class, for example, you use problem-solving and reasoning skills. In English class, you use your language, reading, and verbal skills. Do you think you would enjoy a job that used those same skills?

Think of your experiences, projects, interests, and activities. Do you like outdoor activities such as biking? Or would you prefer to read a novel? Do you like to travel? Do you like to work with your hands? Consider all the activities you like to do. Your list can include hobbies, school subjects, clubs or organizations, volunteer work, jobs, family activities, and sports.

Looking at your interests and experiences can help you identify your abilities.

Ask people who know you to help you identify your interests and abilities. These people might include your school counselor, rehabilitation counselor, and family members. All are good resources to assist you in discovering your abilities. Once you have considered the activities you enjoy, you can think about the abilities you need to do each activity. For example, a person may pick camping as a favorite activity. This person might be good at planning and organizing. He or she would probably enjoy working outdoors and solving problems. A person who enjoys building models might be good at reading, problem solving, and math. A person who loves surfing the Internet might be good at reading, writing, looking up information, and using a computer.

## How Do You Feel About Work?

● ● ● ● ● ● ● ● ● ●

**What are some things you do that reflect your values?**

Knowing what you value is key to choosing an occupation that is right for you. Work-related values refer to how you like to work and the results you produce. People's values can help determine their career decisions. Examine your values closely—both personal and work related—and how you want to express those values in your career.

Don't feel bad if you have trouble defining your values. Often, the process of finding out what we truly value takes years of life experience. Sometimes the things we think we value are not as important to us when we examine them closely. We may find that other values are even more important. Some of our values change as we grow older and have more experiences. A young, single person may value excitement and the chance to travel around the country or even the world. She may actively seek opportunities for new experiences at this stage in her career. Later in life, when she has a family to support, her values may change. She may find she values job security, a good salary, and flexible hours.

## Work-Related Values

Look at this list of work-related values and think about the five that are most important to you. Why are these values important to you? You will be happiest in an occupation that includes most or all of your values.

- variety
- working with your hands
- job security
- working alone
- helping others
- pleasant surroundings
- good salary
- working with people
- challenging work
- being part of a team
- being creative
- opportunities for advancement
- high status
- doing something that benefits others

## Lesson 1 Review

Write the answers to these questions on a sheet of paper, using complete sentences.

1) What is the difference between a quality and a skill?

2) What is self-assessment?

3) Why is self-assessment an important first step in career planning?

4) What is one way to identify your abilities?

5) What are values?

# Examine Career Requirements and Rewards

**Ideal**
*Perfect, or the best you can think of*

Before you apply for a job, consider whether it is the kind of work you want. Think about the satisfaction or happiness that working in that job could bring day after day. Then ask yourself the following questions. Your answers will help you decide whether or not a certain job is right for you.

1. Is this the kind of work I will enjoy doing?

2. Will I make enough money to meet my needs and feel good about the work I'm doing?

3. Can I get to this place easily and on time?

When you can identify the job you want, you will be one step closer to finding it.

## How Can You Tell If a Job Is Right for You?

New employment opportunities appear every day. If you can identify the job you want, you are more likely to find it. Start by thinking about your **ideal,** or perfect, job. Your ideal job combines three main characteristics. First, it includes the activities you most like to do. Second, it takes place in the environment that you are most comfortable in. Finally, it allows you to express your values. In the real world, you may have to compromise. Your ideal job may not exist. But if you do not have an ideal job as a goal, you may end up with a job that is not even close.

Write a description of your ideal job. Start with a statement that describes the purpose of your ideal job. In other words, how does this job benefit the community?

Then think about how you would work with others in your ideal job. Do you like working alone or with others only occasionally? Do you like being a member of a team?

How much responsibility do you want? For example, do you prefer to **supervise,** or give directions, to other people? Or would you rather receive and follow directions? Do you like making decisions? Or would you prefer to leave the big decisions to someone else?

Consider your ideal work environment. Do you prefer working inside or outside? How do you feel about interruptions?

Finally, the heart of the job description is the job's main responsibilities. What skills would you use in a job? Think about your interests, abilities, and values, and how they could translate to a job.

Now that you have thought about your ideal job, give it a title. It might be a title that already exists or one you create. Don't worry if you have never seen a job title like it—you may have just invented it.

● ● ● ● ● ● ● ● ●

**Why is it unlikely that an ideal job exists?**

## Lesson 2 Review

Write the answers to these questions on a sheet of paper, using complete sentences.

1) What is one question to ask yourself when deciding if a job is right for you?

2) What is your ideal job?

3) How can describing your ideal job help you in your job search?

4) What does it mean to compromise when it comes to finding your ideal job?

5) How would your ideal job benefit your community? Where would it take place? What would your main responsibilities be?

# Identify Occupations ● ● ● ● ● ● ● ● ● ● ●

**Nontraditional**
*Seen in a way today that is different from the way it was seen in the past*

Y ou examined your qualities and skills, interests, abilities, and values. You considered your ideal job. Now use that knowledge to pinpoint occupations that interest you. It is time to research some existing occupations.

As you research occupational titles, be open-minded to **nontraditional** careers. They may be good matches with your abilities and interests. Something is nontraditional if it is seen differently today than it was in the past. For example, a nontraditional career choice for a man might be administrative assistant, nurse, or flight attendant. A nontraditional career choice for a woman might be auto mechanic, pilot, or construction worker. Don't limit yourself by thinking "that's a man's job," or "that's a woman's job." Keep an open mind. Many jobs are no longer closed to either men or women.

## What Should You Know About Each Occupation?

● ● ● ● ● ● ● ● ● ●

**Why do you think certain occupations were once closed to men or women?**

To get the most out of your research, keep a few general questions in mind about each occupation. Ask yourself:

• Does this occupation fit with my interests?

• How does this occupation agree with my values?

• How would this occupation make use of my abilities?

Here are a few more specific questions to keep in mind as you research occupational titles:

• What abilities and skills does this occupation require?

• What is the average monthly or yearly salary for this occupation?

• Where is it performed (in an office, in a manufacturing facility, outdoors at different sites)?

• What other occupations are like this one?

• Will this occupation be in demand in the future?

- Is there room to grow in this occupation?

- Do I need more training or education for this occupation?

What else would you like to know about the occupation? You may want to write down postsecondary courses you might need to take to prepare for the occupation. Some occupational resources list agencies or organizations you can contact to get more information.

## Where Can You Find Information About Different Occupations?

Many resources are available to help you gather information about different occupations. Libraries offer a variety of occupational resources. The guidance counselor at your school may have access to occupational resources. You can also find information online by searching a few keywords such as *careers* or *career planning*. Once you have discovered some attractive occupational titles, consider interviewing people who work in those occupations to get firsthand information.

### Some Occupational Resources

- *Dictionary of Occupational Titles (DOT)*
  The DOT lists every commonly held occupation in the United States. It includes a description of each occupation. The DOT also helps you identify activities you might do in your ideal occupation.

- *Occupational Outlook Handbook (OOH)*
  The OOH is an encyclopedia of more than 800 occupations described in detail. The OOH also lists sources of career information such as professional and trade organizations.

- *Guide for Occupational Exploration (GOE)*
  The GOE groups occupations by interest areas. For example, suppose you have not chosen an occupation, but you know you like to help people and repair machines. The GOE can help you find occupations that match your interests.

• • • • • • • • • • •
**Why is it important to know whether an occupation will be in demand in the future?**

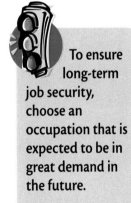

To ensure long-term job security, choose an occupation that is expected to be in great demand in the future.

• *The Occupational Information Network (O\*NET)*
O\*NET is a new online occupational resource. It is an automated replacement for the DOT (mentioned above). O\*NET is an easy-to-use database that contains information on more than 1,100 occupations. It can match an individual's skill requirements to occupations.

## Use the Library

You can find almost any resource in the library. Business directories, industry trade journals and magazines, or books on job hunting are available. Many libraries also have videos and computer programs about occupations.

Check your library for a listing of trade and professional organizations. These organizations can help if you are interested in a particular trade or profession. Some trade organizations may offer information about on-the-job training.

As you continue researching occupational titles, you may find that resources list other occupations with similar titles. A group of occupations that share similar titles and duties is often called an **occupational grouping,** or cluster. Take time to explore all the titles in the occupational grouping. You may discover an occupation that is even better suited to you than the one you started with. You may also discover some interesting occupational titles you didn't know existed.

Use the library to research different occupations.

## The Informational Interview

In an **informational interview,** you can get firsthand information about an occupation by talking with someone who has that occupation. It is also a great way to create contacts for possible job openings in that field. You can have an informational interview face-to-face or by telephone. Getting information about an occupation firsthand is sometimes more useful than reading about it.

The first step in an informational interview is to identify people to interview. Do you have friends or relatives who work in any of the occupations you are interested in? If so, they would be good candidates for an informational interview. Teachers and school counselors may also know people you could contact. Telephone directories, libraries, civic organizations, city or county offices, and unions are excellent resources for finding contacts. Contact a few people to interview. Explain your purpose: You are gathering information about specific occupations that interest you. Ask each person if he or she would be available for an informational interview to discuss his or her occupation.

Before the interview, learn as much about the occupation and the company as you can. Learn about the workplace, or the place where the work is done. Try to learn something about the person you will be interviewing. Then prepare a list of questions to ask.

Dress appropriately for the workplace you are visiting. Be prepared: Bring your interview questions, a notebook, and a pen or pencil. Arrive on time. If possible, be a few minutes early. Be friendly and courteous. Greet the person you are meeting with "good morning" or "good afternoon" and say the person's name. Give your name and the reason you are there.

> **Informational interview**
> *A talk with a person about his or her occupation to learn more about it*

What one or two
questions would
you add to the
informational
interview
questions list?

Before beginning the interview, ask how much time the person plans to spend with you. Do not go past that time. Ask the questions that are most important to you first. If you run short of time, you can skip the rest. You may want to save time toward the end of the interview to ask the person for job-seeking tips.

As the interview ends, summarize how you benefited from the interview. This requires some quick thinking. Be prepared to comment on what you found most interesting or most helpful about the interview. As you leave, thank the person for his or her time and shake hands.

Follow up your informational interview with a thank-you letter. It shows your appreciation for the knowledge, experience, and time the person shared with you. Try to mail the thank-you letter within 24 hours of the interview.

## Some Informational Interview Questions

- What activities and responsibilities does your job include?
- What skills and education are needed for this job?
- What kinds of jobs are available in this field?
- What do you like best about your job?
- What do you like least about your job?
- What types of entry-level jobs are available in this field?
- Are there any other ways to enter this field such as part-time work, volunteer work, or changing from another career?
- What opportunities do you think will be available in this field in the future?
- Can you refer me to other professionals in the field who may be able to help with my job search?

## Lesson 3 Review

On a sheet of paper, write the word or words in parentheses that correctly complete each sentence.

**1)** An occupational choice that may not have been available for a man or a woman in the past is called _____. (sexist, prejudiced, nontraditional)

**2)** A good place to start researching occupational titles is the _____. (library, newspaper, supermarket bulletin board)

**3)** A group of jobs that share similar titles and duties is called _____. (a job group, an occupational grouping, a job title)

**4)** In _____ , a job seeker talks with a person to learn about a job. (a job interview, a research trip, an informational interview)

**5)** A good handshake is gentle but _____. (firm, soft and limp, powerful and long-lasting)

### Your Handshake

While a handshake may seem unimportant, it reveals a great deal about you. A handshake that is too strong makes you appear insecure or too eager. A weak handshake could make you seem to lack confidence. The best handshake is one in which you grip the person's whole hand then squeeze gently but firmly. Shake briefly, then let go. Be sure to make and keep eye contact with the other person, smile, and speak in a pleasant tone.

## Lesson 4

# Consider Education and Training Requirements

**M**ost, if not all, of the occupations that interest you will probably require some training and education. Specific programs may range from ten weeks to two or more years. It depends on the education you need to perform the job. Even if you are not sure what your career will be, you may have decided to continue your education.

## Will You Need More Training?

The following questions can help you decide if you need more education or training for a certain occupation. Ask yourself:

1. Do I have the education required?

2. Can I work the hours and days required?

3. Do I have the skills needed?

4. Am I able to operate the equipment needed for this occupation?

5. Can I use the tools and/or resources needed to do this occupation?

6. Can I meet all the other occupation requirements?

Think of an occupation you would like to have. What kind of training do you think you need to prepare for that occupation?

## How Can You Get More Training?

You need more training for the occupation you want, so you must find out where and how to get it. You have many resources for obtaining information about schools and training programs.

### Postsecondary Schools

To get information about schools and colleges, you can read their catalogs and brochures. You can view laser discs and videotapes or use computer programs to learn about specific colleges and schools.

Here are some other things you can do:

- Obtain guidebooks that describe and compare different schools.

- Visit campuses and meet with school personnel.

- Attend college fairs.

- Talk to friends, relatives, counselors, and teachers about colleges, vocational/technical schools, and trade schools.

- Meet with postsecondary school representatives who visit your high school.

- Visit postsecondary schools' Web sites on the Internet.

## Apprenticeships

An **apprenticeship** can be a great way to train for a skilled profession. An apprentice learns a trade by working with someone who has mastered that trade. More than 800 skilled fields have apprenticeship programs. You can enter an apprenticeship for a variety of occupations, including carpentry, cabinetmaking, and construction. Trade unions, companies, labor organizations, and educational institutions all sponsor apprenticeships. To learn about apprenticeship programs in your state, call your State Department of Labor.

An apprenticeship is a combination of on-the-job training and classroom education. A sponsor pays the cost of the apprenticeship. The apprentice usually earns a wage of about 40 percent of what a skilled worker in that trade would earn.

Hundreds of fields offer apprenticeship programs.

After completing an apprenticeship, you are awarded a certificate of completion. The certificate is recognized by employers nationwide.

## Internships

An **internship** is a temporary job, usually for students, that can provide valuable work experience. Many internships are unpaid. Even without a salary, however, internships have many benefits. They offer work experience in a field that interests you. They can build confidence in your skills. They provide a way to make contacts in your chosen field. They also give you a chance to find out firsthand if a certain job is right for you.

Finding an internship is similar to finding a job. Many internships are offered during the summer. Positions for internships fill up fast. You want to start looking for an internship three to four months before you will be ready to start.

## Lesson 4 Review

On a sheet of paper, write the word or words in parentheses that correctly complete each sentence.

1) For most occupations, some _____ will be required. (college, training, computer skills)

2) To determine if you are qualified for a job, ask yourself, "Will I be able to _____ ?" (work the equipment required, pay for the training, work with the boss)

3) A _____ is awarded after completion of an apprenticeship. (certificate of completion, diploma, license)

4) An internship is a _____ job. (permanent, part-time, temporary)

5) Many _____ are unpaid. (internships, apprenticeships, college professors)

# Create Job-Search Materials ● ● ● ● ● ● ● ●

**Y**ou have identified the occupation you are most interested in. Now you need to prepare job-search materials. Job-search materials are a current **resume,** cover letter, and reference list. For people seeking jobs in certain fields, a current portfolio is also part of the job-search package. For example, someone seeking a job in the graphic arts field would compile a portfolio of his or her artwork.

## How Do You Prepare a Resume?

A resume is the most important job-search piece. Your resume is a written summary of your work-related skills, experience, and education organized in an easy-to-read form. It is an effective way to "sell" yourself to possible employers. A sample resume appears on the next page. A typical resume has four main sections:

- Personal information—This section tells who you are and where you can be contacted.

- Objective—This section tells what you want to do.

- Work experience—This section describes the jobs you have had.

- Education—This section lists the education and training you have completed or are in the process of obtaining.

You may also add a section describing nonwork-related activities you have participated in and awards and honors you have achieved.

### Personal Information

Personal information appears first in a resume. Personal information includes your name, address, and telephone number. Be sure to include your ZIP code with your address and your area code with your telephone number.

A resume

## Objective

An objective describes your career goal. It should be broad enough to allow you to be considered for more than one job. For example, suppose you are looking for a job as a plumbing apprentice. Your long-range career objective might be "to become a master plumber." An objective that is too narrow might exclude a person from being considered for a job he or she would enjoy.

## Work Experience

Work experience should include all full-time and part-time jobs that you have had for more than three months. This section should also include any jobs you performed as a volunteer. Volunteer jobs might include babysitting, snow shoveling, lawn mowing, or similar nonpaid jobs you have done for neighbors and friends. Work experience shows you are responsible and dependable and can do things on your own.

If you are a recent graduate, you may have little or no work experience. If so, do not put this section at the top of your resume. Place it further down the page under the education section. People who have had several jobs, however, should put the work experience section near the top of their resume. This shows that they have experience and are qualified for a new job.

## Education

If you have recently graduated from school, this section can be especially important on your resume. List the names and locations—city and state—of the high school and postsecondary school you attend or attended. Put the years you were there. Be sure to list any special courses you have taken that relate to the job you are seeking. You should also mention areas or courses in which you got good grades.

## Resume Checklist

When preparing your resume, ask yourself:

1. Have I listed the information on my resume in the best order?
2. Have I worded my career objectives so that they match the job I want?
3. Have I listed all of my education, including any additional courses? Have I stated the things I did well in school? Have I highlighted courses that relate to the job I want?
4. If I have work experience, have I listed the specific skills I have used that relate to the job I want?
5. Have I listed extracurricular activities and/or community activities that show my interest in areas related to the job I want?
6. Are the section headings clear? Do they stand out on the page?
7. Is all my information correct?
8. Have I corrected spelling and typing errors?
9. Have I corrected punctuation and capitalization errors?
10. Did I enter my name, address, and phone number at the top of the page?
11. Have I kept my resume on one or two pages?
12. Is my resume neat, attractive, and readable?

**Extracurricular activities** *Activities done in addition to attending school classes*

**What information would you list first on your resume?**

### Extracurricular Activities, Awards, and Honors

**Extracurricular activities** are school activities people do in addition to attending school classes. These activities include sports, the school newspaper, band, and student government. If you have been out of high school for several years, you probably should not list high school activities.

Do you participate in any community groups or activities? Be sure to list them. This includes volunteer work and such things as community theater groups or religious activities. Employers often feel that people who are active in the community will be hardworking, dependable, and caring.

September 12, 2000

Ms. Helen White
MNO Company
4671 Highland Road
Palatine, IL 60067

Dear Ms. White:

I am writing in response to the ad for an office administrator that appeared in the Sunday Tribune. I am enclosing my resume for your review.

For the past two years, I have worked as an office assistant at Lakeland Corporation. In that time, I have taken on more responsibility. I am a hard worker who is looking for new challenges.

I would welcome the opportunity to talk with your personally about the office administrator position. You can reach me at 847/555-1234. I will follow up with you on September 20. Thank you for your time and consideration.

Sincerely,

*Leslie Strom*

Leslie Strom

A cover letter

# What Is a Cover Letter?

A cover letter introduces you to a potential employer. When you submit a resume to an employer, include a cover letter. A sample cover letter is shown here. The cover letter needs to be tailored to the job opening you are applying for. It tells the employer you are interested in that job and why you are qualified to do the work. Direct a cover letter to the person who does the hiring. If you do not know that person's name, call the company and ask. If you are responding to an ad, direct the cover letter to the person or department listed in the ad. A cover letter is most effective when it is addressed to the correct person.

You want to include the following information in your cover letter:

• The reason you are writing—the job you are interested in.

• Your qualifications—what you can do for the company.

• The action you plan to take to pursue your interest in the job—"I will call you on . . ."

• A thank-you to the person for his or her time and consideration.

## Cover Letter Checklist

1. Have you identified the job title and stated how you found out about the job?

2. Have you listed the skills you have that would help you do the job?

3. Have you checked for and corrected any spelling errors?

## How Do You Choose a Reference?

You will want to create a reference list similar to the one shown here. References are people you know who will speak well of you to an employer. A reference can describe the kind of person you are, things you do well, and how you get along with others. Good references include former employers, religious leaders, coaches, club sponsors, teachers, neighbors, and other adults who know you.

Relatives are not usually good choices for references. Employers may think that relatives will say nice things about you because you are related to them. You will want to get permission from your references before putting them in your reference list.

Leslie Strom
113 South Marlow Road
Palatine, IL 60067
847/555-1234

**REFERENCES**

Ms. Sally Turner, Owner
Lakeland Corporation
445 Emerson Road
Palatine, IL 60067
847/555-3214

Ms. Carol Walstrom, Neighbor
115 South Marlow Road
Palatine, IL 60067
847/555-6656

Rev. Robert Walker, Pastor
First Community Church
8912 Malcolm Avenue
Palatine, IL 60067
847/555-9281

A reference list

When employers ask for references, they usually request three. Select at least three people you have asked for permission to list. Type their names, occupations, addresses, and daytime phone numbers on a sheet of paper. Add your name at the top and use the heading "References." Keep in mind that previous employers can legally discuss only job-related issues when giving a reference.

## Lesson 5 Review

Write the answers to these questions on a sheet of paper, using complete sentences.

1) What are two types of information included in a resume?

2) Why are relatives not a good choice for references?

3) What four pieces of information should you include in a cover letter?

4) Which section of a resume describes the person's career goal?

5) How does a resume help you "sell" yourself to employers?

# *Begin Your Job Search* ● ● ● ● ● ● ● ● ● ● ●

People find jobs in many ways. Some methods will work well for you. Others will not. Try out a couple and continue with the ones that work best. Begin by identifying businesses or other places that have the types of jobs you want. Create a list of possible employers to help you keep your job search focused.

## What Are Some Sources for Finding Available Jobs?

You are ready to apply for jobs and you need to find out what jobs are available. There are a variety of sources you can use to identify available jobs. You may need to use more than one source.

• State Job Service—Most states offer a job service through the state employment office. Many job services provide job listings on computer. Job services also offer counseling, free literature, and information about training programs.

• Employment agencies—These companies work with people to help them find jobs. The agencies collect fees for their efforts. Sometimes the fee is paid by the hiring company, but often it is the individual's responsibility. Be sure you know about any fees you may be charged if you choose to use an employment agency.

• Career and vocational counselors—These counselors help you choose a profession based on your skills and interests. Many school placement offices offer the services of these counselors, usually free of charge. Counselors in private practice charge for their services. If you decide to hire a counselor, first ask for his or her track record for placing people in jobs.

• Headhunters—A company usually hires a headhunter to find a qualified candidate for a position with very specific requirements. An individual who is looking for a job can also hire a headhunter.

- Vocational Rehabilitation services—Vocational Rehabilitation (VR) is a nationwide federal and state program. It helps people with disabilities plan suitable employment goals and find jobs. Look under the state listings in your telephone directory.

- Telephone book—Start here if you plan to send your resume to employers who have not advertised an opening. Suppose you are a paralegal, and you want to work for a private law firm. The Yellow Pages will list most of the law firms in your city, with addresses and phone numbers.

- Chamber of Commerce—This is a good source of information on local businesses. The chamber may have a job board or directory.

- Networking—Tell everyone you know, including family, friends, and acquaintances, about your job search, and ask them to tell others. Soon, you will have a network of people helping you find a job.

- Classified ads—Read the want ads in your local newspaper, but do not depend on this source alone. Some experts say that only about 5 percent of people looking for work find jobs through the want ads.

## What Is Networking?

Many career experts believe that **networking** is the best way to find a job. Networking is the sharing of information or services among individuals, groups, or institutions. Many jobs are part of the "hidden job market." This means that the jobs are not advertised. The only way to learn about these jobs is through personal contact with people who know about them.

Most employers like to hire people who have been recommended to them. This is where networking comes in. Create a group of people who can help you in your job search. You can find these people through friends, family, or coworkers. Ask people in your network for job leads and for information about occupations and companies. Request introductions to other people who may become part of your network.

**Networking**
*The sharing of information or services among people or institutions*

Start a networking file using index cards and a recipe box. Write the name, occupation, address, and phone number of each contact on a card. Note how you know them. Record any help they gave you and dates of contact.

To be a successful networker, you need to stay in contact with your network. Keep a file of names, mailing and e-mail addresses, and phone numbers of everyone in your network. Get in touch with your contacts regularly. Give them a friendly phone call just to say hello. Drop them an e-mail with a question. Keep an organized record of all contacts you make with your network. Write down when you communicate with someone, how you contacted that person, and what information was exchanged.

● ● ● ● ● ● ● ● ● ● ●
**Why would an employer want to hire someone who is recommended to her by someone she knows?**

## How Do You Conduct a Job Search?

You have a resume, references, and a list of job possibilities. The following tips can help you in your job search:

• Treat your job search like a full-time job. Each day, make a list of tasks related to your search. Include contacts you plan to make, meetings or interviews you must attend, and thank-you notes to write. Keep notes of your conversations.

• Make brief calls to different people in your network every day. Tell them what you are looking for and ask for other contacts. Follow up on the leads you get.

• Maintain a file to track your job-search efforts. File a copy of the letters you send to contacts or potential employers.

| Date | Contact's Name | Communication Method | Outcome of Contact | Action to be Taken | Completed |
|------|----------------|----------------------|--------------------|--------------------|-----------|
| 9/6 | Sarah Carr | phone call | Contact at ARF Company: Bill Larson 651/555-1234 | Call Bill to ask about possible job openings in his company. Ask if he knows other people in the field I can contact. | 9/8 |
| 9/8 | Bill Larson | phone call | Gave me a lead on an opening at ARF. Also suggested I call Andrew Hall 651/555-1544 at Rumball. | Apply for an opening at ARF. Contact Andrew Hall. | |

A sample networking file

- Keep a record of your contact people, the outcome of your communication with them, and actions you take.

- Check want ads and other employment sources. However, spend most of your time networking.

- Tailor your resume to each job you apply for so it is more specific to that job. Sending the same resume to every possible employer will not offer the best results.

Finding a job is a full-time job. Most people who get jobs they want have put a lot of effort into finding them.

Keep copies of all letters you send during your job search.

## Lesson 6 Review

Write the answers to these questions on a sheet of paper, using complete sentences.

**1)** What are two services that charge a fee for job placement?

**2)** What is networking?

**3)** Name three people who could be part of your network. Explain why you chose them.

**4)** What percent of people looking for jobs find them through the classified ads?

**5)** According to many career experts, what is the best way to find a job?

# The Job Application and Interview ● ● ● ●

If your job-search efforts are successful, sooner or later you will fill out an application and have an interview.

## What Is a Job Application?

A job application is a standard form a person fills out when applying for a job. The application gives those involved in the hiring process some specific information about you. It provides information about your education and work experience. You must be honest about the information you give on an application. Some companies will fire you if they find out that your application was dishonest. A sample page from a job application appears below.

**Equal Opportunity Employer**
ABC Corporation does not discriminate in hiring or employment on the basis of race, color, creed, religion, national origin, ancestry, age, disability, marital status, status with regard to public assistance, veteran status, sexual or affectional preference, or other factors identified and protected by federal, state, or local legislation. No question on the application is intended to secure information to be used for such discrimination.

*Please print in ink and answer every question.*

**PERSONAL INFORMATION**

Name: _____
       Last                    First                  Middle

Date of Application: _____    Social Security Number: _____

Present Address: _____
                 Street              City        State      ZIP

Permanent Address: _____
                   Street            City        State      ZIP

Telephone:    Home: _____    Business: _____

**EMPLOYMENT DESIRED**

Type of work or position desired:   ☐ FT   ☐ PT   ☐ Temporary

Date available for work: _____

How were you referred to us? _____

**EDUCATION**

| Type of School | Name and Location of School | Major Course | Minor Course | Did You Graduate? | Degree | GPA |
|---|---|---|---|---|---|---|
| High School | | | | | | |
| College or University | | | | | | |
| Graduate or Law School | | | | | | |
| Business or Vocational | | | | | | |
| Other | | | | | | |

List any courses/subjects studied that you feel would help you in the position for which you are applying. _____

A job application

Sometimes, an employer will expect you to fill out an application on the spot. Be prepared to give your personal information and education and work history before you walk into the employer's place of business. A pocket resume can help you with these tasks. A pocket resume is a brief version of your formal resume. It contains information you need to fill out applications. A pocket resume may be on note cards or in a small, spiral notebook.

List your name, address, phone number, Social Security number, special skills and talents, awards, and activities on the first index card.

Use the second card for your work experience. List the names and addresses of your current and former employers, your job titles, and your responsibilities. Also list the dates you held the jobs, your salary for each one, and your reason for leaving your current position. Use as many cards as you need. Then, on another card, list your references' names, occupations, business addresses, and daytime phone numbers.

When filling out an application, read and follow the directions. Provide as much information as you can. If part of an application does not apply to you, write N/A, for "not applicable" in that section. This tells the person reading the application that you have not accidentally left something out.

Write neatly. If you make a mistake, erase carefully, use correction fluid, or ask for another application and start over. Remember that an application tells people a great deal about you, and you want to make the best possible impression.

To make yourself stand out from other job applicants, always submit a resume along with a job application.

## How Can You Make the Most of a Job Interview?

When you get an interview at a company, you have a good chance of getting a job there. Making a good impression at the interview is important. The people who interview you will notice your appearance and that will figure into their impression of you. You want to look professional and be respectful.

Be polite to everyone you meet. When asked, introduce yourself and explain why you are there. Listen carefully to questions you are asked. Stay calm and answer questions clearly and briefly.

Looking professional and acting respectful can help you make a good impression.

During the interview, remain positive and confident. Maintain good posture. Speak clearly and avoid slang. Bring a few copies of your resume. At the end of the interview, give your resume to the person or people who interviewed you.

## What Should You Do After a Job Interview?

Follow up each job interview with a thank-you letter to each person who interviewed you. Mail thank-you letters within 24 hours of the interview. In the letter, thank the person for his or her time. Also, restate your interest in the position. You may want to restate any points that you feel you did not express clearly in the interview. Or you can briefly remind the interviewer about the skills you could bring to the job.

If a week or so passes and you have not heard from the employer, follow up with a phone call. You may politely ask whether he or she has made a decision. You may also let the employer know again that you are interested in the job.

### Looking Your Best for an Interview

- Wash, dry, and comb your hair.
- Trim and clean your fingernails, use deodorant, and brush your teeth.
- Keep jewelry to a minimum. Many chains or long, dangling earrings do not look professional.
- Select clothes that are clean, pressed, and look professional. A suit is a good choice. A skirt or pants with a dress shirt and jacket or sweater are some other good options. Avoid loud colors; they can be distracting. You want people to tune in to you, not your clothes.
- When you are dressed and ready for the interview, check how you look in a mirror. Arrive at the workplace a little early and visit the bathroom to freshen up.

Some jobs, though they seem like a good fit, may not be a good match for you. Even interviews that go well do not always result in job offers. Don't be discouraged. Remain positive, continue your job search, and you will find the right job.

## Lesson 7 Review

Write the answers to these questions on a sheet of paper, using complete sentences.

**1)** Why should you be honest when filling out a job application?

**2)** What is a pocket resume?

**3)** When you write "N/A" on a job application, what does it mean?

**4)** When you are in an interview, what are some things you want to do?

**5)** What kind of information should you include in a thank-you letter for a job interview?

## Technology In Our Lives

### Scannable Resumes

Many companies use computer scanners to read typewritten resumes and record the important information in them. The information is stored in a computer file. When the company needs a person with certain skills, it can search the computer file for people with those skills.

A scannable resume needs to be simpler than a formal resume. Remove design elements. Make the action words into nouns. For example, change *managed* to *manager*. For more information about preparing a scannable resume, search the Internet using the term *scannable resumes*.

## Lesson 8    *Negotiate Employment Needs* ● ● ● ● ● ●

**Compensation**
*The wages and benefits that an employer provides to its employees in exchange for their work*

**Negotiation**
*The process of arranging for things you need, usually by giving in on some issues but not on all issues*

If your first interview has gone well, the employer may consider hiring you. You may be called back for a second interview. At this stage, the subject of **compensation** may come up. Compensation is the wages and benefits that an employer provides to its employees in exchange for their work. A combination of wages and benefits is often called a compensation package.

### What Are Benefits?

Benefits are often called "fringe benefits" because they are offered in addition to wages. Some jobs include many benefits. Other jobs offer few or none. Benefits may include health insurance, paid vacation and sick days, retirement pensions, and investment options. Benefits can be a valuable part of a compensation package.

### How Do You Negotiate for What You Need?

The discussion of compensation between you and an employer may take the form of **negotiation.** Negotiation is the process of arranging for things you need, usually by giving in on some, but not all, issues. It is similar to compromising.

Be prepared to negotiate compensation before you are offered a job. Figure out how much money you need for living expenses plus savings. If possible, find out the salary range in the market for the position you are interviewing for. Understand how valuable your skills are in the job you are seeking. For example, you may be able to find out the current wage or salary for an entry-level office administrator. Then you can decide if the compensation you are offered is in line with that of other entry-level office administrators.

This information will tell you how much money to ask for and how much you can expect to receive. This is your starting point for negotiations.

The employer may ask you what your wage or salary is at your current job, if you have one. Currently, you may be making less than you would like to make in your new job. Be prepared to explain why your skills are now worth more.

The employer may state a salary range for the position. He or she may also describe the benefits package. When you examine this compensation package, figure out how much the benefits are worth in dollars. Add that amount to the yearly wage or salary the employer offers. This is your total compensation package.

Some job candidates request a higher salary figure that is still within the acceptable pay range for the job. This gives the job candidate room to negotiate with the employer. If the employer counteroffers with a lower figure, the candidate can accept the lower offer and still make a reasonable salary. This approach lets both people feel they met each other halfway.

Sometimes people choose to negotiate for other things besides money. Flexible work hours, parking fees, parking space, or more vacation days are just a few negotiable things. Negotiation is not required in accepting a job. It is something you can choose to do or not do. Check the job-search section in your local library for more information about negotiating.

**What is one thing you may ask for during compensation negotiations in exchange for accepting a lower salary?**

A person with a disability may need an accommodation to perform a task or job responsibility.

## Do You Need Accommodations?

People who have disabilities do many things well. A disability hinders a person from doing a task the same way most people do it. Some disabilities affect how a person learns and functions. Other disabilities are physical. In a job situation, a person with a disability may need an accommodation in order to complete a task or job responsibility.

The Americans with Disabilities Act (ADA) protects people with disabilities. In the employment arena, the law prohibits discrimination against qualified job candidates with disabilities. A qualified individual with a disability must be able to perform the essential functions of the position, with or without a reasonable accommodation.

The law requires employers to make accommodations if they would not impose an "undue" or extreme hardship on the business. For example, an employer must make nonwork areas used by employees accessible to people with disabilities. Such areas include cafeterias, lounges, and employee buses.

Some other examples of accommodations include the following:

• Making existing employee buildings accessible to people with disabilities by including wheelchair ramps, elevators, or similar accommodations.

• Modifying work schedules.

• Changing equipment.

• Modifying examinations, training materials, or policies.

• Providing sign-language translators for the hearing impaired.

Let your employer know if you need an accommodation to do your job. Employers are required to provide reasonable accommodations only if they are aware of a person's disability. Working out job accommodations requires cooperation between the employee, the employee's supervisor, and human resources.

● ● ● ● ● ● ● ● ● ●

**Based on your career investigation, what types of accommodations would you need for the job you are interested in?**

## Lesson 8 Review

On a sheet of paper, write the word or words in parentheses that correctly complete each sentence.

**1)** Another term for wages or salary is _____. (profit sharing, fringe benefits, compensation)

**2)** A way to arrange for things you need in a job is through _____. (negotiation, compensation, accommodation)

**3)** Medical insurance, paid vacation days, and profit sharing are things you would find in a _____. (grocery store, benefits package, resume)

**4)** It is _____ to refuse to hire a qualified person because that person has a disability. (legal, illegal, best)

**5)** On-the-job assistance for a person with a disability is known as _____. (a fringe benefit, a compensation package, an accommodation)

### Online Resources

**Occupational Information Network (O*NET)**
**U.S. Department of Labor**

*www.doleta.gov/programs/onet/*

Descriptions of more than 1,100 occupations.

**Occupational Outlook Handbook (OOH)**
**U.S. Department of Labor**

*stats.bls.gov/ocohome.htm*

Descriptions of what workers do on the job, working conditions, required training and education, and more.

**U.S. Department of Labor**
**Employment and Training Administration**

*www.doleta.gov/*

Information about jobs and apprenticeships.

# *Travel to and from Work* • • • • • • • • •

Accoring to the Federal Highway Administration, almost 75 percent of U.S. workers drive to work alone. About 10 percent ride to work in a two-person car pool. About 5 percent take public transportation and another 4 percent walk.

No matter how you get to work, find out in advance how long your trip will take. Allow a little extra time for unexpected delays. Check on available parking and parking costs if you plan to drive.

For many people, public transportation is less expensive than driving. Public transportation includes bus services, trains, ferryboats, and other services. According to the American Automobile Association, in 1998 it cost between $5,000 and $10,000 per year to operate a vehicle. Costs varied depending on the size of the vehicle and the number of miles driven. Yearly costs for using public transportation range from $200 to $2,000 per person.

Public transportation provides a less expensive alternative to driving to work.

## How Do You Plan Your Route?

Larger cities have public transportation systems. To use public transportation, first find out what services exist between your home and work. You can call your local transit, or transportation, authority for schedules, maps, and other information. You can often find these materials in train and subway stations. Signs at bus stops usually provide specific routes and times they run. Buses and trains operate on set schedules. They operate most often during weekday morning and evening rush hours.

Many cities are linked to suburbs by regional trains and buses. You may have to drive to a train station if you are traveling between the suburbs and the city. Parking lots at train stations provide parking spaces for a fee.

Within the city, you may be able to walk to a bus stop or train station and catch one bus or train to your job. Or you may have to transfer, or switch, to a second bus or train to reach your destination. Transferring may be free, or you may have to pay a small fee. Be sure to ask about the transfer process before you get on the bus or train.

## How Do You Pay for Public Transportation?

You may pay for rides on public transportation with transit cards, tokens, passes, or cash. Transit cards are electronically programmed cards with a prepaid dollar value. You slide the card through an electronic "reader" at a train turnstile or on a bus. The fare is then automatically subtracted from the card's value. Tokens are small metal "coins" that are good for one trip.

If you take more than two trips a day, an unlimited-use pass may be your most economical choice. Unlimited-use passes allow you to take as many trips as you want to during a set period of time. Unlimited-use passes are usually available for one day, one week, or one month.

**Describe the route you take to work or school. What kind of public transportation could you use to get there?**

Paying for public transportation with cash may be slightly more expensive than using passes or transit cards. Also keep in mind that if you use cash, you may be required to have exact change, especially on buses.

## Lesson 9 Review

Write the answers to these questions on a sheet of paper, using complete sentences.

**1)** How do most people travel to and from work?

**2)** What is the yearly cost range for using public transportation?

**3)** What does transferring mean in public transportation?

**4)** How do you use a transit card?

**5)** What form of transportation do you think is best? Give two reasons to support your opinion.

## Current Day

### Vanpools

You have probably heard of car pools. But what about vanpools? A vanpool is a group of about seven to 15 people who ride to work together in a van. For some people, vanpooling is a better choice than driving to work alone or taking public transportation. Vanpooling usually costs less than driving alone. In addition, vanpools contribute to less traffic and pollution because one vehicle takes the place of four or more individual vehicles. Many vanpoolers enjoy the relaxing ride and the companionship of their fellow riders.

Groups of employees who live and work near each other may start a vanpool on their own. They might lease a van from a rental car agency that has a vanpool program. Some communities and employers also run vanpool programs. In some cities, certain parking ramps offer better parking rates to vanpools and car pools.

# Chapter 10 Summary

● ● ● ● ● ● ● ● ● ● ● ● ● ● ● ● ● ● ● ● ●

■ Discovering your abilities, interests, and work-related values through self-assessment is the first step in making a good job choice.

■ Researching possible jobs involves finding out a number of things: What skills and training does a job require? What activities does it involve? Where does it take place? Once you have researched jobs, you can use what you have learned through self-assessment to choose jobs that suit you.

■ Library research and informational interviews are two ways to learn about different jobs.

■ Good interviewing skills include being prepared, being polite, showing enthusiasm, and following up.

■ Postsecondary schools, internships, and apprenticeships are three ways to get job education, experience, and training.

■ A neat, well-organized resume clearly presents your skills, experience, and education.

■ Many sources of job information are available. They include job services, employment agencies, career and vocational counselors, and your network of personal contacts.

■ Networking, or using personal contacts, to find the hidden job market is often considered the best way to find a job.

■ A compensation package includes wages and benefits. Compensation is often agreed on by means of negotiation between an employer and a job applicant.

■ Most people drive to work alone, but public transportation may be less expensive.

## Comprehension: Identifying Facts

On a sheet of paper, write the correct word or words from the Word Bank to complete each sentence.

> **WORD BANK**
>
> accommodations
> application
> apprenticeship
> cover letter
> extracurricular
>
> ideal
> informational
>   interview
> internship
> networking
> nontraditional
>
> occupational
>   grouping
> public
>   transportation
> qualities
> skills

1) Honesty and laziness are examples of people's _____.

2) Writing and fixing machines are examples of _____.

3) Because your _____ job may not exist, you may have to compromise.

4) For a man, a _____ career might be preschool teacher.

5) Nurse, nurse's aide, and dental assistant may belong to the same _____.

6) To learn about an occupation from a person who works in it, you may conduct an _____.

7) On-the-job training under a skilled master is called an _____.

8) A temporary job that is often unpaid is called an _____.

9) Student government, sports, and other activities done in addition to school work are called _____.

10) You can find out about the hidden job market through _____.

11) You may be fired for writing false information on a job _____.

12) A _____ introduces you to a potential employer.

13) _____ help people with disabilities perform job tasks.

14) About 5 percent of all workers use _____ to travel to their jobs.

## Comprehension: Understanding Main Ideas

On a sheet of paper, write the answers to the following questions using complete sentences.

15) What are two of the sections on a resume? What information does each of them contain?

16) How do an employer and employee reach agreement on wages and benefits?

17) What is the difference between an internship and an apprenticeship?

18) List four people you know who could be references.

## Critical Thinking: Write Your Opinion

On a sheet of paper, write the answers to the following questions using complete sentences.

19) Why should people who have been out of high school for awhile not list high school extracurricular activities on their resume?

20) Should people with disabilities be able to work in any type of job? Explain your answer.

# Self-Assessment

**Can you answer the following questions?**

- ☑ What kind of information can be found in an employee handbook?
- ☑ What does peer pressure mean in the workplace?
- ☑ What happens in a layoff?
- ☑ What is a performance assessment?
- ☑ In a harassment situation, where would you turn for help?
- ☑ What can you expect the first day of a new job?
- ☑ Why is it helpful to have a career plan?
- ☑ What is one example of a workplace barrier?
- ☑ What does it take to be a good team member?
- ☑ What steps can you take to resolve conflict with a coworker?

# The Employment Setting

**Y**ou've been hired for the job you always dreamed of. You know that many people applied for the job. But you are the one who was hired. You feel special and proud of yourself.

Tomorrow is your first day at work. You are excited and a little nervous. Everything will be new to you. New people. New building. New rules. How will you remember everything? How will you show your boss you are a good worker?

In this chapter, you will explore skills that every worker needs. You will learn how to use your time in a wise manner. You will discover how to build good relationships with other workers. You will learn how to set—and reach—your career goals.

## Goals for Learning

▶ To describe a typical first day at work

▶ To develop time management strategies

▶ To explore ways of developing healthy relationships with others

▶ To understand the need for personal career goals

▶ To identify actions one can take to achieve career goals

## *Beginning a New Job* ● ● ● ● ● ● ● ● ● ●

**E**veryone feels a bit nervous on the first day of a new job. That's because a new job is a big change in your life. Change is difficult. It means doing things differently. It means breaking old patterns. That's hard, but change also helps you grow. It helps you become the person you want to be.

### What Can You Do to Have a Great First Day?

You can do certain things to help your first day go smoothly. First, try to relax. Remember that you were chosen for the job. Your employer believes that you have the skills needed to be a good worker. Your employer is confident that you can do the job. You should be confident, too.

On your first day, be sure to arrive at work on time. You might even try to report a few minutes early, if possible. This sends a message to your employer. It says that you value your new job and are eager to start learning.

Make sure that you dress properly for work. If your job requires wearing a uniform, make sure that it is neat and clean. If a uniform is unnecessary, make sure your outfit is suitable. For males, that might mean wearing a dress shirt and tie. Avoid wearing torn and wrinkled clothes. Females should avoid wearing very short skirts or tight-fitting clothes. Remember, you are going to your job— not to a dance.

On your first day of work, you will meet your coworkers.

## What Can You Expect on the First Day?

On your first day, you will probably meet many new people, including **coworkers.** Your coworkers are the people who work in the same company. Pay attention when you are introduced to them. Try to remember their names. Shake their hands firmly, and make eye contact. These actions will send a powerful message. They will tell your coworkers that you want to develop good relationships with them.

On your first day, a coworker will probably show you around. You will be shown where to put your things, like your coat or lunch. You will be brought to your workstation, or place where you work. You probably will be given some tasks to do. If you are unsure of anything, ask questions. Asking lots of questions is better than doing the work incorrectly. Learning a new job takes time.

You may also be asked to fill out several forms. These forms might include tax forms for the state and U.S. government. You might not have some of the information with you. Don't put down just anything to get the forms finished. Ask if you can take the forms home with you. Fill them out correctly and bring the completed forms to work the next day.

**Coworker**
*A person who works for the same company*

**Employee handbook**
*A book describing the rules of a company*

## What Is an Employee Handbook?

Many companies give new workers an **employee handbook.** This book describes the company's rules and job benefits. Look through the handbook. Notice the kind of information it contains. Then, when you have a question, look for the answer in your handbook.

**ABC CORPORATION**

**Employee Handbook**

An employee handbook

Suppose you don't understand a form given to you on the first day of work. You ask to take it home and reread it. But you still don't know how to complete it. Who could help you with the form?

Be sure to review the company rules in the handbook. Some rules explain what to do if you are sick and cannot come to work. Other rules describe the company's smoking or phone policies. Not following these rules could cost you your job. You could be **fired,** or dismissed from the company. Then you might have a hard time finding another job. If you don't understand something in the handbook, ask your supervisor about it. It is important that you understand and follow all the rules listed in the employee handbook.

## What Is a Probation Period?

• • • • • • • • • • •

**Your three-month probation period is over. Your supervisor hasn't rated you or set a time to do so. What would you do?**

Some companies have a **probation period** for new workers. This is a test period when a worker must show that he or she is able to do a job. Most probation periods last two or three months. During that time, the worker is trained for the job and gets paid for the work. At the end of the probation period, the company rates the worker. If the company is pleased with the worker's progress, the person continues in the job. If not, the person is dismissed, or let go.

During the probation period, the new worker is also assessing the company. This test period gives the worker time to get a feel for the job, supervisor, coworkers, and the company. It is a good time for the worker to get to know the job requirements and what is expected of him or her. Is the job what he or she expected or is it very different? Does the worker look forward to coming to work each day? This is also a good opportunity to get to know the people who work for the company. Are they supportive of each other and the company? The worker should consider his or her needs, and determine if this is the right place to be.

## What Is a Labor Union?

When you start a new job, you may be asked to join a **labor union.** A labor union is an organization of people who do similar jobs. Members of the union elect officials. Their job is to protect the union members. Union officials make sure that their workers are treated fairly. They check the places where union members work to make sure the places are safe. Union officials meet with company officials to discuss workers' problems. If you decide to join a union, you will have to pay dues, or a small fee.

> **Labor union**
> *An organization of workers who do similar jobs*

## Lesson 1 Review

Write the answers to these questions on a sheet of paper, using complete sentences.

1) What are some things you can do to have a great first day at work?

2) How can you show your coworkers that you value them?

3) Why is it important to read an employee handbook?

4) What is a probation period?

5) Suppose a coworker asks you to join a labor union. You are saving for a new car and really don't want to have to pay union dues. But you know that being a union member protects you from being treated unfairly. What will you tell your coworker?

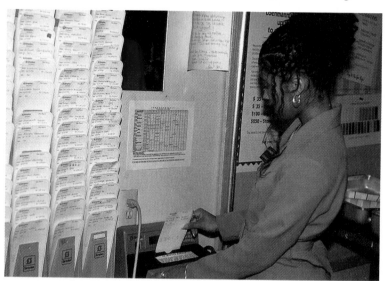

# Employing Time-Management Techniques ●

**H**as a friend or family member ever kept you waiting? How did it make you feel? Probably angry! Time is something most people need more of. It is valuable. You don't like it when someone wastes your time. Your company won't like it if you waste its time.

## Why Is It Important to Be Punctual?

Every company expects its workers to be **punctual.** Being punctual means reporting for work on time. It also means leaving for lunch and breaks at the correct time—and returning promptly. A worker who is punctual shows others that he or she is responsible and takes the job seriously.

## How Can You Manage Your Time Effectively?

Most people try to be punctual. They don't intend to be late for work or meetings. But things come up to delay them. The trip to work takes longer than expected. A sudden errand must be taken care of. An unexpected telephone call comes in. All these things take up time and can make a person late.

To avoid these problems, try to manage your time effectively. Write down the amount of time you spend each day on required activities.

At some companies, employees punch a time clock to record the hours they work.

Then look at the time you spend doing things you enjoy, such as watching television or talking on the phone. Use this information to make a schedule. Making a personal schedule that includes required activities and free time will help you use your time wisely.

## What Are Deadlines?

You might work in a job that has **deadlines.** A deadline is the latest time when something must be done. If you work in a mailroom, you might have to deliver all the mail by 1:00 P.M. If you work in a restaurant, you might have to set all the tables by 4:30 P.M.

Workers who are able to follow a schedule and meet deadlines are valuable. Workers who are often late and miss deadlines might get fired. People who are fired because they couldn't follow schedules and meet deadlines may have a hard time getting another job.

## What Is a Time Clock?

Most companies want to know when their workers arrive and when they leave work. At some companies, workers keep track of their hours by writing them down on a time sheet. Other companies use a time clock. Each worker has a time card next to the time clock. The card is slipped into a slot in the time clock. The clock prints the time on the card. A worker slips his or her card into the clock at the beginning and the end of each workday. This way, the company has a record of the time a worker began and ended the workday.

## What Are Shifts?

If you work at a place that stays open 24 hours a day, you might work a certain **shift.** A shift is a work period in a company. The morning shift might be 7:00 A.M. to 3:00 P.M. The evening shift might be 3:00 P.M. to 11:00 P.M. The night shift might be 11:00 P.M. to 7:00 A.M. People who work in hospitals, police stations, nursing homes, and factories often work shifts.

**Deadline**
*The latest time when something must be done*

**Shift**
*A work period in a company*

Would you rather work a morning shift or nighttime shift? Explain your answer.

## What to Do When You Can't Get to Work on Time

Each company has its own policy about what to do when you will be late, or when you are ill. Read your employee handbook and ask your supervisor so you know the correct procedure to follow. In both situations, you need to call your supervisor to let him or her know why you will not be at work on time. If you are running late, call before you are expected to be at work. Don't wait until you are already late to make contact. Try to estimate your time of arrival and give your supervisor that information. If you wake up ill, call and talk to your supervisor. Explain that you are sick and won't be at work that day.

Do not wait for your supervisor to call you. It is your responsibility to contact your supervisor when you know you will be late or when you are ill.

## Lesson 2 Review

On a sheet of paper, write the word or words in parentheses that correctly complete each sentence.

1) A person who is punctual is _____. (always late, generally on time, usually fired)

2) Making a _____ helps you manage your time wisely. (telephone directory, television log, personal schedule)

3) A deadline is the latest time _____. (something has to be done, you can report to work, you can take your lunch break)

4) Workers put their time cards into a time clock when they _____. (apply for a job, are ill, begin and end a workday)

5) A supermarket that is open 24 hours a day probably hires workers to work _____. (for 24 straight hours, different shifts, every other day)

## *Coping with Barriers* • • • • • • • • • • • •

**H**ave you ever driven down a road and suddenly discovered that it was blocked off? If so, you probably felt impatient. The roadblock, or barrier, stopped you from moving forward.

Sometimes roadblocks occur in the workplace. They are barriers that stop workers from reaching their goals. But these workplace roadblocks can be overcome. Just like on the highway, you can move around them to keep your career on track.

### What Are Some Workplace Barriers?

Most workers have supervisors who guide their work. Listen to your supervisor and follow his or her instructions. Disagreeing with a supervisor can create a workplace barrier.

As you learn your job, you may think of a better way to complete a task. Some supervisors welcome new ideas. Your supervisor may want to hear yours. Other supervisors think their ideas are best.

Some supervisors welcome new ideas.

● ● ● ● ● ● ● ● ● ●

**Have you ever had to spend time with someone who had a bad attitude? How did you feel being around this person?**

They are not eager to hear suggestions for improvement. Before offering a suggestion, think about your supervisor. Plan how you will share your idea. Be sure to show respect for the supervisor and his or her ideas. Don't act like you know more than your supervisor does.

A bad attitude is another type of workplace barrier. A worker who is constantly grumpy and complaining about work has a bad attitude. A worker who tries to cover mistakes by making excuses or putting blame on coworkers has a bad attitude.

Good workers have positive attitudes. They do not put down the company, its products, or other workers. They do not gossip. Workers with good attitudes are willing to learn new skills. They know these skills will help them do a better job. When they are asked to do something a different way, they don't insist the old way is better. They try the new way.

## What Are Good Communication Skills?

Good workers communicate with others in a healthy way. When people communicate, one person explains a thought, feeling, or idea. Another person listens and understands the message. Listening is an important part of healthy communication. Good listeners encourage others to express themselves. Good listeners look directly at the speaker. They do not interrupt the speaker. When the speaker has finished, they ask questions. They make sure they understand the speaker's message. Workers who are good listeners are usually good communicators.

## Who Can Help You Overcome Workplace Barriers?

Even with good communication skills, it can be hard to get along with some people at work. If you have a problem with a coworker or supervisor, contact the company's **human resources (HR) department.** The human resources department handles employees' work-related issues. HR staff people will help you work out problems with others.

They will also make sure you are being treated fairly. A company must follow laws that protect workers' rights. The HR staff will make sure that you are treated in the manner described by these laws.

## Lesson 3 Review

On a sheet of paper, write the word or words in parentheses that correctly complete each sentence.

**1)** A workplace barrier can _____ you from reaching your goals. (help, prevent, slow)

**2)** A good worker _____. (lets a bad mood affect work, communicates with others in a healthy way, gossips about coworkers)

**3)** An important part of healthy communication is _____. (listening, writing, shouting)

**4)** A company's human resources staff makes sure that workers _____. (start work on time, join a union, are treated fairly)

**5)** By asking a speaker questions, you show that _____. (you are interested in what the speaker said, the speaker didn't send a clear message, you know more than the speaker)

## *Handling Workplace Conflict* • • • • • • • •

> **Resolve**
> *To settle a disagreement*

**M**ost people try to get along with others. They do not look for arguments or conflicts. Yet problems do occur. That is because no two people are exactly alike. They have different ways of doing things. They have different feelings and opinions. Sometimes these differences lead to conflict.

### How Can You Avoid Conflict in the Workplace?

A conflict is a disagreement or an argument. Some conflicts are small. Others can lead to a fight. Any type of conflict can cause problems in the workplace. Try to avoid conflicts whenever you can. Sometimes the best way to deal with conflict is to walk away. Ask yourself: Is the problem really a big deal? Is it worth fighting about? How will I feel if I just forget it? If you can ignore the situation, do so.

After you walk away, think about what happened. Take responsibility for your actions. Note how you may have added to the trouble. Think about what you might have done differently to lessen the conflict.

### How Can Conflicts Be Resolved?

Some conflicts cannot be ignored. They must be resolved. When you **resolve** a conflict, you find a way to settle the disagreement. The solution is acceptable to all people involved. Here are some steps you can follow to resolve conflict:

1. Stay cool. Take a breath or go for a walk. When you feel calm, approach the other person.

Most conflicts can be resolved.

2. Identify the problem. Use good listening skills while the other person speaks. Do not interrupt. When the other person has finished, ask questions to make sure you understand his or her feelings. Then explain how you feel. Be honest and avoid insults.

3. Find out what the other person needs. Determine what he or she would like to have happen. Then say what you need and would like to have happen. Try to use "I" messages.

4. Together with the other person, make a list of possible solutions. Write down everything you think of, even if some of your ideas seem silly. Something that seems silly at first just might end up being the best solution.

5. Look through the list. Circle the ideas that are fair to everyone. Remember that a good solution often involves compromise.

6. Discuss the circled ideas. Try to agree on one that is best. If you reach an agreement, be sure to do what you promise. If you cannot reach an agreement, ask another person for help. For workplace conflicts, this help might come from the HR department.

● ● ● ● ● ● ● ● ● ●
**Think about the last conflict you had with someone. How did your actions contribute to the disagreement?**

## How Do Good Communication Skills Help Resolve Conflict?

You use words to send messages to others. You also send messages with your body through body language. Tapping your fingers, crossing your arms, smiling, and frowning are examples of body language. Each of these actions sends a message to those around you.

Listeners may pay more attention to your body language than to your words. That's because your body language often shows your true feelings. When you talk, you might try to hide your feelings. However, your body language gives them away.

Good communication includes making sure your words and body language match. If they don't, the listener will get a mixed message. For example, frowning while telling a coworker that she did a good job sends a mixed message. The coworker will be confused. She might think you are making fun of her. This can lead to conflict, which is what you want to avoid.

## Do All People Communicate the Same Way?

In the workplace, you will encounter people with different backgrounds and experiences. You may also encounter people from different cultures. Remember that the way people from another country communicate may be very different from what you are used to. In some countries, looking away from a speaker is a way of showing respect. When you speak with someone from another country, try to understand and honor such differences. Failing to do so may lead to conflict.

## Lesson 4 Review

Write the answers to these questions on a sheet of paper, using complete sentences.

1) How can you avoid a conflict about something that is not very important to you?

2) What are two steps you can follow to resolve a conflict?

3) What is body language? Give two examples.

4) What should you think about when speaking with a person from another country?

5) As a coworker tells you that "you look great," she frowns and crosses her arms over her chest. What message do you receive?

## *Building Work Relationships*  ● ● ● ● ● ● ● ●

**O**nce you have a job, you need to be a good employee. You must be responsible, follow instructions, and do your best. Doing your best means getting along with others and learning new skills. It also means being an active, contributing member of a team.

### How Can You Build a Positive Relationship with Your Supervisor?

Most workers report to a supervisor who guides their work. Your supervisor expects you to be a responsible worker. Responsible workers come to work on time every day. They try to find better ways to do their jobs. They do not take long breaks, make personal phone calls, or waste company time in other ways.

Responsible workers are willing to do extra work to get the job done. They will do extra tasks that are not part of their job. Most important, they do what they promise. This is important to a supervisor. Honoring your promises shows that you are dependable. It also builds trust between you and your supervisor.

Develop a positive relationship with your supervisor.

## How Can You Build Positive Relationships with Coworkers?

You may like some coworkers better than others. Still, you must try to get along with everyone. Good communication skills can help. Good communicators are able to share their ideas and opinions without annoying others. They are also good listeners. They listen to other people the way they want others to listen to them. This is part of what is sometimes called the Golden Rule. Treat others the way that you want to be treated. This is a good rule not only for communicating, but also for living. Work to understand what is being said and what people are feeling. When you know what others think and care about, it is easier to get along with them.

●　●　●　●　●　●　●　●　●　●

**Did you ever deal with negative peer pressure? What did the person or people want you to do?**

## What Is Peer Pressure?

Your coworkers may pressure you, or strongly encourage you, to do things. These demands are **peer pressure.** Peer pressure is positive when the activities suggested are healthy or helpful. An example of positive peer pressure is a coworker urging you to take brisk walks with her at lunchtime.

Some of your coworkers might pressure you in negative ways. Negative peer pressure is being urged to do something harmful, unsafe, or against the law. You might face negative peer pressure from a coworker who encourages you to leave work early or take very long breaks. Giving in to this negative peer pressure can lead to problems—even losing your job.

## How Do You Deal with Negative Peer Pressure?

You can learn to identify negative peer pressure. When a coworker suggests an activity, ask yourself if the activity goes against your beliefs. Ask if the activity makes you feel uncomfortable. Decide if the activity could be dangerous for you or someone else. If the answer to any of these questions is "yes," the peer pressure is negative.

You need to say "no" calmly and confidently. Don't anger or embarrass the person asking. Simply look the person in the eye. Use a firm voice to show that you have made up your mind. Don't bother giving the person a long explanation. Explaining your reasons may start an argument. Just say "no" and walk away. You might risk a friendship, but you will be true to yourself and your feelings.

Don't use your sick days as vacation days. Use sick days only when you really are ill.

## What Does It Take to Be a Good Team Member?

Any group that works together forms a team. A family is a team. You and your coworkers are a team. Certain qualities will make you a valuable member of your work team.

Team members listen to one another. They respect each other's opinions. Team members realize that each person on the team has different ideas and skills. They use these differences to get a job done. Each member contributes by doing a task that he or she does well. Dividing the work this way helps the team complete a task with little stress.

Team members recognize that each person on the team has different ideas and skills.

Team members depend on each other. They trust one another. If one member does not do his or her job, the entire team suffers. Being a good team member means doing your share of the work to the best of your ability. Taking pride in your part of the job helps your team be successful.

## Lesson 5 Review

On a sheet of paper, write the word or words in parentheses that correctly complete each sentence.

**1)** A responsible worker _____. (takes long breaks, makes personal telephone calls, is on time for work)

**2)** Honoring your promises shows a supervisor that you _____. (are dependable, like your job, want to be a leader)

**3)** Peer pressure is negative when the activities suggested are _____. (harmful, helpful, healthy)

**4)** An example of a team is a _____. (supervisor, family, worker)

**5)** If one member of a team doesn't finish his or her job, the entire team _____. (is successful, works harder, suffers)

## *Dealing with Discrimination and Harassment* • • • • • • • • • • • • • •

**H**ave you ever been singled out or treated differently than others? If so, you probably did not like the experience. It may have left you feeling angry or hurt. You might have felt as if you were being picked on. Everyone wants to be treated fairly. Unfortunately, not everyone is.

### What Is Discrimination?

Sometimes discrimination occurs in the workplace. When this happens, a person is treated differently because of something other than his or her individual worth. Some people are discriminated against because of their gender. Others are discriminated against because of their race, religion, or age. The law forbids discrimination in the workplace.

A good worker behaves professionally and keeps comments to coworkers businesslike.

# What Is Harassment?

Another unjust practice that sometimes happens in the workplace is **harassment.** Harassment is repeatedly bothering or annoying a person at work. It also means saying or doing things to make a coworker uneasy or unhappy. Because of the harassment, the worker does not feel comfortable in the workplace. The worker becomes anxious or worried. This prevents the worker from doing his or her job properly.

## How Do You Handle Discrimination or Harassment?

Often, the first step in stopping harassment is to politely but firmly ask the harasser to stop. Unfortunately, that does not always work. Every company has a policy on discrimination and harassment. If you feel you are being discriminated against or harassed, get a copy of your company's policy on these problems. It is often included in the employee handbook. If you do not have an employee handbook, ask the HR department for the policy.

Once you have a copy of the policy, read it carefully. It will explain how to report the problem. Follow the steps described in the proper order. If you are unsure of something, make an appointment with someone in the HR department. Explain your situation and ask questions. The HR worker will guide you.

Remember that you have a right to be treated fairly at work. Don't let anyone take this right away from you. Speak up for yourself. The law is on your side, and so is your company.

**What are some behaviors that are not suited for the workplace?**

## Lesson 6 Review

On a sheet of paper, write the word or words in parentheses that correctly complete each sentence.

**1)** Harassment makes a worker feel _____ in the workplace. (comfortable, successful, uncomfortable)

**2)** You can get a copy of your company's discrimination and harassment policy from _____. (your supervisor, the person who hired you, the human resources department)

**3)** Fair treatment in the workplace is every worker's _____. (opinion, wish, right)

**4)** When at work, you should behave _____. (in a businesslike manner, like you are with family members, as if you are talking with friends)

**5)** Not promoting a worker because of his or her age is an example of _____. (harassment, discrimination, peer pressure)

## Current Day

### Harassment in Today's Workplace

Today, harassment is a much broader issue than it was in the past. Harassment can take many forms. Repeated comments about a coworker's appearance may be seen as harassment. Constantly telling jokes about ethnic groups can be called harassment. You may touch a coworker in what you think is a casual manner. However, if the person you touch feels uncomfortable about it, the touch may be considered harassment.

Sometimes such actions are innocent. Sometimes they are not. A good worker avoids any kind of behavior that might be questionable. Keep your comments to coworkers businesslike. Don't behave as informally as you would if you were out with friends. Otherwise, you might say or do something that sends a negative message. Remember that you are at work to work. Always behave professionally.

## *Setting Career Goals* • • • • • • • • • • • •

O nce you have a job, it is time to look ahead. It is time to think about a career, or the profession you choose to do to earn a living. Successful careers do not happen by accident. They are the result of planning and work.

### What Are Career Goals?

What was the first job you ever had? If you are like many workers, it probably was part-time work. It may not have been doing something you really enjoyed. You took the job just as a way to earn money.

At some point, you will want to get a better job. You will want to find a job that lets you do something that you enjoy. You will want to find a job that is more rewarding and pays more money. To find such a job, you will want to set a career goal. Setting a career goal gives you something to aim for. It can help you make the most of your abilities.

### How Do You Set Career Goals?

You are a unique person. You do certain things well and have certain interests. You are skilled in some ways. Think about your special traits. Then think of a career that will use these

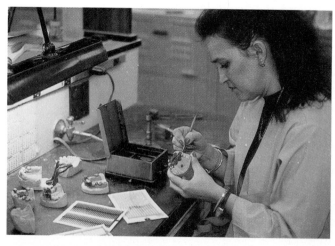

Set a realistic career goal.

traits. This will help you find a job that interests you. Also think about what you want from a job. Don't limit yourself to what you want right now. Think about what you might want in the future. For example, you might want to have your own business. You know that you are skilled at working on cars. Your career goal might be to own a car repair shop.

## What Are Realistic Goals?

A career goal needs to be realistic. Many people would like to become famous actors or athletes. However, only a few people have the skills necessary to reach those goals. They are not realistic goals for most people. A good career goal is one with a good chance of being reached.

A career goal should also be specific. It should describe exactly what you want to do and when you want to do it. *Working in Florida within two years* is not a specific career goal. It does not identify the type of job you want. A better career goal would be *Working as a lab technician in Florida within two years.*

## What Is a Career Plan?

After you choose a specific and realistic career goal, you need a **career plan.** A career plan is a step-by-step way to reach your goal.

**Career plan**
*A step-by-step way to reach your career goals*

• • • • • • • • • •
**What is your career goal?**

Creating and following a career plan helps you reach your career goals.

The following steps can help you make a career plan.

1. Write down your career goal. Write down your current job. Is it in the right field for your career goal? Writing it down helps you keep a record of your progress.

2. List the steps needed to reach your goal. You might need to find a job in your chosen field to get some experience. You might need to take some classes.

3. Set up a time line for completing each step. Decide how long each step should take. Some steps might take years.

4. Note any potential obstacles that might slow you down. Then list some ways you could overcome the obstacles.

5. Check your progress as you work toward your goal. Make changes in the plan when needed. A career plan is flexible.

Maintain contact with your rehabilitation counselor.

## Maintaining Communication with Rehabilitation Services

Many students with disabilities have an assigned rehabilitation counselor when they exit high school. A student will want to maintain contact with this counselor for the purposes of career planning, job seeking, and retaining employment. Keeping in contact is also important for a student who continues with postsecondary education at a two- or four-year institution. If a student moves to another county or state, the student may have the file transferred to continue services.

A student's high school might not set up services before the student leaves high school. The student can do this independently or with family assistance. Rehabilitation services help individuals who are blind, physically impaired, learning disabled, or have other disabilities. Rehabilitation services have specific criteria to determine who qualifies for these lifetime services. Even if an individual is diagnosed with a disability, he or she is not guaranteed the services. Ongoing communication between the individual and rehabilitation services is critical. Contact the county office or the state's Department of Economic Security for more information.

## What Else Can You Do to Further Your Career?

Making and following a career plan helps you reach your career goals. Another way to reach your goals is to always make the most of any job you have. Even if the job is not part of your career plan, try to be a responsible worker. This will help you earn your employer's trust.

Show your employer that you can be counted on to do a good job. Always be on time. Try to do a little more than what is required. Be flexible and willing to try new things. Your employer will notice and appreciate these actions.

## Lesson 7 Review

On a sheet of paper, write the word or words in parentheses that correctly complete each sentence.

**1)** The profession a person chooses to do to earn a living is a
_____. (skill, job, career)

**2)** A realistic career goal is _____. (impossible to reach, likely to be achieved, the same for all people)

**3)** A specific career goal states what you want to do and
_____. (when you want to do it, the tools you need, who to ask for help)

**4)** A career plan is a step-by-step way to meet your
_____. (new boss, coworkers, career goals)

**5)** An example of an unrealistic career goal is wanting to
become _____. (a nursery school teacher in your hometown, the highest-paid professional football player, a computer programmer)

# *Requesting Performance Assessment* ● ● ●

**Performance assessment**
*A report that rates how well you do your job*

A child in grade school gets a report card. The report card rates the youngster in different areas. It identifies things the child does well. It also notes areas where the child needs to improve.

Reports on an individual's progress are not limited to schools. Most companies give workers a type of report card, too.

## What Is a Performance Assessment?

After you have worked for several months, your supervisor may give you a **performance assessment.** A performance assessment, or review, is a report that rates how well you do your job. It is much like a school report card.

Most performance assessments have a rating scale. Your supervisor gives you a score for different work tasks. A certain score shows that you do a task very well. Another score shows that you need to do a task better.

A performance assessment rates how well you do your job.

Your supervisor will meet with you and go over the performance review. He or she will explain the rating scale. Then your supervisor will describe what you are doing right and what you need to improve.

Listen carefully to your supervisor during this meeting. Note the areas in which your supervisor wants you to improve. Try not to argue or give excuses. Show that you are eager and willing to be a better worker. If you do not understand something, politely ask questions. This indicates to your supervisor that you are serious about your job.

At the end of your meeting, you will probably be asked to sign the review. This shows that you met with your supervisor and discussed the report. Never sign the paper without reading it first. Be sure that you understand everything it contains. The document is important. A copy of it will be placed in your work file. Make sure you get a copy, too.

Keep important work-related documents, such as copies of your performance assessments, in one work folder at home.

**PERFORMANCE REVIEW**

**SELF REVIEW:** The performance review process is composed of three parts: self review, manager's review and the review discussion. In the manager's review you are asked to evaluate the job performances of each of the people who report directly to you. Below are 8 to 12 job components that are important to success in the job responsibilities for this position.

REVIEW PERIOD:   FROM  January 2000   TO  January 2001

DATE REVIEW HELD:   January 5, 2001

Audrey Coopers                    PROJECT MANAGER          MARKETING
name                              position                 division

**2000 GOALS:** List the top 2 goals or achievements for 2000. Comment on achievement of each goal.

1. LITERATURE BOOK MANAGEMENT
– Facilitate profitability of the books.
– Take over conversion of printed books to the Internet.

2. ADVERTISER BONUS
– Successfully transitioned sections to client services and editorial.

**PERFORMANCE RATING FACTORS:** Evaluate the individual's performance in each category below and circle the appropriate rating. Ratings and comments need to focus on how each factor translates into observed behaviors in getting the job done. Comments and ratings must relate directly to your performance of job responsibilities or accomplishment of annual goals. Comments must provide specific examples and, as appropriate, emphasize strengths or areas needing improvement.

EXCEPTIONAL:     Excels in all aspects of job component on a sustained basis. Very high expertise. Model of excellence and coach for others.

COMMENDABLE:   Performance consistently exceeds criteria and standards needed to achieve goals.

EFFECTIVE:       Performance meets standards for almost all aspects of job component. Work is steady, reliable and requires minimal supervision. Consistently reaches goals.

NEEDS            Usually meets job requirements, but occasionally performance falls below minimum
IMPROVEMENT:     standard. Applies to people in new jobs, or those needing to brush up on skills or learn new ones.

UNACCEPTABLE:   Performance falls below minimum requirements.

1. **JOB & MARKET KNOWLEDGE:** Clear understanding of how marketing relates to sales, production, circulation and editorial. Understands positioning of booklets. Understands products promoted and industries served. Requires minimal supervision. Uses resources effectively. Sets deadlines and ensures all components are completed on time.

Unacceptable     Needs Improvement     Effective     Commendable     Exceptional

A performance assessment

What type of body language would you use when asking a supervisor for a performance assessment?

## How Often Do Performance Assessments Occur?

Each company has its own policy on performance assessments. Some companies rate new employees after three or six months. Other companies have yearly performance assessments for all employees. Most employee handbooks have information about the company's policy. Read this section carefully. It will describe how often a worker is assessed and who does the rating. The handbook might also include a copy of the rating form.

## What If Your Supervisor Does Not Review Your Work?

Sometimes a supervisor forgets to review a worker. If this happens, ask your supervisor for a performance assessment. Let your supervisor know that you realize he or she has a busy schedule. Explain that a performance assessment will help you improve your work skills and tell you what you need to do better. If your supervisor does not conduct the review, go to human resources. Ask a worker in that department to help you.

## Lesson 8 Review

Write the answers to these questions on a sheet of paper, using complete sentences.

1) What is a performance assessment?

2) What type of information is contained in a performance assessment?

3) How can you find out about your company's policy on performance assessments?

4) What should you do if you do not receive a performance assessment after working for a year?

5) Suppose your supervisor asks you to sign your performance assessment without giving you a chance to read it first. What should you do?

## Lesson 9

# Requesting Additional Education and Training • • • • • • • • •

If you were to look at a photograph of yourself taken five years ago, what would you see? You would probably see a person who looks quite different from the way you are today. You have changed physically in the last five years. You have changed inside, too. You are wiser and can do different things. Change is one thing you can count on. Nothing ever stays the same—not even your job.

## Why Should You Learn New Skills?

Your job can change over time just as you do. New tools are created. Improved ways of doing a task are identified. The skills that you need to do your job today may be different from those you will need in five years.

Take steps to make sure that your skills change as your job changes. If you don't, a day may come when you can no longer do your job well.

## How Can You Learn New Skills?

There are many ways to learn new skills. Some companies offer courses at work. The courses are designed to help workers develop skills the company feels are important. For example, the company might offer a computer course because some workers will be using computers to do their jobs. Or a customer service seminar to teach workers how to provide quality service to customers.

Your community may offer courses, too. Night courses for members of the community are often held at local schools. Some courses can help you develop a hobby such as photography or sewing. Other courses help you brush up on skills you haven't used much such as geometry or typing.

Some courses can help you master life skills such as making a personal budget or improving your reading skills. Other courses can help you develop new workplace skills such as supervising others or writing a marketing plan. You can learn more about courses offered in your community by calling your city hall, library, or a local school.

You can also learn new skills right in the workplace. This form of learning is called on-the-job training. A coworker or supervisor becomes your teacher. He or she shows you how to do something new. You learn how to do tasks that may or may not be part of your regular job. On-the-job training is a great way to learn new things. You get to try the new task and the person training you is right there to answer your questions.

Learning new skills that you can use to help your company grow makes you a valuable worker. It also shows your supervisor that you are willing to learn and take on new challenges. And it helps you grow as a person. You add another skill to the list of skills you already have.

On-the-job training helps workers learn new skills right in the workplace.

## Lesson 9 Review

Write the answers to these questions on a sheet of paper, using complete sentences.

**1)** Why is it important to keep learning new skills?

**2)** Why do some companies offer courses in the workplace?

**3)** Suppose you work in a company that does not offer courses for its workers. Where can you take courses?

**4)** What is on-the-job training?

**5)** Suppose your supervisor asks you to come in on your day off for some on-the-job training. You will not be paid for this time, however. What would you do?

## Technology In Our Lives

### Taking Courses Online

Do you think it is possible to take a college course without ever leaving your home? It is if you have a home computer and access to the Internet. Many colleges offer courses online. Students log on to a site and get information from an instructor. Some sites allow the students to interact with one another—just like in a chat room. Teachers and students can have online conversations, too.

Colleges are not the only places that offer online instruction. There are companies and institutes that offer a wide variety of courses, too. Many of the courses are designed to develop skills for the workplace.

In order to take an online course, you must register with the place offering it. You also will have to pay a fee. But if the course helps you gain skills that get you a better job, that money is well spent.

## Lesson 10

### *Obtaining a Raise or Promotion* ● ● ● ● ●

> **Promotion**
> *A new job with more responsibility and more pay*

S tudents who do their schoolwork well receive an A. Insurance companies charge good drivers lower insurance rates. Volunteers who donate time to the community might be rewarded with a note of appreciation. People who do their jobs well are often given some kind of recognition. They receive raises and promotions.

### How Can You Earn a Raise or Promotion?

When you are hired for a job, you are told how much money you will be paid. Some workers are paid a wage, or a certain amount of money, for each hour they work. The more hours they work, the more money they earn. Other workers are paid a salary, or a certain amount each week, no matter how many hours they work.

Always do your best to leave a job on good terms. Future employers might call the company to check on your work habits and ability to be part of a team.

The longer you work, the more valuable you are to the company. You become more independent and can do your job without being supervised. You become more skilled at the job. Most companies show appreciation for such improvements. One sign of appreciation is a raise, or an increase in pay. The amount of a raise is based on different things. Some raises are determined by the worker's performance assessment. The more improvement the assessment shows, the higher the raise. Other raises are a percentage of the worker's salary. A company might decide to reward all its workers with a 4 percent raise. So, each worker's salary is increased by 4 percent.

A company may recognize a good employee with a **promotion.** A promotion is a new job with more responsibility and more pay. Promotions are sometimes determined by a worker's performance assessment.

Sometimes a promotion is given when an opening comes up in the company. For example, a supervisor might take another job elsewhere. This creates an opening in the company. Company officials might offer the job to the most responsible worker who had reported to the supervisor. Or they could give the job to the worker with the best performance assessment.

Many companies have a schedule for giving workers raises and promotions. Your employee handbook contains this information. You can also ask someone in the HR department about the company's raise and promotion policies.

## Can You Ask for a Raise or Promotion?

If you think you deserve a raise or promotion, meet with your supervisor. Explain why you think you deserve the raise or the promotion. Focus on specific things you have done that prove you are a responsible worker. Communicate clearly and be confident. By asking for the meeting, you show that you believe in yourself and your skills. Accept your supervisor's decision. Don't argue if you are turned down. Ask your supervisor for suggestions on what you need to do to get the raise or the promotion in the future.

● ● ● ● ● ● ● ● ● ● ●
**Why is it important to do the best job possible beginning on your first day at work?**

## Lesson 10 Review

Write the answers to these questions on a sheet of paper, using complete sentences.

**1)** What are two ways that a worker's salary is determined?

**2)** What is a promotion?

**3)** How can a good performance assessment lead to a raise or promotion?

**4)** How can a worker find out about the company policy on raises and promotions?

**5)** Suppose your supervisor tells you that the company has decided to give each worker a 5 percent raise. What does that mean?

## Coping with a Layoff • • • • • • • • • • • • •

Have you ever had an outdoor event halted suddenly by a rainstorm? If so, you know that things don't always go as planned. That's true of the workplace, too. Every once in awhile, something can occur to interrupt your career plan.

### What Is a Layoff?

At some point, through no fault of your own, you may lose your job. You might be working hard and doing everything right. But you and your coworkers could be out of work because of a **layoff.** A layoff is when a company has no work for certain employees for a period of time. Some layoffs last a few months. Some layoffs are permanent.

• • • • • • • • • •

**Do you know anyone who has experienced a layoff? How did being out of work affect the person?**

Layoffs occur for many reasons. Suppose a company decides to move from Chicago to Atlanta. The company lays off all the workers in Chicago. New workers are hired in Atlanta. Perhaps a product that the company makes isn't selling well. The company decides to stop making the product. It lays off all the workers in the department that makes the item. It may even shut down an entire plant. Every worker in the plant is out of a job.

If you lose your job because of a layoff, you may feel upset or angry. You were a responsible worker. You did everything your supervisor asked, yet you still lost your job. It doesn't seem fair.

Keep your resume up to date so it is ready when you need it.

You may also feel as if you were to blame for being laid off, but you shouldn't. The layoff was not your fault. It has nothing to do with your ability to do your job. A layoff is simply one of those things that happen in life.

You can do some things to help you get through a layoff. First, don't feel guilty. Keep telling yourself that losing your job wasn't your fault. Second, think of your past job as a learning experience. It helped you develop new skills and provided you with work experience. Your skills and knowledge will help you find a new job.

**Unemployment benefits**
*Money and services that are available to unemployed workers seeking new jobs*

## How Do You Find Another Job?

If the layoff is permanent, you need to find a new job. Begin by updating your resume to include your previous job. Be sure to note that you no longer work at the job because of a company layoff.

Some companies that have layoffs help workers find new jobs. Check to see if your company offers this service. Another way to find a new job is through an unemployment office in your state. Usually these offices have listings of jobs available locally. You may also be entitled to receive state **unemployment benefits.** Unemployment benefits are money and services that are available to unemployed workers while they seek new jobs.

While looking for a new job, you might do temporary work. Temporary workers fill in for regular workers who are sick or on vacation. They also fill positions that have become available within a company. Temporary work is a good way to get more work experience. It also is a way of showing a company that you are a good worker. Sometimes a company will offer a temporary worker a full-time job.

The best time to look for a job is when you still have one. If you think a layoff might be coming, start looking for a new job. When you respond to an ad, note that you are job hunting because your company might have a layoff.

## Lesson 11 Review

Write the answers to these questions on a sheet of paper, using complete sentences.

**1)** What is a layoff?

**2)** What are some reasons for a layoff?

**3)** Is it a worker's fault that he or she loses a job because of a layoff? Explain your answer.

**4)** How can a worker find a new job after a layoff?

**5)** Why is it important to do your best when working as a temporary worker?

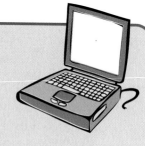

### Online Resources

**America's Job Bank**
**U.S. Department of Labor and the Public Employment Service**

*www.ajb.org/seeker*

A state-operated program that matches employers and job seekers.

**Don't Work in the Dark! Campaign**
**U.S. Department of Labor**

*www.dol.gov/dol/wb/public/NRICDWID.htm*

Part of a public education campaign to inform working women of their rights in the workplace.

**U.S. Department of Education**
**Office of Special Education and Rehabilitative Services**

*www.ed.gov/offices/OSERS*

Information about programs for children, youth, and adults with disabilities.

# Chapter 11 Summary

● ● ● ● ● ● ● ● ● ● ● ● ● ● ● ● ● ● ●

■ Your first day in a new job can be both exciting and scary. Try to stay calm and be confident. Remember that you were chosen for the job.

■ An employee handbook contains valuable information about the company's work policies. Read through it carefully. Be sure to keep it where you can easily find it.

■ Responsible workers come to work on time. They work hard and look for ways to do their jobs better.

■ Good communication skills help build positive relationships with coworkers and supervisors.

■ Follow your beliefs and feelings. Don't give in to negative peer pressure. When a coworker strongly urges you to do something you feel is wrong, simply say no.

■ Every worker has certain rights. These rights are protected by the law. If you feel that your rights have been denied, seek help from the company's HR department.

■ Develop a career plan that identifies your career goals and how and when you will reach them.

■ Learn from your performance assessment. Note your supervisor's suggestions for improving your work. Take steps to follow these suggestions.

■ Improve your workplace skills. Take courses and get on-the-job training to help you do your current job better. This can also prepare you for better jobs.

■ Don't feel guilty if your company has a layoff. Think about the skills and experience you gained from the job. Use them to find a new position.

## Comprehension: Identifying Facts

On a sheet of paper, write the correct word or words from the Word Bank to complete each sentence.

> **WORD BANK**
>
> career
> career goal
> career plan
> communicate
> deadline
>
> employee
>   handbook
> human resources
> layoff
> peer pressure
>
> performance
>   assessment
> promotion
> shift

1) A company has a _____ when it lacks work for some of its workers.

2) If you work in a company that is open 24 hours a day, you might work the 11:00 P.M. to 7:00 A.M. _____ .

3) The work a person does throughout his or her life to earn a living is the person's _____.

4) When you receive a _____, you get a new job with more responsibility and more pay.

5) An _____ contains information about a company and its policies.

6) A _____ is the latest time something can be done.

7) When coworkers strongly urge you to do something, they use _____ to get you to act a certain way.

8) A _____ is a step-by-step way to meet your career goals.

**Test-Taking Tip**

Take time to organize your thoughts before writing answers to short-answer questions.

9) When you share thoughts, feelings, and ideas with others, you _____.

10) The type of work you would like to be doing several years from now is your _____.

11) A report that rates how well you do your job is a _____.

12) You can turn to _____ for help if a coworker is harassing you.

## Comprehension: Understanding Main Ideas

On a sheet of paper, write the answers to the following questions using complete sentences.

13) What are traits of a realistic career goal?

14) How are a career goal and a career plan related?

15) What are two kinds of workplace barriers?

16) What are some positive steps you can take if you are laid off?

17) What are three steps you can take to resolve conflict?

18) How are a performance assessment and a raise related?

## Critical Thinking: Write Your Opinion

On a sheet of paper, write the answers to the following questions using complete sentences.

19) Whenever a certain coworker sees you, he makes a comment about your appearance and winks. His behavior is beginning to make you feel uncomfortable. What can you do to solve the problem?

20) What type of body language would you use when asking a supervisor for a raise?

## Self-Assessment

Can you answer the following questions?

☑ What do you need to consider when selecting a postsecondary setting?

☑ What are two kinds of postsecondary schools?

☑ What is the average cost of tuition for one year of college?

☑ What are four things you might want to do during a college visit?

☑ What kinds of services are available in many colleges to students with learning disabilities?

☑ What are five study strategies?

☑ What are three kinds of financial aid?

☑ What is financial aid and how do you apply for it?

☑ Why would you want to meet with an admissions officer at schools you are interested in?

☑ What are three things schools typically look for in a student's enrollment application?

# The Educational Setting

**W**here do you see yourself in a year? In two years? In four years? Do your plans for the future include a degree from a postsecondary school such as college? If not, maybe they should. A college education does not guarantee happiness in life. But it does provide you with many more opportunities than if you did not go to college. In college, you learn the skills and gain the knowledge necessary to obtain jobs that interest you and pay well. You also meet new people and learn more about yourself.

Maybe you think your high school grades are not good enough to get you into college. Or maybe you think college is too expensive. The truth is that if you want to go to college, you probably can. In this chapter, you will learn how to find the college that is right for you. You will learn how to apply to colleges and how to get financial aid. You will also learn study skills that will help you be successful in any educational setting.

## Goals for Learning

▶ To use library resources to gather information about colleges

▶ To know what questions to ask before choosing a college

▶ To describe the types of special services available at colleges

▶ To use study techniques that will be helpful in college

▶ To explain ways to obtain financial aid for college

# Selecting a Postsecondary Setting ● ● ● ● ●

**Postsecondary education**
*Any type of formal education after you graduate from high school*

**H**igh school is referred to as secondary education. Any type of formal education after you graduate from high school is called **postsecondary education.** For most people, postsecondary education means college. Whether you are a freshman in high school or completing your high school diploma, now is a good time to start thinking about college.

## What Are Some Different Kinds of Colleges?

Postsecondary education includes military training and apprenticeships. However, most types of postsecondary education involve college. There are about 3,500 colleges in the United States. About 1,900 of them offer four-year bachelor's degrees. Many of the others offer two-year associate degrees. The chart on the next page compares different kinds of postsecondary school programs.

Spend time researching postsecondary schools to find one that is right for you.

Types of postsecondary programs

| | Technical College/ Vocational School | Community College/ Junior College | Four-Year College/ Liberal Arts | University |
|---|---|---|---|---|
| Focus of Program | Specialized training for particular occupation | Two-year degree in career area or academic course credit that transfers to a four-year college | Four-year degree; general academic courses plus focus on major | Four-year degree plus graduate programs |
| Length of Program | Nine months to two years | Two years | Four years or more | Four years or more |
| Admissions Requirements | Public—usually open enrollment Private—high school diploma; may be other requirements | Public—usually open enrollment to high school graduates Private—high school diploma, GPA, SAT or ACT; may be other requirements | GPA, class rank, SAT or ACT; essay, interview; may be other requirements | GPA, class rank, SAT or ACT; essay, interview; may be other requirements |
| High School Coursework Recommended | Basic skills in math, science, English, and computers Higher levels in some programs Courses in program area helpful | English—four years Math—four years Science—three years Social Studies— three years Arts—two years Computer Science— one year Foreign Language— two years Study Skills | English—four years Math—four years Science—three years Social Studies— three years Arts—two years Computer Science— one year Foreign Language— two years Study Skills | English—four years Math—four years Science—three years Social Studies— three years Arts—two years Computer Science— one year Foreign Language— two years Study Skills |
| Approximate Tuition (for state residents) | Public—$1,000 to $2,200 Private—$2,300 to $10,000 | Public—$1,200 to $1,800 Private—$2,000 to $10,000 | Public—$2,500 to $5,500 Private—$4,000 to $22,000 | Public—$2,500 to $5,500 Private—$4,000 to $22,000 |

Other sources of training include apprenticeships, on-the-job training, and military training.

## What Are Some Sources of College Information?

How do you begin your search for a college? You will find that many sources of information are available.

### *Directories*

You might begin your search by looking through a college directory. Several college directories exist. They contain information about all the colleges in the United States. Here you can learn a college's size, location, admission requirements, majors, and much more. *The College Handbook* and *Peterson's Guide to Four-Year Colleges* are the most popular college directories. You can find them in high school counseling offices and libraries.

Why would it be helpful to know your family's income before meeting with someone in the financial aid office?

### *Internet*

Information about many colleges is accessible, or available, on the Internet. You can call each college you are interested in to get its Web site address.

### *Brochures*

If you are a junior or senior in high school, you have probably been receiving college brochures in the mail. These brochures are a nice introduction to the colleges. However, remember that they are a form of advertisement. They try to present the schools in the best light.

### *Counselors and Teachers*

Seek advice from high school counselors and teachers. If they know you, they may be able to point you in the direction of colleges where you will be successful.

# What Should You Know About a College?

The following list of questions shows some of the things you should know about a school before choosing it. Some of these questions you must ask other people. Here are some questions you must ask:

1. Does the college offer a degree in my field of interest?

2. Where is the school? Do I want to go to college while living at home? Do I want to be in a small town or a large city?

3. How large is the college? Do I want to go to a small school or a large one with more than 20,000 students?

4. How expensive is the college?

5. Can I get in? Is my GPA in high school high enough to meet the school's standards? Are my ACT or SAT scores high enough? Do I have a job and do volunteer work, which shows school admissions officers that I am a responsible and caring person?

6. Can I get a degree in two or four years? Can the school guarantee that all the courses I need for my degree will be available throughout the two or four years? If not, might I have to stay an extra year, and pay more tuition?

7. How will the class schedule fit in with my work schedule? What if I go to school part time and work full time? Can I take classes in the evening and on weekends?

8. How safe is the campus? (Ask to see the college's crime statistics and security measures. If you can, ask students how safe they feel on campus.)

9. What is campus life like? What kinds of clubs and extracurricular activities are available?

10. Can I get along with the students? Do my personality and values match fairly well with those of the students in general?

> ## Things to Do on a College Visit
>
> - Meet with an admissions officer.
> - Meet with a financial aid officer.
> - Meet with a learning disability (LD) specialist or other special services personnel if appropriate.
> - Tour the campus.
> - Talk with students.
> - Stay overnight in a dorm.
> - Sit in on classes that interest you.
> - Talk with a professor.
> - Visit the bookstore and look at textbooks.

## What Is the Next Step?

When you have whittled down your choices to a handful of schools, the next step is to check them out in person. Visit the colleges you have chosen to find out what they are really like. A college visit is like test-driving a car before you buy it.

Start planning your college visit by calling the admissions office of the college. Ask to speak to an admissions officer, and tell the officer you would like to visit the campus. Make an appointment to meet with the officer when you visit. See if the admissions officer can arrange to have you spend the night in a dorm. That will give you a more realistic idea of how students live.

After calling the admissions officer, call the financial aid office and make an appointment with a financial aid officer. Talking with a financial aid officer will give you an idea of how much financial aid you may qualify for.

Be sure to spend time talking with students. They will likely be open about their opinions of the school. If you are leaning toward a certain field of study, talk to students in that field. Ask the admissions office to help you arrange to meet students in your field during your campus visit.

## What Will an Admissions Officer Ask?

Most colleges do not require an interview with an admissions officer. But it helps to have one. You can get many of your questions answered during the interview. It is a chance to leave a good impression with the person or one of the people who will review your application.

Below are some questions typically asked in a college interview. Plan what you will say in response to these questions and practice your answers out loud. But don't try to memorize them. Remember that the interview is a conversation, not a rehearsed play.

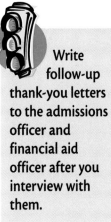

Write follow-up thank-you letters to the admissions officer and financial aid officer after you interview with them.

- Why do you want to go to college?
- What are your career goals?
- What do you hope to major in?
- Why are you interested in this school?
- Why should this school accept you?
- What were your favorite courses in high school?

### Tips for a College Interview

- Bring a pad and pen to take notes during the interview.
- Bring a list of questions to ask. You might want to include some of those listed earlier in the lesson.
- Be pleasant and smile.
- Look at the admissions officer when talking.
- Speak clearly and intelligently. Don't use "like" and "you know" in every sentence if you tend to use these words a lot.
- Do not chew gum.
- Answer questions in complete sentences. Try not to give one-word responses.
- Dress casually, but not in jeans or shorts.
- Be honest, even if you think the truth sounds bad.

- What extracurricular activities have you participated in?

- What are your hobbies and talents?

- What jobs have you had?

- Do you plan to work while going to college?

## Lesson 1 Review

Write the answers to these questions on a sheet of paper, using complete sentences.

**1)** What are three things you might want to do during a college visit?

**2)** How is a community college different from a university? How are they the same?

**3)** What are four sources for information about colleges?

**4)** Why is a college interview important?

**5)** What are four things that are most important for you to consider when choosing a college?

## Technology In Our Lives

### Computer Software for Gathering College Information

Some software programs will allow you to create lists of schools that meet characteristics that you set. For example, you may ask for a list of colleges that are within 100 miles of your home, have fewer than 5,000 students, and offer a degree in business.

These software programs are expensive—about $400. However, your high school or public library may have them.

## Lesson 2 | *Completing the Enrollment Process* ● ● ● ●

**Y**ou have investigated many schools and visited the ones you can. Now it is time to narrow the choices. You might end up with four or five schools that you would feel comfortable attending. You think you would be successful at any of them. They would help you grow as a person. The next step is to apply to them.

### How Do You Apply to Postsecondary Schools?

When you visit a school, you can pick up an application form. Or you can write a letter to the admissions office to request a form. The deadline to fill out and send in the application will be noted on the application form. Most deadlines are in January or February for classes beginning the following September. It is wise to send in your application a few weeks before the deadline. That way you can be sure that the classes won't fill up before your application is considered.

Complete the college application form and send it in a few weeks before the deadline.

Many colleges accept an application called the **Common Application.** This is an eight-page form that many colleges use as their official application form. Find out if the schools you are applying to accept this form. If they do, you have to fill it out only once. Then you can copy it for every school you apply to.

Most of the application will take about an hour to fill out. You can ask a parent, counselor, or teacher to help you. Parts of the application need to be filled out by a counselor and a teacher.

## What Do Colleges Look for on an Application?

One of the most important parts of an application is your **transcript.** This is a record of the courses you took in high school and the grades you earned. Your transcript is attached to the part of the application your counselor fills out.

Of course, the better your grades, the better your chances of being accepted by the college. However, schools like to see improving grades. So if you start poorly as a high school freshman, you can help yourself by improving steadily.

Scores that you received on standardized tests (ACT or SAT) are part of the application. These scores are not as important as your high school grades. Many admissions officers know that some people simply do not do well on tests.

Part of the application asks you to list activities that you have participated in. Colleges like to have students who get involved. But do not join numerous clubs in high school just so you can list them on an application. Colleges like students who contribute to an organization, not just join it. Actively contributing to the school newspaper for four years is better than joining ten clubs and contributing nothing to them.

• • • • • • • • • •

**What activities— including school, community, religious, family, or personal—could you participate in or contribute to?**

Postsecondary schools look for students who actively participated in high school clubs or organizations.

Another part of your application includes **recommendations.** In these, a teacher and a counselor write about you and say why you should be admitted to the college. You can choose which teacher writes your recommendation. Give the teacher and the counselor a few weeks' notice so that they can write thoughtful, helpful recommendations.

The essay is the part of the application where you are asked to write about yourself. Colleges want an essay for three reasons:

1. to learn more personal information about you.

2. to learn how you think.

3. to learn how well you write.

Some applications assign a specific topic for the essay. Others, such as the Common Application, let you choose from a list of topics. One of the topics may be to write about an experience that has special meaning to you. Do not hurry through the essay. Think about an experience and why you remember it. Organize your thoughts into sentences and paragraphs. Colleges are not so interested in the experience itself but in why it is important to you.

> **Recommendation**
> *A written statement that tells why a person should be considered for something such as a college or job*

 Do as much community service as you can. You might volunteer in a hospital, nursing home, or homeless shelter. You will not only help others but you will help yourself when colleges look at your contributions to the community.

## Lesson 2 Review

Write the answers to these questions on a sheet of paper, using complete sentences.

1) How can you get an application form to a postsecondary school?

2) What is a Common Application?

3) What information is on a transcript?

4) What does an essay tell a school about you?

5) Suppose you do volunteer work at a hospital. Why is this a good thing to list on a college application?

*Finding Out About Special Services* ● ● ● ●

Sometimes people with learning disabilities think that they will not be successful in college. However, most colleges have a variety of special services to help students be successful.

## What Is a Precollege Preparatory Program?

Many colleges offer a precollege preparatory program. This is a program taken before entering the college, usually in the summer. It prepares you for your first year of college. The program emphasizes study skills and reading, writing, math, and study skills. The program also gives you a taste of campus life.

## What Kinds of Special Services Are Offered?

The college may have a program specifically for students with learning disabilities. In some schools services are offered through the Disability Services Office. Generally, the programs are headed by a learning disabilities (LD) specialist. Usually the student will be required to self-disclose and apply to the program in addition to the college. The student will need to provide documentation of the disability. There might be an additional fee.

The services offered include all or most of the following:

- diagnostic testing
- academic advising
- tutoring
- proofreading

Many postsecondary schools offer support services to students.

- assistance in using a computer
- texts put on audiotapes
- lectures put on audiotapes
- tests read aloud
- assistance with note-taking
- support group
- personal counseling

When you interview at a college, bring your parents or guardians along. They may think of questions you hadn't thought of.

Many colleges offer some support services to all students. For example, every student is assigned to an academic adviser who will help the student plan his or her classes. Most schools have a resource center, where students can seek assistance with their schoolwork.

Staff people in these centers generally are not trained in a disability area. They are more likely to be trained in a subject area, such as writing or math. Students can usually seek academic assistance on a drop-in basis. No documentation is required.

Students can find out about a college's special services when they interview with the admissions officer. It is also a good idea to meet with an LD specialist, if possible, during a campus visit.

• • • • • • • • • •

Why is it important to self-disclose to the college you choose?

## Lesson 3 Review

Write the answers to these questions on a sheet of paper, using complete sentences.

**1)** What is the purpose of a precollege preparatory program?

**2)** What are the possible requirements for participating in a program specifically for students with learning disabilities?

**3)** What are five special services typically offered in colleges?

**4)** How can you find out about a college's special services?

**5)** What is one question a student with a learning disability might ask an admissions officer during an interview?

# Applying Study Strategies ● ● ● ● ● ● ● ● ●

**H**ave you ever wondered why some people learn new things more easily than other people do? It is true that some people simply learn more easily than others. But more often than not, people who do well in school work at it. Good students use study strategies to learn, remember, and apply new information. A strategy is a careful plan or method.

## What Are Some Study Strategies?

You can apply different study strategies to different learning situations. For example, some strategies can help you memorize facts. Other strategies can help you take notes. Still other strategies can help you plan and organize your study time.

### General Strategies

• Sit near the front of class to improve your attention.

• Take notes in class.

Good students use study strategies to learn, remember, and apply new information.

- Set a daily study goal. For example, your goal might be to complete your homework and review that day's nutrition lesson.

- Find a quiet place to study, or use earplugs.

### Strategies for Memory

- Study your notes right after class or that evening.

- To memorize a list, group similar items and study them in a rhythm.

- Make flash cards with a key idea on one side and a definition or an explanation on the other side.

- Make up sentences in which the first letter of each word stands for what you are memorizing.

**Think of something you had to memorize recently. What sentence can you create to help you remember?**

### Strategies for Listening and Note-Taking

- Listen for clues that tell you the speaker is giving a key point. For example, the speaker might say, "The first point is . . ."

- Group a lecture into parts. For example, the speaker might say that a certain event had five causes. Then you know five topics will be discussed.

- Underline or star main points.

- Use abbreviations for commonly used words. For example, use the letter *r* for the word *are,* or *tcr* for *teacher.*

### Strategies for Planning and Organization

- Keep a calendar listing daily responsibilities. Include your work hours and study time.

- Write assignments and due dates in an assignment notebook and on a calendar.

- Make a list of things you have to do, and number the items in order of their importance.

- Break a large project into smaller steps, and set deadlines for each step.

### Strategies for Test Preparation and Test-Taking

- Make sure you know what the test will cover and what kind of test it will be (multiple-choice, true/false, essay).

- Don't wait until the night before to study. Study a little bit each evening for several days before the test.

- Use relaxation techniques right before the test. For example, close your eyes, breathe deeply, and imagine a peaceful scene.

- Read directions carefully and follow them.

- Check your answers.

- Look over the whole test before you start and plan how much time you will need for each section.

- Save any questions you are not sure of for last.

### Strategies for Using Textbooks and Other Resources

- Read objectives or study questions before you read the text, to set a purpose for your reading.

- Find and use all study aids in the book, such as the table of contents, index, appendix, and chapter outline.

- Seek assistance from the reference librarian when looking for resources.

- Seek out all possible resources such as indexes, periodicals, reference books, pamphlets, and the Internet.

## Lesson 4 Review

Write the answers to these questions on a sheet of paper, using complete sentences.

**1)** What are two general study strategies?

**2)** When is the best time to study your notes from class?

**3)** How can you make taking notes easier during a lecture?

**4)** What is a good way to study for a test?

**5)** What two study strategies do you think would be the most helpful to you? Explain your answer.

# *Obtaining Financial Aid* • • • • • • • • • • •

**H**ave you ever had sticker shock? That is when you are unpleasantly surprised by the high cost of something, like a car. It is easy to experience sticker shock over the cost of college and other postsecondary schools. Between tuition, room and board, books, and personal expenses, going to a typical four-year college can cost $15,000 or more per year. But most students do not pay the full price. They can receive **financial aid.**

## What Is Financial Aid?

Financial aid is anything that lowers the cost of college for a student. Financial aid usually comes from the government, private organizations, and the colleges themselves.

About $43 billion is available from the government each year to help pay for college. Colleges give away another $10 billion in the form of tuition discounts to people who qualify. Scholarships add millions more. That is a lot of money to help people go to college. And some of it is available to you.

## What Are Some Kinds of Financial Aid?

Most financial aid from the government is based on need. A computer formula says you (and your parents or guardians) can afford to pay a certain dollar amount. That amount is subtracted from the cost of attending a college. The difference is your financial need. Some kinds of financial aid follow.

### *Grants*

A grant is an amount of money from the government to help pay your college tuition. The amount is based on need. The less income a person or person's family has, the more grant money that person qualifies for. It usually ranges from a few hundred dollars to more than $3,000 per year.

**If you are the first in your family to go to college, say so in the application. You might mention it in the essay. Colleges look kindly on first-in-the-family students. It gives the college a more diverse population, which colleges like.**

## Loans

Each year, the government gives a large sum of money to colleges to lend to students. These loans have to be repaid with interest, but the interest rate is lower than that of a typical loan. You start repaying the loan after you leave college. It is assumed that you will then have a good job and be able to pay off the loan.

## College Jobs

You can get a job working for the college. It may be working in the cafeteria, the library, maintenance, the admission offices, or other areas. The government gives the college money to help pay your wages.

## Current Day

### Private Scholarships

Each year thousands of companies, clubs, religious organizations, and service groups award **scholarships.** These monetary gifts for tuition are often awarded for academic excellence and community service. Other factors might depend on the organization. Some companies award scholarships to the children of their employees. A store that sells musical instruments might award scholarships to musicians who win a talent contest.

You can find directories of private scholarships in a library, counseling office, or bookstore. These directories list scholarships, the rules for them, and contact information. Some directories are on computer. You answer about 20 questions. Then the computer produces a list of scholarships for which you might qualify and contact information.

A lot of financial aid is available. But you have to go out and apply for it.

## How Do You Apply for Financial Aid?

To apply for most financial aid, you have to fill out a form. The four-page form is called the **Free Application for Federal Student Aid (FAFSA).** You can get the FAFSA at a high school counseling office or a college financial aid office.

The FAFSA asks for your financial information. This includes your income, how much tax you have paid, and how much money you have in the bank.

Free Application for Federal Student Aid (FAFSA)
*The form used to apply for financial aid from the federal government*

## When Should You Apply?

The best time to begin filling out applications for financial aid is in late December. This will give you time to gather the information that you will need to fill out the FAFSA. Then you can mail it right after New Year's Day. This is the earliest time you can apply for financial aid for the following school year.

It is important to apply for financial aid early. If you apply later, such as in spring, no money may be left to give you for that year.

• • • • • • • • • •

**Why would you want your parent or guardian to help you complete the FAFSA?**

## What Happens After You Apply?

When the government gets your FAFSA, a computer uses the information to figure out your expected family contribution. This is the amount of money that you and your family are expected to be able to pay for your education. This information is sent to you as well as to the colleges that you listed on the FAFSA. The colleges use the information to figure out your need and decide how much money to give you. Between grants, loans, jobs, and scholarships, you could have thousands of dollars deducted from the sticker price of college.

## Lesson 5 Review

Write the answers to these questions on a sheet of paper, using complete sentences.

1) Why do most students pay less than the full price for college?

2) What are five types of financial aid?

3) How does a loan for education differ from a typical loan?

4) What is the FAFSA?

5) What would you tell someone who didn't want to apply for financial aid because he or she didn't like to fill out forms?

## Online Resources

**U. S. Department of Education**

*www.ed.gov/*

Includes information on discretionary grant applications, financial aid, direct loans, and more.

**U.S. Department of Education**
**Free Application for Federal Student Aid (FAFSA)**

*www.ed.gov/offices/OPE/express.html*

Provides information on FAFSA and a link for applying online.

**U.S. Department of Education**
**Think College**

*www.ed.gov/thinkcollege*

Provides information on preparing and planning for college. It includes links to directories for four-year colleges and universities, two-year colleges, business and technical schools, ACT, and more.

# Chapter 12 Summary

- Some sources of information about colleges include directories, the Internet, college brochures, and counselors and teachers.

- Consider a few things when choosing a college, including location, courses offered, tuition, and what campus life is like.

- Before you choose a college, visit it and meet with the admissions officer.

- Colleges consider many things when reviewing an application. These include high school grades, test scores, activities in school and in the community, and recommendations.

- Colleges offer many special services, including tutoring, help with note-taking, help with computers, and counseling.

- Using study strategies can help you be successful in college.

- A lot of financial aid is available for students to help them pay the cost of college.

- Financial aid comes in the form of grants, loans, jobs, discounts, and scholarships.

- You fill out a form called the Free Application for Federal Student Aid to apply for financial aid.

## Comprehension: Identifying Facts

On a sheet of paper, write the correct word or words from the Word Bank to complete each sentence.

---

**WORD BANK**

Common Application

community college

expected family contribution

Free Application for Federal Student Aid (FAFSA)

financial aid

grant

postsecondary education

recommendation

scholarship

transcript

tuition discount

university

---

1) A private organization may award a _____ to help a student pay for college.

2) A four-year college that gives advanced degrees is usually called a _____ .

3) A college where you get a two-year degree is usually called a _____ .

4) Anything that lowers the cost of college for a student is a form of _____.

5) Your counselor attaches a copy of your _____ , or high school grades, to your application.

6) Many colleges accept a _____ instead of their own application.

7) The amount of money that you and your family are expected to be able to pay for your education is your _____ .

8) The _____ is the name of the form used to qualify for financial aid from the federal government.

**Test-Taking Tip**

Try to answer all questions as completely as possible. When asked to explain your answer, do so in complete sentences.

9) A _____ is an amount of money from the government for college tuition.

10) Any formal education after high school is called _____ .

11) A break in the price of college given by the college itself is a _____ .

12) Part of a college application includes a _____ , in which a teacher or counselor writes about you.

## Comprehension: Understanding Main Ideas

On a sheet of paper, write the answers to the following questions using complete sentences.

13) What are eight special services that colleges usually offer?

14) What are six things you should do on a college visit?

15) How might becoming involved in your community help you get into college?

16) How might you use a calendar as a study aid?

17) How are grants and loans different? How are they the same?

18) When is the best time to start filling out an application for financial aid? Explain your answer.

## Critical Thinking: Write Your Opinion

On a sheet of paper, write the answers to the following questions using complete sentences.

19) What are some characteristics of your ideal college? Why are these characteristics important to you?

20) What would you say to an admissions officer who asks you why you want to go to college?

## Self-Assessment

Can you answer the following questions?

- [x] What are the different learning styles called?
- [x] What are two things that contribute to a successful marriage?
- [x] What does it mean to be a custodial parent?
- [x] What is one unhealthy reason to get married?
- [x] What are two signs that a couple may be ready to start a family?
- [x] What are three examples of good parenting skills?
- [x] What is the most common family type today?
- [x] What is a blended family?
- [x] What are four characteristics of a healthy family?
- [x] Is the number of single-parent families in the United States growing?

# *Other Areas of Transition*

**W**hen we are young, it seems as though we grow and change every day. As we get older, the changes happen more slowly. But we really never stop changing. We leave the home we grew up in and make a home of our own. Most of us get married. We may have children. Some of us get divorced. We may leave jobs and get new ones. These transitions, or changes, are exciting, but they can also present challenges.

In this chapter, you will find out about some of the areas of transition that people experience. You'll learn how people decide to get married and start families. You'll learn about the challenges involved in marriage and parenting. You'll also read about the different ways people learn. Finally, you will discover how understanding your own ways of learning can help you become a successful lifelong learner.

## *Goals for Learning*

▶ To understand what makes a successful marriage

▶ To identify the characteristics of healthy and unhealthy marriages

▶ To understand the responsibilities involved in parenting and the skills needed

▶ To describe different kinds of families

▶ To define three learning styles and the learning methods related to each of them

# *Marriage* • • • • • • • • • • • • • • • • •

In our society, most people decide to get married at some time. There are many healthy and unhealthy reasons to get married. Some healthy reasons include knowing and loving a person and wanting to have a family with that person. If two people understand themselves and each other, they have a good chance for a healthy marriage. Their marriage can help them feel happy and fulfilled.

Two people who understand themselves and each other have a good foundation for a healthy marriage.

## Why Do People Marry?

Marriage has benefits for couples. The partners give each other companionship. They enjoy communicating with each other and working together on their home and family. They enjoy developing a social life together with other couples and families. Staying together as marriage partners takes effort, which is usually worthwhile. Communication and division of chores help a couple to stay together.

Some people decide to marry because other people strongly encourage them. Others get married because they are trying to escape an unpleasant home life. They think that marriage will solve their problems.

Sometimes people decide to marry because of an unexpected pregnancy. This usually puts a strain on a marriage from the start. The decision to have children is an important one. The couple can best make that decision when they are ready to handle the responsibility.

> **Divorce**
> *The legal end of a marriage*

## When Do People Marry?

In the past, people often married when they were quite young. Today, however, the average age at which men marry is 26. For women, the average age is 24. One reason people are waiting longer to get married is that they usually live longer now. Also, people have found that they need more education to get the jobs they want. They wait until they are finished with school to get married. Some people wait to marry because they want to earn enough money to support themselves and their family.

Studies show that marriages are healthier and last longer if the couple is older. For example, for every four teenage marriages, three end in **divorce**. Divorce is the legal end of a marriage.

Some people choose not to marry. Others choose a career or close friendships over married life. This does not mean that their lives are less happy or healthy.

**What is one way a couple may work out a disagreement over how to spend money?**

## What Contributes to a Successful Marriage?

At some time or another, good and bad things affect a marriage. Moving to a new home or starting a new job is an exciting event. Losing a job or facing an illness is difficult. Partners who are supportive of each other are more able to cope with these changes.

A successful marriage usually requires more than just love. Partners have to communicate. They have to trust each other and agree on many issues. They must be willing to work out problems. Some common problems in marriage include handling money, getting along with relatives, and raising children. Some couples also have trouble working out a fair way to divide household tasks.

# Characteristics of a Healthy Marriage

No one quality or combination of qualities means that a marriage will work for sure. However, studies show that the following qualities are important in a healthy marriage:

- agreeing on money matters.
- having similar interests.
- knowing each other well before marriage.
- accepting and supporting each other.
- agreeing about having children.
- agreeing on how to **discipline** children, or teach them good behaviors and limit bad ones.
- having common goals.
- sharing household tasks.
- having similar family backgrounds and good relationships with parents.

Marriages are more successful when the two people know and understand themselves. Then they are better able to understand each other. They can have a stronger relationship.

## What Are Separation and Divorce?

Sometimes when a husband and wife believe they cannot live together, they separate. **Separation** may be an agreement between the two people, or it may be a court decision. During the separation, a couple usually thinks about the marriage. They try to decide if they are better off living apart or whether their problems can be worked out. If they believe the marriage cannot be saved, they may decide to divorce.

## Lesson 1 Review

Write the answers to these questions on a sheet of paper, using complete sentences.

**1)** What is one healthy reason to get married?

**2)** What is one unhealthy reason to get married?

**3)** What is the average age for women to get married? For men?

**4)** What is a separation?

**5)** Why are teen marriages more likely to end in divorce?

## Current Day

### Benefits of Marriage

Most people accept the belief that marriage is a good thing. But new research has shown just how good marriage really is for people. A 1998 study by a researcher from the University of Chicago drew the following conclusions about marriage:

- Marriage lengthens life. Ninety percent of married men and women lived to age 65. Only 60 to 70 percent of divorced or never-married people lived that long.

- Marriage increases physical and emotional health. Far fewer married people reported alcohol or drug problems or depression than did single or divorced people.

- Marriage raises income. Married people have, on average, more than twice as much money as single people.

## Lesson 2    *Parenting*

The birth of a child is a major event in a family. The decision to have children is an important one. People choose to have a child for healthy and unhealthy reasons.

### When Is a Couple Ready to Become Parents?

When a husband and wife decide they are ready to have a child, they are likely to feel good about their decision. Here are some signs that a couple is ready to start a family:

• They have a strong, loving marriage.

• They have a secure home.

• They have enough money to support a child.

Sometimes, however, couples have a baby for other reasons. They may give in to pressure from friends or parents. They may simply want to pass on the family name. Some couples have children because they believe it will make their marriage stronger. Often, the opposite happens. If a marriage already has problems, the stress of having a baby usually makes the problems worse.

Some couples have a baby that they didn't plan to have. Perhaps the baby comes at a time when the couple is struggling with other problems. Then the parents may not be able to meet the responsibilities of parenting.

Parents are responsible for the health and well-being of their children.

## What Does It Mean to Be a Parent?

When a baby is born, the parents' lives change. Parents are responsible for the health, safety, and well-being of their children. They must plan for the care of their children. They must pay the expenses of raising children, including food, clothing, and medical care.

Parents need to have good parenting skills. They must know how to take care of the physical health of their child. They also must know how to help their child grow emotionally. They need to help and encourage their children to begin to do things for themselves. Parents who grew up in loving, secure homes may already have many of the necessary skills. Other parents may need to learn these skills by attending classes or reading books or articles on child care.

**Conception**
*The beginning of a pregnancy*

## Technology In Our Lives

### A Child's Brain Development

Scientists have learned a great deal about the way children's brains develop. One source of new information about the brain is a medical technology called positron emission tomography, or PET. A PET scan shows which parts of the brain are active at different times—and how active they are.

Scientists who have studied PET scans of children's brains have made an interesting discovery. Between **conception** and three years of age, the number of connections between cells in a child's brain increase 20 times. Conception is the beginning of a pregnancy. These connections are what allow thinking and learning to take place. At no other time in a person's life does brain development happen so quickly.

What does this mean for parents? It means that providing lots of positive, healthy attention helps kids' brains develop in positive, healthy ways. Such attention includes a lot of touching and hugging, reading, talking, and singing songs and nursery rhymes.

**Consequence**
*What happens as a result of something*

Parents can set fair limits. Children learn at an early age that they must follow certain rules. If children break the rules, parents should provide a **consequence.** A consequence is what happens as a result of something. For example, if a child misbehaves, the consequence may be to sit alone for a few minutes. Providing a consequence is one way to discipline children. Experts agree that discipline should be fair and not harmful.

## What Are Some Family Types?

The most common type of family today is a family with only two people—a *married couple* without children. The second most common type is the *nuclear family.* A nuclear family is made up of one or two adults and their children.

A nuclear family with just one adult who cares for the children is a *single-parent family.* Mothers are most often the head of these families. Another family type is the *blended family.* In this family, one or both parents have been in relationships before that produced children. When children from an earlier relationship live with the new couple, the result is a *blended family.*

Family members enjoy spending time together.

A fourth family type is the *extended family.* An extended family is a nuclear family plus other relatives, such as grandparents, aunts, uncles, and cousins.

## Characteristics of a Healthy Family

Any type of family can be healthy or unhealthy. Studies show that healthy families have these six important qualities:

1. Commitment—Family members support and encourage one another.

2. Appreciation—Family members show appreciation for one another.

3. Communication—Everyone in the family talks to and listens to everyone else.

4. Time—Family members spend time together, either working or having fun.

5. Shared beliefs—Family members use their common beliefs to give them strength and purpose.

6. Coping ability—Family members are better able to handle problems because they get help and support from one another.

**Custodial parent**
*The parent who is responsible for children after a divorce*

**Joint custody**
*Both parents sharing the responsibilities of raising and caring for children*

When children are adopted, they become part of an *adoptive family*. Some children may join a foster family for awhile. A *foster family* cares for children who need short-term parenting when their birth parents cannot care for them.

Sometimes children have two families. The parent who is responsible for children after a divorce is the **custodial parent.** In blended and some single-parent families, children live with the custodial parent. They may spend time with the noncustodial parent in another home. This is true when parents have **joint custody** of children. Joint custody means that both parents share the responsibilities of raising and caring for the children.

Any of these family systems can be healthy or unhealthy. In a healthy family system, the family members work well together.

● ● ● ● ● ● ● ● ● ●

**What is one way divorce can affect children in a family?**

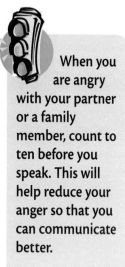

When you are angry with your partner or a family member, count to ten before you speak. This will help reduce your anger so that you can communicate better.

## How Is the Family Changing?

The family lifestyle is changing. Many families are smaller today than they were many years ago. Parents may decide to have fewer children because of the cost or because of their jobs. They may believe that they can provide a healthy home for only one or two children, rather than four or five.

Many families want or need extra money. To help support the family, both parents may have jobs outside the home. When both parents work, some difficulties may result. For example, parents may find it harder to decide how to divide the household chores. Many parents must leave their children in a daycare center while they work.

The number of single-parent families is increasing in the United States. A single-parent family may have some problems because parenting responsibilities fall on just one adult.

In single-parent families, parenting responsibilities fall on just one adult.

## Where Can Families Turn for Help?

Problems in a family can affect the health of each member. A family may need help to solve a problem. Dealing with a problem is better than trying to avoid it. Family members can do several things to get help dealing with their problems.

Many communities operate special counseling centers. Families can get help at these centers for little or no cost.

A couple whose marriage is in trouble can talk with a marriage counselor. Marriage counselors are trained to help couples improve or save their marriage. Family counselors work with problems in families. These counselors talk with family members and offer suggestions to help solve conflicts.

Many communities have several kinds of support groups. These are groups of people who share a common problem and offer each other encouragement in dealing with it. Many support groups help people who have had a death in the family. Other support groups help people deal with alcohol or drug problems.

## Lesson 2 Review

Write the answers to these questions on a sheet of paper, using complete sentences.

1) What are four things that parents must provide for their children?

2) What does it mean to discipline a child?

3) How does a nuclear family differ from an extended family?

4) How are families today different from families of long ago?

5) How might the lack of a job for a single parent affect the health of the family?

## Online Resources

### U.S. Department of Health and Human Services

*www.hhs.gov/kids/*

Fun and educational Web pages for kids.

### U.S. Department of Health and Human Services Administration for Children and Families

*www.acf.gov/programs*

Provides links to information on adoption, foster care, youth development, fun Web pages for kids about the government, and more.

**Auditory**
*Having to do with hearing*

**Tactile**
*Having to do with touching*

**Visual**
*Having to do with seeing*

Learning is a lifelong process. It does not end just because a person has become an adult. Adults may return to school to get a degree or learn a new job skill. They may get a new job that requires more training. Or they may simply want to learn new subjects or skills on their own.

Adults are often faced with the need to learn things on their own. They may not always have a teacher to help them. Everyone learns differently. Learning is easier when you are able to work with your own learning style. For this reason, adult learners may find it helpful to identify their own learning style.

Learning is a lifelong process.

## What Are Learning Styles?

A learning style is simply a way of learning. Researchers and educators have identified three major learning styles but there are others. The three major ones are **visual, auditory,** and **tactile.** Visual has to do with seeing. Visual learners take in information best by seeing it. Auditory has to do with hearing. Auditory learners take in information best by hearing it. Tactile has to do with touching. Tactile learners learn best by touching things.

No single learning style is better than any of the others. Each has its own strengths and weaknesses. What is important is that each person understand his or her own learning style. Then the person can use learning methods that are easiest, most natural, and most comfortable for that person.

## Visual Learners

Visual learners have excellent imaginations. They think in pictures and remember things best if they have seen them. They are usually good spellers and may have art skills.

Visual learners may need to hear spoken instructions more than once before they understand them. Using visual aids is a good way for visual learners to learn new information. Visual aids include charts, illustrations, maps, notes, and videos. These learners often find it helpful to mark information as they are learning new material. They may use brightly colored highlighters or sticky notes. Visual learners in class might find it helpful to sit at the front of a classroom. Then they can see the teacher's facial expressions clearly.

## Auditory Learners

Auditory learners listen well. They like to talk about what they are learning. They follow spoken instructions better than written ones. They are likely to be good at giving speeches and presentations.

Listening to lectures or cassette tapes works well for auditory learners. Reciting information aloud helps auditory learners remember information. Auditory learners usually need spoken explanations of charts, diagrams, and graphs. They often find it helpful to use rhymes, raps, or musical jingles to remember information. Speaking ideas aloud while another person writes them down is a good way for auditory learners to organize their ideas.

## Tactile Learners

Tactile learners express themselves physically. For example, they may move their hands around a lot when they speak. They may be poor listeners and lose interest in long speeches. Tactile learners often learn best by relating information to real-life situations.

Stress and nervousness are barriers to learning for anyone. To be a better learner, make sure you are healthy, fit, and well rested. Do this by eating a well-balanced diet, exercising regularly, and getting enough sleep.

• • • • • • • • • •

Which learning style describes you best? How do you know?

Tactile learners may have difficulty learning in school. This is largely because they learn best by doing rather than just listening. It is also because they need to move around, act things out, and touch things in order to understand them.

Tactile learners may find it helpful to take frequent breaks and move around while studying. They may also learn better if they study while standing up, or even snack or chew gum while studying. Tactile learners may benefit from tracing words with their finger as they study them. Writing down facts several times also helps.

Learning is easier when you know your learning style.

## Lesson 3 Review

On a sheet of paper, write the word or words in parentheses that correctly complete each sentence.

1) A _____ style is a way of or approach to learning. (visual, study, learning)

2) Visual learners learn best through their sense of _____. (sight, hearing, touch)

3) _____ learners need to touch things in order to understand them. (Visual, Auditory, Tactile)

4) The best way for an auditory learner to understand new information is by _____. (doing, touching, listening)

5) Visual learners usually _____. (move their hands around when they talk, are good spellers, understand spoken instructions best)

# Chapter 13 Summary

• • • • • • • • • • • • • • • • • • • • • • • • • •

- Most people in the United States marry at some time. People get married for both healthy and unhealthy reasons.

- People today are waiting longer to get married.

- Some elements that usually lead to a healthy marriage include having similar family backgrounds, more education, and secure jobs.

- People have babies for both healthy and unhealthy reasons.

- Parents are responsible for the health, safety, and well-being of their children. They pay the expenses of raising children.

- Parents need to learn certain skills to help their children grow physically and emotionally. They must set rules and provide discipline.

- Some qualities of healthy families are commitment, appreciation, time, communication, shared beliefs, and coping ability.

- There are several kinds of families. These include nuclear, blended, single-parent, extended, adoptive, and foster families. The most common type of family is a married couple with no children.

- Many organizations help married couples and families with problems.

- Learning is a lifelong process.

- People learn best by following their own learning style—visual, auditory, or tactile.

- Visual learners take in information best through their sense of sight. Auditory learners take in information best through their sense of hearing. Tactile learners take in information best through their sense of touch.

## Comprehension: Identifying Facts

On a sheet of paper, write the correct word or words from the Word Bank to complete each sentence.

> **WORD BANK**
>
> auditory learners
> average
> blended families
> companionship
> consequence
>
> custodial
> divorce
> learning style
> money matters
> nuclear families
> parenting skills
>
> separation
> single-parent families
> touch
> visual learners

1) One benefit of marriage is _____.

2) The legal end of a marriage is known as _____.

3) In a _____, a couple spends time apart to think about their troubled marriage.

4) Agreeing on _____ is one characteristic of a healthy marriage.

5) The _____ age for a man to marry in the United States today is 26.

6) Good _____ may be learned from a couples' own parents or from classes or books.

7) If a child misbehaves, the _____ might be to have to sit alone for awhile.

8) _____ are made up of one or two adults and their children.

9) After a divorce, the _____ parent takes responsibility for caring for the children.

**Test-Taking Tip**

Drawing pictures and diagrams is one way to help you understand and solve problems.

10) Most _____ are headed by a woman.

11) _____ include children from an earlier relationship.

12) Understanding your own _____ can help you find the best ways to learn new information.

13) Learners who learn best by seeing things are called _____.

14) Speaking ideas aloud while another person writes them down is a good way for _____ to organize their ideas.

15) Tactile learners absorb information best through their sense of _____.

## Comprehension: Understanding Main Ideas

On a sheet of paper, write the answers to the following questions using complete sentences.

16) What is one healthy and one unhealthy reason to get married?

17) In what way is discipline part of good parenting?

18) Name the three learning styles and one characteristic of each.

## Critical Thinking: Write Your Opinion

On a sheet of paper, write the answers to the following questions using complete sentences.

19) In what ways do you think families today are healthier than families in the past? How do you think they are less healthy?

20) Why do tactile learners often have more difficulties in school than visual or auditory learners?

## Most Common Sites for Cancer in Men and Women

| Men | | Women | |
|---|---|---|---|
| Prostate | 179,300 | Breast | 175,000 |
| Lung & bronchus | 94,000 | Lung & bronchus | 77,600 |
| Colon & rectum | 62,400 | Colon & rectum | 67,000 |
| Urinary bladder | 39,100 | Uterine corpus | 37,400 |
| Non-Hodgkin's lymphoma | 32,600 | Ovary | 25,200 |
| Skin—melanoma | 25,800 | Non-Hodgkin's lymphoma | 24,200 |
| Oral cavity | 20,000 | Skin—melanoma | 18,400 |
| Kidney | 17,800 | Urinary bladder | 15,100 |
| Leukemia | 16,800 | Pancreas | 14,600 |
| Pancreas | 14,000 | Thyroid | 13,500 |
| All sites | 623,800 | All sites | 598,000 |

*Source: American Cancer Society, 1999.*

## Cancer Deaths, by Site, in Men and Women

| Men | | Women | |
|---|---|---|---|
| Lung & bronchus | 90,900 | Lung & bronchus | 68,000 |
| Prostate | 37,000 | Breast | 43,300 |
| Colon & rectum | 27,800 | Colon & rectum | 28,800 |
| Pancreas | 13,900 | Pancreas | 14,700 |
| Non-Hodgkin's lymphoma | 13,400 | Ovary | 14,500 |
| Leukemia | 12,400 | Non-Hodgkin's lymphoma | 12,300 |
| Esophagus | 9,400 | Leukemia | 9,700 |
| Liver | 8,400 | Uterine corpus | 6,400 |
| Urinary bladder | 8,100 | Brain | 5,900 |
| Stomach | 7,900 | Stomach | 5,600 |
| All sites | 291,100 | All sites | 272,000 |

*Source: American Cancer Society, 1999.*

# The ABCDs of Melanoma

Melanoma is usually curable if you find it early. Follow this A-B-C-D self-examination guide adapted from the American Academy of Dermatology:

■ **A is for asymmetry**—Symmetrical round or oval growths are usually benign. Look for irregular shapes where one half is a different shape than the other half.

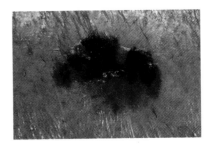

■ **B is for border**—Irregular, notched, scalloped, or vaguely defined borders need to be checked out.

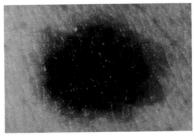

■ **C is for color**—Look for growths that have many colors or an uneven distribution of color. Growths that are the same color all over are usually benign.

■ **D is for diameter**—Have your doctor check out any growths that are larger than 6 millimeters, about the diameter of a pencil eraser.

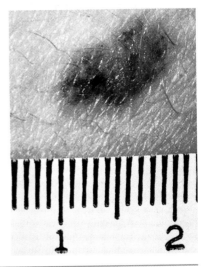

## The Six Essential Nutrient Classes

| NUTRIENT | BEST FOOD SOURCES | WHY THEY ARE NEEDED |
|---|---|---|
| Protein | Cheese, eggs, fish, meat, milk, poultry, soybeans, nuts, dry beans, and lentils. | To promote body growth and repair and maintain tissue. |
| Carbohydrate | Bread, cereal, flour, potatoes, rice, sugar, dry beans, and fruit. | To supply energy, furnish heat, and save proteins to build and regulate cells. |
| Fat | Butter, margarine, cream, oils, meat, whole milk, nuts, and avocado. | To supply energy and furnish heat. To save proteins to build and regulate cells. To supply necessary fat-soluble vitamins and other nutrients. |
| **MINERALS** Calcium | Milk, cheese, leafy green vegetables, oysters, and almonds. | To give rigidity and hardness to bones and teeth. Also for clotting of blood, osmosis, action of heart and other muscles, and nerve response. |
| Iron | Meats (especially liver), oysters, leafy green vegetables, legumes, dried apricots or peaches, prunes, and raisins. | To carry oxygen in the blood. |
| Iodine | Seafood and iodized salt. | To help the thyroid gland regulate cell activities for physical and mental health. |
| **VITAMINS** Vitamin A | Whole milk, cream, butter, liver, egg yolk, leafy green vegetables, dark yellow fruits and vegetables. | To promote health of epithelial tissues. For health of eyes and development of teeth. |
| Thiamin | Present in many foods, abundant in few; pork, some animal organs, some nuts, whole grains, yeast, dry beans, and peas. | To promote healthy nerves, appetite, digestion, and growth. To metabolize carbohydrates. |
| Riboflavin | Milk, lean meats, cheese, eggs, leafy green vegetables, and whole grains. | To make for better development, greater vitality, freedom from disease, and metabolism of carbohydrates, fats, and proteins. |
| Niacin | Lean meats, liver, poultry, peanuts, legumes, and yeasts. | To promote good digestion, healthy skin, and a well-functioning nervous system. |
| Vitamin C | Citrus fruits, strawberries, tomatoes, broccoli, cabbage, and green peppers. | To enhance iron absorption. Also for deposit of intercellular cement in tissues and bone. |
| Vitamin D | Milk, cheese, cream, salmon, tuna, and fortified cereal. | To help absorb and use calcium and phosphorus. |
| **WATER** | Drinking water, fruit juice, and food. | To supply body fluids and regulate body temperature. |

# Fiber Content of Selected Foods

**GRAINS**

**FRUITS**

**VEGETABLES**

**LEGUMES**

| | Serving size | Dietary Fiber (g) |
|---|---|---|
| Bread, white | 1 slice | 0.6 |
| Bread, whole wheat | 1 slice | 1.5 |
| Oat, bran, dry | 1/3 cup | 4.0 |
| Oatmeal, dry | 1/3 cup | 2.7 |
| Rice, brown, cooked | 1/2 cup | 2.4 |
| Rice, white, cooked | 1/2 cup | 0.8 |
| | | |
| Apple, with skin | 1 small | 2.8 |
| Apricots, with skin | 4 fruit | 3.5 |
| Banana | 1 small | 2.2 |
| Blueberries | 3/4 cup | 1.4 |
| Figs, dried | 3 fruit | 4.6 |
| Grapefruit | 1/2 fruit | 1.6 |
| Pear, with skin | 1 large | 5.8 |
| Prunes, dried | 3 medium | 1.7 |
| | | |
| Asparagus, cooked | 1/2 cup | 1.8 |
| Broccoli, cooked | 1/2 cup | 2.4 |
| Carrots, cooked, sliced | 1/2 cup | 2.0 |
| Peas, green, frozen, cooked | 1/2 cup | 4.3 |
| Potato, with skin, raw | 1/2 cup | 1.5 |
| Tomato, raw | 1 medium | 1.0 |
| | | |
| Kidney beans, cooked | 1/2 cup | 6.9 |
| Lima beans, canned | 1/2 cup | 4.3 |
| Pinto beans, cooked | 1/2 cup | 5.9 |
| Beans, white, cooked | 1/2 cup | 5.0 |
| Lentils, cooked | 1/2 cup | 4.7 |
| Peas, blackeye, canned | 1/2 cup | 4.7 |

# Calcium and Fat Content of Dairy Products*

| Product | Calories | Fat (grams) | Calcium (milligrams) |
|---|---|---|---|
| **Skim milk (also called nonfat or fat free)** | | | |
| Plain | 86 | 0 | 301 |
| Chocolate | 144 | 1 | 292 |
| **1% milk (also called lowfat or light)** | | | |
| Plain | 102 | 2½ | 300 |
| Chocolate | 158 | 2½ | 288 |
| **2% milk (now called reduced fat)** | | | |
| Plain | 121 | 5 | 298 |
| Chocolate | 179 | 5 | 285 |
| **Whole milk** | | | |
| Plain | 150 | 8 | 290 |
| Chocolate | 209 | 8 | 280 |
| Buttermilk (lowfat) | 100 | 2 | 300 |
| Buttermilk (whole) | 150 | 8 | 300 |
| Sweetened condensed milk | 246 | 7 | 217 |

*Nutrition information is based on a one-cup serving; only sweetened condensed milk is based on a quarter-cup serving

# Eating Disorders

| Disorder | Description | Characteristics | Consequences |
|---|---|---|---|
| **Anorexia** | Emotional problem characterized by severe weight loss | Affects more females than males<br><br>Extreme dieting, food rituals, not eating<br><br>Compulsive exercising<br><br>Frequent weighing<br><br>Intense fear of becoming fat when actually too thin<br><br>Treatable with medicine, psychotherapy when found early | Malnutrition<br><br>Menstruation stops<br><br>Lowered metabolic rate<br><br>Poor temperature regulation<br><br>Heart problems<br><br>Death |
| **Bulimia** | Emotional problem involving bingeing (eating large amounts of food in a short time) followed by purging (ridding one's body of the food) or severe dieting | Fear of or inability to stop eating<br><br>Secret vomiting or use of laxatives<br><br>Constantly thinking about food<br><br>Secretly storing up food<br><br>Person wants help but won't ask<br><br>Extreme concentration on appearance<br><br>Feeling of being out of control<br><br>Depression<br><br>Treatable with medicine, psychotherapy | Enlarged or ruptured stomach<br><br>Eroded tooth enamel<br><br>Pneumonia from inhaling vomit<br><br>Other physical problems<br><br>Behavioral problems<br><br>Psychological problems<br><br>Danger of substance abuse |
| **Compulsive overeating** | Emotional problem involving bingeing but no purging | Continually snacking<br><br>Large meals and frequent snacks while bingeing<br><br>Great feelings of guilt and shame for feeling out of control<br><br>Inability to stop eating during binges<br><br>Possible family tendency to be overweight<br><br>Treatable with medicine, psychotherapy | Obesity (condition of having extreme body fat)<br><br>Heart disease<br><br>Diabetes<br><br>Some kinds of cancer<br><br>Reduced life span |

## Appendix C   *Physical Fitness*   ● ● ● ● ● ● ● ● ● ● ● ● ●

### Frame Size

To determine your frame size:

1. Extend your arm in front of your body bending your elbow at a ninety-degree angle to your body (your arm is parallel to your body).

2. Keep your fingers straight and turn the inside of your wrist to your body.

3. Place your thumb and index finger on the two prominent bones on either side of your elbow, measure the distance between the bones with a tape measure or calipers.

4. Compare to the medium frame chart below. Select your height based on what you are barefoot. If you are below the listed inches, your frame is small. If you are above, your frame is large.

### Elbow Measurements for Medium Frame

| Height in 1" Heels | Elbow Breadth |
|---|---|
| **Men** | **Men** |
| 5'2"–5'3" | $2^1/2$"–$2^5/8$" |
| 5'4"–5'7" | $2^5/8$"–$2^7/8$" |
| 5'8"–5'11" | $2^3/4$"–3" |
| 6'0"–6'3" | $2^3/4$"–$3^1/8$" |
| 6'4" | $2^7/8$"–$3^1/4$" |
| **Women** | **Women** |
| 4'10"–4'11" | $2^1/4$"–$2^1/2$" |
| 5'0"–5'3" | $2^1/4$"–$2^1/2$" |
| 5'4"–5'7" | $2^3/8$"–$2^5/8$" |
| 5'8"–5'11" | $2^3/8$"–$2^5/8$" |
| 6'0" | $2^1/2$"–$2^3/4$" |

## Top 10 Fat-Blasting Exercises

| Activity | Calories Burned (per 30 minutes) | Activity | Calories Burned (per 30 minutes) |
|---|---|---|---|
| Bicycling, vigorous (15 MPH) | 340 | Spinning class (indoor cycling) | 312 |
| Jogging (10- to 12-minute miles) | 340 to 272 | Jumping rope, slowly | 272 |
| Swimming, vigorous | 340 | Tennis, singles | 272 |
| Cross-country ski machine | 323 | Hiking, uphill | 238 |
| | | Inline skating | 238 |
| | | Walking, uphill (3.5 MPH) | 204 |

## Recommended Height and Weight for Women

| Height Feet Inches | Small Frame | Medium Frame | Large Frame |
|---|---|---|---|
| 4'10" | 102–111 | 109–121 | 118–131 |
| 4'11" | 103–113 | 111–123 | 120–134 |
| 5'0" | 104–115 | 113–126 | 122–137 |
| 5'1" | 106–118 | 115–129 | 125–140 |
| 5'2" | 108–121 | 118–132 | 128-143 |
| 5'3" | 111–124 | 121–135 | 131–147 |
| 5'4" | 114–127 | 124–138 | 134–151 |
| 5'5" | 117–130 | 127–141 | 137–155 |
| 5'6" | 120–133 | 130–144 | 140–159 |
| 5'7" | 123–136 | 133–147 | 143–163 |
| 5'8" | 126–139 | 136–150 | 146–167 |
| 5'9" | 129–142 | 139–153 | 149–170 |
| 5'10" | 132–145 | 142–156 | 152–173 |
| 5'11" | 135–148 | 145–159 | 155–176 |
| 6'0" | 138–151 | 148–162 | 158–179 |

Weights at ages 25–59 based on lowest mortality.

Weight in pounds according to frame (in indoor clothing weighing 3 lbs.; shoes with 1" heels).

## Recommended Height and Weight for Men

| Height Feet Inches | Small Frame | Medium Frame | Large Frame |
|---|---|---|---|
| 5'2" | 128–134 | 131–141 | 138–150 |
| 5'3" | 130–136 | 133–143 | 140–153 |
| 5'4" | 132–138 | 135–145 | 142–156 |
| 5'5" | 134–140 | 137–148 | 144–160 |
| 5'6" | 136–142 | 139–151 | 146–164 |
| 5'7" | 138–145 | 142–154 | 149–168 |
| 5'8" | 140–148 | 145–157 | 152–172 |
| 5'9" | 142–151 | 148–160 | 155–176 |
| 5'10" | 144–154 | 151–163 | 158–180 |
| 5'11" | 146–157 | 154–166 | 161–184 |
| 6'0" | 149–160 | 157–170 | 164–188 |
| 6'1" | 152–164 | 160–174 | 168–192 |
| 6'2" | 155–168 | 162–178 | 172–197 |
| 6'3" | 158–172 | 167–182 | 176–202 |
| 6'4" | 162–176 | 171–187 | 181–207 |

Weights at ages 25–59 based on lowest mortality.

Weight in pounds according to frame (in indoor clothing weighing 5 lbs.; shoes with 1" heels).

*Adopted in Congress July 4, 1776*
*The Unanimous Declaration of the*
*Thirteen United States of America*

When, in the course of human events, it becomes necessary for one people to dissolve the political bands which have connected them with another, and to assume among the powers of the earth, the separate and equal station to which the laws of nature and of nature's God entitle them, a decent respect to the opinions of mankind requires that they should declare the causes which impel them to the separation.

We hold these truths to be self-evident, that all men are created equal, that they are endowed by their Creator with certain unalienable rights, that among these are life, liberty, and the pursuit of happiness. That to secure these rights, governments are instituted among men, deriving their just powers from the consent of the governed. That whenever any form of government becomes destructive of these ends, it is the right of the people to alter or to abolish it, and to institute new government, laying its foundation on such principles and organizing its powers in such form, as to them shall seem most likely to effect their safety and happiness. Prudence, indeed, will dictate that governments long established should not be changed for light and transient causes; and accordingly all experience hath shown that mankind are more disposed to suffer, while evils are sufferable, than to right themselves by abolishing the forms to which they are accustomed. But when a long train of abuses and usurpations, pursuing invariably the same object evinces a design to reduce them under absolute despotism, it is their right, it is their duty, to throw off such government, and to provide new guards for their future security.

Such has been the patient sufferance of these colonies; and such is now the necessity which constrains them to alter their former systems of government. The history of the present King of Great Britain is a history of repeated injuries and usurpations, all having in direct object the establishment of an absolute tyranny over these states. To prove this, let facts be submitted to a candid world.

He has refused his assent to laws, the most wholesome and necessary for the public good.

He has forbidden his governors to pass laws of immediate and pressing importance, unless suspended in their operation till his assent should be obtained; and when so suspended, he has utterly neglected to attend to them.

He has refused to pass other laws for the accommodation of large districts of people, unless those people would relinquish the right of representation in the legislature, a right inestimable to them and formidable to tyrants only.

He has called together legislative bodies at places unusual, uncomfortable, and distant from the depository of their public records, for the sole purpose of fatiguing them into compliance with his measures.

He has dissolved representative houses repeatedly, for opposing with manly firmness his invasions on the rights of the people.

He has refused for a long time, after such dissolutions, to cause others to be elected; whereby the legislative powers, incapable of annihilation, have returned to the people at large for their exercise; the state remaining in the mean time exposed to all the dangers of invasion from without, and convulsions within.

He has endeavored to prevent the population of these states; for that purpose obstructing the laws for naturalization of foreigners; refusing to pass others to encourage their migrations hither, and raising the conditions of new appropriations of lands.

He has obstructed the administration of justice, by refusing his assent to laws for establishing judiciary powers.

He has made judges dependent on his will alone, for the tenure of their offices, and the amount and payment of their salaries.

He has erected a multitude of new offices, and sent hither swarms of officers to harass our people, and eat out their substance.

He has kept among us, in times of peace, standing armies without the consent of our legislatures.

He has affected to render the military independent of and superior to the civil power.

He has combined with others to subject us to a jurisdiction foreign to our constitution, and unacknowledged by our laws; giving his assent to their acts of pretended legislation:

For quartering large bodies of armed troops among us:

For protecting them, by a mock trial, from punishment for any murders which they should commit on the inhabitants of these states:

For cutting off our trade with all parts of the world:

For imposing taxes on us without our consent:

For depriving us in many cases, of the benefits of trial by jury:

For transporting us beyond seas to be tried for pretended offenses:

For abolishing the free system of English laws in a neighboring province, establishing therein an arbitrary government, and enlarging its boundaries so as to render it at once an example and fit instrument for introducing the same absolute rule into these colonies:

For taking away our charters, abolishing our most valuable laws, and altering fundamentally the forms of our governments:

For suspending our own legislatures, and declaring themselves invested with power to legislate for us in all cases whatsoever.

He has abdicated government here, by declaring us out of his protection and waging war against us.

He has plundered our seas, ravaged our coasts, burned our towns, and destroyed the lives of our people.

He is at this time transporting large armies of foreign mercenaries to complete the works of death, desolation and tyranny, already begun with circumstances of cruelty and perfidy scarcely paralleled in the most barbarous ages, and totally unworthy the head of a civilized nation.

He has constrained our fellow citizens taken captive on the high seas to bear arms against their country, to become the executioners of their friends and brethren, or to fall themselves by their hands.

He has excited domestic insurrections amongst us, and has endeavored to bring on the inhabitants of our frontiers, the merciless Indian savages, whose known rule of warfare, is an undistinguished destruction of all ages, sexes, and conditions.

In every stage of these oppressions we have petitioned for redress in the most humble terms: our repeated petitions have been answered only by repeated injury. A prince, whose character is thus marked by every act which may define a tyrant, is unfit to be the ruler of a free people.

Nor have we been wanting in attentions to our British brethren. We have warned them from time to time of attempts by their legislature to extend an unwarrantable jurisdiction over us. We have reminded them of the circumstances of our emigration and settlement here. We have appealed to their native justice and magnanimity, and we have conjured them by the ties of our common kindred to disavow these usurpations, which would inevitably interrupt our connections and correspondence. They too have been deaf to the voice of justice and of consanguinity. We must, therefore, acquiesce in the necessity, which denounces our separation, and hold them, as we hold the rest of mankind, enemies in war, in peace friends.

We, therefore, the representatives of the United States of America, in General Congress, assembled, appealing to the Supreme Judge of the world for the rectitude of our intentions, do, in the name, and by authority of the good people of these colonies, solemnly publish and declare, that these united colonies are, and of right ought to be free and independent states; that they are absolved from all allegiance to the British Crown, and that all political connection between them and the state of Great Britain, is and ought to be totally dissolved; and that as free and independent states, they have full power to levy war, conclude peace, contract alliances, establish commerce, and to do all other acts and things which independent states may of right do. And for the support of this declaration, with a firm reliance on the protection of Divine Providence, we mutually pledge to each other our lives, our fortunes, and our sacred honor.

*Signed by John Hancock of Massachusetts as President of the Congress and by the fifty-five other Representatives of the thirteen United States of America:*

### New Hampshire

Josiah Bartlett
William Whipple
Matthew Thornton

### Connecticut

Roger Sherman
Samuel Huntington
William Williams
Oliver Wolcott

### Massachusetts Bay

Samuel Adams
John Adams
Robert Treat Paine
Elbridge Gerry

### Rhode Island

Stephen Hopkins
William Ellery

### Pennsylvania

Robert Morris
Benjamin Rush
Benjamin Franklin
John Morton
George Clymer
James Smith
George Taylor
James Wilson
George Ross

### Delaware

Caesar Rodney
George Read
Thomas M'Kean

### New York

William Floyd
Philip Livingston
Francis Lewis
Lewis Morris

### Virginia

George Wythe
Richard Henry Lee
Thomas Jefferson
Benjamin Harrison
Thomas Nelson, Jr.
Francis Lightfoot Lee
Carter Braxton

### North Carolina

William Hooper
Joseph Hewes
John Penn

### South Carolina

Edward Rutledge
Thomas Heyward, Jr.
Thomas Lynch, Jr.
Arthur Middleton

### Georgia

Button Gwinnett
Lyman Hall
George Walton

### Maryland

Samuel Chase
William Paca
Thomas Stone
Charles Carroll of
    Carrollton

### New Jersey

Richard Stockton
John Witherspoon
Francis Hopkinson
John Hart
Abraham Clark

## Preamble

We the people of the United States, in order to form a more perfect Union, establish justice, insure domestic tranquility, provide for the common defense, promote the general welfare, and secure the blessings of liberty to ourselves and our posterity, do ordain and establish this Constitution for the United States of America.

## Article I
## The Legislative Branch*

### Congress

**Section 1**

All legislative powers herein granted shall be vested in a Congress of the United States, which shall consist of a Senate and House of Representatives.

### The House of Representatives

**Section 2**

(1) The House of Representatives shall be composed of members chosen every second year by the people of the several states, and the electors in each state shall have the qualifications requisite for electors of the most numerous branch of the state legislature.

(2) No person shall be a representative who shall not have attained to the age of twenty-five years, and been seven years a citizen of the United States, and who shall not, when elected, be an inhabitant of that state in which he shall be chosen.

(3) Representatives and direct taxes shall be apportioned among the several states which may be included within this Union, according to their respective numbers, [which shall be determined by adding to the whole number of free persons, including those bound to service for a term of years, and excluding Indians not taxed, three-fifths of all other persons]. The actual enumeration shall be made within three years after the first meeting of the Congress of the United States, and within every subsequent term of ten years, in such manner as they shall by law direct. The number of representatives shall not exceed one for every thirty thousand, but each state shall have at least one representative; [and until such enumeration shall be made, the state of New Hampshire shall be entitled to choose 3, Massachusetts 8, Rhode Island and Providence Plantations 1, Connecticut 5, New York 6, New Jersey 4, Pennsylvania 8, Delaware 1, Maryland 6, Virginia 10, North Carolina 5, South Carolina 5, and Georgia 3].

* Headings and paragraph numbers have been added to help the reader. The original Constitution has only the article and section numbers.

(4) When vacancies happen in the representation from any state, the executive authority thereof shall issue writs of election to fill such vacancies.

(5) The House of Representatives shall choose their speaker and other officers; and shall have the sole power of impeachment.

## *The Senate*

### Section 3

(1) The Senate of the United States shall be composed of two senators from each state, [chosen by the legislature thereof,] for six years; and each senator shall have one vote.

(2) Immediately after they shall be assembled in consequence of the first election, they shall be divided as equally as may be into three classes. The seats of the senators of the first class shall be vacated at the expiration of the second year, of the second class at the expiration of the fourth year, and of the third class at the expiration of the sixth year, so that one-third may be chosen every second year; [and if vacancies happen by resignation, or otherwise, during the recess of the legislature of any state, the executive thereof may make temporary appointments until the next meeting of the legislature, which shall then fill such vacancies].

(3) No person shall be a senator who shall not have attained to the age of thirty years, and been nine years a citizen of the United States, and who shall not, when elected, be an inhabitant of that state for which he shall be chosen.

(4) The Vice President of the United States shall be president of the Senate, but shall have no vote, unless they be equally divided.

(5) The Senate shall choose their other officers, and also a president pro tempore, in the absence of the Vice President, or when he shall exercise the office of President of the United States.

(6) The Senate shall have the sole power to try all impeachments. When sitting for that purpose, they shall be on oath or affirmation. When the President of the United States is tried, the Chief Justice shall preside: and no person shall be convicted without the concurrence of two-thirds of the members present.

(7) Judgment in cases of impeachment shall not extend further than to removal from office, and disqualification to hold and enjoy any office of honor, trust, or profit under the United States: but the party convicted shall nevertheless be liable and subject to indictment, trial, judgment, and punishment, according to law.

## Organization of Congress
### Section 4
(1) The times, places, and manner of holding elections for senators and representatives, shall be prescribed in each state by the legislature thereof; but the Congress may at any time by law make or alter such regulations, [except as to the places of choosing senators].

(2) The Congress shall assemble at least once in every year, [and such meeting shall be on the first Monday in December,] unless they shall by law appoint a different day.

## Rules and Procedures
### Section 5
(1) Each house shall be the judge of the elections, returns and qualifications of its own members, and a majority of each shall constitute a quorum to do business; but a smaller number may adjourn from day to day, and may be authorized to compel the attendance of absent members, in such manner, and under such penalties as each house may provide.

(2) Each house may determine the rules of its proceedings, punish its members for disorderly behavior, and, with the concurrence of two-thirds, expel a member.

(3) Each house shall keep a journal of its proceedings, and from time to time publish the same, excepting such parts as may in their judgment require secrecy; and the yeas and nays of the members of either house on any question shall, at the desire of one-fifth of those present, be entered on the journal.

(4) Neither house, during the session of Congress, shall, without the consent of the other, adjourn for more than three days, nor to any other place than that in which the two houses shall be sitting.

## Payment and Privileges
### Section 6
(1) The senators and representatives shall receive a compensation for their services, to be ascertained by law, and paid out of the treasury of the United States. They shall in all cases, except treason, felony, and breach of the peace, be privileged from arrest during their attendance at the session of their respective houses, and in going to and returning from the same; and for any speech or debate in either house, they shall not be questioned in any other place.

(2) No senator or representative shall, during the time for which he was elected, be appointed to any civil office under the authority of the United States, which shall have been created, or the emoluments whereof shall have been increased during such time; and no person holding any office under the United States, shall be a member of either house during his continuance in office.

### How a Bill Becomes a Law
**Section 7**

(1) All bills for raising revenue shall originate in the House of Representatives; but the Senate may propose or concur with amendments as on other bills.

(2) Every bill which shall have passed the House of Representatives and the Senate, shall, before it becomes a law, be presented to the President of the United States; if he approve he shall sign it, but if not he shall return it, with his objections to that house in which it shall have originated, who shall enter the objections at large on their journal, and proceed to reconsider it. If after such reconsideration two-thirds of that house shall agree to pass the bill, it shall be sent, together with the objections, to the other house, by which it shall likewise be reconsidered, and if approved by two-thirds of that house, it shall become a law. But in all such cases the votes of both houses shall be determined by yeas and nays, and the names of the persons voting for and against the bill shall be entered on the journal of each house, respectively. If any bill shall not be returned by the President within ten days (Sundays excepted) after it shall have been presented to him, the same shall be a law, in like manner as if he had signed it, unless the Congress by their adjournment prevent its return, in which case it shall not be a law.

(3) Every order, resolution, or vote to which the concurrence of the Senate and House of Representatives may be necessary (except on a question of adjournment) shall be presented to the President of the United States; and before the same shall take effect, shall be approved by him, or being disapproved by him, shall be repassed by two-thirds of the Senate and House of Representatives, according to the rules and limitations prescribed in the case of a bill.

### Powers Granted to Congress
**Section 8**

The Congress shall have power:

(1) To lay and collect taxes, duties, imposts, and excises, to pay the debts and provide for the common defense and general welfare of the United States; but all duties, imposts, and excises shall be uniform throughout the United States;

(2) To borrow money on the credit of the United States;

(3) To regulate commerce with foreign nations, and among the several states, and with the Indian tribes;

(4) To establish a uniform rule of naturalization, and uniform laws on the subject of bankruptcies throughout the United States;

(5) To coin money, regulate the value thereof, and of foreign coin, and fix the standard of weights and measures;

(6) To provide for the punishment of counterfeiting the securities and current coin of the United States;

(7) To establish post offices and post roads;

(8) To promote the progress of science and useful arts, by securing for limited times to authors and inventors the exclusive right to their respective writings and discoveries;

(9) To constitute tribunals inferior to the Supreme Court;

(10) To define and punish piracies and felonies committed on the high seas, and offenses against the law of nations;

(11) To declare war, grant letters of marque and reprisal, and make rules concerning captures on land and water;

(12) To raise and support armies, but no appropriation of money to that use shall be for a longer term than two years;

(13) To provide and maintain a navy;

(14) To make rules for the government and regulation of the land and naval forces;

(15) To provide for calling forth the militia to execute the laws of the Union, suppress insurrections and repel invasions;

(16) To provide for organizing, arming, and disciplining, the militia, and for governing such part of them as may be employed in the service of the United States, reserving to the states respectively, the appointment of the officers, and the authority of training the militia according to the discipline prescribed by Congress;

(17) To exercise exclusive legislation in all cases whatsoever, over such district (not exceeding ten miles square) as may, by cession of particular states, and the acceptance of Congress, become the seat of the government of the United States, and to exercise like authority over all places purchased by the consent of the legislature of the state in which the same shall be, for the erection of forts, magazines, arsenals, dockyards, and other needful buildings; —And

(18) To make all laws which shall be necessary and proper for carrying into execution the foregoing powers, and all other powers vested by this Constitution in the government of the United States, or in any department or officer thereof.

## Powers Denied Congress

**Section 9**

(1) The migration or importation of such persons as any of the states now existing shall think proper to admit, shall not be prohibited by the Congress prior to the year one thousand eight hundred and eight, but a tax or duty may be imposed on such importation, not exceeding ten dollars for each person.

(2) The privilege of the writ of habeas corpus shall not be suspended, unless when in cases of rebellion or invasion the public safety may require it.

(3) No bill of attainder or ex post facto law shall be passed.

(4) No capitation, [or other direct,] tax shall be laid, unless in proportion to the census or enumeration herein before directed to be taken.

(5) No tax or duty shall be laid on articles exported from any state.

(6) No preference shall be given by any regulation of commerce or revenue to the ports of one state over those of another: nor shall vessels bound to, or from, one state, be obliged to enter, clear, or pay duties in another.

(7) No money shall be drawn from the treasury, but in consequence of appropriations made by law; and a regular statement and account of the receipts and expenditures of all public money shall be published from time to time.

(8) No title of nobility shall be granted by the United States: And no person holding any office of profit or trust under them, shall, without the consent of the Congress, accept of any present, emolument, office, or title, of any kind whatever, from any king, prince, or foreign state.

## Powers Denied the States

**Section 10**

(1) No state shall enter into any treaty, alliance, or confederation; grant letters of marque and reprisal; coin money; emit bills of credit; make anything but gold and silver coin a tender in payment of debts; pass any bill of attainder, ex post facto law, or law impairing the obligation of contracts, or grant any title of nobility.

(2) No state shall, without the consent of the Congress, lay any imposts or duties on imports or exports, except what may be absolutely necessary for executing its inspection laws: and the net produce of all duties and imposts, laid by any state on imports or exports, shall be for the use of the treasury of the United States; and all such laws shall be subject to the revision and control of the Congress.

(3) No state shall, without the consent of Congress, lay any duty of tonnage, keep troops, or ships of war in time of peace, enter into any agreement or compact with another state, or with a foreign power, or engage in war, unless

actually invaded, or in such imminent danger as will not admit of delay.

# ARTICLE II
## The Executive Branch

### *The President*

#### Section 1

(1) The executive power shall be vested in a President of the United States of America. He shall hold his office during the term of four years, and, together with the Vice President, chosen for the same term, be elected, as follows:

(2) Each state shall appoint, in such manner as the legislature thereof may direct, a number of electors, equal to the whole number of senators and representatives to which the state may be entitled in the Congress: but no senator or representative, or person holding an office of trust or profit under the United States, shall be appointed an elector.

[The electors shall meet in their respective states, and vote by ballot for two persons, of whom one at least shall not be an inhabitant of the same state with themselves. And they shall make a list of all the persons voted for, and of the number of votes for each; which list they shall sign and certify, and transmit sealed to the seat of the government of the United States, directed to the president of the Senate. The president of the Senate shall, in the presence of the Senate and House of Representatives, open all the certificates, and the votes shall then be counted. The person having the greatest number of votes shall be the President, if such number be a majority of the whole number of electors appointed; and if there be more than one who have such majority, and have an equal number of votes, then the House of Representatives shall immediately choose by ballot one of them for President; and if no person have a majority, then from the five highest on the list the said House shall in like manner choose the President. But in choosing the President, the votes shall be taken by states, the representation from each state having one vote; a quorum for this purpose shall consist of a member or members from two-thirds of the states, and a majority of all the states shall be necessary to a choice. In every case, after the choice of the President, the person having the greatest number of votes of the electors shall be the Vice President. But if there should remain two or more who have equal votes, the Senate shall choose from them by ballot the Vice President.]

(3) The Congress may determine the time of choosing the electors, and the day on which they shall give their votes; which day shall be the same throughout the United States.

(4) No person except a natural-born citizen, or a citizen of the United States at the time of the adoption of this Constitution, shall be eligible to the office of President; neither shall any person be

eligible to that office who shall not have attained to the age of thirty-five years, and been fourteen years a resident within the United States.

(5)  In case of the removal of the President from office, or of his death, resignation, or inability to discharge the powers and duties of the said office, the same shall devolve on the Vice President, and the Congress may by law provide for the case of removal, death, or resignation or inability, both of the President and Vice President, declaring what officer shall then act as President, and such officer shall act accordingly, until the disability be removed, or a President shall be elected.

(6)  The President shall, at stated times, receive for his services, a compensation, which shall neither be increased or diminished during the period for which he shall have been elected, and he shall not receive within that period any other emolument from the United States, or any of them.

(7)  Before he enter on the execution of his office, he shall take the following oath or affirmation:  —"I do solemnly swear (or affirm) that I will faithfully execute the office of President of the United States, and will to the best of my ability, preserve, protect, and defend the Constitution of the United States."

## Powers of the President
### Section 2
(1)  The President shall be commander in chief of the Army and Navy of the United States, and of the militia of the several states, when called into the actual service of the United States; he may require the opinion, in writing, of the principal officer in each of the executive departments, upon any subject relating to the duties of their respective offices, and he shall have power to grant reprieves and pardons for offenses against the United States, except in cases of impeachment.

(2)  He shall have power, by and with the advice and consent of the Senate, to make treaties, provided two-thirds of the senators present concur; and he shall nominate, and by and with the advice and consent of the Senate, shall appoint ambassadors, other public ministers and consuls, judges of the Supreme Court, and all other officers of the United States, whose appointments are not herein otherwise provided for, and which shall be established by law: but the Congress may by law vest the appointment of such inferior officers, as they think proper, in the President alone, in the courts of law, or in the heads of departments.

(3)  The President shall have power to fill up all vacancies that may happen during the recess of the Senate, by granting commissions which shall expire at the end of their next session.

## Duties of the President

### Section 3

He shall from time to time give to the Congress information of the state of the Union, and recommend to their consideration such measures as he shall judge necessary and expedient; he may, on extraordinary occasions, convene both houses, or either of them, and in case of disagreement between them, with respect to the time of adjournment, he may adjourn them to such time as he shall think proper; he shall receive ambassadors and other public ministers; he shall take care that the laws be faithfully executed, and shall commission all the officers of the United States.

## Impeachment

### Section 4

The President, Vice President, and all civil officers of the United States, shall be removed from office on impeachment for, and conviction of, treason, bribery, or other high crimes and misdemeanors.

# ARTICLE III
# The Judicial Branch

## Federal Courts and Judges

### Section 1

The judicial power of the United States, shall be vested in one Supreme Court, and in such inferior courts as the Congress may from time to time ordain and establish. The judges, both of the Supreme and inferior courts, shall hold their offices during good behavior, and shall, at stated times, receive for their services, a compensation, which shall not be diminished during their continuance in office.

## Jurisdiction of United States Courts

### Section 2

(1) The judicial power shall extend to all cases, in law and equity, arising under this Constitution, the laws of the United States, and treaties made, or which shall be made, under their authority; — to all cases affecting ambassadors, other public ministers and consuls; — to all cases of admiralty and maritime jurisdiction; — to controversies to which the United States shall be a party; — to controversies between two or more states; — [between a state and citizens of another state;] — between citizens of different states; — between citizens of the same state claiming lands under grants of different states, and between a state, or the citizens thereof, and foreign states, [citizens or subjects].

(2) In all cases affecting ambassadors, other public ministers and consuls, and those in which a state shall be party, the Supreme Court shall have original jurisdiction. In all the other cases before mentioned, the Supreme Court shall have appellate jurisdiction, both as to law and fact, with such exceptions, and under such regulations as the Congress shall make.

(3) The trial of all crimes, except in cases of impeachment, shall be by jury; and such trial shall be held in the state where the said crimes shall have been committed; but when not committed within any state, the trial shall be at such place or places as the Congress may by law have directed.

## Treason

### Section 3

(1) Treason against the United States, shall consist only in levying war against them, or in adhering to their enemies, giving them aid and comfort. No person shall be convicted of treason unless on the testimony of two witnesses to the same overt act, or on confession in open court.

(2) The Congress shall have power to declare the punishment of treason, but no attainder of treason shall work corruption of blood, or forfeiture except during the life of the person attainted.

# ARTICLE IV
# The States and the Federal Government

## State Acts and Records

### Section 1

Full faith and credit shall be given in each state to the public acts, records, and judicial proceedings of every other state. And the Congress may by general laws prescribe the manner in which such acts, records, and proceedings shall be proved, and the effect thereof.

## Rights of Citizens

### Section 2

(1) The citizens of each state shall be entitled to all privileges and immunities of citizens in the several states.

(2) A person charged in any state with treason, felony, or other crime, who shall flee from justice, and be found in another state, shall on demand of the executive authority of the state from which he fled, be delivered up, to be removed to the state having jurisdiction of the crime.

(3) [No person held to service or labor in one state, under the laws thereof, escaping into another, shall, in consequence of any law or regulation therein, be discharged from such service or labor, but shall be delivered up on claim of the party to whom such service or labor may be due.]

## New States and Territories

### Section 3

(1) New states may be admitted by the Congress into this Union; but no new state shall be formed or erected within the jurisdiction of any other state; nor any state be formed by the junction of two or more states, or parts of states, without the consent of the legislatures of the states concerned as well as of Congress.

(2) The Congress shall have power to dispose of and make all needful rules and regulations respecting the territory or other property belonging to the United States; and nothing in this Constitution shall be so construed as to prejudice any claims of the United States, or of any particular state.

### *Protection of States Guaranteed*

### Section 4

The United States shall guarantee to every state in this Union a republican form of government, and shall protect each of them against invasion; and on application of the legislature, or of the executive (when the legislature cannot be convened) against domestic violence.

# ARTICLE V
# Amending the Constitution

The Congress, whenever two-thirds of both houses shall deem it necessary, shall propose amendments to this Constitution, or, on the application of the legislatures of two-thirds of the several states, shall call a convention for proposing amendments, which, in either case, shall be valid to all intents and purposes, as part of this Constitution, when ratified by the legislatures of three-fourths of the several states, or by conventions in three-fourths thereof, as the one or the other mode of ratification may be proposed by the Congress; provided [that no amendment which may be made prior to the year one thousand eight hundred and eight shall in any manner affect the first and fourth clauses in the ninth section of the first article; and] that no state, without its consent, shall be deprived of its equal suffrage in the Senate.

# ARTICLE VI
# General Provisions

(1) All debts contracted and engagements entered into, before the adoption of this Constitution, shall be as valid against the United States under this Constitution, as under the Confederation.

(2) This Constitution, and the laws of the United States which shall be made in pursuance thereof; and all treaties made, or which shall be made, under the authority of the United States, shall be the supreme law of the land; and the judges in every state shall be bound thereby, anything in the constitution or laws of any state to the contrary notwithstanding.

(3) The senators and representatives before mentioned, and the members of the several state legislatures, and all executive and judicial officers, both of the United States and of the several states, shall be bound by oath or affirmation, to support this Constitution; but no religious test shall ever be required as a qualification to any office or public trust under the United States.

## ARTICLE VII
## Ratifying the Constitution

The ratification of the conventions of nine states shall be sufficient for the establishment of this Constitution between the states so ratifying the same.

Done in convention by the unanimous consent of the states present the seventeenth day of September in the year of our Lord one thousand seven hundred and eighty-seven and of the independence of the United States of America the twelfth. In witness thereof we have hereunto subscribed our names.

George Washington,
  President and
  deputy from Virginia

**Delaware**

George Read
Gunning Bedford, Jr.
John Dickinson
Richard Bassett
Jacob Broom

**Maryland**

James McHenry
Dan of St. Thomas
  Jenifer
Daniel Carroll

**Virginia**

John Blair
James Madison, Jr.

**North Carolina**

William Blount
Richard Dobbs
  Spaight
Hugh Williamson

**South Carolina**

John Rutledge
Charles Cotesworth
  Pinckney
Charles Pinckney
Pierce Butler

**Georgia**

William Few
Abraham Baldwin

**New Hampshire**

John Langdon
Nicholas Gilman

**Massachusetts**

Nathaniel Gorham
Rufus King

**Connecticut**

William Samuel
  Johnson
Roger Sherman

**New York**

Alexander Hamilton

**New Jersey**

William Livingston
David Brearley
William Paterson
Jonathan Dayton

**Pennsylvania**

Benjamin Franklin
Thomas Mifflin
Robert Morris
George Clymer
Thomas FitzSimons
Jared Ingersoll
James Wilson
Gouverneur Morris

**Attest:**

William Jackson,
  Secretary

## The Bill of Rights

### AMENDMENT 1
### *Religious and Political Freedoms (1791)*

Congress shall make no law respecting an establishment of religion, or prohibiting the free exercise thereof; or abridging the freedom of speech, or of the press; or the right of the people peaceably to assemble, and to petition the government for a redress of grievances.

### AMENDMENT 2
### *Right to Bear Arms (1791)*

A well-regulated militia, being necessary to the security of a free state, the right of the people to keep and bear arms shall not be infringed.

### AMENDMENT 3
### *Housing of Soldiers (1791)*

No soldier shall, in time of peace be quartered in any house, without the consent of the owner, nor in time of war, but in a manner to be prescribed by law.

### AMENDMENT 4
### *Search and Arrest Warrants (1791)*

The right of the people to be secure in their persons, houses, papers, and effects, against unreasonable searches and seizures, shall not be violated, and no warrants shall issue, but upon probable cause, supported by oath or affirmation, and particularly describing the place to be searched, and the persons or things to be seized.

### AMENDMENT 5
### *Rights in Criminal Cases (1791)*

No person shall be held to answer for a capital, or otherwise infamous crime, unless on a presentment or indictment of a grand jury, except in cases arising in the land or naval forces, or in the militia, when in actual service in time of war or public danger; nor shall any person be subject for the same offense to be twice put in jeopardy of life or limb; nor shall be compelled in any criminal case to be a witness against himself, nor be deprived of life, liberty, or property, without due process of law; nor shall private property be taken for public use, without just compensation.

### AMENDMENT 6
### *Rights to a Fair Trial (1791)*

In all criminal prosecutions, the accused shall enjoy the right to a speedy and public trial, by an impartial jury of the state and district wherein the crime shall have been committed, which district shall have been previously ascertained by law, and to be informed of the nature and cause of the accusation; to be confronted with the witnesses against him; to have compulsory process for obtaining witnesses in his favor, and to have the assistance of counsel for his defense.

## AMENDMENT 7
### Rights in Civil Cases (1791)

In suits at common law, where the value in controversy shall exceed twenty dollars, the right of trial by jury shall be preserved, and no fact tried by a jury, shall be otherwise re-examined in any court of the United States, than according to the rules of the common law.

## AMENDMENT 8
### Bails, Fines, and Punishments (1791)

Excessive bail shall not be required, nor excessive fines imposed, nor cruel and unusual punishments inflicted.

## AMENDMENT 9
### Rights Retained by the People (1791)

The enumeration in the Constitution, of certain rights, shall not be construed to deny or disparage others retained by the people.

## AMENDMENT 10
### Powers Retained by the States and the People (1791)

The powers not delegated to the United States by the Constitution, nor prohibited by it to the states, are reserved to the states respectively, or to the people.

## AMENDMENT 11
### Lawsuits Against States (1795)

The judicial power of the United States shall not be construed to extend to any suit in law or equity, commenced or prosecuted against one of the United States by citizens of another state, or by citizens or subjects of any foreign state.

## AMENDMENT 12
### Election of the President and Vice President (1804)

The electors shall meet in their respective states and vote by ballot for President and Vice President, one of whom, at least, shall not be an inhabitant of the same state with themselves; they shall name in their ballots the person voted for as President, and in distinct ballots the person voted for as Vice President, and they shall make distinct lists of all persons voted for as President, and of all persons voted for as Vice President, and of the number of votes for each, which lists they shall sign and certify, and transmit sealed to the seat of the government of the United States, directed to the president of the Senate; — the president of the Senate shall, in the presence of the Senate and House of Representatives, open all the certificates and the votes shall then be counted; — the person having the greatest number of votes for President, shall be the President, if such number be a majority of the whole number of electors appointed; and if no person have such majority, then from the persons having the highest numbers not exceeding three on the list of those voted for as President, the House of Representatives shall choose immediately, by ballot, the President.

But in choosing the President, the votes shall be taken by states, the representation from each state having one vote; a quorum for this purpose shall consist of a member or members from two-thirds of the states, and a majority of all the states shall be necessary to a choice. And if the House of Representatives shall not choose a President whenever the right of choice shall devolve upon them, [before the fourth day of March next following,] then the Vice President shall act as President, as in the case of the death or other constitutional disability of the President.

The person having the greatest number of votes as Vice President, shall be the Vice President, if such number be a majority of the whole number of electors appointed, and if no person have a majority, then from the two highest numbers on the list, the Senate shall choose the Vice President; a quorum for the purpose shall consist of two-thirds of the whole number of senators, and a majority of the whole number shall be necessary to a choice. But no person constitutionally ineligible to the office of President shall be eligible to that of Vice President of the United States.

## AMENDMENT 13
### Abolition of Slavery (1865)
**Section 1**
Neither slavery nor involuntary servitude, except as a punishment for crime whereof the party shall have been duly convicted, shall exist within the United States, or any place subject to their jurisdiction.

**Section 2**
Congress shall have power to enforce this article by appropriate legislation.

## AMENDMENT 14
### Civil Rights (1868)
**Section 1**
All persons born or naturalized in the United States, and subject to the jurisdiction thereof, are citizens of the United States and of the state wherein they reside. No state shall make or enforce any law which shall abridge the privileges or immunities of citizens of the United States; nor shall any state deprive any person of life, liberty, or property, without due process of law; nor deny to any person within its jurisdiction the equal protection of the laws.

**Section 2**
Representatives shall be apportioned among the several states according to their respective numbers, counting the whole number of persons in each state, [excluding Indians not taxed]. But when the right to vote at any election for the choice of electors for President and Vice President of the United States, representatives in Congress, the executive and judicial officers of a state, or the members of the legislature thereof, is denied to any of the male inhabitants of such state, being twenty-one years of age, and citizens of the United States, or in any way abridged, except for participation in rebellion, or

other crime, the basis of representation therein shall be reduced in the proportion which the number of such male citizens shall bear to the whole number of male citizens twenty-one years of age in such state.

## Section 3

No person shall be a senator or representative in Congress, or elector of President and Vice President, or hold any office, civil or military, under the United States, or under any state, who, having previously taken an oath, as a member of Congress, or as an officer of the United States, or as a member of any state legislature, or as an executive or judicial officer of any state, to support the Constitution of the United States, shall have engaged in insurrection or rebellion against the same, or given aid or comfort to the enemies thereof. But Congress may by a vote of two-thirds of each House, remove such disability.

## Section 4

The validity of the public debt of the United States, authorized by law, including debts incurred for payment of pensions and bounties for services in suppressing insurrection or rebellion, shall not be questioned. But neither the United States nor any state shall assume or pay any debt or obligation incurred in aid of insurrection or rebellion against the United States, or any claim for the loss or emancipation of any slave; but all such debts,

obligations, and claims shall be held illegal and void.

## Section 5

The Congress shall have power to enforce, by appropriate legislation, the provisions of this article.

## AMENDMENT 15
### Right to Vote (1870)

## Section 1

The right of citizens of the United States to vote shall not be denied or abridged by the United States or by any state on account of race, color, or previous condition of servitude.

## Section 2

The Congress shall have power to enforce this article by appropriate legislation.

## AMENDMENT 16
### Income Taxes (1913)

The Congress shall have power to lay and collect taxes on incomes, from whatever source derived, without apportionment among the several states, and without regard to any census or enumeration.

## AMENDMENT 17
### Direct Election of Senators (1913)

(1) The Senate of the United States shall be composed of two senators from each state, elected by the people thereof for six years; and each senator shall have one vote. The electors in each state shall have the qualifications requisite for electors of the most numerous branch of the state legislatures.

(2) When vacancies happen in the representation of any state in the Senate, the executive authority of such state shall issue writs of election to fill such vacancies: provided, that the legislature of any state may empower the executive thereof to make temporary appointments until the people fill the vacancies by election as the legislature may direct.

(3) This amendment shall not be so construed as to affect the election or term of any senator chosen before it becomes valid as part of the Constitution.

## AMENDMENT 18
## *Prohibition of Liquor (1919)*

### Section 1
After one year from the ratification of this article the manufacture, sale, or transportation of intoxicating liquors within, the importation thereof into, or the exportation thereof from the United States and all territory subject to the jurisdiction thereof for beverage purposes is hereby prohibited.

### Section 2
The Congress and the several states shall have concurrent power to enforce this article by appropriate legislation.

### Section 3
This article shall be inoperative unless it shall have been ratified as an amendment to the Constitution by the legislatures of the several states, as provided in the Constitution, within seven years from

the date of the submission hereof to the states by the Congress.

## AMENDMENT 19
## *Women's Suffrage (1920)*

### Section 1
The right of citizens of the United States to vote shall not be denied or abridged by the United States or by any state on account of sex.

### Section 2
Congress shall have power to enforce this article by appropriate legislation.

## AMENDMENT 20
## *Terms of the President and Congress (1933)*

### Section 1
The terms of the President and Vice President shall end at noon on the 20th day of January, and the terms of senators and representatives at noon on the third day of January, of the years in which such terms would have ended if this article had not been ratified; and the terms of their successors shall then begin.

### Section 2
The Congress shall assemble at least once in every year, and such meeting shall begin at noon on the third day of January, unless they shall by law appoint a different day.

### Section 3
If, at the time fixed for the beginning of the term of the President, the President elect shall have died, the Vice President elect shall become President. If a

President shall not have been chosen before the time fixed for the beginning of his term, of if the President elect shall have failed to qualify, then the Vice President elect shall act as President until a President shall have qualified; and the Congress may by law provide for the case wherein neither a President elect nor a Vice President elect shall have qualified, declaring who shall then act as President, or the manner in which one who is to act shall be selected, and such person shall act accordingly until a President or Vice President shall have qualified.

## Section 4
The Congress may by law provide for the case of the death of any of the persons from whom the House of Representatives may choose a President whenever the right of choice shall have devolved upon them, and for the case of the death of any of the persons from whom the Senate may choose a Vice President whenever the right of choice shall have devolved upon them.

## Section 5
Sections 1 and 2 shall take effect on the 15th day of October following the ratification of this article.

## Section 6
This article shall be inoperative unless it shall have been ratified as an amendment to the Constitution by the legislatures of three-fourths of the several states within seven years from the date of its submission.

## AMENDMENT 21
### Repeal of Prohibition (1933)

### Section 1
The eighteenth article of amendment to the Constitution of the United States is hereby repealed.

### Section 2
The transportation or importation into any state, territory, or possession of the United States for delivery or use therein of intoxicating liquors, in violation of the laws thereof, is hereby prohibited.

### Section 3
This article shall be inoperative unless it shall have been ratified as an amendment to the Constitution by conventions in the several states, as provided in the Constitution, within seven years from the date of the submission hereof to the states by the Congress.

## AMENDMENT 22
### Limitation on Presidential Terms (1951)

### Section 1
No person shall be elected to the office of the President more than twice, and no person who has held the office of President, or acted as President, for more than two years of a term to which some other person was elected President shall be elected to the office of the President more than once. But this article shall not apply to any person holding the office of President when this article was proposed by the Congress, and shall not prevent any person who may be holding

the office of President, or acting as President, during the term within which this article becomes operative from holding the office of President or acting as President during the remainder of such term.

## Section 2

This article shall be inoperative unless it shall have been ratified as an amendment to the Constitution by the legislatures of three-fourths of the several states within seven years from the date of its submission to the states by the Congress.

## AMENDMENT 23
### Suffrage in the District of Columbia (1961)

## Section 1

The district constituting the seat of government of the United States shall appoint in such manner as the Congress may direct: A number of electors of President and Vice President equal to the whole number of senators and representatives in Congress to which the district would be entitled if it were a state, but in no event more than the least populous state; they shall be in addition to those appointed by the states, but they shall be considered, for the purposes of the election of President and Vice President, to be electors appointed by a state; and they shall meet in the district and perform such duties as provided by the twelfth article of amendment.

## Section 2

The Congress shall have power to enforce this article by appropriate legislation.

## AMENDMENT 24
### Poll Taxes (1964)

## Section 1

The right of citizens of the United States to vote in any primary or other election for President or Vice President, for electors for President or Vice President, or for senator or representative in Congress, shall not be denied or abridged by the United States or any state by reason of failure to pay any poll tax or other tax.

## Section 2

The Congress shall have power to enforce this article by appropriate legislation.

## AMENDMENT 25
### Presidential Disability and Succession (1967)

## Section 1

In case of the removal of the President from office or of his death or resignation, the Vice President shall become President.

## Section 2

Whenever there is a vacancy in the office of the Vice President, the President shall nominate a Vice President who shall take office upon confirmation by a majority vote of both houses of Congress.

## Section 3

Whenever the President transmits to the president *pro tempore* of the Senate and the Speaker of the House of Representatives his written declaration that he is unable to discharge the powers and duties of his office, and until he transmits to them a written declaration to the contrary, such powers and duties shall be discharged by the Vice President as acting President.

## Section 4

Whenever the Vice President and a majority of either the principal officers of the executive departments or of such other body as Congress may by law provide, transmit to the president pro tempore of the Senate and the Speaker of the House of Representatives their written declaration that the President is unable to discharge the powers and duties of his office, the Vice President shall immediately assume the powers and duties of the office as acting President.

Thereafter, when the President transmits to the president pro tempore of the Senate and the speaker of the House of Representatives his written declaration that no inability exists, he shall resume the powers and duties of his office unless the Vice President and a majority of either the principal officers of the executive department or of such other body as Congress may by law provide, transmit within four days to the president pro tempore of the Senate and the Speaker of the House of Representatives

their written declaration that the President is unable to discharge the powers and duties of his office. Thereupon Congress shall decide the issue, assembling within forty-eight hours for that purpose if not in session. If the Congress, within twenty-one days after receipt of the latter written declaration, or, if Congress is not in session, within twenty-one days after Congress is required to assemble, determines by two-thirds vote of both houses that the President is unable to discharge the powers and duties of his office, the Vice President shall continue to discharge the same as acting President; otherwise, the President shall resume the powers and duties of his office.

## AMENDMENT 26
## *Suffrage for 18-Year-Olds (1971)*

### Section 1

The right of citizens of the United States, who are eighteen years of age or older, to vote shall not be denied or abridged by the United States or by any state on account of age.

### Section 2

The Congress shall have power to enforce this article by appropriate legislation.

## AMENDMENT 27
## *Congressional Pay (1992)*

No law, varying the compensation for the services of the senators and representatives, shall take effect, until an election of representatives shall have intervened.

# Glossary

## A

**Abnormal** (ab nôr´ məl) Unusual; different from normal (p. 155)

**Abstinence** (ab´ stə nəns) A voluntary choice to avoid something (p. 251)

**Accommodation** (ə kom ə dā´ shən) An adjustment that helps a person successfully complete a task (p. 162)

**Acquired immunodeficiency syndrome (AIDS)** (ə kwir´ d imyü nō di fish´ ən sē sin´ drōm) A disorder of the immune system (p. 28)

**Addictive** (ə dik´ tiv) Habit forming (p. 46)

**Additive** (ad´ ə tiv) A substance added to food in small amounts (p. 129)

**Aerobic exercise** (âr ō´ bik ek´ sər sīz) Activity that increases a person's heart rate (p. 133)

**Affective disorder** (ə fek´ tiv dis ôr´ dər) A mental problem characterized by disturbed or uncontrolled emotions (p. 159)

**Aftershock** (af tėr shäk´) A small earthquake that follows a larger earthquake (p. 109)

**Agency** (ā´ jən sē) A department or an office (p. 294)

**Alcoholism** (al´ kə hȯl liz əm) A disease in which a person is dependent on alcohol (p. 48)

**Alert** (ə lėrt´) Paying attention and being wide awake (p. 97)

**Amino acid** (ə mē´ nō as´ id) A small chemical unit that makes up protein (p. 123)

**Anabolic steroid** (an ə bol´ ik ster´ oid) A synthetic drug that resembles the male sex hormone testosterone (p. 51)

**Anaerobic exercise** (an ə rō´ bik ek´ sər sīz) Activity that quickly uses up oxygen in the body (p. 133)

**Analgesic** (an l jē´ zik) A medicine that relieves pain (p. 41)

**Antibiotic** (an ti bī ot´ ik) A medicine that controls infection by destroying bacteria and other pathogens (p. 42)

**Antibody** (an´ ti bod ē) A protein that kills a specific kind of pathogen (p. 30)

**Antivirus program** (an´ tī vī´ rəs prō´ gram) A program that protects a computer from viruses (p. 226)

**Anxiety disorder** (ang zī´ ə tē dis ôr´ dər) A mental problem that makes normal life difficult because of intense anxiety (p. 158)

**Apprenticeship** (ə pren´ tis ship) A way to learn a trade by working with a master at that trade (p. 315)

**Arthritis** (är thri´ tis) A group of diseases that result in swelling of the joints and rubbing on the bones (p. 26)

**ATM card** (ATM kärd) A card that allows you to use an ATM (p. 184)

**Auditory** (ȯ´ də tôr´ ē) Having to do with hearing (p. 416)

**Automated teller machine (ATM)** (ȯ´ tə māt ed te´ lər mə´ shēn) A machine that lets you put money into a bank account or take money out (p. 184)

## B

**Balance** (bal´ əns) The amount of money left in an account after the withdrawals are subtracted from the deposits (p. 181)

**Ballot** (bal´ ət) A card or paper on which a person marks his or her vote (p. 289)

**Barbiturates** (bär bich´ ər itz) A category of sedative-hypnotic drugs (p. 49)

**Behavior modification** (bi hā´ vyer mod ə fə kā´ shən) A form of psychotherapy that teaches a person to replace an unhealthy behavior pattern with a healthy one (p. 158)

**Benign** (bi nīn´) Not harmful to health (p. 23)

**Bipolar disorder** (bi pō´ lər dis ôr´ dər) A mental problem involving wide uncontrollable shifts in a person's feelings (p. 160)

**Blizzard** (bliz´ ərd) A strong winter snowstorm (p. 106)

**Body language** (bod´ ē lang´ gwij) Facial expressions, hand gestures, and other forms of communication that do not use words (p. 245)

**Bookmark** (bùk´ märk) A shortcut to an Internet site (p. 223)

**Budget** (buj´ it) A plan for spending money (p. 175)

## C

**Calcium** (kal´ sē əm) Mineral important for maintaining strong bones and teeth (p. 124)

| | | | | | | | | | | |
|---|---|---|---|---|---|---|---|---|---|---|
| a | hat | e | let | ī | ice | ô | order | ù | put | sh | she |
| ā | age | ē | equal | o | hot | oi | oil | ü | rule | th | thin |
| ä | far | ėr | term | ō | open | ou | out | ch | child | ŦH | then |
| â | care | i | it | ȯ | saw | u | cup | ng | long | zh | measure |

ə { a in about / e in taken / i in pencil / o in lemon / u in circus }

**Calorie** (kal´ ər ē) A unit that measures the amount of energy in food (p. 116)

**Candidate** (kan´ də dāt) A person running for government office such as mayor or president (p. 288)

**Carbohydrate** (kär bō hī´ drāt) A nutrient that provides energy and includes sugar or starch (p. 120)

**Carbon monoxide** (kär´ bən mə nok´ sīd) A colorless, odorless gas that can cause death within minutes (p. 92)

**Cardiac arrest** (kär´ dē ak ə rest´) A condition in which the heart has stopped beating and there is no pulse (p. 14)

**Cardiopulmonary resuscitation (CPR)** (kär dē ō pul´ mə ner ē ri sus´ ə tā shen) An emergency procedure for cardiovascular failure (p. 14)

**Cardiovascular** (kär dē ō vas´ kyə lər) Relating to the heart and blood vessels (p. 20)

**Career plan** (kə rir´ plan) A step-by-step way to reach your career goals (p. 363)

**Cartilage** (kär´ tl ij) A cushion in the joints (p. 26)

**Certificate of deposit (CD)** (sər tif´ ə kit ov di poz´ it) A savings account in which the money has to stay in the account for a period of time (p. 204)

**Cervix** (sėr´ viks) Narrow outer end of the uterus (p. 262)

**Chancre** (shang´ kər) A painless, hard sore with a small amount of yellow discharge (p. 261)

**Check register** (chek rej´ ə stər) A booklet in a checkbook to keep track of checks and deposits (p. 183)

**Chlamydia** (klə mid´ ē ə) A sexually transmitted disease with symptoms similar to gonorrhea (p. 261)

**Cholesterol** (kə les´ tə rol) A waxy, fatlike substance in the cells of all animals (p. 122)

**Citizen** (sit´ ə zən) A member of a country (p. 288)

**Classified ad** (klas´ ə fīd ad) Notice that describes property available for sale or rent (p. 58)

**Clinical depression** (klin´ ə kəl di presh´ ən) An affective disorder involving long-lasting, intense sadness (p. 159)

**Common Application** (kom´ ən ap´ lə kā´ shən) A form to request admission that is accepted by many colleges (p. 389)

**Communicable disease** (kə myü´ nə kə bəl də zēz) A disease that can be passed from one person to another (p. 27)

**Compensation** (kom pən sā´ shən) The wages and benefits that an employer provides to its employees in exchange for their work (p. 330)

**Compromise** (kom´ prə mīz) Both sides give in a little to reach an agreement (p. 150)

**Conception** (kən sep´ shən) The beginning of a pregnancy (p. 411)

**Conflict** (kon´ flikt) A disagreement between two or more people who have different ideas (p. 246)

**Consequence** (kon´ sə kwens) What happens as a result of something (p. 412)

**Consumer** (kən sü´ mər) A person who buys goods and services (p. 195)

**Cope** (kōp) To deal with or overcome problems and difficulties (p. 138)

**Cosigner** (kō sī nər) A person with a good credit history who will pay a credit card bill if the cardholder cannot pay it (p. 191)

**Coworker** (kō´ wėr kər) A person who works for the same company (p. 343)

**Credit** (kred´ it) Money that is borrowed with the promise to pay it back (p. 190)

**Credit card** (kred´ it kärd) A card that allows a person to buy something now and pay for it later (p. 172)

**Credit report** (kred´ it ri pôrt´) A summary of a person's credit history (p. 194)

**Curfew** (kėr´ fyü) A time by which people must be off the streets (p. 295)

**Cursor** (kėr´ sər) A blinking line that indicates where you are working within a document (p. 213)

**Custodial parent** (ku stō´ dē əl per´ ənt) The parent who is responsible for children after a divorce (p. 413)

**Cytomegalovirus retinitis** (sī´ tə me gə lō vī rəs ret ən´ īd əs) An eye infection that can lead to blindness (p. 260)

# D

**Daily Value (DV)** (dā´ lē val´ yü) The percent of a nutrient in a food product compared with the total amount of that nutrient needed daily (p. 127)

**Deadline** (ded´ līn) The latest time when something must be done (p. 347)

**Deductible** (di duk´ tə bəl) A specified amount of medical expenses an individual must pay each year before insurance pays anything (p. 36)

**Deduction** (di duk´ shən) Money taken out of a paycheck (p. 188)

**Default** (di fôlt´) Preprogrammed information within a software program (p. 216)

**Defense mechanism** (di fens´ mek´ ə niz əm) A mental device one uses to protect oneself (p. 156)

**Defensive driving** (di fen´ siv drīv´ ing) Driving safely by watching out for other drivers and adjusting to unsafe road conditions (p. 102)

**Deficiency** (di fish´ ən sē) Lack of a certain nutrient in the diet (p. 117)

**Delusion** (di lü´ zhən) A false belief (p. 160)

**Denial** (di nī´ əl) A conscious refusal to take something seriously (p. 157)

**Dental hygienist** (den´ tl hī jē´ nist) A dental professional who is trained to clean teeth, give dental exams, and teach patients good oral hygiene (p. 40)

**Deposit** (di poz´ it) The money an apartment owner holds until you move out of the apartment (p. 62)

**Deposit** (di poz´ it) Money put into a bank account (p. 180)

**Deposit slip** (di poz´ it slip) A slip of paper you fill out to show how much money you are putting into a bank account (p. 180)

**Depressant** (di pres´ nt) A drug that slows down the central nervous system (p. 47)

**Designer drug** (di zin´ er drug) An illegal drug with a slightly different chemical makeup than a similar legal drug (p. 51)

**Destination** (des´ tə nā´ shən) A place a person is going (p. 283)

**Diabetes** (dī ə bē´ tis) A disease in which the body is not able to use glucose from food (p. 25)

**Diet** (dī´ ət) The food that you regularly eat and drink (p. 116)

**Digestion** (də jes´ chən) To change food into a form the body can use (p. 120)

**Direct deposit** (də rekt´ di poz´ it) Having a paycheck deposited directly into a bank instead of receiving the check (p. 189)

**Disability** (dis´ ə bil´ ə tē) A condition that causes a person to be unable to do a task in the usual way (p. 162)

**Discipline** (dis´ ə plin) To teach children acceptable behaviors and limit unacceptable ones (p. 408)

**Discriminate** (dis krim´ ə nāt) To treat differently on the basis of something other than individual worth (p. 255)

**Diskette** (dis ket´) A small square made of plastic and metal, used to store information (p. 217)

**Displacement** (dis plās´ mənt) Shifting an emotion from its real object to a safer or more immediate one (p. 157)

**Divorce** (də vôrs´) The legal end of a marriage (p. 407)

**Document** (dok´ yə mənt) A page of text in a word processor file or a spreadsheet (p. 213)

**Download** (doun´ lōd) To move a copy of a file from one computer to another (p. 225)

**Drag** (drag) Point to an item, then press and hold the mouse button as you move the mouse to a new location (p. 214)

**Drug** (drəg) A chemical substance other than food that changes the way the mind and body work (p. 41)

**Dysfunctional** (dis fungk´ shə nəl) Not working properly (p. 243)

## E

**Earthquake** (ėrth´ kwāk) A shaking of the land that occurs when huge areas of rock move (p. 109)

**Eating disorder** (ēt´ ing dis ôr´ dər) An attempt to deal with psychological problems through eating habits (p. 161)

**Electrical fire** (i lek´ trə kəl fīr) A fire caused by a problem with the flow of electricity (p. 91)

**Electrical shock** (i lek´ trə kəl shok) A flow of electric current through the body that may cause serious burns, other injuries, and even death (p. 92)

**Electrocution** (i lek´ trə kyü´ shən) Death by electrical shock (p. 92)

**E-mail** (ē´ māl) Electronic mail; messages that are written and/or read on-screen and sent through a modem (p. 228)

**Empathy** (em´ pə thē) Identifying with and trying to understand someone else's feelings (p. 255)

**Emphysema** (em fə sē´ mə) A serious respiratory disease that makes breathing difficult (p. 46)

**Employee handbook** (em ploi´ ē hand búk´) A book describing the rules of a company (p. 343)

**Evacuate** (i vak´ yü āt) To leave home and go to a safe place (p. 106)

**Exchange** (eks chānj´) The trading of one item at a store for another item (p. 198)

**Exemption** (eg zemp´ shən) A tax deduction for each member of a family (p. 202)

**Extracurricular activities** (ek strə kə rik´ yə lər ak tiv´ ə tēz) Activities done in addition to attending school classes (p. 319)

| a | hat | e | let | ī | ice | ô | order | ù | put | sh | she | ə | { a in about |
|---|-----|---|-----|---|-----|---|-------|---|-----|----|-----|---|-----|
| ā | age | ē | equal | o | hot | oi | oil | ü | rule | th | thin | | e in taken |
| ä | far | ėr | term | ō | open | ou | out | ch | child | ṯẖ | then | | i in pencil |
| â | care | i | it | ȯ | saw | u | cup | ng | long | zh | measure | | o in lemon |
| | | | | | | | | | | | | | u in circus |

## F

**Fee** (fē) Money charged for a service (p. 179)

**Fiber** (fī′ bər) A substance that helps you digest food; it is found in foods that contain carbohydrates (p. 121)

**File** (fīl) A text document, spreadsheet, database, or program that is identified by a unique name (p. 218)

**Finance charge** (fə nans′ chärj) A fee you pay based on the amount of money you have borrowed from the credit card company (p. 192)

**Financial aid** (fa nan′ shəl ād) Anything that lowers the cost of college for a student, including grants and loans (p. 397)

**Fire extinguisher** (fīr ek sting′ gwish ər) A portable device containing chemicals that will put out a small fire (p. 95)

**Fired** (fīr′ ed) To be dismissed from a company (p. 344)

**First aid** (fėrst ād) The immediate emergency care given to a sick or injured person before professional medical care arrives (p. 8)

**Flammable** *or* **inflammable** (flam′ ə bel)(in flam′ ə bel) Easily catches on fire (p. 91)

**Flash flood** (flash flud) When a body of water quickly overflows without warning and covers dry land (p. 108)

**Folder** (fōl′ dər) A section in a computer's hard drive where documents are stored (p. 218)

**Fracture** (frak′ chər) A broken bone (p. 19)

**Free Application for Federal Student Aid (FAFSA)** (frē ap lə kā shen fôr fed′ ər əl stüd′ nt ād) The form used to apply for financial aid from the federal government (p. 399)

**Frostbite** (frôst′ bīt) A tissue injury caused by exposure to extreme cold (p. 18)

## G

**Genital herpes** (jen′ ə təl hėr′ pēz) A sexually transmitted chronic disease (p. 262)

**Gonorrhea** (gon ə rē′ ə) A sexually transmitted disease that does not always show symptoms (p. 260)

**Good Samaritan Laws** (gùd sə mar′ ə tən lôs) Laws that protect people who assist victims in an emergency (p. 9)

**Gross pay** (grōs pā) Total amount of money earned before deductions (p. 188)

## H

**Hallucination** (hə lü sn ā′ shən) A distorted idea about a person or event that is not real (p. 160)

**Hallucinogen** (hə lü′ snə jen) A drug that confuses the central nervous system (p. 50)

**Harassment** (har′ əs mənt ) Repeatedly bothering or annoying a person (p. 360)

**Hard drive** *or* **hard disk** (härd drīv) (härd disk) A data storage device that is usually installed in the computer base unit (p. 213)

**Hardware** (härd′ wer) The equipment that makes up a computer—the base unit, monitor, mouse, keyboard, and printer (p. 212)

**Health care facility** (helth kâr fə sil′ ə tē) A place where people go for medical, dental, and other care (p. 34)

**Health insurance** (helth in shùr′ əns) A plan that pays all or part of a person's medical costs (p. 35)

**Health maintenance organization (HMO)** (helth mān′ tə nəns ȯr gə nə zā′ shən) A form of managed care (p. 36)

**Health-related fitness** (helth ri lā′ tid fit′ nis) The parts of physical fitness that help you stay healthy; they include cardiovascular fitness, strength, muscular endurance, flexibility, and body fat (p. 132)

**Heat exhaustion** (hēt eg zȯs′ chən) A condition resulting from physical activity in a very hot environment (p. 17)

**Heatstroke** (hēt′ strōk) A condition resulting from being in the heat too long (p. 17)

**Heimlich maneuver** (hīm′ lik mə nü′ vər) Firm upward thrusts below the rib cage to force an object out of the airway (p. 11)

**Heroin** (her′ ō ən) An illegal narcotic made from the opium poppy (p. 50)

**Hospice** (hos′ pis) A long-term care facility for people who are dying (p. 35)

**Hospital** (hos′ pi təl) A facility where sick and injured people receive medical care (p. 35)

**Human immunodeficiency virus (HIV)** (hyü′ mən i myü nō di fish′ ən sē vi′ rəs) The pathogen that causes AIDS (p. 257)

**Human Resources (HR) department** (hyü′ mən ri sȯrs′ ez di pärt mənt) A part of a company that handles employees' work-related issues (p. 350)

**Hurricane** (hėr′ ə kān) A strong tropical storm with heavy rains and winds above 75 miles per hour (p. 106)

**Hypertension** (hī pər ten′ shən) High blood pressure (p. 20)

**HyperText Transfer Protocol (http)** (hi′ pər tekst trans fėr′ prō′ tə kol) A computer language or coded text that can transfer formatted text and graphics (p. 222)

**Hypothermia** (hī pō thėr′ mē ə) A serious loss of body heat from being too cold too long (p. 18)

## I

**Icon** (i´ kon) A small image on a computer screen that represents something stored on the computer (p. 213)

**Ideal** (ī dē´ əl) Perfect, or the best you can think of (p. 306)

**Immune** (i myün´) Resistant to infection (p. 28)

**Immunity** (i myü´ nə tē) The body's ability to resist infectious diseases (p. 30)

**Income tax** (in´ kum taks) A tax paid on the money that people earn (p. 200)

**Incubation** (ing kyə bā´ shən) Time between the initial infection and the appearance of symptoms of a disease (p. 28)

**Individual retirement account (IRA)** (in də vij´ ü əl ri tīr´ mənt ə kount´) A savings account that is set up to encourage people to save for their retirement (p. 204)

**Informational interview** (in´ fər mā´ shən əl in´ tər vyü) A talk with a person about his or her occupation to learn more about it (p. 311)

**Inhalant** (in hā´ lənt) A chemical that is breathed in (p. 51)

**Inpatient** (in pā´ shənt) Someone receiving health care who stays overnight or longer (p. 35)

**Insulin-dependent diabetes** (in´ sə lən di pen´ dənt dī ə bē´ tis) Diabetes that usually causes a person to depend on daily injections of insulin; type I diabetes (p. 25)

**Insurance policy** (in shür´ əns pol´ ə sē) A written agreement between an insurance company and a buyer (p. 72)

**Interest** (in tər´ ist) Money that a bank pays you for keeping your money in the bank (p. 178)

**Internet service provider (ISP)** (in´ tər net sėr´ vis prə vid´ r) A company that connects a telephone line to the Internet for a fee (p. 222)

**Internship** (in´ tėrn ship) A temporary job that can provide valuable work experience (p. 316)

**Intimate** (in´ tə mit) Very personal or private (p. 242)

**Intoxication** (in tok sə kā´ shən) The excitement or stimulation caused by use of a chemical substance (p. 48)

**Isokinetic exercise** (ī sə ki net´ ik ek´ sər sīz) Activity that builds muscle strength when muscles resist tension through a full range of slow motions (p. 133)

**Isometric exercise** (ī´ sə met´ rik ek´ sər sīz) Activity that uses muscle tension to build strength (p. 133)

**Isotonic exercise** (ī sə ton´ ik ek´ sər sīz) Activity that builds muscle strength with weights (p. 133)

**Issue** (ish´ ü) A question or problem that people discuss and make a decision about (p. 288)

## J

**Jaywalking** (jā´ wȯk ing) Crossing a street at a place other than a corner or crosswalk (p. 104)

**Joint custody** (joint kus´ tə dē) Both parents sharing the responsibilities of raising and caring for children (p. 413)

**Jury** (jür´ ē) A group of people chosen to listen to both sides of a case in a trial and give a verdict (p. 291)

## K

**Kaposi's sarcoma** (kä´ pə sēz sär kō´ mə) A rare type of cancer that affects the skin or internal organs (p. 260)

## L

**Labor union** (lā´ bər yü´ nyən) An organization of workers who do similar jobs (p. 345)

**Layoff** (lā´ ȯf) A period of time when a company has no work for employees (p. 374)

**Lease** (lēs) A written contract that describes a rental agreement (p. 58)

**Littering** (lit´ ər ing) Leaving trash on property that is not your own (p. 295)

**Loan** (lōn) Money borrowed for a certain amount of time (p. 190)

**Lymph nodes** (limf nōdz) Knotlike lumps in the body that contain disease-fighting cells (p. 260)

## M

**Malignant** (mə lig´ nənt) Harmful to health (p. 23)

**Malignant melanoma** (mə lig´ nənt mel ə nō´ mə) A common form of skin cancer often caused by the sun (p. 25)

**Malnutrition** (mal nü trish´ ən) A condition that results from a diet that lacks nutrients (p. 117)

**Managed care** (man´ ijed kâr) Health insurance organizations that are go-betweens for patients and doctors (p. 36)

**Manual** (man´ yü əl) A booklet that explains how to use and care for a piece of equipment (p. 64)

**Marijuana** (mar ə wä´ nə) An illegal drug made from a hemp plant (p. 51)

| a | hat | e | let | ī | ice | ô | order | ù | put | sh | she | ə | a in about |
|---|-----|---|-----|---|-----|---|-------|---|-----|----|-----|---|-----------|
| ā | age | ē | equal | o | hot | oi | oil | ü | rule | th | thin | | e in taken |
| ä | far | ėr | term | ō | open | ou | out | ch | child | ᵺ | then | | i in pencil |
| â | care | i | it | ȯ | saw | u | cup | ng | long | zh | measure | | o in lemon |
| | | | | | | | | | | | | | u in circus |

**Mature** (mə chur´) Reaches full value (p. 204)

**Maximum heart rate** (mak´ sə məm härt rāt) Heartbeats per minute during hard, fast, and long exercise (p. 134)

**Medicaid** (med´ ə kād) State and federally funded health insurance for people with incomes below a certain level (p. 37)

**Medicare** (med´ ə kâr) Health insurance for people age 65 and older and people with disabilities who receive Social Security benefits (p. 37)

**Medicine** (med´ ə sən) A drug that is used to relieve, treat, cure, prevent, or identify a disease or problem (p. 41)

**Menu** (men´ yü) List of operations or directions (p. 213)

**Mineral** (min´ ər əl) A substance formed in the earth, needed for fluid balance, digestion, and other body functions (p. 123)

**Minimum balance** (min´ ə məm bal´ əns) The smallest amount of money a person can keep in a bank account without having to pay a fee (p. 179)

**Minimum payment** (min´ ə məm pā´ mənt) The least amount of money you must pay on a bill (p. 192)

**Modem** (mō´ dem) Hardware that connects a personal computer to a telephone line (p. 222)

**Mucous membrane** (myü´ kəs mem´ brān) The moist lining of body passages (p. 29)

**Mucus** (myü´ kəs) Fluid the mucous membranes secrete (p. 29)

## N

**Narcotic** (när kot´ ik) A psychoactive drug made from the opium poppy and used to relieve pain (p. 50)

**Natural disaster** (nach´ ər əl di zas´ tər) A sudden emergency that results from acts of nature (p. 106)

**Negotiation** (ni gō shē ā´ shən) The process of arranging for things you need, usually by giving in on some issues but not on all issues (p. 330)

**Net pay** (net pā) The amount of money an employee receives after deductions have been taken out of the gross pay (p. 188)

**Networking** (net´ wėr king) The sharing of information or services among people or institutions (p. 323)

**Nicotine** (nik´ ə tēn) A chemical in tobacco to which people become addicted (p. 46)

**Non-insulin–dependent diabetes** (non´ in´ sə lən di pen´ dənt dī ə bē´ tis) Diabetes that usually does not cause a person to depend on insulin; type II diabetes (p. 25)

**Nonskid** (non skid) Rubber, plastic, or another sticky material that does not slip (p. 90)

**Nontraditional** (non trə dish´ ə nəl) Seen in a way today that is different from the way it was seen in the past (p. 308)

**Nurture** (nėr´ chər) Helping someone or something grow or develop (p. 242)

**Nutrient** (nü´ trē ənt) A substance in food that your body needs to work properly (p. 116)

**Nutrition facts** (nü trish´ ən fakz) The section of a food label that provides information about the product (p. 127)

## O

**Obstacle** (ob´ stə kəl) Something that interferes with achieving a goal (p. 264)

**Occupational grouping** (ok yə pā´ shə nəl grü´ ping) A group of jobs that share similar titles and duties (p. 310)

**Online** (on´ līn) Connected to the Internet (p. 223)

**Operating system software** (op´ ə rāt´ ing sis təm sȯft wâr) Software that runs the computer (p. 213)

**Optimism** (op´ tə miz əm) Tending to expect the best possible outcome (p. 150)

**Option** (op´ shən) A choice (p. 267)

**Optional feature** (op´ shə nəl fē´ chər) Device on a vehicle that a buyer pays extra to have (p. 101)

**Osteoarthritis** (os tē ō är thrī´ tis) A condition in which the cartilage in joints wears away (p. 26)

**Outpatient clinic** (out´ pā shənt klin´ ik) A place where people receive health care without staying overnight (p. 35)

**Overdose** (ō´ vər dōs) An amount of a drug that is too large for the body to use (p. 49)

## P

**Panic attack** (pan´ ik ə tak´) A feeling of terror that comes without warning and includes chest pains, rapid heartbeat, shaking, sweating, or shortness of breath (p. 158)

**Pathogen** (path´ ə jen) An agent that causes disease (p. 28)

**Paycheck** (pā´ chek) A check from an employer to an employee (p. 186)

**Paycheck stub** (pā´ chek stub) A piece of paper attached to a paycheck that has information about the money earned (p. 187)

**Pedestrian** (pə des´ trē ən) A person who walks (p. 104)

**Peephole** (pēp´ hōl) A small hole in a door that allows someone to see out but does not allow others to see in (p. 93)

**Peer pressure** (pir presh´ ər) Urging from others to do something (p. 356)

**Penalty** (pen´ l tē) A sum of money you forfeit for not meeting all the requirements of an agreement (p. 205)

**Performance assessment** (pər fôr məns ə ses´ mənt) A report that rates how well you do your job (p. 366)

**Personal computer** (pėr´ sə nəl kəm pyü´ tər) A small computer used by one person at a time (p. 212)

**Personal identification number (PIN)** (pėr´ sə nəl ī den tə fə kā´ shən num´ bər) A code that lets your ATM card work (p. 184)

**Pessimism** (pes´ ə miz əm) Tending to expect the worst possible outcome (p. 150)

**Pharmacist** (fär´ mə sist) A druggist (p. 41)

**Phobia** (fō´ bē ə) An irrational or unreasonable fear of something (p. 156)

**Phosphorus** (fos´ fər əs) Mineral that works with calcium to maintain strong bones and teeth (p. 124)

**Physical fitness** (fiz´ ə kəl fit´ nis) The body's ability to meet the demands of everyday living (p. 131)

**Pilot light** (pī´ lət līt) A small stream of burning gas that leads into a stove (p. 69)

**Plaque** (plak) A sticky film of bacteria that grows on the teeth and gums (p. 38)

**Pneumonia** (nü mō´ nyə) A lung infection (p. 260)

**Postsecondary education** (pōst sek´ ən der ē ej´ ə kā´ shən) Any type of formal education after you graduate from high school (p. 382)

**Preferred provider organization (PPO)** (pri fėr´ d prə vīd´ er ôr gə nə zā´ shən ) A form of managed care (p. 37)

**Prejudice** (prej´ ə dis) Negative, or unfavorable, opinions formed without grounds or sufficient knowledge (p. 255)

**Prescription** (pri skrip´ shən) A written order from a medical person for a medicine or other treatment (p. 34)

**Primary care physician (PCP)** (prī´ mer ē kâr fə zish´ ən) A doctor who treats people for routine medical problems (p. 32)

**Probation period** (prō bā´ shən pir´ ē əd) A test period when a worker must prove to a company that he or she can do the job (p. 344)

**Procedure** (prə sē´ jer) A way of doing something (p. 97)

**Procrastination** (prō kras´ tə nā shən) Putting off things you need to do until the last minute (p. 269)

**Projection** (prə jek´ shən) Accusing someone of having your attitudes, feelings, or purposes (p. 157)

**Promotion** (prə mō´ shən) A new job with more responsibility and more pay (p. 372)

**Psychoactive drug** (sī kō ak´ tiv drəg) A drug that affects the mind and mental processes (p. 47)

**Psychologist** (sī kol´ ə jist) A person who studies people's mental and behavioral characteristics (p. 155)

**Psychotherapy** (sī kō ther´ ə pē) Psychological treatment for mental or emotional disorders (p. 158)

**Punctual** (pungk´ chü əl) To be on time for appointments (p. 346)

## R

**Rate** (rāt) A fee charged for a certain amount of a product (p. 67)

**Rational** (rash´ ə nəl) Reasonable (p. 151)

**Recommendation** (rek ə men dā´ shən) A written statement that tells why a person should be considered for something such as a college or job (p. 391)

**Recreation** (re krē ā´ shən) Activities people do for enjoyment (p. 97)

**Rectum** (rek´ təm) Lower part of the large intestine (p. 260)

**Recycle** (rē sī´ kəl) To use something over again (p. 68)

**Refund** (ri fund´) A return of money (p. 198)

**Register** (rej´ ə stər) To sign up to vote (p. 289)

**Rehabilitation** (re hə bil´ ə tā shən) Therapy needed for recovery from surgery or an illness or injury (p. 35)

**Rent** (rent) To pay a fee in order to use something (p. 58)

**Renter's insurance** (ren tərs in shùr´ əns) A policy that protects the value of your property and your ability to replace it (p. 72)

**Repression** (ri presh´ ən) The unconscious dismissal of painful impulses, desires, or fears from the conscious mind (p. 157)

**Rescue breathing** (res´ kyü brē´ thing) Putting oxygen from the rescuer's lungs into an unconscious person's lungs to help the person breathe (p. 13)

**Reservation** (rez ər vā´ shən) An arrangement made to keep something available for your use (p. 284)

**Resolve** (ri zolv) To settle a disagreement (p. 352)

**Responsibility** (ri spon sə bil´ ə tē) A duty (p. 288)

| | | | | | | | | | | | |
|---|---|---|---|---|---|---|---|---|---|---|---|
| a | hat | e | let | ī | ice | ô | order | ù | put | sh | she | ⎧ a | in about |
| ā | age | ē | equal | o | hot | oi | oil | ü | rule | th | thin | e | in taken |
| ä | far | ėr | term | ō | open | ou | out | ch | child | ᴛʜ | then | ə ⎨ i | in pencil |
| â | care | i | it | ȯ | saw | u | cup | ng | long | zh | measure | ⎩ o | in lemon |
| | | | | | | | | | | | | u | in circus |

**Resume** (re zə´ mā) A written summary of your work-related skills, experience, and education in a well-organized, easy-to-read form (p. 317)

**Rheumatoid arthritis** (rü´ mə toid är thrī´ tis) A destructive inflammation of the joints (p. 26)

**Risk factor** (risk fak´ tər) A habit or trait that is known to increase a person's chances of having a disease (p. 21)

## S

**Safe-deposit box** (sāf di poz´ it boks) A secure box at the bank for keeping special items (p. 178)

**Safety feature** (sāf´ tē fē´ chər) Device on a vehicle that helps prevent accidents or protects the driver and passengers during accidents (p. 100)

**Sales tax** (sālz´ taks) A small amount of money added to the price of goods and some services (p. 201)

**Saturated fat** (sach´ ə rā tid fat) A type of fat usually found in animal sources of food (p. 122)

**Savings account** (sā´ vings ə kount´) Money that earns interest in a bank (p. 179)

**Savings bond** (sā´ vings bond) A certificate of a loan to the government (p. 204)

**Savings book register** (sā´ vings bùk rej´ ə stər) A small book you use to record each deposit and withdrawal (p. 181)

**Scholarship** (skol´ ər ship) A gift of money for tuition, often awarded by private organizations (p. 398)

**Scroll** (skrōl) To move the mouse up, down, left, or right on a computer screen (p. 214)

**Search engine** (sėrch en´ jən) A site that offers an index of other sites (p. 233)

**Security** (si kyùr´ ə tē) Safety system to keep people safe from harm (p. 60)

**Select** (si lekt´) To click on a character, word, or words using a mouse, which highlights that item so you can change it (p. 212)

**Self-advocacy** (self´ ad´ və kə sē) The ability to identify and meet needs connected to one's disability without loss of dignity to oneself or others (p. 162)

**Self-assessment** (self´ ə ses´ mənt) The process of studying your own interests, needs, abilities, and values (p. 302)

**Self-defeating behavior** (self´ di fēt´ ing bi hā´ vyər) An action that blocks a person from reaching a goal (p. 156)

**Self-esteem** (self´ e stēm´) How one feels about oneself; self-respect (p. 149)

**Separation** (sep ə rā´ shen) A married couple's agreement, or a court decision, to stop living together (p. 408)

**Sexually transmitted disease (STD)** (sek´ shü əl´ lē tranz mit´ ed da zēz) Any disease that is spread through sexual activity (p. 257)

**Shift** (shift) A work period in a company (p. 347)

**Shock** (shok) Failure of the circulatory system to provide enough blood to the body (p. 15)

**Software** (sȯft´ wâr) Program that tells the computer how to take in and process information (p. 213)

**Specialist** (spesh´ ə list) A doctor who works only in a particular branch of medicine (p. 32)

**Splint** (splint) A rigid object that keeps a broken bone in place (p. 19)

**Sprain** (sprān) A tearing or stretching of tendons or ligaments connecting joints (p. 18)

**Standard deduction** (stan´ dərd di duk´ shən) An amount of money set by the government that takes the place of separate tax deductions (p. 201)

**Standard feature** (stan´ dərd fē´ chər) Device that comes in all vehicles of a certain model (p. 101)

**Sterility** (stə ril´ ə tē) The inability to produce a child (p. 261)

**Stimulant** (stim´ yə lənt) A drug that speeds up the central nervous system (p. 46)

**Stress** (stres) A state of physical or emotional pressure (p. 137)

**Stroke** (strōk) A cardiovascular disease that occurs when the blood supply to the brain is stopped (p. 21)

**Substance abuse disorder** (sub´ stəns a byüz dis ȯr´ dər) An unhealthy dependence on alcohol or other drugs (p. 158)

**Suicide** (sü´ ə sīd) Killing oneself (p. 159)

**Supervise** (sü´ pər vīz) To give direction to another person (p. 307)

**Syphilis** (sif´ ə lis) A sexually transmitted disease (p. 261)

## T

**Tactile** (tak´ təl) Having to do with touching (p. 416)

**Tax** (taks) Money that people pay to the government (p. 200)

**Tax deduction** (taks di duk´ shən) A cost that you can subtract from your income when figuring out your income taxes (p. 201)

**Tax-deferred** (taks di fėr´ red) Not taxed until withdrawn (p. 205)

**Telephone etiquette** (tel´ ə fōn et´ ə ket) Courteous behavior for speaking on the telephone (p. 78)

**Thermostat** (ther´ mə stat) A device that controls temperature (p. 68)

**Thought disorder** (thŏt dis ôr´ dər) A mental problem characterized by distorted or false ideas and beliefs (p. 160)

**Tooth decay** (tüth di kā´) The softening and wearing away of the hard part of the tooth (p. 38)

**Tornado** (tôr nā´ dō) A cone-shaped cloud with winds of up to 500 miles per hour (p. 106)

**Toxic** (tok´ sik) Harmful to health; poisonous (p. 24)

**Tranquilizers** (trang´ kwə lī zərs) A category of sedative-hypnotic drugs (p. 49)

**Transcript** (tran´ skript) A record of the courses you took in high school and the grades you earned (p. 390)

**Traveler's check** (trəv´ ə lers chek) A check that is bought from a bank and can be replaced if lost or stolen (p. 285)

**Tumor** (tü´ mər) A mass of tissue formed from the abnormal growths of cells (p. 23)

## U

**Unemployment benefits** (un em ploi´ mənt ben´ ə fits) Money and services that are available to unemployed workers seeking new jobs (p. 375)

**Universal precautions** (yü nə vėr´ səl pri kö´ shəns) Methods of self-protection that prevent contact with blood or body fluids (p. 10)

**Unsaturated fat** (un sach´ ə rā tid fat) A type of fat usually found in plant sources of food (p. 122)

**Utility company** (yü til´ ə tē kum´ pə nē) A business that provides water, electricity, or gas to homes and businesses (p. 67)

## V

**Vaccination** (vak sə nā´ shən) An injection of dead or weakened virus to make the body immune to the virus (p. 30)

**Visual** (vizh´ ü əl) Having to do with seeing (p. 416)

**Vitamin** (vī tə mən) A substance needed in small amounts for growth and activity (p. 123)

**Volunteering** (vol ən tir´ ing) Giving your time, without pay, to help others (p. 291)

## W

**Warning** (wôr´ ning) A dangerous storm is expected soon (p. 106)

**Warranty** (wôr´ ən tē) A written statement that promises the product will work for a certain amount of time (p. 199)

**Watch** (wäch) A dangerous storm is possible (p. 106)

**Web browser** (web brouz´ er) A software program that allows a personal computer to read and understand the language used on the Internet (p. 222)

**Web site** (web sīt) A file server (hard drive) on a remote computer network (p. 221)

**Withdrawal** (with drò´ əl) A physical reaction to the absence of a drug in the body (p. 47)

**Withdrawal** (with drò´ əl) Money taken out of a bank account (p. 180)

**Withdrawal slip** (with drò´ əl slip) A slip of paper you fill out to show how much money you are taking out of a bank account (p. 180)

| a | hat | e | let | ī | ice | ô | order | ù | put | sh | she | | a | in about |
|---|-----|---|-----|---|-----|---|-------|---|-----|----|-----|---|---|----------|
| ā | age | ē | equal | o | hot | oi | oil | ü | rule | th | thin | | e | in taken |
| ä | far | ėr | term | ō | open | ou | out | ch | child | ฺTH | then | ə | i | in pencil |
| â | care | i | it | ȯ | saw | u | cup | ng | long | zh | measure | | o | in lemon |
| | | | | | | | | | | | | | u | in circus |

# Index

# C

calcium, 124

calmness, 8

calorie, 116

camping, 281

cancer, 22–23
  risk factors for, 24–25
  treatment for, 24

carbon monoxide, 92

carbohydrates, 120–121

cardiac arrest, 14

cardiovascular diseases, 20–21
  risk factors for, 21–22

career, 337. *See also* job; occupation
  abilities and, 302–304
  education for, 314–315
  examining requirements of, 306–307
  goals for, 362–365
  ideal, 306
  objective of, 318
  planning for, 301, 363–365, 377
  resources for, 309–310
  rewards of, 306–307
  skills and, 302–303
  values and, 304–305

cartilage, 26

cash, 172–174, 207

CD (certificate of deposit), 204

Centers for Disease Control and Prevention
  Division of Sexually Transmitted Diseases, 270
  National Center for HIV, STD, and TB Prevention, 270

cervix, 262

chancre, 261–262

checking accounts, 181–183

chemotherapy, 24

chest compression, 14

chewing, 12

chlamydia, 261

choking, 11–12, 12, fig. 1.1

cholesterol, 22, 122

citizenship, 148, 288, 297

classified ads, 58–59

clothing
  care of, 81–84
  dry cleaning of, 82
  washing/drying of, 83–84

*College Handbook, The,* 384

colleges, 371, 401
  admissions office of, 386–387
  application to, 389–391

financial aid for, 397–400
  information about, 382–385
  Internet, 384
  interview at, 387, 393
  precollege prep program for, 392–393
  software for, 388
  special services for, 392–393
  studying at, 394–396
  technical, 383
  visiting, 386

communication, 148, 154, 245–246
  conflict and, 246–248
  intimate, 242
  skills for, 350, 353–354, 377

community, 297
  involvement in, 291–296
  laws for, 294–296
  service to, 391

community centers, 291–292

compensation, 330–331, 372–373

compromise, 150–151

computer(s), 211
  creation of document for, 212–214
  deletion of document for, 216
  e-mail and, 228–231
  hardware of, 212
  Macintosh, 214–217, 219–220
  management of files/folders for, 218–220
  personal, 212–220, 237
  printing from, 216–217
  saving of document for, 214–215
  scanning by, 329
  virus in, 226

conception, 413

conflict, 246–248
  job, 352–354
  resolution of, 352–353

consequence, 414

*Consumer Reports,* 196

consumer(s), 84, 195, 236
  advantages for, 196
  influences on, 196–197
  wise, 195, 207

coping, 138–139

cosigner, 191

counselor, 304, 311, 322, 337, 384, 401

cover letter, 320

coworkers, 343, 356, 359, 370, 377

CPR (cardiopulmonary resuscitation), 14, 16

credit, 190–191, 207
  reports of, 194

credit cards, 80, 85, 172, 190–191
  finance charges for, 192–193

minimum payment of, 192
wise use of, 193–194
crime
    pedestrian and, 105
    prevention of, 93, 286
curfew, 295
cursor, 213–214
custody, joint, 413
cytomegalovirus retinitis, 260

## D

Daily Value (DV), 127
dating, 250–251, 271
deadlines, 347
decision making, 264–267
deductions, 188
default, 216
defense mechanisms, 156–157, 167
delusion, 160
denial, 157
dental hygiene, 38–40
Department of the Treasury, Internal Revenue Service, 206
depressant, 47
depression, clinical, 159
destination, 283
diabetes, 25–26
*Dictionary of Occupational Titles (DOT)*, 309
diet. *See* nutrition
digestion, 120
directories, 384
disabilities, 154, 162–166, 332, 364, 376
disasters, natural, 106–110
    warning for, 106
    watch for, 106
discipline, 410
discrimination, 254–255, 359–360
disease(s), 53, 270. *See also* names of specific diseases
    acquiring of, 27–28
    common, 20
    infectious, 27–28, 28, fig. 1.4
    protection from, 29
    sexually transmitted (STD), 257–263, 270, 271
diskette, 217, 225
disorder(s), 157–161
    affective, 159–160
    anxiety, 158
    bipolar, 160
    eating, 161, 167
    substance abuse, 158, 167
    thought, 160

treatment of, 157–161
displacement, 157
distress signal, choking, 11
divorce, 409
doctor. *See* physician
document, 213–218
download, 225
drag, 214
driving
    alcohol affect on, 48–49
    defensive, 102–103
    insurance and, 74–75
    safe, 102–103
    work and, 334–336
drug(s), 41, 46–52
    AIDS and, 259
    designer, 51
    family and, 415
    other dangerous, 50–52
    overdose with, 49
    psychoactive, 47–50, 53
    withdrawal from, 47
dry cleaning, 82

## E

earthquakes, 109
education, postsecondary, 382–388
electrical fires, 91
electrical shock, 92–93
electrocution, 92–93
e-mail, 228–231, 237
emergencies
    contact with, 94–95
    life-threatening, 11–15
    plan for, 107
    supplies for, 102
emergency medical service (EMS), 8, 10, 13–15, 16
emotions
    health and, 145, 149, 152
    management of, 151
empathy, 255
emphysema, 46
employee
    handbook for, 343–344, 360, 377
    paychecks of, 186–189
employer, 365
employment, 341. *See also* job; occupation
employment agencies, 322
endurance, heart and lung, 132, 134
evacuate, 106
exemptions, 202

## S

safe-deposit box, 178–179
safety, 60, 89
 bicycle, 98–99, 111
 cellular phones and, 103
 home, 90–96
 in-line skating, 98–99
 natural disasters and, 106–109
 pedestrian, 104–105
 recreational, 97–99
 sports, 98
 vehicle, 100–103, 111
 water, 97–98
 workplace, 97
salary, 330–331
 raise of, 372–373
SAT, 383, 385, 390
savings, 176, 179–181, 203–205, 207
savings bonds, 204
scholarships, 397–398
schools, violence in, 152
search engine, 233
seat belts, 100, 103
security
 apartment, 60
 home, 93
 telephones and, 80, 85
sedative-hypnotics, 50
self-acceptance, 242
self-advocacy, 162–164
self-assessment, 6, 56, 88, 114, 144, 170, 210, 240, 274, 300, 302, 340, 380, 404
self-esteem, 149, 167, 242
self-expression, 275
sexual activity, 250–251, 258, 271
shock, 15
shopping
 food, 127–129
 online, 232
skating, in-line, 98–99
smoke detectors, 64, 91, 93
smoking, 22, 24, 46–47
social awareness, 241
Social Security, 80, 85, 188, 203, 207
social skills, 148
socializing, 249–250
software, 213, 388
splint, 19
sports, 98
sprain, 18

standard deduction, 201
State Home Page, 296
sterility, 261
steroids, anabolic, 51–52
stimulant, 46
stress, 141
 management of, 138–140, 152
 reaction to, 137–140
 teenagers and, 138
stroke, 14, 21
student financial aid, 399–401
studying, 394–396
sugars. *See* carbohydrates
suicide, 159
sunlight, 25
supervisor, 307, 355, 366–368, 370
support system, 147
syphilis, 261–262

## T

tactile learning, 416–419
tags, emergency medical, 8
tax-deferred savings plans, 205
taxes, 200, 207
 deductions for, 201–202
 exemptions for, 202
 income, 200
 sales, 201
teams, 357–358
teenagers, 141
 credit cards and, 193
 dietary needs of, 126
 marriage of, 407
 socializing by, 249–250
 stress and, 138
telephone(s), 76, 85
 cellular, 77, 79, 103
 directory book for, 323
 emergency numbers for, 8
 etiquette on, 78–79
 security and, 80
 setting up service of, 76–78, 80
tenants, 60, 62
tests
 standardized, 390
 taking of, 396
textbooks, 396
The College Handbook. *See College Handbook, The*
thermostat, 68–69
thinking
 healthy, 152
 positive, 153